DOING QUALITATIVE RESEARCH ONLINE

For Hannah and Zac, Sammy, Oliver, and Alex, whose natural curiosity inspires me to work for a better future for us all, and for Cole, who helps keep the home fires burning while I am burning up the keyboard.

DOING QUALITATIVE RESEARCH ONLINE

Janet E. Salmons

2nd Edition

Los Angeles | London | New Delhi
Singapore | Washington DC | Melbourne

Los Angeles | London | New Delhi
Singapore | Washington DC | Melbourne

SAGE Publications Ltd
1 Oliver's Yard
55 City Road
London EC1Y 1SP

SAGE Publications Inc.
2455 Teller Road
Thousand Oaks, California 91320

SAGE Publications India Pvt Ltd
B 1/I 1 Mohan Cooperative Industrial Area
Mathura Road
New Delhi 110 044

SAGE Publications Asia-Pacific Pte Ltd
3 Church Street
#10-04 Samsung Hub
Singapore 049483

Editor: Alysha Owen
Assistant editor: Charlotte Bush
Production editor: Prachi Arora
Copyeditor: Christine Bitten
Proofreader: Elaine Leek
Indexer: Martin Hargreaves
Marketing manager: Ben Sherwood
Cover design: Shaun Mercier
Typeset by C&M Digitals (P) Ltd, Chennai, India
Printed in the UK

Library of Congress Control Number: 2021938478

British Library Cataloguing in Publication data

A catalogue record for this book is available from the
British Library

ISBN 978-1-5297-1413-5
ISBN 978-1-5297-1412-8 (pbk)
eISBN 978-1-5297-6577-9

At SAGE we take sustainability seriously. Most of our products are printed in the UK using responsibly sourced
papers and boards. When we print overseas we ensure sustainable papers are used as measured by the PREPS
grading system. We undertake an annual audit to monitor our sustainability.

Contents

List of Figures

List of Tables

About the Author

Dr Janet Salmons is a free-range scholar, writer, coach, and artist through Vision2Lead. Her areas of interest include emerging research methods, and teaching and collaborative learning in the digital age.

Janet's most recent books are: *What Kind of Researcher are You?* (2021), *Reframing and Rethinking Collaboration in Higher Education and Beyond: A Practical Guide for Doctoral Students and Early Career Researchers* with Narelle Lemon (2021), *Publishing from your Doctoral Research: Create and Use a Publication Strategy* with Helen Kara (2020), *Learning to Collaborate, Collaborating to Learn* (2019), *Find the Theory in your Research* (2019), *Getting Data Online* (2019), and *Doing Qualitative Research Online* (2016).

Janet serves as the Methods Guru and lead writer for SAGE Publishing's research community, MethodSpace. She is an honorary member of the TAA Council of Fellows (2019) and received the Mike Keedy Award (2018) in recognition of enduring service to authors. She lives and works in Boulder, Colorado.

Acknowledgments

Thanks to trail-blazing researchers whose work helps us understand the world. Particular thanks to Naomi Clarke, Natalia Reinoso Chavez, Bea Gardener, and Louise Couceiro for discussing their online research approaches with me. Special thanks go to my patient and supportive editor, Michael Ainsley. Thanks also to the Cornell University Library for allowing alumni access to the database that makes my desk research possible.

Preface to the Second Edition

WHAT HAS CHANGED SINCE THE 1ST EDITION WAS PUBLISHED IN 2016? EVERYTHING, AND NOTHING

Everything has changed because higher education and academic research were rocked by the COVID-19 pandemic. This disruption will undoubtedly have far-reaching consequences not yet visible, but three points relevant to this book are glaringly obvious now:

1. **Online and technology-mediated communication is essential to modern life**
   When face-to-face meetings were not possible, everything from work life and health care to children's schooling and happy hours shifted online. For many people, online interactions were their only interactions. People who were accustomed to a limited range of electronic communications had an immersion course in videoconferencing and other forms of online exchange.

2. **The Digital Divide is real**
   Alas, not everyone had the opportunity to fully participate. Those without broadband-connected computers and digital literacy skills were left behind. Those with little or no broadband found slow Internet incompatible with media-intensive platforms and expectations for video exchanges. The skills needed to text chat or use social media are inadequate for sophisticated telehealth appointments or multi-stage applications for government assistance.
   Those who previously accessed computers at work, libraries or other public spaces could no longer connect. People who had moved away from home computers and embraced smartphones as their only device found the inherent limitations made it difficult to fulfill the tasks at hand.

3. **Even those who were previously skeptical about online research have come to accept its usefulness**
   While academia as a whole has long embraced some forms of technology, many would-be online researchers have encountered obstacles when reviewers looked skeptically at their proposals. However, attitudes changed when researchers could no longer select research sites, recruit participants, or collect data in person. More openness to online research will undoubtedly open the door to more innovation.

What do these points mean for you? I would say it is mostly good news. You are likely to encounter less resistance from reviewers of your research proposal. If you want to study the digital footprints people leave online, the increased level of Internet use means you will have more potential data available. If you are interested in using methods that entail direct interaction with human participants, you are more likely to find individuals you can engage in rich communication. Where in the past you might have homed in on simple interviews, you might be able to use more complex and collaborative approaches now that your participants are comfortable with diverse communication technologies.

At the same time, the opposite is true. Depending on your research interests, you might find that potential participants have limited or no Internet access, and little record of online engagement. If so, you may need to be flexible in order to communicate in the way they prefer. And certainly, online research is not the best approach for every study.

Social Justice, Inclusion, and Equality: Not Enough Change!

Issues where we might have wished for change have stubbornly resisted adequate forward momentum. Alas, racism, sexism, and other forms of discrimination persist. While I do not directly address cultural competence directly, the emphasis in this book is on ethical research. Please extend respect to all gatekeepers and partners, communities, and participants.

While Usage has Changed, Communications Technologies Have Not Changed Very Much

When I wrote the first edition, we could communicate electronically with text-based chat, email or posts, with video chats or videoconferencing, shared images or files – and those are the same forms we use today. The devices might be smaller and lighter, the platforms have different brand names, but the ways we use technology to communicate with words and images continues.

WHAT THE BOOK IS AND IS NOT

In this book I endeavor to provide both the background and the how-to for doing qualitative research online. The book offers an overview of methods including some that involve no direct interaction with participants and others that involve intensive, collaborative interactions. The book provides principles any online qualitative researcher can apply. However, it is beyond the scope of this book to dig deeply into Big Qual or post-qualitative methodologies.

I present a holistic approach that invites you to look at ways each choice influences the direction of the study. I encourage you to venture into less-traveled spheres and try creative approaches that make use of the possibilities the Internet affords researchers. I hope the book is useful to you – and I look forward to seeing the innovations you bring to the field as you collect the deep data needed to understand our complex and continually changing world.

Janet Salmons, PhD
Boulder, Colorado

qualitative researcher can apply. However, it is beyond the scope of this book to dig deeply into Qual or post-qualitative methodologies.

I present a holistic approach that invites you to look at ways each choice influences the direction of the study. I encourage you to venture into less-traveled spheres and try creative approaches that make use of the possibilities the Internet offers researchers. I hope the book is useful to you – and I look forward to seeing the innovations you bring to the field as you collect the deep data needed to understand our complex and continually changing world.

Janet Salmons, PhD
Boulder, Colorado

Organization of the Book

The book launches with Chapter 1, an overview of online qualitative research and the Qualitative e-Research Framework. This chapter will help you think about the type of study you want to design and conduct. It is the stage for five major sections of the book:

Section I: Designing Online Qualitative Studies

This section includes chapters about making decisions on the methodologies, methods, and technologies for the study.

Section II: Becoming an Ethical Online Researcher

Essential to all design choices is consideration of ethical foundations for the research design and ethical principles that guide the way the research is conducted. These are the topics covered in Section II. This section also invites you to think about the perspectives you bring to your role as a researcher, and the position you will take in relation to the study.

Section III: Preparing to Collect Data Online

What do you need to know and do to get ready for the actual research? Most researchers will need a sampling strategy and plan that guides selection of participants or other data sources. Those collecting data will need to choose who will participate and prepare to interact with them. Chapters in Section III address the decision-making factors and practical steps needed when preparing to collect data online.

Section IV: Collecting Qualitative Data Online

Without data there is no study, so options for collecting extant data, eliciting data and/or using enacted methods are discussed in Section IV.

Section V: Working with Data and Reporting Findings

Once data has been collected the researcher needs to analyze the diverse materials assembled throughout the study, determine the findings, and then think about how to write about them. These topics are covered in Section V.

The book concludes with an Appendix that includes suggested readings on qualitative research and a Glossary of terms. In the online resources you will find an Instructor's Guide with additional materials, including media, templates, exercises, and up-to-date references to literature using online qualitative methods.

Research Cameos

In each chapter of this book, hypothetical research scenarios are used to illustrate stages of the research process. The four cameos differentiate between four different types of qualitative online research, and the kinds of decisions researchers might make. Use them to think through your own research plans.

RESEARCHER 1

Researcher 1 is designing a study using extant data. They plan to analyze Big Data from journal databases as well as mission statements and editorials from selected journals to understand how and where qualitative research is published. They see their role as one of a 'miner,' who digs into source materials. They will use a case study methodology. They will define spatial boundaries by selecting databases that include journals from social sciences, humanities, education, and business disciplines. They will define the temporal parameters as 2015 to the present. They will define relational boundaries in terms of authors who conduct qualitative studies and publish articles in indexed journals. Researcher 1 has chosen to look at these issues at a societal, global level by looking at a crowd of published articles in many journals, across disciplines. To collect data, they plan to search and export lists of references from journal databases as the first stage, then sort by keywords for methodologies, methods, and publication dates. In this study the technology is entwined with the research phenomena since they are studying qualitative publication trends in electronic journals. They feel this study, using databases of published journal articles as extant data, offers few ethical dilemmas or risks. They will follow guidelines from their institution and research supervisor, so feel at this stage that an ethical approach drawn from deontological theory will be appropriate.

Since they are using peer-reviewed journal databases, they will not need to inform anyone or obtain consent agreements. It will be legitimate for Researcher 1 to cite sources from the journals for selected examples they choose to include.

They will be working within their university library system. They will familiarize themselves with any library regulations and adhere to them. People skills will be important when interacting with librarians, research supervisors, and other stakeholders. They are more concerned with the need for self-awareness and cultural competence. They do not want to overlook indigenous scholarship or writings from emerging researchers.

Given the nature of the study, Researcher 1 is coming from an outsider position. Their challenge for building credibility will come later in the research process when they are writing, presenting, and/or publishing results.

They begin with criterion-based sampling. The inclusion criteria will be implemented as key word searches that include 'qualitative,' and terms that describe methodologies that are typically qualitative such as 'ethnography' and 'phenomenology.' Researcher 1 could decide that given the specificity of these criteria, they will aim for a heterogeneous set of sources. These could include those from discipline-specific journals, such as *Business & Society* or *British Journalism Review*, as well as research-oriented journals that cover all types of research, such as *Research Ethics* or *Methodological Innovations*. They will also look at databases for journals specific to qualitative research, such as *Qualitative Inquiry*. They will use an existing sample frame, that is, the journal databases. Given that they plan to look at trends over a period of time, they will encompass both historical and contemporary data. They will be reviewing records from scholarly journals originally published in print, then scanned in or digitized, as well as journals published in the digital era. While some journals are open access, they will use private databases, available through an academic library. Researcher 1 is enrolled at a university where they can utilize this private database.

Researcher 1 is designing a study using extant data, so they are not preparing to interact with participants. Still, they will be interacting with others so are looking at ways to improve online communication skills. They realize that the informal, casual communications they are accustomed to using with friends will not be appropriate when discussing access to databases.

Researcher 1 plans to conduct the analysis using a linear-sequential approach to begin coding after all data are collected. First, they will code references from journal databases by discipline and location of the lead author's academic institution. They will categorize accordingly, creating two sets of lists. Next, they will code by keywords for methodologies, methods, and publication dates. Researcher 1 will use a case study methodology and plan to construct cases based on the coding categories of discipline, geographic location, methodology, methods, and dates. They will develop case descriptions, as suggested by Yin (2018). They will construct a time-series analysis with data organized by date, and will conduct keyword cluster analysis to identify methodological and disciplinary trends (Ebrahim, Poshtan, Jamali, & Ebrahim, 2020). The data, bibliographic entries in journal databases, will be in text form.

RESEARCHER 2

Researcher 2 is designing a study that involves eliciting data through one-to-one and group online interviews with qualitative researchers who have successfully published their studies. They plan to exemplify the 'gardener' metaphor by cultivating rapport with each participant. They will use a phenomenological methodology to study the lived experience of qualitative researchers who go through the process of conducting and reporting on research in journal articles and other publications. They have chosen to look at the research question at an individual level by studying the experiences of researchers going through the publication process and plan to conduct online interviews with individual researchers. The technology serves primarily as a medium to communicate and interact with participants about their experiences. At the same time, they are interested in the social media sites, shared folders, and other tools used by researchers to develop an understanding of the user experience. They feel drawn to the ethics of care, because they want to work from a respectful stance and avoid situations that could make participants feel uncomfortable.

Because they will elicit data through one-to-one and group online interviews they will need consent agreements from all participants. They plan to observe the non-verbal cues during interviews and include that visual data as well as the verbal responses. They will need consent agreements from all participants. They will create a visual infographic depicting the stages of the study from preparation for the interview, the interview, potential follow-up questions, member checking, through to any needed discussions about presentations or publications. They will create a simple blog about the study and include basic information about timing for each stage and any logistical information participants might need. They will also verbally review the expectations at the beginning of each interview to make sure any participants' questions have been fully answered.

Although designing a study that involves eliciting data through one-to-one and group online interviews with consenting participants, to understand some of the issues and dilemmas academic writers face, they plan to conduct unobtrusive observation of social media posts to hashtags such as #acwri or observations of open discussions on social networking sites. They do not intend to collect data in these settings, simply to gain some background on the issues, challenges, and topics being discussed. While they share some characteristics as a qualitative researcher, they will approach the study as an outsider.

They will conduct the interviews using a video conference platform and they will make sure that they have selected an online setting that is accessible and easy to use. They will create a setting conducive to interviews. They know that people skills will be essential in this study in order to establish rapport with interviewees and to convey to them the importance of their contributions to the research.

They know that self-awareness, and self-control, will be needed in order to respond appropriately and respectfully to participants. To build credibility they will create a research blog to share their research journey. They will discuss their motivations for conducting the study, links to their academic institution, and relevant affiliations. If they have publications, or online posts participants can view, they will share links.

For sampling, they will start with a convenience sample of participants they know from professional networking circles. After the initial set of interviews, they might use a snowball approach, asking participants to get the word out about the study to their circles of friends and colleagues. This means they will use an existing sample frame, that is, their professional network. They are planning for a sample size of 20 participants, all qualitative researchers who have successfully published their studies.

- *Inclusion*: Academic writers with a doctoral degree and three to five publications in peer-reviewed scholarly journals.
- *Exclusion*: Student writers with no publications in peer-reviewed scholarly journals.

In addition to clear inclusion/exclusion criteria, it is important for Researcher 2 to spell out what they expect from participants. Are they looking for specific expertise or experience? Using the same example, we could offer more specific criteria:

- *Inclusion*: Academic writers who have published qualitative research based on organizational ethnography in the business sector.
- *Exclusion*: Academic writers who have published qualitative ethnographic research about individuals, the public sector, or NGOs

When recruiting participants, Researcher 2 wants to avoid giving the impression that they will be judgmental about struggles and feelings of failure potential participants might have about falling short on meeting publication goals. They want to convey openness to a range of academic writing competence and success. Researcher 2 will look for volunteers who respond to a promotional post they will include on their social media pages. However, they are not confident that enough participants will respond, so they are planning to use a commercial panel. They will review Mechanical Turk and other options to find one that can help recruit participants willing to engage through a video interview.

While they have participated in video calls and chats, they have not been responsible for managing the platform for serious matters. They have not led groups on a videoconference platform. They are scheduling at least two one-to-one and small group pre-interview practice sessions. While they typically have a 'just do it' attitude about technology, they plan to watch tutorials on the platform to ensure they know all the features and are able to address any problems.

Researcher 2 plans to elicit data from consenting participants using multiple types of synchronous and asynchronous interviews to understand their experiences and plans for publishing qualitative research.

Semi-structured questions: For a synchronous interview on a videoconferencing platform, they articulate main questions, and will develop follow-up and probing questions depending on the answers:

- Briefly describe your qualitative research.
- What are your publishing goals?
- What will help you meet these goals?
- What obstacles will you need to overcome?
- Who do you communicate to help you meet your goals?

Unstructured questions: Tell me why it is important to publish your qualitative study?

Structured questions: They articulate questions and will post them to each participant by text message at 6pm each day for one week. For this near-synchronous exchange they craft the following questions:

- Did you work on writing you hope to publish, or take other actions to move your publication process forward?
- In a few words, how do you feel about progress made today toward meeting your goals?
- What steps will you take tomorrow?

Researcher 2 plans to elicit data from consenting participants using multiple types of synchronous and asynchronous interviews to understand their experiences and plans for publishing qualitative research. They have prepared main questions for the semi-structured interviews, questions to be spoken in a videoconference setting using audio and webcams. They have written out the questions to be posed in the text messaging application the participant is accustomed to using. They have checked to make sure that the participants have the technical capability to participate in both kinds of interactions.

They plan to use a videoconference platform, with webcams on. However, this data is for their own use only, since the participant will be visible and recognizable. They will protect the data and will not use it for presentations of the study. They have clarified the researcher-only review of recordings. They have also verified that the text messaging data will not be shared in any way that could reveal the participants' identities.

They have practiced using the platform, and stuck a note in an obvious place as a reminder to start recording. They have positioned the webcam to promote the best eye contact and minimized distractions in the background. Even though they have core questions, they are prepared to ask them in a conversational way. They will have the guide on hand but will not read the questions. They have practiced conducting the interview and asked for feedback from their colleague. Do I seem friendly but professional? Do I seem interested in your response? Do I avoid facial expressions that convey approval or disapproval of your responses? After a couple of practice interviews, they are confident about conducting the interview.

Researcher 2 will use a phenomenological methodology. They will collect all interview data, and then begin the stages of Phenomenological Reduction, Imaginative Variation, and Synthesis. For the first stage, they will listen to and view recordings, making notes and memoing. If participants shared any visuals in the interviews, such as pictures of their journals or diagrams of their writing process, they will set those aside. They will make sure they have permission to use non-representational images in publications or presentations. Next, they will transcribe the interviews into text files and move to the next stage of coding to find themes and contexts that reflect on the phenomenon of writing with group support and exchange.

RESEARCHER 3

Researcher 3 is designing a study that will involve generating data with aspiring and successful qualitative researchers', enacted approaches. They intend to journey with participants through experiential simulations. The researcher feels the 'traveler' metaphor will best represent their relationship to participants. They will conduct an exploratory qualitative study to engage with researchers and authors, and try to learn the steps they take when deciding how to get qualitative research published, and while engaging in the stages of submission and review. Researcher 3 has chosen to explore the individual experiences and choices of researchers. They plan to offer a publishing workshop online and collect data from the writers who participate. Technology will serve as a setting for data collection, as well as a medium to communicate with participants one-to-one and in a group. They will offer a workshop and collect data from those who join. They intend to proceed in a respectful way and avoid risk to participants, but at the same time, to take a pragmatic approach. They value the outcomes and believe that the outcome of participants' improved publication skills will be worth it even if there is some discomfort along the way.

They will need consent agreements from all participants that will spell out what aspects of the workshop experience will be recorded for the purpose of this study. Researcher 3 is offering this free workshop in exchange for the opportunity to learn from the experiences of workshop participants. In addition to written information about this approach, Researcher 3 will record a short video that participants can watch to fully understand the expectations. In addition, Researcher 3 will verbally review the expectations and answer any questions at the beginning of the first workshop session.

The study will involve generating data with aspiring and successful qualitative researchers in a workshop setting. Researcher 3 plans to openly observe the workshop participants and will note this fact in the consent agreement. They will give participants the option of engaging anonymously if sensitive issues are being discussed that they would rather not be included in the data. They foresee the possibility of secondary participants who engage in conversation with consenting members. They will handle this on a case-by-case basis, either asking for permission to use the quote or paraphrasing it in a way that would not link it back to the non-consenting group member.

They are considering the option of offering this workshop under the aegis of an organization that serves academic writers. They will meet with staff or volunteers from the organization to make sure that plans for data collection are acceptable. After these meetings, they succeeded and now have partnered with a university writing center that will allow them to offer the online workshop for doctoral students and early career faculty and will assist in recruiting participants. They will share findings with the university writing center, making it a win–win project.

Since they will enroll verified members of the university community, credibility issues will not be a concern in terms of being assured that volunteers are legitimate. They will need to be transparent about the dual purpose of the workshop: to help the writers who join, and to collect data. They will need to be self-aware about how they juggle these priorities. They will approach the study from the position as an insider, a fellow qualitative researcher and writer. They will select anecdotes and stories that illustrate ways they succeeded or failed and how they learned from the experience.

For sampling, they will still need to create a plan, but will leverage the university partnership to use a nominated approach. They intend to ask people who supervise doctoral students or early-career researchers to refer individuals who might benefit from the workshop, and who would be willing to commit to the process. They will construct their sample frames. Researcher 3 will aim for a sample of 10 participants, justifying a small sample on the premise that they will interact with participants multiple times.

- *Inclusion*: Doctoral students who are in the dissertation or thesis stage, or early-career researchers who completed their degrees within the last five years.
- *Inclusion*: Doctoral students or early-career researchers who can commit to attending all sessions of the free workshop and complete a written publication plan.
- *Exclusion*: Doctoral students or early-career researchers whose research is quantitative or mixed methods.

The decision to partner for this research project means they will need to use the university's web conferencing and e-learning platform. They are not familiar with this platform, so will take advantage of the tutorials and help sessions offered by the IT department. They will offer the publishing workshop online in three online sessions.

They plan to use visual communication to help the students understand different pathways for getting books or articles published. They will ask students to generate visual maps or diagrams to illustrate the major stages and related obstacles they anticipate. In the third session they want to create a collective visual representation of the journey from completion of a study to publication of findings in a book or article. They will use the shared whiteboard feature to construct the map, then download it so each member has a copy. Researcher 3 will use this collective drawing in conjunction with individual students' drawings to better understand their perceptions of temporal and success factors, and obstacles. In one of the sessions, they will use a role-play exercise that will help writers prepare for a proposal discussion with an acquisitions editor. The role-plays will occur on the class web conferencing platform so will be recorded for review and analysis.

Researcher 3 will conduct an exploratory qualitative study. Because they are interested in the experiences of writers in an online workshop, they will complete research memos after each class to reflect on the tone, progress, and other observations such as participation levels. They will download or transcribe comments from the classroom discussions, and export student writings into folders established for each individual. They will use a narrative analysis on these text-based documents. While they are not looking for plot and character, they do want to see how the participants' writings evolved over the course of the workshop.

RESEARCHER 4

Researcher 4 is designing a study that will include an analysis of extant data from journal archives, and online interviews with selected authors and editors. They expect to take multiple roles and draw from all three metaphors. They will conduct an ethnographic study of a writing group, to observe their process and experiences with getting their work published. Researcher 4 has chosen to look at research publishing at individual and small group levels. They plan to observe the meetings of an online writing group and their related social media interactions. They will also interview selected writers about their experiences. They will also use technology as a communication medium and setting for a writing group that offers support and reviews to each other. They think virtue ethics will be a useful guide, since they are not sure what might emerge and want to be prepared to take a moral stand in any situation that arises.

This study will include observations of an online writing group and their related social media posts. In addition, they will interview selected group members. They expect to make an agreement with the moderator of the group, and offer an opt-out for group members who prefer not to be a part of the study. They will only collect data from members who agree to participate. They will negotiate additional agreements with the interview participants.

Researcher 4 will create a detailed information sheet for the group and for interview participants and update it as the study proceeds. The group moderator will introduce the researcher and allow them time to explain the study. Researcher 4 will need to balance multiple priorities, some with and some without participants. They will approach the study from the position of an insider, a fellow qualitative researcher and writer. They will select anecdotes and stories that illustrate ways they succeeded or failed and how they learned from the experience.

They will construct their sample frame. Researcher 4, given that they will have multiple forms of data, plans for a sample of four to six at the interview stage. This case is a bit different because the researcher must first locate a writing group willing to allow observations. They will select participants from that group for one-to-one interviews. While observing the group, they could look for potential interviewees using these criteria:

- *Inclusion*: Writing group members who post at least twice each week about their publishing journey.
- *Inclusion*: Writing group members who contribute reviews and comments to other members.
- *Exclusion*: Writing group members whose research is quantitative or mixed methods.

Researcher 4 is looking for active writing groups with a blog or social media presence and contacting moderators or organizers to find one willing to participate. They are also contacting qualitative methodologists to ask whether they would be willing to make a referral to a formal or informal writing group. They have created a video recruitment message, noting clear boundaries about the data they will and will not collect. They are open to the possibility of sharing findings or related resources with the group. Their study will involve primarily text-based communications. They do not need to learn new technology to move forward.

Researcher 4 plans to observe a writing group's social media interactions, as well as their online meetings. They categorize this work as being primarily emergent because they will study a group that is currently active. The group is private, members only, so their writings and conversations are not accessible to the public.

They do share tips and resources with each other on social media, but writings and support-related interactions are private.

Researcher 4 wants to observe an online writing group as part of their data collection. While they negotiated permission and consent, they do not plan to interact with the group members during their meetings. They are considering two options:

> **Conduct a structured observation**. They identify specific time frames for the observation. They draw key themes from the literature and align them with what is learned from a preliminary scan of the community. They construct an observation guide so they can track discussions and posts during the planned time frames. They intend to identify interview questions based on this observation and then to conduct the second stage of the study with group members willing to meet one-to-one.

> **Conduct an unstructured observation**. They observe the group with an open mind, recording data specific to the research questions. They plan to keep an open mind to any topic discussed in the group.

They are conducting a multimodal study, including observations of an online writing group and their related posts to social media, plus conducting email interviews with several group members. Like Researcher 3, they want to succinctly communicate steps and editors' expectations associated with the complex process of getting published. They believe a flow-chart would be easier for interviewees to understand than a lengthy written document. They constructed a flow-chart of the publication process for asynchronous email interviewees. They asked participants to annotate the chart in response to questions such as: note the places in the process where you feel confident of success, note the places where you are concerned about success, note your timeline and add dates to the chart.

They plan an iterative approach to data analysis. They will begin coding transcripts, observation notes, and visual artifacts while continuing to collect data. After all interviews are completed, they will do a second round of coding of all the data.

Researcher 4 will conduct an ethnographic study. They will create initial categories when they analyze the data as it is collected and continue to sift the data for new themes and patterns. They will have text-based data from review comments group members made to one another, and email interviews, and will use a content analysis process to gain an understanding of the individuals' experiences and the writing group as a whole.

Discover your online resources

Doing Qualitative Research Online, 2nd Edition is supported by online resources to help you learn. Visit https://study.sagepub.com/salmonsdqro2e to find:

For instructors

- Download **PowerPoint slides** featuring figures and tables from the book, which can be customized for use in your own lectures and presentations.
- An **Instructor's Guide** featuring learning activities, relevant research cases from SAGE Research Methods and research articles from SAGE's Open Access Journals

For instructors and students:

- **YouTube videos** to aid learning and research whether you are using this book for research or to teach

1

Qualitative Approaches for Research in a Data-intensive World

HIGHLIGHTS

Online communication pervades our lives. Now that it has leapt from our desks into our pockets, we communicate with others and access information anytime and anywhere. When we use these same approaches for **qualitative research**, either to communicate with participants or to access posted material, the considerations at play are quite different from those present in social uses of technology. In this chapter, the basic elements of qualitative research are defined and then applied in the online context. We will start to consider the types of information and communications tools we might use for research purposes, including apps and mobile devices as well as sites and platforms on the Internet. We will begin to reflect on the roles and skills needed to conduct qualitative research. The *Qualitative e-Research Framework* is introduced as a tool for thinking through and organizing the key elements of online qualitative **research design**.

OBJECTIVES

After reading and reflecting on this chapter, you will be able to:

- understand the defining characteristics of qualitative research
- analyze the attributes of online and electronic communication

(Continued)

- consider ways qualitative research approaches can use online communications for data collection
- understand key questions for applying the Qualitative e-Research Framework to the research design process.

QUALITATIVE RESEARCH: UNDERSTANDING HOW THE WORLD IS SEEN AND EXPERIENCED

What is qualitative research, and for what kinds of research questions is it appropriate? A common, universally agreed-upon definition is elusive. Qualitative researchers typically eschew simplistic descriptions and do not look for big, generalizable answers. They are interested in the nuanced and the particular in their efforts to understand human experience. Rather than trying to define qualitative research, it might be more useful to understand defining characteristics in order to think about how technology can be used to carry out some or all of the study.

Qualitative inquiry aims to generate new understandings of the meaning people give to their lives and their worlds. This means qualitative researchers are typically focused on the participants' own descriptions of social and material circumstances, their lived experiences and histories, perspectives, and insights. Based in commitment to these broad goals, qualitative researchers operate from the assumption that people construct their own realities and interpret the world in unique ways.

Within these universal principles qualitative researchers have developed more particular approaches that guide the ways they study individuals or groups, organizations, communities or society. These methodological frameworks provide theoretical and practical guidance that helps researchers design studies that can answer questions associated with a research problem.

Qualitative researchers choose data collection methods that allow for close contact and interaction between researchers and participants. Unlike **quantitative research**, which involves large groups of participants, qualitative researchers typically engage small **samples** of participants. They try to dig deeply to fully grasp participants' perceptions of the problem at hand. Qualitative researchers also choose data collection methods that permit indirect contact with individuals through careful review of stories and pictures found in documents and archives. They might use large collections known as Big Data, looking for broad trends and types of experiences rather than particular instances from individual participants.

Qualitative researchers learn about the nature and dimensions of these perceptions, experiences or behaviors by asking the individuals (interviews, focus groups, questionnaires), watching them (participant or unobtrusive **observation**), creating with them (arts-based and creative methods), and/or by reviewing their writings or expressions (documents, written or visual expressions, or records). Researchers may use one or more of these methods within a single study. Once data has been collected, researchers review and analyze it using inductive and abductive reasoning to move from the particular to themes and trends and to generate findings. These approaches are used to generate in-depth, detailed explanations of the research problem or phenomenon based on the perceptions, experiences or behaviors of individuals or groups.

For the purpose of this book, a concise working definition will be used:

Qualitative research is an umbrella term used to describe ways of studying perceptions, experiences or behaviors through their verbal or visual expressions, actions or writings.

QUALITATIVE RESEARCH WITH INFORMATION AND COMMUNICATIONS TECHNOLOGIES

Qualitative research as defined above and the Internet have something in common: for both, communication and exchange are central. They would seem a natural fit! To understand how they fit, we will need to answer two central questions:

- To what extent are communication styles and platforms used for personal, social, and professional purposes suitable for research, given the need for privacy and protection of data?
- What is the potential for using electronic forms of exchange and data retrieval for qualitative data collection?

Let's begin by reflecting on the ways we communicate electronically. We'll also need to think critically about the nature of the online milieu and the places where we engage in Internet-mediated communications. At the same time, we must understand the nature of qualitative inquiry, and consider which approaches can be adapted and where new methodological thinking is called for.

Online Communication Attributes

Communicating online has become a part of everyday life for many people, so the means of doing so has become routine. What motivations underlie our decisions to communicate via **text** or email versus video chat or posts to a social media site? Do we think about what is most convenient or preferable for us, for the person with whom we want to have a conversation, and/or group with whom we want to share? Do we aim to match the medium to the message? Do we consider whether or not the message is private, or whether it could be made public without our authorization? Think about your own technology uses for professional or academic, personal or social life, as well as information and news access. Step back and reflect on what you do each day with your computer, tablet, and/or smartphone, and think about why you make the choices you do. (See the exercise at the end of this chapter for more guidance.)

We can have a conversation with another person, or convey the same message to many 'friends' or 'followers' or to total strangers by sending it to an email list, posting it on a website comment area, **blog**, or on social media. Or we participate in group exchanges where anyone can initiate and/or respond to messages. The first example can be described as a 'one-to-one' dialogue, the second is an example of 'one-to-many', and the third of 'many-to-many'. In Table 1.1 online communication options are distinguished by the type of interaction and notions of one-to-one, one-to-many or many-to-many. These distinctions become fuzzy when individuals can forward or post messages intended as one-to-one to other recipients with or without the permission of the original writer. Still, it is useful to think about how we calibrate our messages differently depending on the purpose, the message recipient(s), and the technology we use.

Table 1.1 ICTs and communication

Communication Options	One-to-One	One-to-Many	Many-to-Many
Text	Email Text messages Chat	Posts to websites, blogs, online communities Email lists	Social networking sites, social media Comment areas Crowdsourcing Discussion forums
Verbal	Voice over Internet Protocol (VoIP) calls	Podcasts	Voice over Internet Protocol (VoIP) conference calls
Visual	Image or media attachments Links to images or media Interaction as visual, digital, or avatar representation	Image or media attachments Links to images or media Vodcast Interaction as visual, digital, or avatar representation	Virtual reality Massively open online games (MOOGs) Interaction as visual, digital, or avatar representation
Mixed or multiple	Videoconference or video chat Web conferencing space	Webinar Online presentation	Virtual reality Massively open online games (MOOGs)

With little forethought, when we want to reach people we know we may elect to tap out a text message, send an email, make a post on a social media site, or turn on the web camera and converse by video chat. We might decide a picture conveys the message and take one with the smartphone camera, pull one from a website, or use emoticons or GIFs.

We choose free platforms or subscription sites with interactive spaces that offer us ways to find and exchange ideas. We interact with people who share common interests or experiences – or those we disagree with on politics and social issues. We might join discussion groups in an online community or on social media. We may create ongoing relationships and enduring bonds with folks we will never meet in person or make comments read by people with whom we will never interact again.

Our fluid meshing of online and offline lifestyles means interactions overlap and blend. We might interact with a friend via social media one minute and then see her in person the next; we might find some forms enhance our relationships while others distract us and disrupt real communication (Lieberman & Schroeder, 2020). You do not need to become a communications scholar, but careful thinking about structure, styles, and options for online communication will be beneficial as you move forward with your research.

Timing from Message to Response

A conversation is different from a letter sent by post, and the same contrast exists when we communicate electronically. Reciprocal **computer-mediated** exchanges of message and response may occur at the same time (**synchronous**) or we may post or send a message not knowing when a response will be received (**asynchronous**). We select among options made available to us by the design and function of the hardware (computers, laptops, mobile devices, or phones), bandwidth of connection, and software interface. The design and function of most information and communications technologies (ICTs) and social networking sites (SNSs) are driven mostly by highly competitive commercial interests. Each has affordances (the ability to communicate anywhere with mobile devices) and restrictions that may be obvious (you can only post certain image formats or message lengths), or subtle (incompatibility of competing software). The features may or may not align with the priorities of those who want to communicate online.

Communicate by Saying, Writing or Seeing

We may communicate online with words alone, through written (text messages, chat, posts, or email) or verbal conversations or recordings (**Voice over Internet Protocol** (VoIP), podcasts). Or we may decide to communicate visually, by sharing a picture or media clip which we have created or found online. Alternatively, we may decide to share applications, enter a **virtual world** or game, and interact through an **avatar** or digital persona we have created.

When we converse face-to-face, we are together in the same place and time. We see and hear each other, sending and receiving complex verbal and **non-verbal** signals. Face-to-face, we see and hear people and things in the environment in a space we experience together. We may have a physical connection – a touch on the arm, handshake or hug. Some of these ways of communicating are replicated online, for example with **videoconferences**, calls or chats we can see and hear each other. We can use gestures and non-verbal signals; we may display emotions. But in this instance, we are in our own respective environments that may be geographically close or on the other side of the globe. We share only what can be seen through the lens of the web camera, which we can choose to direct in such a way as to reveal, disclose, or avoid other elements of the environment. Modern tools allow us to create virtual backgrounds, so the other(s) on the videocall see an image that does not reveal our actual setting.

Quid Pro Quo and Technology Tools

You may have heard the saying, 'there is no such thing as a free lunch.' For Internet and device application users, not only is there no free lunch, but you generally can't choose to pay for your proverbial lunch, either. If you want lunch, you will have to do what the restaurant says, or go home and cook. End user licensing agreements, the fine print users click through, spell out this trade-off. Users must accept the offer made by the company that provides the platform or application in order to use it. Sometimes customization or choices are offered, but typically use of the service is based on allowing the company to access personal data. You don't usually have the option to say, 'I'll pay for my lunch, but leave my information alone.'

Users supply personal information to service providers with every post, query, or click in commercial applications like Google Search, Facebook, and Twitter. Users supply information about their physical whereabouts when their smartphones or wearable technologies beam their locations back to the company.

The user's profile information and record of communication may be available, to some degree, to other users, the company hosting the site, and others. Some users are aware that they are making a choice when they create online identities or settings or select where to participate and what information to share about themselves. Others are unaware of the implications of seemingly innocuous online activities. Users benefit from this data exchange because they can use search technology, social networks, GPS mapping and the like, without charge.

Private, Public, or Somewhere in Between

Another distinction between electronic and face-to-face communication relates to expectations of privacy. Unless we are government spies who suspect that we are being bugged by enemy agents, in a physical room when we close a door we generally expect that the conversation is being conducted in private and no enduring record documents it. We rely on the ability to close the door and have private moments in life. Online, every communication leaves some kind of footprint or trace. We might think a text chat is a one-to-one conversation and expect that it is our private exchange. We might feel more comfortable discussing sensitive or personal matters than we would on a social media page. However, that text message exchange has probably been saved to the company's servers and could be accessed by others.

The concept of privacy can generally be defined as the individuals' ability to control the terms by which their personal information is collected and used. One way this control is exercised is described as the 'right to be forgotten,' meaning we have the right to ask a search engine or platform to remove links to our personal information, or the embarrassing childhood pictures Mom shared or the posts you made about a wild party or inflammatory political views. Larsen explains:

> The right to be forgotten touches upon aspects of what it means to live in a 'network society.' It is about the development of rights at the intersection of technology, personhood, and the public/private divide. The right to be forgotten involves contemporary questions of what it means to be 'human' in a digital, networked age. Who controls or benefits from networked, personal data? Relatedly, who draws the line between what is public and what is private online? (Larsen, 2020, p. 145)

Governments, companies, and other regulators are trying to protect users' privacy and allow the right to control digital records of their activities while allowing a free flow of online communication. The General Data Protection Regulation (GDPR) was enacted by the European Union in 2018, 'imposing obligations onto organizations anywhere, so long as they target or collect data related to people in the EU' (EU, 2018). The GDPR, a complex set of definitions and principles, establishes rules relating to the rights and freedoms people have to expect protection of their data, and the ways data is processed.

These kinds of protections are not consistently available across the globe. If we are conducting research across national borders, it will be important to familiarize ourselves with rules and practices. Additionally, each site has varying policies about the level of privacy users can expect, the degree of protection for information posted using their services, and the ability of users to fully erase posts or profiles.

The intersection of these issues – governmental privacy regulations, privacy practices by technology companies, and styles of communication and expectations of users – is critical for researchers to understand. We'll be looking at these implications throughout the book, as we delve into decisions associated with designing, conducting, and analyzing online research.

QUALITATIVE E-RESEARCH: INQUIRIES IN THE DIGITAL ENVIRONMENT

What do the attributes of online communication mean to qualitative researchers? Qualitative research approaches and online communication share some characteristics since both emphasize the significance of human exchange and expression. This is true whether the researcher interacts directly with participants, or indirectly with records of their ideas or experiences preserved in documents, archives, social media posts, or Big Data.

Our decisions about what ICT to use for personal and social communications or information gathering may be made based on our own preferences, but when using the Internet for research the decisions must be much more strategic. Choices need to be appropriate for the partners and participants with whom we interact, and permit collection of the types of data that will allow us to answer the research questions.

The working definition for qualitative research introduced earlier can be refined to encompass online methods. Qualitative e-research is an umbrella term used to describe methodological traditions for using information and communications technologies to study perceptions, experiences or behaviors through their verbal or visual expressions, actions, or writings.

The presence of the Internet in the study does not necessitate a wholesale redefinition of qualitative inquiry per se. Yet even this subtle shift in definition carries numerous implications for the research design, methodologies and methods, conduct, ethics, and reporting. Online, qualitative researchers have numerous options for selecting and studying participants regardless of geographic location. Given the varied modes of Internet-mediated communication that are possible, researchers also have numerous options for the types of data (text, visual, media) and ways to access it. These wide-ranging possibilities call for new ways to think about research designs that take into account the unique characteristics of the Internet.

Redefining Qualitative Data Collection for Online Research

Rich data is at the heart of a qualitative study. Where and how the data can be found, drawn out or generated online is as broad as the Internet itself. Any way that people can communicate using computers and mobile devices can potentially serve as a means of collecting data.

Qualitative data collection is typically characterized by the method used. At the most basic level the methods are defined as follows:

- **Interviews**. The researcher poses questions or suggests themes for conversation with research participants. Research participants respond to questions and any follow-up prompts. The exchange is recorded and/or the researcher takes notes during the interview. Transcripts of the interview together with researchers' notes are the data analyzed and interpreted to answer the research questions.
- **Observations**. Researchers using observations to collect data take note of whatever may be occurring that relates to the topic of the inquiry. Research observations can take place in a controlled or laboratory setting; naturalistic observations can occur anywhere. Depending on the type of observation, the researcher may or may not engage with those being observed.
- **Document or archival analysis**. Historical or contemporary documents and records of all kinds are analyzed in this type of qualitative research. The term *documents* may also refer to diaries, narratives, journals, and other written materials.

Numerous variations and schools of thought exist about each approach and associated skills, techniques, and practices. Many books are available on each of these types, and a resource list of some excellent ones is included in the Appendix.

Given the unique characteristics of the online environment and communication, different classifications are needed to more accurately define the types of data collection. Three interrelated distinctions to be described in a new system of classifications are:

- where the data resides
- how the researcher accesses the data
- the relationship(s) of the researcher to human participants, archives, or sites where the data can be found.

To address these distinctions and advance a new way of thinking, three types of online data collection are defined here: *extant, elicited,* and *enacted.* The way each type is used in a study has implications for the overall design, role of researcher, and process for analysis. A study may use one approach or combine them in multimethod designs.

Differentiating Online Modes of Data Collection

Extant

Extant data includes documents, visuals, records, Big Data, and other materials the researcher examines to find evidence and background information related to the research problem. See Chapter 10 for more about extant data collection.

- **Where is the data?** Much online communication involves posting text, images or other materials on websites or blogs, social media, or various communications applications. Some of these messages are conveyed through one-to-one channels others ostensibly cannot access. But much of this kind of communication is available for anyone to read, copy, scrape, or download. Materials relevant to the study may also be available through libraries, archives, Big Data, datasets, or databases.
- **How does the researcher access the data?** Collecting this kind of data involves adapting the methods traditional qualitative researchers refer to as observation, **document analysis, archival research, narrative research**, or **discourse analysis**. Data collection can entail scraping or downloading items or sets of materials. Extant data collection can occur either synchronously or asynchronously. The researcher could, for example, observe a synchronous online event, such as a **webinar** or meeting. The live session could be recorded or notes taken. More often the researcher using these approaches works asynchronously, since archived records, documents, or materials may have been posted over a period of time.
- **What is the relationship between researcher and human participants, archives, or sites where the data can be found?** Extant data exists without any intervention or influence by the researcher. The researcher may take field notes or write memos about the data or collection process, but the data itself was generated by users without prompting from the researcher. The researcher has no direct contact with the users unless the study entails consent or permissions. (For more on ethical issues, see Chapters 4 and 5.)

Elicited

Data is collected from consenting participants in response to researchers' questions or other prompts. The researcher can influence the direction or level of specificity and can probe in ways not possible with extant data. See Chapter 11 for more about eliciting data collection.

- **Where is the data?** Participants' responses about lived experiences, perceptions, and perspectives of individuals who have knowledge related to some aspect of the research problem becomes data.
- **How does the researcher access the data?** The researcher poses questions or offers prompts to encourage participants to share verbal, visual, or written data. The researcher may have carefully planned and structured the elicitation to focus on specific questions, or it may be loosely structured to allow ideas to emerge through conversation. Collecting this kind of data involves adapting the methods traditional qualitative researchers refer to as participant observation, interviews, focus groups, or questionnaires. Elicited data collection can occur either synchronously or asynchronously. For example, an interview may be conducted using a synchronous text or video exchange, or an asynchronous email exchange. Researchers using participant observation online may post to a social media or online community site or use synchronous text chat to engage with group members. **Online questionnaires** collect data asynchronously.

- **What is the relationship between researcher and human participants, archives, or sites where the data can be found?** The researcher has direct interactions with participants who consent to participate.

Enacted

The term enacted refers to approaches for generating data through some kind of online activity that engages researcher and participant in the generation of data.

- **Where is the data?** Participants' responses or observed behaviours associated with the lived experiences, perceptions, and perspectives of individuals who have knowledge related to some aspect of the research problem becomes data.
- **How does the researcher access the data?** Researchers construct a situation that allows for data to emerge from within the interaction or event, in response to various kinds of prompts. During these events, the researcher collects data through observations and records field notes. The researcher may also decide to add an elicitation component to the study, with interviews or focus groups. Collecting this kind of data involves adapting the methods traditional qualitative researchers refer to as vignettes, role-plays, simulations, games, or performative, creative, or arts-based research.
- **What is the relationship between researcher and human participants, archives, or sites where the data can be found?** As with elicited data collection, the researcher has a direct interaction with consenting participants.

ROLES FOR QUALITATIVE E-RESEARCHERS

When you imagine your role as a researcher, how would you describe it metaphorically? A way to think about the distinction between styles of data collection is through the stances of the researcher, described metaphorically as the miner, traveler (Kvale, 2007; Kvale & Brinkman, 2014), and gardener (Salmons, 2010, 2015). According to the metaphors Kvale and Brinkman devised to explain various roles that interviewers take, the researcher who digs out facts and feelings from research subjects is characterized as a *miner*. The *traveler* journeys with the participant to experience and explore the research phenomenon. The metaphor of the *gardener* was introduced to describe a nur-turing process often needed when building rapport with participants online. The metaphor alludes to ways a researcher uses questions to plant a seed, and **follow-up** or probing questions to cultivate the growth of ideas and shared perceptions. The researcher-as-gardener is characterized by an attitude of deep listening; the gardener listens for changes in the weather, for needs of the soil, as needed for the plant to grown.

Using Metaphors to Think about Researchers' Roles

The miner, gardener, or traveler metaphors can be used to think about roles we take in any kind of research, but they are particularly relevant to the consideration of the online approaches described here as extant, elicited, or enacted research (see Table 1.2).

Extant

Extant research is clearly aligned with the metaphor of the miner. The researcher has to locate the potentially rich seam and start digging. They may have to burrow through extraneous materials to get to the desired ore. Like miners, researchers may be fortunate to readily locate the rich, relevant records of users' conversation and abundant archives. With more and more historical documents being scanned, and contemporary events being documented online, the availability of high-quality materials has never been better.

Researchers may also find the gold is eluding them. They may discover that materials relevant to the study are not in the anticipated location or readily available online at all. Researchers using extant materials may also encounter access issues, proprietary boundaries or closed, members-only communities. To collect the needed data, researcher might need to get help from archivists or librarians. Don't be afraid to contact gatekeepers; be prepared to explain your research purposes. A proposal was necessary to gain access to one archive where I conducted research.

Again, the researcher using extant data does not influence the substance or nature of the documents or materials collected, using only what has been posted or curated. As a result, the researcher may find that the data is not adequate to achieve the purpose of the study. In a multimethod study the researcher can add an interview or questionnaire component to the study and elicit explanations from participants to fill in missing pieces of the story.

Elicited

Elicited research is most appropriately aligned with the gardener metaphor. The researcher may use verbal or written questions to elicit responses from participants. In a study using participant observation, the researcher may elicit data by informally asking questions or conversing with others engaged in the activity under observation. Researchers using these methods may also use images, graphics, or media that represent some aspect of the research problem or phenomenon to elicit reactions or answers. Elicitation is flexible and, unlike the researcher using extant data, researchers can draw out detailed replies specific to the phenomena being studied.

Enacted

Researchers using enacted research approaches fit the metaphor of the traveler. This kind of study researcher designs and carries out events or activities that require the researcher to be a co-participant. The researcher is thus highly engaged with the participant(s) throughout the process. Enacted approaches are only possible when participants are willing to travel with the researcher. A greater commitment is needed than completion of a single interview or **survey**.

Table 1.2 Typology, metaphors, and research questions

Type	Data Collection	Metaphor(s)	Types of Research Questions
Extant	Studies using existing materials developed without the researcher's influence	Miner	*What? How?*
			What are the activities, types of behaviors, trends in activities exhibited in the ways people post or interact online?
			How do people express themselves or describe their worlds in the writings, images, or media they post?
Elicited	Studies using data elicited from participants in response to the researcher's questions	Gardener	*What? How? Why?*
			What motivates people to act as they do?
			Why do individuals or groups engage in some activities and not others?
			How do they use communications technologies?
			How do they feel about it?
Enacted	Studies using data generated with participants during the study	Traveler	*What? How? Why?*
			What is the experience of participating in online events?
			How do people engage with known or unknown others online?
			What can be learned by interacting with participants using visual, mobile, virtual reality, and other online communication tools or platforms?
			Why are some choices made over others?

WHAT HAPPENS WHEN RESEARCHERS USE THESE IDEAS?

How do these ideas about qualitative online inquiry play out in research designs? You will find exemplars throughout the book that show ways to make decisions about the best approach, and apply key principles, at each stage of the process. The *research cameo* is one type of exemplar. Cameos are hypothetical scenarios designed to illustrate points in each chapter. The *research case* is a second type. Cases are stories from researchers, based on author interviews and their published studies. You will find cameos in every chapter, and research cases in Section III, Preparing to Collect Data Online.

─────────────── RESEARCH CAMEO 1.1 ───────────────

Metaphors and Research Questions

Four hypothetical researchers are designing ways to study the same research question: How and where do qualitative researchers publish their studies? We will follow these researchers throughout the book in order to illustrate ways to apply research concepts.

Researcher 1 will use extant data, Researcher 2 will use elicit data, Researcher 3 will generate data with enacted approaches, and Researcher 4 will use a multimodal design with multiple online approaches.

Researcher 1 is designing a study using extant data. They plan to analyze Big Data from journal databases as well as mission statements and editorials from selected journals to understand how and where qualitative research is published. They see their role as one of a 'miner' who digs into source materials.

Researcher 2 is designing a study that involves eliciting data through one-to-one and group online interviews with qualitative researchers who have successfully published their studies. They plan to exemplify the 'gardener' metaphor by cultivating rapport with each participant.

Researcher 3 is designing a study that will involve generating data with aspiring and successful qualitative researchers' enacted approaches. They intend to journey with participants through experiential simulations. The researcher feels the 'traveler' metaphor will best represent their relationship to participants.

Researcher 4 is designing a study that will include an analysis of extant data from journal archives, and online interviews with selected authors and editors. They expect to take multiple roles and draw from all three metaphors.

A HOLISTIC APPROACH TO DESIGNING AND CONDUCTING QUALITATIVE E-RESEARCH

As an online researcher, you will have many decisions to make when designing a study that will involve collecting data on the Internet or with digital tools. While it is true that all researchers face daunting design challenges, distinctive characteristics about how people interact and behave online mean there are additional factors to consider when designing a study that will be entirely or partially conducted online.

Cooperation and/or approval of proposals is typically needed, and those individuals may not be familiar with the nuances of online research. Student researchers need approvals from dissertation chairs or research supervisors, committees, and ethics boards. Researchers might need to gain access to sites or participants. Scholars need green lights from grant-makers, editors, or peer reviewers. Clarity in the development and presentation of the research design will help to expedite decision-making by the people who need to determine that your study is needed, ethical, and respectful to any participants.

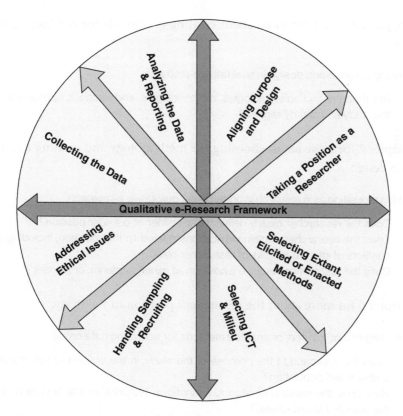

Figure 1.1 Qualitative e-Research Framework

The Qualitative e-Research Framework offers a conceptual schema of qualitative online research that will help you think through the components of the study, and present it in a coherent way (see Figure 1.1). It is comprised of interrelated categories, each with a set of questions and models. When introduced in *Cases in Online Interview Research* (Salmons, 2012) as the E-Interview Research Framework, the central focus was on data collection with **online interviews**. The updated framework encompasses a full range of qualitative online data collection based on the use of extant, elicited, or enacted data – or a mix of these types. In addition to its use at the design stage, the Qualitative e-Research Framework can be used in analytic contexts to evaluate proposed or published studies because it offers guiding topics and questions to review.

The Qualitative e-Research Framework is displayed as a circular system to facilitate a holistic approach to thinking through all elements of a study. While there are sequential phases in a research project, qualitative research is rarely linear.

- Choosing a qualitative e-research approach for the study:

  o Can you provide a compelling rationale for why you are conducting the study online?

See Chapters 2 and 3 for more about creating a rationale for conducting online research.

- Aligning purpose and design in qualitative e-research:

  o Are theories and epistemologies, methodologies, and methods appropriate for the study and clearly aligned?

See Chapter 2 for more about choosing the methodology and creating a coherent research design.

- Taking a position as a researcher undertaking qualitative e-research:

  o Does the researcher clearly delineate an insider or outsider position?
  o Does the researcher explain implications related to that position, including any conflicts of interest or risks of researcher bias?
  o Does the researcher perceive a position as miner, gardener, or traveler?

See Chapter 6 for more about the researcher's position in the study.

- Selecting extant, elicited, or enacted methods for collecting data online:

  o Does the approach fit the purpose of the study, in the context of the research problem and population?
  o How does the researcher align ICT functions, features, and/or limitations with the selected approach(es)?
  o Within each approach, are the specific methods (interviews, observations, etc.) appropriate to the study?

See Chapters 2 and 3 for more about choosing and using the appropriate approach.

- Selecting ICT and setting for qualitative e-research:

  - What ICT features will be used and why?
  - Will the study collect text-based, audio, and/or visual data?
  - Will the setting be in a public or private online milieu?

See Chapter 3 for more about choosing and using ICTs in the study.

- Handling sampling and recruiting in qualitative e-research:

  - Will the study engage human participants? If so, what sampling approaches are appropriate given the purpose of the study and target population?
  - Will participants be recruited online, if so, how?
  - In a study using extant data, how will archives or datasets be selected? What criteria will be used for selection of specific posts or user-generated content?

See Chapter 7 for more about issues related to determining a sampling plan for participants and/or materials for the study using extant, elicited, or enacted methods.

- Addressing ethical issues in qualitative e-research:

  - Has the researcher taken appropriate steps to protect **human subjects** and, where appropriate, their avatars or online representations?
  - Has the researcher obtained proper informed consent?
  - Does the researcher have permission to access and use posts, documents, profiles, or images?
  - Has the researcher committed to acting with integrity in all phases and contacts with others throughout the study?

See Chapters 4, 5, and 6 for more about ethical issues and the role of the researcher.

- Collecting the data online in qualitative e-research:

  - Is the researcher experienced with all features of the selected technology?
  - For studies using extant methods, is the researcher familiar with the setting, archive, databases, or other online environment where the data will be collected? Is the researcher familiar with software tools if they plan to use Big Data or plan to mine or trawl for data? Does the researcher have a guide or plan for recording observations? See Chapter 10.
  - For studies using elicited or enacted methods, does the researcher have a plan for conducting interviews, focus groups, or other interactions with participants with either prepared questions or a guide?

See Chapters 9, 11, and/or 12 for more about collecting data from participants.

- Analyzing the data and reporting on qualitative e-research:
  - Does the researcher have a plan for preparing, organizing, and coding all types of data?
  - Does the researcher have the proper permissions for using excerpts or quotations in published reports?

See Chapters 13 and 14 for more about data analysis and presenting and writing about the findings.

SUMMARY OF KEY CONCEPTS

Chapter 1 offers foundations for the rest of the book by defining qualitative research and qualitative e-research. Given the unique characteristics of online communication, three types of data collection are defined: extant, elicited, and enacted. The type of data collection, including the determination of whether human participants are involved, are decisions with implications for ethical practices and research design. Chapter 1 introduced the Qualitative e-Research Framework as a schema for thinking through design decisions.

DISCUSSION QUESTIONS AND EXERCISES

- **Analyze your online communication choices**. To think through communications choices you might make for research purposes, look more closely at the technologies you typically use. Identify and deconstruct the choices you make for your own personal and social communications. Keep a communications log for three days. Note what form(s) of communication you use, with whom (family member, friend, or colleague). Indicate whether you use visual, verbal, text, or a combination of modes to communicate.
- **Reflect on your potential research projects**. Which questions could best be answered with extant, elicited, or enacted styles of data collection? Why?
- **Think about holistic research designs for online qualitative research**. Look at the Qualitative e-Research Framework. Identify at least one question you would ask a researcher pertaining to each area of the model, in order to understand the design of the study.
- **Compare approaches**. Using your university library or open access journals, locate one article that uses extant data, and one that uses data elicited from participants. Compare and contrast the research questions, approaches, and findings.

Critique and discuss choices the researchers made at the design stage. How would the study have been different if it had been conducted online?

- **Look at emerging online research**. Using your university library or open access journals, locate one article that describes a study that involves an approach described here as 'enacted.' Why did the researcher select the approach? What was gained by collaborating with participants in an arts-based, creative, performative, or experiential study?

SECTION I

DESIGNING ONLINE

QUALITATIVE STUDIES

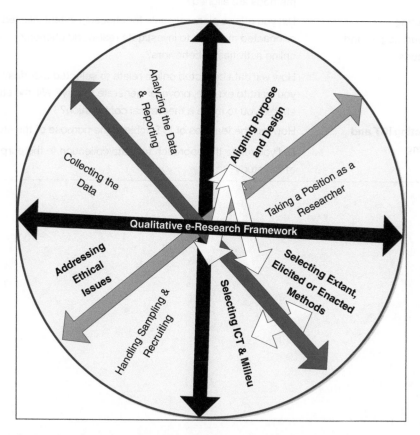

Figure I   Relationships in the Qualitative e-Research Framework

When we are contemplating an 'online study' it is tempting to start by thinking about the technologies first. However, other design decisions need to be made so we can choose the most appropriate tools to carry it out. The Qualitative e-Research Framework helps us do just that!

The Qualitative e-Research Framework is based on the premise that all elements of the inquiry are interrelated and intersubjective (see Figure I.1). Nowhere is this point more relevant than in consideration of how the purpose for the study and selected methodologies align with the methods. In an online study, this includes deciding how selected information and communications technologies fit with the design, and the purpose served.

Some of the questions to consider at this stage are listed in Table I.1.

Table I.1 Design issues in relation to the Qualitative e-Research Framework

	Aligning Purpose and Design
Aligning Purpose and Design	Did you make a coherent case for how the research questions, purpose, theories and epistemologies, methodologies, and methods are aligned?
Selecting Methodologies and Methods	Did you offer a clear rationale for choosing extant, elicited, or enacted methods to investigate real-world phenomena or online activities or behaviors?
	How will data collected online relate to selected theories? Do you want to explore, prove, or generate theory? Will the study enable you to make a theoretical contribution?
Selecting ICT and Setting	How will the features of ICT achieve the purpose of the study?
	Did you relate the approach for data collection to the purpose of the study?

2

Choosing Methodologies and Methods for Online Studies

HIGHLIGHTS

You have many decisions to make when designing and planning to conduct a qualitative inquiry. The same question can be explored from many different perspectives using many different possible approaches. Each choice is significant, and directions taken can change the nature of the study and the findings. Each choice must also fit within a larger framework of the research design. While qualitative research practices in general are referenced throughout the chapter, the discussion here will focus on how to apply them online. Each epistemological perspective and methodological approach has its own history, development, and disciplinary focus. Qualitative, mixed, and multimethods are explored extensively in the literature. Doing justice to each of the full range of related topics is beyond the scope of this book; thus, suggestions for further reading on research foundations are offered if you are interested in pursuing specific methodologies in more depth.

This chapter emphasizes careful decision-making as essential to the role and responsibility of the researcher. With these fundamentals in mind, you will be ready to focus on how to apply your selected approach with online or digital tools in Chapter 3.

OBJECTIVES

After reading and reflecting on this chapter, you will be able to:

- understand the role of the researcher as decision-maker
- comprehend key elements of research design: epistemology, theory, methodology, and methods
- demonstrate the importance of aligning the purpose of the study and the design elements
- consider how the unit of analysis influences decisions about methodology and methods in online studies
- think about the motivation behind conducting the study online, and understand the implications of that decision.

METHODOLOGIES AND METHODS ARE A STARTING POINT

In this chapter you will explore fundamental choices for a qualitative design: the methodologies and methods. You will look at ways to align the purpose of the study with the approach used to conduct it. Once you have chosen the methodologies and methods you intend to use, you can move on to the next steps.

Decisions about the research design need to be made in a systematic way so that you can develop thoughtful rationales and proposals. All researchers must think through and make these decisions, yet the online researcher has an additional set of considerations. Very simply, technology changes the ways we make sense of and communicate about thoughts and experiences. An email is distinctively different from a video chat. We respond differently to a text message from a colleague than to a social media post from someone we've never met. In an online study such distinctions influence the ways we think about how to frame the study, the kinds of data we collect, whether and how we interact with participants.

THINK LIKE AN ARCHITECT

Here is a metaphor to launch your thinking about research design: if you are building a house, you need to start with a blueprint. The blueprint lays out all of the elements of the house and must include the essentials: the kitchen, dining area, living room, and bedrooms. It must show how these rooms connect because if we have a kitchen but no way to get to the dining room it will be hard to serve a meal. If hallways and stairs are lacking, the house will not be functional. The blueprint also needs to take into account the lay of the land and the surroundings. Will the house fit in the sandy or rocky, hilly or flat plot? And will the finished home fit within the neighborhood?

The research designer is the architect for the study. Elements of the study need to make sense together with the appropriate connecting links and clear relationships that show how each element is aligned with the design as a whole. Just as the architect cannot ignore the surrounding terrain or built environment, the research designer needs to keep in mind the context of the study in terms of the discipline or field of study, its literature, theoretical frameworks, and expectations. Architects are design thinkers, decision-makers, and communicators. Just as the architect needs a blueprint that a homeowner can easily understand, the researcher must explain the research design in a way that is understandable by others who lack familiarity with qualitative research in general, and online research in particular.

RESEARCHER AS DECISION-MAKER

In Chapter 1 you were introduced to a variety of options for conducting qualitative research online. As a researcher, it is up to you to make the best choice about what to study, with whom or what sources, using what methodologies, methods, and digital tools. Becoming a successful researcher hinges on your ability to make responsible decisions about research designs, and your integrity for carrying them out in respectful ways.

You might be on a team with co-researchers or have partners. In such situations you might need to develop and use communication, collaboration, and shared decision-making skills. Or, you might be in a situation where you have stakeholders who will have some advisory or oversight roles, such as thesis or dissertation supervisors, or funders. In such situations you will need to be able to defend your decisions and accept input for recommended or required changes. Keep in mind that research collaborators or stakeholders might not be familiar with online methods and need careful explanations for the approaches you want to take.

Throughout this chapter and the remainder of the book you will find tips for developing your capacity to become an ethical, responsive researcher. By building your understanding about the implications of design decisions you will be confident about your ability to solicit important buy-in from others.

ALIGNING PURPOSE AND DESIGN

[W]hat ... is meant by 'knowledge'? What is it, and where is it to be found? If there were a succinct answer to this, there wouldn't be a tradition of inquiry, there wouldn't be theories and theorising about knowledge. (Hay, 2008, p. 9)

Empirical research is conducted to generate new knowledge and deeper understanding of the topic of study. The researcher intends to answer the research question and to generate unique contributions to the literature. Research results inform other scholars who may build on the work, as well as decision makers and practitioners looking for reliable information. Each scholar thinks about this process in a unique way and creates his or her original blueprint for the study. Researchers are guided by the scholarly traditions in the field of study and the conventions of qualitative research. An understanding of methodologies and methods common to qualitative research is essential to online researchers who must take additional factors into account when designing studies.

One of the challenges in the free-thinking world of qualitative methodologists is the inconsistency in terminology. To be clear, we will define four interrelated facets essential to qualitative research – epistemology, theory, methodology, and method. The researcher must decide how each of these four interrelated facets helps to achieve the purpose of the study and be prepared to justify each choice.

- **Theory** refers to 'a unified, systematic causal *explanation* of a diverse range of social phenomena' (Schwandt, 2007, p. 293). Theories central to the design of the study are presented in a theoretical framework. 'A theoretical framework is a broad paradigm on which the researcher stands to look into a problem' (Gaudet & Robert, 2018, p. 30). Ask: What is the place for theory in the proposed study? What *theories* of knowledge and what disciplinary theories have been applied to explain key principles related to my subject of inquiry in past research?
- **Epistemology** refers to the study of the nature of knowledge, or the study of how knowledge is justified (Crotty, 1998). Epistemology defines the criteria used for determining what and what does not constitute valid knowledge (Gray, 2018). Epistemology is based on the researcher's world view, that is, how the researcher understands the world and ways of knowing in the context of the research project. Terminology is not universal or precise, so what we refer to here as *epistemology* may also be called *research paradigms*. Ask: What *epistemic* views justify and guide my choices of methodology and methods?
- **Methodology** refers to the philosophies and systems of thinking that justify the methods used to conduct the research. The methodology explains why you are conducting the study in a particular way (Saldaña, 2014). Methodologies offer 'a way of engaging with the research material ... [A methodology is] made of a series of concepts and axioms, and it also proposes concrete methods and techniques to analyse the material' (Gaudet & Robert, 2018, p. 41). Methodologies emerge from academic disciplines in the social and physical sciences, although considerable cross-disciplinary exchange occurs (Pascale, 2011). What we refer to here as *methodologies* may also be called *research types* or *genres*. Ask: What methodology corresponds to the purpose of the study?
- **Method** refers to the practical, systematic steps used to conduct the study (Anfara & Mertz, 2006; Carter & Little, 2007), the 'how' of the study (Saldaña, 2014). The research design or proposal spells out the methods to be used for sampling, recruiting participants, collecting, analyzing, and interpreting data. Ask: What methods will allow me to carry out the inquiry and answer the research questions?

You must decide how each of these four interrelated facets applies to the study you want to propose. As suggested by the circular Qualitative e-Research Framework, decisions cannot be easily made in a linear way. It might be necessary to revisit each choice in light of other factors or influences. This iterative thinking does not stop when the design stage transitions into action; it may be necessary to adapt to unforeseen circumstances while the study is underway. As illustrated in the Figure 2.1 map, each area of the design is related to the others. We need to think about design as an interative, holistic process.

The epistemological framework may change after you decide what online methods to use. Or the epistemological framework may change if you decide whether the study will test or expand upon existing theory or try to generate new theory. The study-specific goals for collecting data online may influence choices in the overall research design. You will need to comprehend the methodological implications for decisions about methods of data collection. For example, potential participants' access to and comfort with communication technologies may influence choices about the overall research approach (see Chapter 3 for more on choosing ICTs for data collection). Your decisions must encompass the whole process – from the abstract ideas to the practical technology tools. Just as the architect needs a blueprint that a homeowner can easily understand, the researcher must explain the research design in a way that is understandable by others who lack familiarity with qualitative research in general, and online research in particular.

THEORIES AND THEORETICAL CONTRIBUTIONS

If you serve as a peer reviewer, you will notice that one of the first items on the form is, 'Does the study make a theoretical contribution?' Similar questions are included in dissertation reviews as well. What does it mean to make a *theoretical contribution*? If you want to present or publish your study, you will need to be able to answer that question. Start by deepening your understanding about theories and their place in research, then think about how your study can contribute to scholarly thinking.

What Is the Place of Theory in Research?

Theory plays different roles in qualitative and quantitative studies. In quantitative research, theory 'is an inter-related set of constructs (or variables) formed into propositions, or hypotheses, that specify the relationship among variables' (Creswell, 2014, p. 54). Quantitative researchers start with a theory, develop a hypothesis, and collect data to refine or contradict the theory. In contrast, some qualitative researchers frame the study in theoretical terms, while others aim to discover and 'ground' theoretical principles in the data.

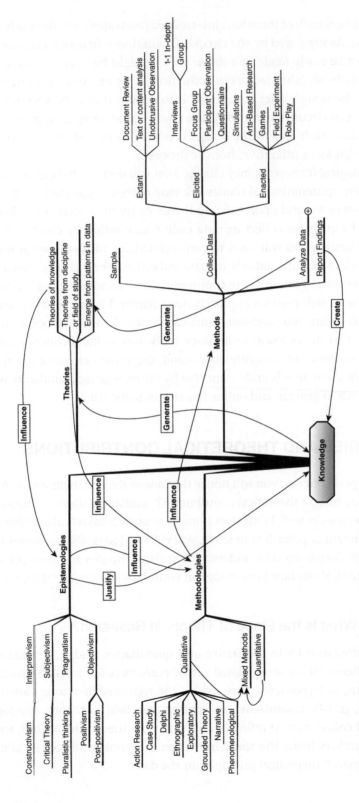

Figure 2.1 Designing studies to generate new knowledge

Corley and Gioia (2011) defined theory as 'a statement of concepts and their inter-relationships that shows how and/or why a phenomenon occurs' (p. 12). While simple, this definition includes three important elements. First, theory is a statement of concepts, definitions, constructs, and propositions. However, these concepts do not stand alone; they are interrelated. So, the second part we need to understand is the type of relationship, such as causal, temporal, or ordinal, that connects these concepts. Third, this system of related concepts has one or more purpose: theory can explain existing phenomena or predict the way phenomena may be expected to unfold.

Empirical research serves to advance the development of theory and in the process to advance our understanding of the phenomena. One way to analyze the ways scholarship makes such advances is by looking at the theoretical contribution each study makes. Sometimes the purpose of the study is to refine or test theory, or to develop or build new theory. Corley and Gioia (2011) suggest two additional dimensions to explore – degrees of originality and utility:

> The idea of [theoretical] contribution rests largely on the ability to provide *original insight* into a phenomenon by advancing knowledge in a way that is deemed to have *utility* or usefulness for some purpose ... Originality can be categorized as either (1) advancing understanding incrementally or (2) advancing understanding in a way that provides some form of revelation, whereas the utility dimension parses into (1) practically useful and (2) scientifically useful. (Corley & Gioia, 2011, pp. 15–16)

As you delve into the literature you will see that theories are not static. When you explore how theories have evolved, you can discern the efforts of researchers to advance understanding in ways that researchers and practitioners find useful. You might look at other kinds of influences on the theory. Changes in culture, society, and technology, mean there are new problems to understand with new or updated theories. On a cultural or personal level, biases can influence the ways scholars define and interpret ideas.

THEORY IN QUALITATIVE RESEARCH

One way or the other, theories underpin the research design, and online studies are no exception. Theories of knowledge will ultimately be used to justify and explain the new understandings that emerge from the study. Theories of knowledge represent different ways of looking at and thinking about ourselves and the world around us ('theory' derives from the Greek verb *theôrein*, meaning 'to gaze upon' [Hay, 2008, p. 9]). Theories from the discipline or field of study may influence not only the choices of methodology, but the nature and questions of the inquiry. Education, sociology, psychology, health business, or humanities researchers will turn to established disciplinary theories when establishing a basis for the study.

They also influence the choice and form of research methodology since some are oriented more toward quantitative or toward qualitative research. This being the case, theories can influence the methods selected to collect and analyze the data.

Where are the gaps in the theories you choose to frame your study? In which areas do earlier explanations no longer apply? Start by delving into the literature about the research problem and questions. How did previous studies explore, develop, and/or test relevant theory? What recommendations made by prior researchers can help prioritize areas where further theory development is needed?

─────────────── SPOT CHECK ───────────────

- Are you familiar with seminal theories in your field of study? If not, background research will be necessary before you begin to design your study.
- When you read scholarly articles, do you look at the way theory is discussed? How did previous studies explore, develop, and/or test relevant theory?
- What recommendations made by prior researchers can help prioritize areas where further theory development is needed?

EPISTEMOLOGIES FOR QUALITATIVE ONLINE RESEARCH

When researchers choose epistemology, methodology, and methods, they draw on accepted concepts and practices to create their own frameworks to use in designing, planning, conducting, analyzing, and reporting on the study.

Positivist, Interpretivist, Critical, and Pragmatic Epistemologies

A positivist perspective presupposes an objective reality that exists apart from the perceptions of those who observe it. A fundamental principle shared by the many schools of positivist thought is that reality is external to the self and can be observed or measured to produce information that can be understood and interpreted by others (Schensul, 2008, p. 517). It makes a separation between the consciousness of the researcher as observer and the nature of the reality observed. The goal of research based in this world view is to discover this objective truth, to better understand reality.

Positivism is the point of view taken by researchers conducting fact-based investigations using the **scientific method**. Positivism is linked to qualitative research through the idea that social situations can be studied, critiqued, and subsequently changed (Schensul, 2008). Critics of positivism think it ignores context and too narrowly excludes 'sources of understanding of the world including those deriving from human experiences, reasoning, or interpretation as inappropriate for scientific enquiry' (Fox, 2008, p. 686). Social researchers have largely rejected strict interpretations of **positivism** in favor of **postpositivism**.

While positivists aim to prove causal relationships, postpositivists rely on deductive logic to build evidence in support of an existing theory (Creswell, 2013; Hesse-Biber & Leavy, 2006). The postpositivist view challenges earlier positivist notions by recognizing that we cannot be 'positive' about our claims of the existence of a common objective reality when studying the behavior and actions of humans because of biases and other limitations of researchers (Creswell & Clark, 2007; Schutt, 2006). Postpositivists fully acknowledge the role of the researcher as interpreter of data and recognize the importance of **reflexivity** in research practice (Fox, 2008).

- **Positivist assumptions about humans and social life**: The 'components of society have an objective existence, they are factual and can be accurately measured. The components of society can influence ... or determine ... human behavior/human understandings' (Loseke, 2013, p. 22).
- **Positivist assumptions about social research**: 'Social researchers must use the scientific method developed in the natural sciences. ... The researcher is a scientist: objective and impartial' (Loseke, 2013, p. 22).

Interpretivist approaches focus on the meanings individuals or groups attribute to events, places, behaviors and interactions, people, and artifacts (Schensul, 2008). Qualitative social researchers operating from a stance influenced by interpretivist perspectives believe that knowledge arises in an individual based on experience and tempered by reason. The premise of **interpretivism** is that, as humans, we 'interpret' our experiences in the social world to produce and reproduce meanings (Blaikie, 2004). From this view, knowledge acquisition occurs when people invent concepts, models, and schemes to make sense of experience and their place in the social and natural world. They continually test and modify these constructions in the light of new experience (Schwandt, 2007).

Each individual interprets meanings and responses in unique ways. By sharing common interpretations communities emerge and define values, cultures, or norms. Yet even when members of a group seem to share the same experiences and perspectives, their interpretations of events or ideas may be different.

- **Interpretive assumptions about humans and social life**: 'While there is an objective world of tangible objects, social research is about the social world, which does not have meaning apart from human understanding of it. ... While human experiences are shaped by the components of society, humans remain creatures who must find meaning in their surroundings' (Loseke, 2013, p. 22).
- **Interpretive assumptions about social research**: 'The goal of research is to understand the complexity of the human experience. The researcher is a student of social life and the researcher is a social member; hence, complete objectivity is not possible' (Loseke, 2013, p. 22).

Critical perspectives are another set of epistemologies qualitative researchers draw on to frame their studies. Critical approaches view individual and group behavior and meaning as shaped by structures and processes of dominance, power, and/or authority (Schensul, 2008, p. 517). Critical perspectives are characterized by an understanding of people as historical agents who are participants in action as well as subject to action (Budd, 2008, p. 175). Critical theorists see research as a means for change to right injustice and for advocacy that may make the world a better place. They engage participants who believe participation in the study will change their lives, or improve the institutions and communities in which they live and work (Bloomberg & Volpe, 2012, p. 29) and sometimes engage participants as co-researchers. Critical approaches are used to study issues related to gender, race, and/or sexual orientation as well as poverty and widespread social problems.

- **Critical assumptions about humans and social life**: The components of society have both an objective existence and subjective meaning. The components of society can be measured, but facts are also embedded in systems of meaning determined by power and politics. All society life is oriented around power relations. These relations determine human behavior and experiences.
- **Critical assumptions about social research**: The methods of science 'are not value-free. Yet these methods can be used when they are in the service of freeing oppressed people' (Loseke, 2013, p. 22).

The goal of critical research is to study, critique, and reveal 'different patterns of locally, nationally, and internationally situated dominance and control; the ways in which they are sustained and reproduced; and the responses of individuals and groups to these structures and power differentials' (Schensul, 2008, p. 517). 'The critical researcher is an advocate for oppressed people' (Loseke, 2013, p. 22) who uses findings to strengthen their case and actualize change.

Sometimes the purpose of the study calls for a balanced, real-world world view and in such cases pragmatic thinking fits. **Pragmatism** holds that the meaning of a concept is determined by its practical implications; and that the truth of any judgment is determined in and through practical activity (Hammersley, 2004, p. 848).

The concept and philosophy associated with pragmatism was introduced in the works of Charles Sanders Peirce (1839–1914), and then further developed by William James (1842–1910) and John Dewey (1859–1952) (McCaslin, 2008, p. 672). As an educator, John Dewey was particularly interested in developing knowledge and fostering learning. His thinking about pragmatism 'points to the importance of joining beliefs and actions in a process of inquiry that underlies any search for knowledge, including the specialized activity that we refer to as research' (Morgan, 2014, p. 1051).

In a research context the pragmatic approach looks for plural, rather than polar, positions. Pragmatists take intersubjective attitudes, moving between objective and subjective viewpoints, 'first converting observations into theories and then assessing those theories through action' (Morgan, 2007, p. 71). Pragmatic researchers recognize problems, develop models that match their observations, check them for logical consistency, and test them through further observation and action. Since the purpose of pragmatic approaches is to locate practical and usable solutions to the stated problem, the research closes when the solution can be articulated (McCaslin, 2008, p. 675).

- **Pragmatic assumptions about humans and social life**: Life and social life operate in a cycle: the origins of our beliefs arise from our prior actions and the outcomes of our actions are found in our beliefs. Experiences create meaning by bringing beliefs and actions in contact with each other (Morgan, 2014, p. 1046).
- **Pragmatic assumptions about social research**: Pragmatism treats research as a human experience that is based on the beliefs and actions of actual researchers. Research never occurs in a vacuum, so researchers should ask and reflect on questions such as: How is it influenced by the historical, cultural, and political contexts in which it is done? How do our research communities come together to emphasize one way of doing things rather than another? (Morgan, 2014, p. 1051)

Interpretivism can readily be used to frame designs for research to be conducted online. This epistemological stance seems like a natural fit for studies that intend to answer questions about Internet users and their experiences. Inherent in the online world is the self-determination of users to find order to construct their own realities to reflect interests, questions, and social engagement. Each Internet user constructs a personally-relevant set of frequently-visited sites and applications. Users find a way to interpret the universe of content in ways that fit their reality. Individuals find and/or build community by sharing ideas and locating others who interpret life in the world in similar ways. Social networking is the term commonly used for many online activities to indicate the importance of sharing and exchange.

Online exchange, whether on an individual, community, or Internet-wide basis occurs with a purpose. Internet users take to social media to highlight problems, to share images and observations on the scenes of the crisis, or to mobilize support for a cause. Critical perspectives can be used by online researchers who design studies with the purpose of creating change or creating a foundation for greater advocacy by revealing the experiences of those who suffer from injustice. This kind of research can demonstrate the prevalence and reach of the problem at hand and rally others of like mind to lobby for or against a decision.

Pragmatic epistemologies provide a framework for explaining scholarly research into actions and behaviors. Many online behaviors involve practical steps to access the technology, use software, operate hardware, and demonstrate information or digital literacy skills. Each epistemology offers a perspective on the study, and a deeper examination of these points of view and their complexities will help the researcher show the scholarly significance of the proposed study. It is up to the researcher to make this design decision and explain it in a way that will clarify and justify the direction of the inquiry.

Epistemologies and Reasoning

Researchers operating from a stance influenced by **constructivism** (or interpretivism) or critical theory believe that knowledge arises in an individual based on experience and reason. Knowledge and meaning exist in communities of people and define what they share as values, culture, or in their relationships to their environment. The researcher can justify the selection of interview methods based on the desire to uncover the interviewee's knowledge on a topic – or to create new understandings with the interviewee through the research process. The researcher may also want to observe how individuals or groups interact with one another and their environments.

Research justified by interpretivist epistemologies typically uses **inductive reasoning** to come to conclusions. Inductive reasoning works from the specific to the general, from a 'particularity (typically a set of observations of some sort) to a broad statement, such as a theory or general proposition concerning a topic' (Fox, 2008a, p. 430). Using inductive reasoning, the researcher looks for patterns, relationships, and associations in the data and constructs generalizations. Researchers use inductive reasoning when they examine how people integrate fragmented phenomena into meaningful explanations of experiences. Qualitative researchers may also use **abductive reasoning**. Abduction is 'a practical reasoning mode whose purpose is to invent and propose ideas and explanations that account for surprises and unmet expectations' (Locke, 2010, p. 4). Researchers use abduction to apply an observation or case to a theory (or vice versa) to generate a plausible interpretation (Schwandt, 2007). A third type, **deductive reasoning**, works from the general to the specific. When researchers use deductive reasoning, they state a hypothesis, then gather data (evidence) to support or refute that hypothesis (Shank, 2008). Deductive reasoning is typically associated with **quantitative research**.

Mixed Methods, Multimethods, and Mixed Epistemologies

The term **mixed methods** describes studies that combine or integrate qualitative and quantitative approaches at different stages of the research process. Researchers might use quantitative surveys or Big Data to understand the scope of a problem, then use qualitative methods to dig below the surface and gain a deeper understanding. Or, after conducting a qualitative study, a researcher could use quantitative methods to learn whether the themes in the data represent a larger trend than could be ascertained from a small interview sample. Some studies carry out both qualitative and quantitative components of the study simultaneously. Mixed methods studies can use qualitative and quantitative methodologies and methods for data collection *and* analysis. For example, it is possible to code qualitative data and analyze it statistically.

Multimethod or **multimodal research** uses more than one method but stays within the respective qualitative or quantitative methodological framework

(Okumus, Olya, Van Niekerk, Taheri, & Gannon, 2020). In qualitative research the term multimodal also refers to studies that utilize more than one type of data. 'A key focus for multimodal research in this area is systematically to document and map the relationship across and between modes in texts, interactions, social practices, artefacts and spaces' (Flewitt, Price, & Korkiakangas, 2019, p. 3). Given the focus of this book, the emphasis is on studies that might include a mix of qualitative research methodologies and methods in online data collection.

Drawing on more than one method may mean mixing epistemologies. Such researchers must reconcile seemingly disparate views of the world. From a positivist or postpositivist view, they want to understand social reality, while from an interpretivist view, they want to understand the meanings people give to reality. They need to identify a world view that encompasses all their methods or use epistemological bricolage, piecing together different ways to make sense of the inquiry and its findings (Freeman, 2007). They might choose to take a pragmatic stance. Pragmatism holds that meaning is determined by the experiences or practical consequences of belief in or use of the idea (Johnson & Onwuegbuzie, 2004). The pragmatic approach looks for plural, rather than polar, positions. Pragmatists take intersubjective attitudes, moving between objective and subjective viewpoints. They rely on abductive reasoning by moving back and forth between inductive and deductive reasoning, 'first converting observations into theories and then assessing those theories through action' (Morgan, 2007, p. 71). Pragmatic researchers develop models that match their observations, check them for logical consistency, and test them through further observation and action. Because they believe that research approaches should be mixed in ways that offer the best opportunities for answering important research questions, pragmatists mix epistemologies, methodologies, and methods.

SPOT CHECK

- Do you understand the differentiation between different epistemological perspectives? If not, background research will be necessary before you begin to design your study.
- Do you think about your proposed research from a positivist, postpositivist, interpretivist, or pragmatic perspective?
- What form of reasoning do you anticipate will fit best given what you know about the research you want to propose?

CHOOSING METHODOLOGIES FOR ONLINE QUALITATIVE RESEARCH

Epistemologies offer one way to think about and situate the study. Methodologies offer additional ways to think through the basis for organizing, planning and conducting the study, and analyzing the results. Each qualitative methodology is a distinct school of thought, with its own philosophers and practitioners. Each offers a different vantage point from which to view the research phenomena, the environment or social context, the participants, and their thoughts, feelings, experiences, or expressions. These vantage points may readily fit into a particular field of research or discipline; however, the sense of fit may evolve when research questions and contexts change. For example, ethnography, a methodology associated with studies of culture, was previously the domain of anthropologists. Now ethnography is being conducted by business researchers to study organizational cultures, or by market researchers to study how products are assimilated into the culture. New forms include visual and sensory ethnography, digital and virtual ethnography. **Phenomenological** approaches previously used in psychology or social work disciplines to gain first-person perceptions are now used in education or health-related fields. To encourage this kind of creative adaptation and boundary-crossing, the discussion is not discipline-specific.

Qualitative methodologies are quite diverse. Some offer detailed guidelines about how to design and carry out every stage of the study from identifying the research question to determining the sample, collecting the data, and analyzing it. Others are broadly philosophical and offer only sketchy guidance for the novice researcher. Some have been widely used in online studies while others have not – offering opportunities for creative researchers to apply them in new ways that take advantage of the characteristics of the digital world.

A brief overview of methodologies and design considerations is offered in Table 2.1. The options are offered as food for thought, not as a prescription for matching methodologies, epistemologies, and online options. Given the focus and scope of this book, fundamental definitions of major schools of thought are simply introduced. See additional resources about qualitative methodologies in the Appendix to delve more deeply into the ones that interest you. The focus here is on ways to use or adapt qualitative methodologies in online research.

───────────── SPOT CHECK ─────────────

- Are you familiar with the basic principles of qualitative methodologies? If not, background research will be necessary before you begin to design your study.
- Are some methodologies more prevalent than others in your field of study? To what extent will you need to defend your choices?
- When you read scholarly articles, do you look at how the methodologies are explained?
- What opportunities or limitations do you perceive in the methodologies presented here when thinking about online research?

Table 2.1 An overview of qualitative research methodologies

Methodology	Online Options	Epistemological Options
Action Research		
Action research is a method of systematically examining behavior in an effort to improve practice. The *action* refers to doing something. The *research* refers to thinking critically and logically about a problem (Duesbery & Twyman, 2020, p. 3).	You could conduct action research online to study ways to improve an online community, course, or discussion group. Or you could conduct action research online to engage participants in a convenient way, in order to study changes needed to a real-world community or organization.	Action research can employ a pragmatic epistemology since the purpose of such research is to improve policies and practices rather than to make a theoretical contribution.
Action research involves a process of collaboration between researchers and participants. When the emphasis on shared decision-making rises to the point where participants become co-researchers, the term *participatory action research* is used. Action research studies aim to identify and develop interventions and change by its process or outcome (Blum et al., 2010, p. 449).		
Autoethnography		
In autoethnographic studies the researcher reflects on and writes an account of his or her own life as an ethnographer (Denzin, 2014). While autoethnography places the self within a social and cultural context, such studies are not primarily about the self, and in this way, it differs from autobiography (Reed-Danahay, 2019).	You could design an autoethnography to study online social and cultural contexts, and your place within them. Alternatively, you could use online tools for an autoethnographic study of broader contexts, including offline experiences or phenomena.	Autoethnographies can utilize an interpretivist epistemology since individual researchers discern meaning from their own lived experience.

(Continued)

Table 2.1 (Continued)

Methodology	Online Options	Epistemological Options
Exploratory Qualitative Study Jupp defined exploratory research as a methodological approach wedded to the notion of exploration and the researcher as explorer. In this context exploration might be thought of as a perspective, 'a state of mind, a special personal orientation' toward approaching and carrying out social inquiry (Jupp, 2006, p. 11). Studies are designed to maximize the discovery of generalizations leading to a detailed and profound understanding of the group, process, or activity under study (Stebbins, 2001, p. 3).	Exploratory online studies allow you to look into a new or emerging phenomenon, or to try new approaches that do not fit into an established methodology.	You could employ interpretivist epistemology since the study depends on understanding how participants construct meaning about the situation or phenomena under investigation. Given the flexibility of exploratory research, a pragmatic or critical epistemology could fit.
Case Study A study of one or more 'cases' which are clearly defined and bounded exemplars of the research phenomenon (Yin, 2018). Yin defined three types of case studies: • An explanatory case study is designed to explain how or why some condition came to be, or why a sequence of events occurred. • An exploratory case study is designed to identify research questions to be used in a subsequent study. • A descriptive case study is designed to describe a phenomenon in context.	You could choose to study cases of online phenomena, or choose to collect data online about cases that occur on or offline. Gallagher (2019) notes the importance of bounding the online case. Boundaries could be spatial (where data will be collected), temporal (time frame for the study), and/or relational (who is being studied, and how they relate to others) in an online case study design.	Online case studies can use interpretivist, pragmatic, or critical epistemologies.

Methodology	Online Options	Epistemological Options
Delphi		
When dealing with novel fields of studies that remain unexplored, the Delphi method can be a useful technique (Ouariachi, Gutiérrez-Pérez, & Olvera-Lobo, 2018). Delphi studies are designed to find consensus from a panel of experts on a present or future issue or topic (Hsu & Sandford, 2010).	The rounds of review and discussion common to Delphi studies could occur synchronously and asynchronously. Synchronous online meetings would be appropriate for the stage where participants aim to achieve consensus on the solution determined from the data collected in the study.	If you choose this approach you could apply pragmatic epistemologies, given that the purpose of most Delphi studies is to develop a practical solution to a current or future problem.
Ethnography		
A study of culture(s), cultural influences, or cultural sense-making. Studies aim to describe and interpret cultural behavior (Schwandt, 2007, pp. 97–98) by emphasizing the importance of understanding the meanings and cultural practices of people from within everyday contexts (Griffin & Bengry-Howell, 2010).	There are many options for using ethnography online using extant, elicited, and/or enacted approaches. Most digital or virtual ethnographers use observational data collection, but questionnaires, surveys, or interviews can be employed as well.	Ethnographic researchers typically choose interpretivism as the epistemological framework.
Ethnographic methods are widely used in online research. Virtual ethnography (Hine, 2020a), digital ethnography or netnography (Kozinets, 2019) have slightly different approaches for studying online cultures and communities.		
Grounded Theory		
A study designed to generate a new theory, new theoretical constructs, or models (Charmaz, 2014; Corbin & Strauss, 2015).	Grounded theory approaches can be used in online research to develop models or frameworks that depict relationships in online cultures, communities, or organizations.	The researcher using grounded theory typically chooses an interpretivist epistemology.
Phenomenology		
A study of the ways individuals experience and give meaning to an event, concept or phenomenon (Giorgi, 2009; Moustakas, 1994).	Phenomenological researchers usually depend on interviews for data collection. Conducting online interviews allows for flexibility of time and location.	The epistemology guiding most phenomenological research comes from interpretivism.

—————————————— RESEARCH CAMEO 2.1 ——————————————

Four researchers are designing ways to study how and where qualitative research is published collecting extant data (Researcher 1), eliciting data (Researcher 2), generating data with enacted approaches (Researcher 3), or collecting data with more than one method (Researcher 4).

Researcher 1 will use a case study methodology. They will define spatial boundaries by selecting databases that include journals from social sciences, humanities, education, and business disciplines. They will define the temporal parameters as 2015 to the present. They will define relational boundaries in terms of authors who conduct qualitative studies and publish articles in indexed journals.

Researcher 2 will use a phenomenological methodology to study the lived experience of qualitative researchers who go through the process of conducting and reporting on research in journal articles and other publications.

Researcher 3 will conduct an exploratory qualitative study to engage with researchers and authors and try to learn the steps they take when deciding how to get qualitative research published, and while engaging in the stages of submission and review.

Researcher 4 will conduct an ethnographic study of a writing group, to observe their process and experiences with getting their work published.

The decision to adopt a methodology is a significant one. The guidelines offered here are just that; there are no hard and fast rules about which methodology fits which unit of analysis, research purpose, or question. It is worthwhile to take the time to sketch out how the proposed problem and question can be studied from various epistemological options before finalizing the choice. Which option fits, and why? How can you justify your decision?

Methodology and Units of Analysis

One way to organize our thinking about qualitative methodologies is to look at how each approach corresponds to the *unit of analysis* for the study. Some methodologies are more aligned to the study of the individual's lived experiences, while others are more generally used to study community or societal issues. How does each respective qualitative methodology align with our interests in individuals, groups, crowds, or the global society which contains people who are not online?

Globe, society or crowd. At the broadest level researchers are interested in global, societal, or cultural issues. These researchers want to understand major trends and common or divergent experiences of a large group or crowd of people. They may be interested in systems or events that touch many lives. They are interested in regions of the world, in specific countries, or in social networking sites that engage people from across the globe. Topics might include political, social or environmental events or crises, poverty, epidemics, immigration, multinational business operations, economic developments, social movements or the environment.

Community, organization or institution. At the next level of analysis researchers are interested in one or more communities, organizations, institutions, agencies and/or businesses. While this category may also involve large groups of people, they operate within some shared set of parameters. Researchers want to understand the systems, roles, policies, practices or experiences of those who are working, learning or living together within some shared set of policies or norms. Topics might include reform efforts, social responsibility, management or leadership styles, or acceptance of change.

Group, Family or team. On a smaller scale, when researchers study groups, teams or families they are exploring relationships, interpersonal dynamics, and interactions among people who know each other. Topics might include communication or collaboration styles or practices, conflict resolution, parenting or family issues.

Individuals. At the most fundamental level, qualitative researchers study attitudes, perceptions, or feelings of individuals. Topics could include any aspect of the lived experience.

RESEARCH CAMEO 2.2

Let's look at how each of the hypothetical researchers we are tracking in research cameos handles decisions about the unit of analysis.

Researcher 1 has chosen to look at these issues at a societal, global level by looking at a crowd of published articles in many journals, across disciplines.

Researcher 2 has chosen to look at the research question at an individual level by studying the experiences of researchers going through the publication process.

Researcher 3 has also chosen to explore the individual experiences and choices of researchers.

Researcher 4 has chosen to look at research publishing at individual and small group levels.

As noted in Chapter 1, research design is a holistic process. And as noted in the introduction to this chapter, becoming a researcher means becoming a decision-maker. If these researchers made different decisions about the unit of analysis, they would alter the entire focus and nature of the study, the presence of and kind of participants, type(s) of data collected, and so on.

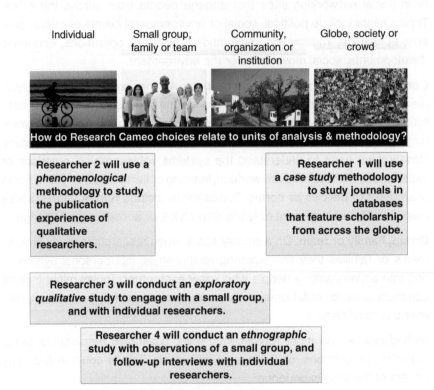

Figure 2.2 Units of analysis and methodologies

METHODS: WAYS TO CONDUCT THE STUDY

Methods are the techniques used to conduct the collection and analysis of data. Chapter 1 introduced extant, elicited, and enacted types of methods for collecting data.

The typology of qualitative online methods (see Table 2.2) associates the types of data and data collection with the type of method. The respective types and methods will be explored in greater depth in Sections III and IV of this book.

Each way to collect data offers both opportunities and limitations. In studies using *extant* data there is the obvious advantage that participants do not need to be recruited and interviews do not need to be scheduled. Depending on the topic of research, extensive material may be available to review. As more historical texts and images are scanned, researchers have access to them through libraries and archives.

Posts range from isolated comments to sustained discussions that involve diverse perspectives. Researchers can follow the reactions to current events in the real-time posts users make to publicly accessible social media or news organization comment areas. In addition to users' posts, numerous government, agency, or company reports are readily accessible. Materials available include print, audio podcast, and video. Big Data and databases are sources that encompass large quantities of extant data.

A disadvantage in using this type of data is that without being able to ask questions the researcher is limited by the scope of relevant material available. It is possible that posts made by users do not accurately or fully reflect their experiences or true points of view. The inability to ask questions means the researcher is unable to probe more deeply, uncover motivations, relationships or the back story behind the user's activity. This may mean the researcher could find him- or herself

Table 2.2 Typology of qualitative online methods

Typology of Online Methods		Data Collected Online from:	Researcher and Participant
Extant	Studies using existing materials developed without the researcher's influence	• Posts, discussions, and archives on websites, blogs, social networking sites including written materials, drawings, graphics or other images, photographs, and/or recorded audio or audio-visual media • Archives • Published literature or books • Documents and reports • Datasets and databases • Unobtrusive observation of sites, communities, or events	No direct contact with individual participants
Elicited	Studies using data elicited from participants in response to the researcher's questions or prompts	• Interviews (one-to-one or group) • Focus groups • Written interviews or questionnaires • Participant observation of sites, communities, or events	Interaction between researcher and one or more participants
Enacted	Studies using data generated with participants during the study	• Vignette, scenario or problem-centered interviews • Simulations, role-plays or dramatic activities • Arts-based or creative methods • Games	Interaction and collaboration involving researcher and one or more participants

buried in data that simply does not go into the level of specificity or offer the kind of substance needed to answer the research question.

Researchers using *elicitation* approaches have a different set of opportunities and limitations. Unlike those using extant data, they *can* ask questions. They are able to redirect, follow up and probe as needed to encourage participants to share their experiences and stories. The researcher can use visual and other types of elicitation methods as well as spoken questions. The researcher may discover new dimensions of the phenomenon that take the study in different directions and allow for innovative discoveries.

The main limitation is that the researcher must be able to find, recruit, and gain consent from suitable participants. As with any enterprise that involves human beings, there is a possibility the person will not live up to expectations. Participants willing to be a part of the study may lack the depth of experience or ability to share it in a clear and articulate way.

Researchers using methods described here as *enacted* share many of the opportunities and limitations described for studies using elicited data. Additionally, these researchers need to find participants willing to engage more deeply and most likely be involved in multiple interactions. These participants need to have more sophisticated technology skills and be willing to try out experiential techniques. In both elicited and enacted methods the participant who changes his or her mind about being a part of the study can simply click the button to close the interview window or just refuse to respond to the researcher's emails or requests to schedule time together.

These pros and cons are weighed when deciding what method or combination of methods to use given the unit(s) of analysis chosen for the study (see Figure 2.3). Some methods lend themselves to **in-depth**, one-to-one communication, while others fit studies where many-to-many communication is involved.

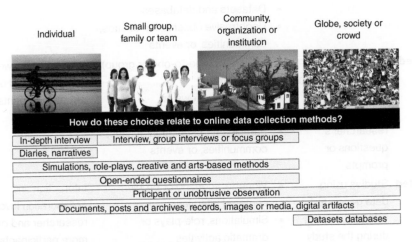

Figure 2.3 Matching method with unit of analysis

—————————— RESEARCH CAMEO 2.3 ——————————

Initial Plans for Data Collection

Researcher 1 plans to search and export lists of references from journal databases as the first stage, then sort by keywords for methodologies, methods, and publication dates.

Researcher 2 plans to conduct online interviews with individual researchers.

Researcher 3 plans to offer a publishing workshop online and collect data from the writers who participate.

Researcher 4 plans to observe the writing group's social media interactions, and their online meetings. They will also interview the researchers about their experiences.

In deciding what methods to use to collect data for the study with what technology, it is helpful to think about why the study is being conducted online. This foundational determination will guide decisions about methods as well as the technologies that allow the researcher to collect data.

DOES TECHNOLOGY SERVE AS THE MEDIUM, SETTING, OR PHENOMENON?

Researchers choose to collect data online for a variety of reasons. The choice can be analyzed by considering one or more of three broad possibilities (see Figure 2.4):

1. **Medium**: Information and communications technologies (ICTs) are chosen as a medium for communication. Just as a telephone conversation is not *about* the telephone per se, the online communication between researcher and participants could be any aspect of the lived experience – online or in person.
2. **Setting**: In addition to functioning as the communication medium, the ICT serves as the electronic research milieu. Just as conventional researchers choose whether to conduct interviews in their offices versus participants' homes, or whether to observe people at a park versus a shopping mall, online researchers need to think about setting. The researcher may have an interest in using specific features of a platform such as availability of a shared **whiteboard** or webcam, so chooses the electronic setting accordingly. A setting could be chosen because it meets the need for privacy and easy access by participants. An online setting could be selected because it is a space where discussions occur about the topics being studied, or because it is a space that attracts users that meet the demographic

or other criteria for the study. An online setting for a study involving adolescents might be different from one involving parents.

3. **Phenomenon**: When characteristics of the communication medium or of the setting are of interest to the researcher we can say the technology is itself part of the phenomenon the study is designed to investigate. In these cases the researcher is interested in the ways users engage with the technology. The purpose of these studies is to analyze activities, experiences, and behaviors on or with ICTs.

If I am a researcher using ICTs as a medium, the nature of the tool or platform is valuable only in its potential for communication with participants. If I am a researcher using ICTs as a setting, I am interested in ways the tool or platform is conducive to specific types of interactions with participants, in a form they are accustomed to participating in for social or professional reasons. If I am a researcher using ICTs as the phenomenon, I want to know how or why users communicate, using what tools, how often, for what purpose.

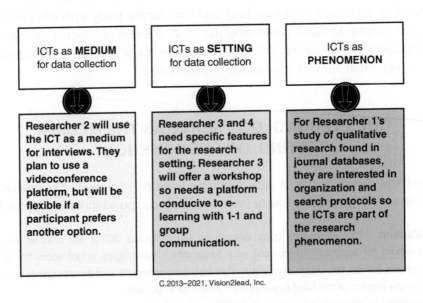

C.2013–2021, Vision2lead, Inc.

Figure 2.4 Reasons for cameo researchers' ICT choices

────────── RESEARCH CAMEO 2.4 ──────────

Choosing to Conduct the Study Online

Four researchers are designing ways to study the publication of qualitative research by collecting extant data (Researcher 1), eliciting data (Researcher 2), generating data with enacted approaches (Researcher 3), and a mix of online qualitative approaches (Researcher 4).

For **Researcher 1**, the technology is entwined with the research phenomena since they are studying electronic journals.

For **Researcher 2**, the technology serves primarily as a medium to communicate and interact with participants about their experiences. At the same time, they are interested in the social media sites, shared folders, and other tools used by researchers to develop an understanding of the user experience.

Researcher 3 will use technology as a workshop setting, as well as a medium to communicate with participants.

Researcher 4 will also use technology as a communication medium and setting for a writing group that offers support and reviews to each other.

Researchers sometimes choose ICTs as a medium for interviews or observations because online communications allow for significant reduction or elimination of constraints that would make in-person data collection impractical. An increased pool of study participants is possible, including geographically dispersed, international, disabled, or socially isolated individuals and hard-to-reach populations. Researchers can use a virtual presence in settings where a physical presence would not be allowed, such as hospitals or closed workplaces, or in settings where the presence of an outsider might be disruptive.

Participants may find such methods less stressful and more convenient because they can be interviewed at home or at work, in a familiar and non-threatening physical environment (Gruber, Szmigin, Reppel, & Voss, 2008, pp. 257–258). They may be more relaxed because they are communicating with the researcher in the comfort of a familiar online setting.

What we know as 'Internet studies' fall into this category, that is, they are studies of the Internet as the phenomenon. The availability and usage of diverse forms of online communication by people of all ages has extended far beyond the early adopters, academics, and scientists. This expanding usage offers greater potential for the Internet and digital tools as mediums or settings for a wider range of research.

SUMMARY OF KEY CONCEPTS

This chapter has introduced a four-part way to think about research design. These four areas are interrelated and need to be considered in a holistic, systems-thinking way. The researcher should approach these design decisions with the understanding that it may be necessary to go around in circles because a linear approach will not be effective. In answering some questions, other questions may be raised so it is important to circle back and make sure all the parts of the study will fit together.

- What *epistemology* will underpin my study, justify and guide my choices of methodology and methods?
- What *theories* of knowledge and what disciplinary theories can explain key principles related to my subject of inquiry in past research? Will the study test, build on, or update existing theory? Or will it generate new theory?
- What *methodology* corresponds to the purpose of the study?
- What *method* or combination of methods will allow me to collect and analyze the data I need to answer the research questions?

While these principles apply to any qualitative research, they are particularly pertinent when the study will be conducted online. In the next chapter, you will explore technology choices in more detail and add to the key questions online research designers need to think through when designing and planning a new study.

DISCUSSION QUESTIONS AND EXERCISES

- Using your library database or open access scholarly journals, find two qualitative peer-reviewed articles based on data collected through interviews. Select one example of a study based on data collected in live, face-to-face interviews and one based on data collected through some kind of online interaction.

   o   Identify the epistemology, main theories, methodologies, and methods used for each study.

   o   Assess whether these elements were aligned in this research design. What would you recommend to improve alignment?

   o   Discuss how the online research exemplar used technology as medium, setting, or phenomenon.

- Review the research cameos for Chapter 2. Choose one and design a different qualitative online research approach. Compare and contrast with the examples given in this chapter.

3

Choosing Information and Communications Technologies for Online Studies

HIGHLIGHTS

Almost any ICT can be adapted for qualitative research. Naturally, the researcher looking for extant data or activities to observe will have different requirements than the researcher who wants to interact with participants. But, whether you are communicating with participants or partners, librarians or gatekeepers, as an online researcher you will need to match needs, purpose, preferences, access, and skills with one of more Information and Communications Technology (ICT). While more about ICTs specific to types of data collection will be covered in Chapters 9–12, this chapter focuses on the nature of online communication. In this chapter a variety of technologies are first reviewed, then discussed in terms of research potential.

OBJECTIVES

After reading and reflecting on this chapter, you will be able to:

- compare and contrast characteristics of online communication tools
- differentiate between synchronicity, synchronous, near-synchronous or asynchronous ICTs for data collection
- evaluate ways to use non-verbal communication online
- assess options for online research settings.

The Internet is continually expanding our ability not only to communicate, but also to create open or private spaces where we can meaningfully interact, inform people across the world about our perspectives, learn from and with each other, and collaborate. Other Information and Communications Technology tools, such as interactive applications, or apps, allow us to track our steps and diets, keep track of household or professional details, communicate with others, and form groups.

The Internet and Internet-enabled tools also permit less benign types of exchanges, including privacy violations, bullying, soliciting participation in criminal or even terrorist activities. Whether for friendly or intrusive reasons, individuals do more than access materials others have posted; we can post comments, pictures, and media or generate material that known or unknown people may view. Now that mobile devices allow for a full range of online activities and locational information, users can share what they see and report on their perceptions in the moment. With these tools readily at hand, we are seeing a change in the flow of information, with individuals both consuming and creating content.

When users experience the creative, generative aspects of online communication, they adapt technologies for their own purposes and create new means of exchange. In the process, they become more comfortable with tools and approaches that may be used in methods that are chosen by researchers to elicit or generate data. At the same time, the active participation in online discussions and social networking means that those who want to collect extant data have a wide range of options in terms of places where user-generated content can be accessed and types of written, audio or multimedia materials to review.

INFORMATION AND COMMUNICATIONS TECHNOLOGIES: TOOLS AND FEATURES FOR QUALITATIVE ONLINE RESEARCH

ICTs are generally known by their brand names. But given the constant changes in the technology industry, and the fact that the same brands are not popular in all parts of the world, we will focus on the features rather than products. We can categorize the options by the affordances for communication, exchange, observation, record-keeping, ability to create and share content, access to or downloading of posted content. Some sites or tools may work for multiple purposes, while others are more limited. ICTs may be freely available on the open, public World Wide Web or as subscriptions. They might be found on social networking sites (SNSs) that require membership or registration, or they may operate as closed, proprietary online environments.

Some types of ICT primarily use text. Some of these technologies also allow for use of visual elements such as *emoticons* or *emoji,* or allow images or links

Table 3.1 ICT features for online research

Text-Based Communication	Multiple Channels for Communication
Blog A blog is a personal online journal where entries are posted chronologically. Microblogs allow for very short entries. Blogs can be text only or include links, images or media. Viewing may be public or limited to specified group of subscribers or friends. Researchers can create blogs to share information about the study with participants or other stakeholders. Researchers can collect extant data from blogs.	**Global Positioning System (GPS) or Global Information Systems** Researchers identify locations of interview-related events, or map location-related data.
Email Researchers can send and receive questions and answers. Researchers can also collect extant data from email discussion archives.	**Podcast or Vodcast** Researchers ask and answer questions by exchanging recorded audio or video files. **Shared Applications** Researchers and participants view and discuss documents, media, or examples by logging in together and using web-based software applications, research tools, or forms. Participants can generate responses by writing, drawing, or diagramming ideas on whiteboards or in shared documents.
Forum A forum (also known as a bulletin board or threaded discussion) is a public or private site where posts and responses are organized in sequential order. Researchers can post and respond to questions and answers in a forum in an online community or on a site restricted to participants. Researchers can observe activities or collect extant data from current discussions or archives.	**Social Media or Social Networking Site** Commercial platform used for posting text, images, or media for others to view and comment upon. May include circles or groups of friends or networks. Researchers can communicate with participants or collect extant data.
Questionnaire Researchers can craft open or closed questions for participants' written responses.	**Video** Researchers and/or participants post, view, and respond to video clips. Researchers can collect extant data from sites where user-generated videos are posted.
Text Message or Chat Researchers can post and respond to questions and answers. Researchers can collect extant data from current discussions or archives.	**Videoconferencing, Video Chat or Call** Researchers and participants see each other while conversing. They may use mobile devices, laptops or computers with webcams or videoconference facilities that allow for an entire group to participate. Researchers can observe videoconference events or webinars. They can collect extant data from archived records of events.

(Continued)

Table 3.1 (Continued)

Text-Based Communication	Multiple Channels for Communication
Wiki	**Virtual Reality or Virtual World**
Multiple authors add, remove, and edit content on a **wiki** website. It can include a blog, **forum** or a space for text chat, used as described above. Researchers can collect extant data from current discussions or archives.	Researchers and/or participants ask and respond to questions through the physical form and identity of an avatar, experience immersive events or phenomena, and/or view examples or demonstrations. Researchers can set up simulations, and observe such exchanges.
	Voice over Internet Protocol (VoIP)
	Researchers and participants ask and answer questions using live audio over the Internet (as opposed to calls using the telephone.)
	Web Conferencing
	Private platforms that typically include multiple features such as videoconferencing, chat, shared whiteboard, shared applications, and the ability to display slides, documents, the desktop, or websites. We will use the term *videoconferencing* to refer to platforms that are primarily used for video calls or chats, and *web conferencing* to refer to platforms that include a wider range of collaboration and meeting tools.

to be shared. Other technologies allow for audio or voice, video, and/or visual communications exchanges. In some settings, such as virtual worlds or games, highly visual interactions may be complemented by text chat. Here these are distinguished as *multichannel* ICTs. See Table 3.1 for an overview of communication technology features in a research context. Think about your research needs, then look for the platforms and applications that will work for you.

─────────── RESEARCH CAMEO 3.1 ───────────

Researcher 1 plans to collect extant data from journal databases. They will use databases available from their university library, so no special arrangements are needed. However, they need to maintain communication with their supervisor and doctoral committee. They plan to create a blog to track major stages, so the research process is transparent to committee members. The blog might also be shared with fellow doctoral students or other potential co-authors for future research articles or presentations.

Researcher 2 plans to conduct online interviews with individual researchers. They expect to communicate via text messaging, email, and videoconferencing.

Researcher 3 plans to offer a publishing workshop online and collect data from the writers who participate. They plan to use email, a web conferencing platform, and a questionnaire tool.

Researcher 4 plans to observe the writing group's social media interactions, and their online meetings. They will also interview the researchers about their experiences. They will conduct interviews using a series of email exchanges.

SYNCHRONOUS OR ASYNCHRONOUS COMMUNICATION

A distinguishing factor of online communication is the timing of message and response. Online interaction is typically categorized according to the ability to send, receive, and respond to messages at the same time (synchronous communication) or at different times (asynchronous communication). In-person, synchronous real-time communication occurs when people meet or talk on the telephone, and asynchronous communication occurs when they write letters.

Synchronous communications use ICTs for written, verbal, and/or visual exchange. By attaching a headset and logging onto a free online service, you can use VoIP instead of telephone, making it possible to have free conversations with anyone in the world with similar access to a computer. By adding a webcam, researchers and participants can use desktop videoconferencing and see each other while they converse. You can adopt platforms designed for online meetings for elicitation or data generation purposes, using shared whiteboards and other tools that allow them to see materials and artifacts in addition to talking with and seeing each other. Or they can interact in immersive 3D virtual worlds or games where they are represented by the avatars they design.

Asynchronous communications do not constrain interactions with the need to participate at the same time. Online asynchronous communications occur when people correspond by email or communicate when they make posts and respond to others in discussion forums, on social media sites, wikis, or blogs.

MEDIA RICHNESS THEORY

Media Richness Theory (MRT) was devised in the 1980s (Daft & Lengel, 1986; Daft, Lengel, & Trevino, 1987). MRT suggests that communication works best when we match the *richness* of the communication channel with the *equivocality* of the task. Rich communication is characterized by (a) immediate feedback, (b) multiple cues, (c) language variety, and (d) personal focus. *Equivocality* refers to confusion or lack of understanding, which can be reduced by the quality or richness of information (Daft et al., 1987). Simply stated, according to MRT, when we can ask for and receive feedback, and use multiple cues to get the message across, we can reduce confusion. According to this line of thinking (Eisenberg, Glikson, & Lisak, 2021), media that is rich in cues (e.g., video calls or web conferencing) is usually synchronous, allowing an immediacy of feedback through verbal and non-verbal (facial expressions and voice) exchanges. In contrast, communication that is lean in cues, such as written media, could be either asynchronous (e.g., email) or synchronous (e.g., text chat). At the same time,

> [C]onstantly evolving technology has been enriching 'lean' media in multiple ways and transforming communication. For example, the recent diffusion of mobile devices such as smartphones in a society has facilitated the 'speed' and 'convenience' of communication ... to facilitate the use of multiple channels. In addition, the embedded technological features in 'lean' media often facilitate interactivity between communicators, which can make a significant contribution to perceived media richness. (Ishii, Lyons, & Carr, 2019, p. 128)

It is important to avoid a simplistic interpretation of MRT and assume that rich communication is better. For example, research by Eisenberg et al. (2021) showed that when some members had less proficiency in the language being used by the team (in the case of this study, English), seemingly rich verbal communication was not always more beneficial than written communication. Those with less comfort in the dominant language could 'hide their differences behind lean written media, enabling them to reduce ingroup versus outgroup categorizations based on language proficiency' (p. 18). This same issue could occur with diverse participants, gatekeepers or other collaborators, so careful thought should precede your choice of channel for communications. Let's explore some of the factors to consider when matching the ICTs to your research task.

ONLINE COMMUNICATION IS RARELY EITHER/OR

The terms 'synchronous' and 'asynchronous' have until recently represented an either–or principle: communication at either the same time or a different time.

One additional refinement is the concept introduced by Dennis et al. (2008): *synchronicity*. Dennis et al. proposed media synchronicity theory (MST) to build on Daft and Lengel's work. They offered a definition for synchronicity that describes a high level of mutual focus and attention in communication. Dennis et al. observed that it is not simply the choice of medium, but

> the *manner* in which individuals use media [that] influences their communication perfor-
> mance (the development of shared understanding). Generally speaking, convergence
> processes benefit from the use of media that facilitate *synchronicity*, the ability to sup-
> port individuals working together at the same time with a shared pattern of coordinated
> behavior. (Dennis et al., 2008, p. 576)

In other words, it is not the medium that dictates whether shared understandings can be achieved – it is the way the medium is used. An ICT may have the potential for rich communication and immediate give and take but be used in ways that allow users to multitask without giving the communication partner full and undivided attention. Synchronicity occurs when communications partners are devoting full attention to the dialogue – no multitasking or other simultaneous conversations. *Synchronous*, then, describes a more basic activity with a technology that allows for real-time message and response but does not necessarily imply a single focus on reciprocity of exchange. Making clear your expectations for synchronous communication or synchronicity can improve communication effectiveness and reduce confusion, or equivocality.

Another refinement to the synchronous–asynchronous polarity is a concept we will call *near-synchronous* conversations (Salmons, 2012). In near-synchronous communication one party may post, text, or send a comment, update, or question to another with the expectation that the receiving party will respond soon – the next time he or she is online. Near-synchronous communications may take the form of an extended conversation. The term *asynchronous* remains a descriptor for communications where there is an expectation of a time gap between message and response.

———————————————— SPOT CHECK ————————————————

- How would you distinguish between synchronicity and synchronous modes? Why might the distinction be important in research communication?
- How would you distinguish between near-synchronous and asynchronous communication? Why might the distinction be important in research communication?

These communication options are presented here as a *time–response continuum*. This model offers a way to categorize the level of immediacy and timing of response in a way that offers more subtle gradations than the prior synchronous–asynchronous dichotomy. As illustrated in Figure 3.1, some ICTs offer flexibility across the entire continuum while others are more limited. Some offer the potential for synchronicity or synchronous exchange which can be recorded and archived for asynchronous access.

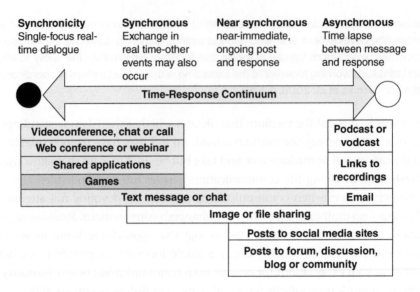

Figure 3.1 Time–response continuum

CHOOSING TIME–RESPONSE COMMUNICATIONS FOR YOUR STUDY

The choice between time–response modes – or the choice to blend them – is significant. Because the online environment offers many modes of communication, you can match the characteristics of the media to specific design requirements of your inquiry. Researchers base their choices on a need for robust communication that allows interviewers to ask questions and interpret immediate responses, written modes that allow interviewees to take time to think about the question and respond, or for access to archived or recorded material.

——————————————— SPOT CHECK ———————————————

In Chapter 1, you were asked to keep a diary of your online communications. Take another look!

- What communication features did you use? Why?
- Which features did you feel best matched the communication task or purpose? Why?

- Did the ICTs afford rich or lean communication?
- If you experienced confusion in your exchange, how did you address it?
- Were the ICTs open-access, free, or did they require a subscription or membership?

Each ICT has its own set of opportunities and limitations. Online asynchronous communication entails two types of displacement – time and space – while synchronous communication entails one type of displacement – space (Bampton & Cowton, 2002). While synchronous modes are rich, and bring people one step closer together, many people find the reflective pause between message and response leads to deeper consideration of the matter at hand. What will work for your participants, collaborative partners, or others associated with your research?

─────────────── RESEARCH CAMEO 3.2 ───────────────

Researcher 1 plans to collect extant data from journal databases. This process is asynchronous.

Researcher 2 plans to conduct online interviews with individual researchers. They want synchronicity in online interviews but will also use near-synchronous text messaging to make interview arrangements and build rapport, and asynchronous email to send documents like the consent agreement.

Researcher 3 plans to offer a publishing workshop online and collect data from the writers who participate. They plan to use asynchronous email, a synchronous web conferencing platform, and an asynchronous questionnaire tool.

Researcher 4 plans to observe the writing group's near-synchronous social media interactions, and their synchronous online meetings. They will conduct follow-up interviews using a series of asynchronous email exchanges.

NON-VERBAL COMMUNICATIONS ONLINE

One of the most common complaints about online communication is: 'you miss the non-verbal cues!' Online researchers *can* grasp meaning from non-verbal cues. To do so they must understand the variations of non-verbal signals that can be made online and make strategic decisions about the ICTs used in order to maximize the potential value.

Non-verbal communication affects the ways we use methods to elicit or generate data with participants through interviews, observations, and other kinds of interactive research events. Ong (1990) observed that '"words, words, words" mean nothing unless built into a nonverbal context, which always controls meanings of words' (p. 1). Grahe and Bernieri (1999) studied the development of rapport as established through verbal, auditory, and non-verbal modes. In the discussion of results, they showed that 'visual information' was critical to the establishment of rapport:

> Overall, we have found little evidence to suggest that conversation content improves judgments of rapport over and above those judgments that are made immediately through the decoding of nonverbal behavior. A question arises as to why visual information was so important for rapport when other researchers have found auditory and verbal cues to be so influential in person perception. The most parsimonious reason may be that rapport is primarily a physically manifested construct; it is a construct that is visible at the surface and readily apparent. (Grahe & Bernieri, 1999, p. 265)

Of course, non-verbal communication is not limited to visual cues. Four modes of non-verbal communication are summarized briefly as:

- *Chronemics* refers to the use of pacing and timing of speech, and the length of silence before a response in conversation.
- *Paralinguistic* communication describes variations in volume, pitch, and quality of voice.
- *Kinesic* communication includes facial expressions, eye contact or gaze, body movements, or postures.
- *Proxemic* communication describes the use of interpersonal space to communicate attitudes.

How are these forms present in online communication? (See Table 3.2.) When people chat or send text messages in real time the length of time between post and response provides pacing and turn-taking in the conversation. In an interview, the timing of response, silence, or non-response provides researchers with *chronemic* non-verbal data. Network latency and multitasking by participants introduce effects that are different from face-to-face contexts, and which can lead to misinterpretation of temporal cues. The interviewer may believe the participant is reflecting on the question or struggling with a slow response, when in fact he or she has been distracted by an incoming email or had a technical glitch.

In an email interview exchange within a forum or SNS, the delay in interaction between researcher and subject can range from seconds to hours or days. In planning an interaction with participants, the researcher usually wants to accommodate the participant by allowing some degree of freedom to determine pace of response. The way participants exercise such freedoms may or may not offer chronemic insight. Slower responses may or may not indicate more powerful reflection on the deeper meanings of the inquiry (Fritz & Vandermause, 2018; Hawkins, 2018; James, 2016). On the other hand, quick replies may indicate lack of adequate consideration by the interviewee. Uncertainty of meaning for chronemic

Table 3.2 Non-verbal communications online

	Chronemic	Paralinguistic	Kinesic	Proxemic
Blog or microblogs	Timing of post and response	Style and tone of writing Sound, tone, and inflection of voice if the link to recording is posted	N/A	N/A
Email	Timing of email and response	Style and tone of writing	N/A	N/A
Forum	Timing of post and response	Style and tone of writing Sound, tone, and inflection of voice if the link to recording is posted	N/A	N/A
Social networking site	Timing of post and response	Style and tone of writing Sound, tone, and inflection of voice if the link to recording is posted	N/A	N/A
Text messaging or chat	Timing of post and response	Style and tone of writing	N/A	N/A
Web conferencing	Natural speech using VoIP	Natural speech using VoIP	Natural communication style seen via webcam	N/A
Videoconferencing	Natural speech using VoIP	Natural speech using VoIP	Natural communication style seen via webcam	N/A
Virtual worlds	Timing of post and response Responses may be communicated by the avatar	Style and tone of writing	Expressions and gestures may be conveyed by the avatar	Movement, sense of space may be communicated by the avatar

cues in email or text interviews, or in SNS exchanges may be addressed by creating some protocols for timing and follow-up, and for the anticipated length of the interview.

The use of videoconferencing or web conferencing tools allows for more natural communication styles that allow for robust non-verbal cues. As Grahe and Bernieri noted (1999), visual information can help to build rapport. In interviews conducted with web-based applications together with audio through VoIP or telephone, researchers listen to interviewees and collect data on chronemic and paralinguistic aspects of their responses. Researchers using videoconferencing or video calls can use some level of kinesic communication, such as facial expressions and gestures, although eye contact may be more difficult to attain.

Proxemic communication, interpreted as physical distance between communicators, is not applicable in most online contexts. However, in environments such as virtual worlds or games where avatars interact, proxemic and kinesic cues can be conveyed. Kotlyar and Ariely describe an example from a study conducted in a virtual world:

> [T]he characters exhibited automated responses to certain words and phrases (e.g., lip movements in response to text inputs, subtle nods in response to 'yes,' question-like gestures in response to sentences that started with 'how,' 'why,' 'what' and 'who' and ended with a question mark, etc.), which were designed to enrich text messages with nonverbal cues. Third, the characters 'acted out' user-triggered emoticon messages (e.g., smile, wink, laugh, sad shocked, roll eyes, huh), which were controllable by either entering common text inputs, such as ':)' and 'lol' or clicking the emoticon buttons on the menu. (Kotlyar & Ariely, 2013, p. 547)

While non-verbal cues can be interpreted from the gestures and facial expressions presented online, the online researcher has fewer options for reading distress or discomfort on the part of participants. In a face-to-face interview or interaction the researcher could see evidence of a problem with a particular question or the research engagement as a whole. The online interviewer has fewer options for recovering a difficult interaction (such as apologizing for an inappropriate question, requesting that the interviewee remain, or retracting a line of questioning) before the interviewee simply logs out (James & Busher, 2009). An online interviewer has less control over the interviewee deciding to terminate the interview since it can be brought to an end with the press of a button. If the study addresses sensitive issues and non-verbal responses are important, the researcher might prefer to use the videoconferencing or web conference tools when interacting with participants to allow for a more natural communication experience.

More challenging is the interpretation of nuances conveyed in writing in text-based exchanges in forum discussions or SNSs. Participant observers can simply ask for clarification. However, researchers using unobtrusive observation techniques and researchers using extant data, such as recorded events, have few options to clarify ambiguous meanings.

--------------------- RESEARCH CAMEO 3.3 ---------------------

Researcher 1 will not rely on non-verbal cues in this study.

Researcher 2 plans to conduct online interviews with individual researchers. They are choosing videoconferencing for the interviews in order to access all four types of non-verbal cues. They will observe cues from the auditory pacing, silences, and facial expressions. While they will not be in the same space as needed to see proxemic cues, they will be aware of cues visible on camera in the participants' setting.

Researcher 3 plans to offer a publishing workshop online and collect data from the writers who participate. They will look for paralinguistic and kinesic cues in the discussion.

Researcher 4 plans to observe the writing group's near-synchronous social media interactions, their synchronous online meetings, with follow-up email interviews. The main non-verbal cues possible in this study will be chronemics in the timing of posts and responses.

ALIGNING FEATURES WITH RESEARCH PURPOSES

Researchers interacting directly with participants for data collection will need several exchanges and may decide to use a variety of communication tools throughout the study. Every stage should be seen as an opportunity to build trust with, and learn about, the research participant. A mix of synchronous, near-synchronous, and asynchronous methods may allow for flexibility, variety, and convenience.

The research relationship is initiated with the initial contact, in the sampling and selection of the research participants. Depending on the nature of the study, asynchronous tools such as email lists, posts on blogs, or websites may be useful for sharing background on the research, information about the researcher(s), and links to institutions or foundations that sponsor, support, or provide supervision for the study. Researchers can discuss details for participation using synchronous tools such as chat, VoIP calls (especially in multinational studies where telephone calls are costly), or desktop videoconferencing. The researcher may choose to include a follow-up stage for member checking, where participants have a chance to review what they have said or to elaborate on or correct responses. Asynchronous tools can be used to send documents by email or to discuss any unresolved issues. These steps may be used at the planning stage by researchers who plan to conduct observations, collect records or documents from consenting participants. Researchers who will interact directly with participants to collect data have additional decisions to make about the ICTs best suited to the study. More specific discussion for each type is given in Chapters 9–12.

CHOOSING, FINDING, OR CREATING A CONDUCIVE MEETING SPACE

Researchers need a safe, neutral location for collecting data from participants. A preferred location will be comfortable and accessible for the participants. Ideally the setting is private with minimal distractions or interference. The setting should not itself become a factor in the participants' responses because of negative associations or feelings of intimidation. It is important to remember that selecting ICTs is about more than simply deciding what tools will be used to transfer messages back and forth between researcher and participant. Technology choices influence the characteristics and feeling of the online space that serves as the research setting. Choices specific to settings for various types of research are discussed in Chapters 6–8.

Some general questions researchers should consider when choosing technologies to use when communicating with participants include the following:

- Do people in the target demographic generally have access to the type of technology to be used, or will a particular choice of technology exclude many potential participants?
- Will the participant feel comfortable, or will additional preparation time be needed to familiarize the participants with the ICT?
- If the setting involves an online community or social media site, are there codes of conduct or norms that allow for (or restrict) researchers? Is there a community manager or host who needs to give permission?

Platforms for Elicited and Enacted Interactions

Throughout this book I discuss ICT *features* rather than specific brands. However, in this box I will name names, given that decisions about the platform have implications for ethical review as well as for the style of interaction. Features discussed here are not limited to these specific platforms, but this analysis will help you identify the questions you need to ask when choosing a platform. If you have access to a different platform through your university, look closely at the privacy information or contact tech support to get answers about recording options. Find more about tools for collecting and analyzing extant data in Chapters 10 and 13.

Platforms that Allow You to Record to Your Hard Drive

Zoom allows you to choose whether to record to your computer or to the cloud. Zoom tech support assured me that when you make that choice, no records are saved to the cloud. I inadvertently tested this theory when I had an outage in the middle of recording to my hard drive. Yes, it was gone and there was no way to retrieve it from the server. You can also record to the cloud and set a password to add security to your files. You can record to the cloud, transcribe or download, then permanently delete the files.

In Zoom you can choose automatic transcriptions for the audio of a meeting or webinar that you record to the cloud, which is very useful for research purposes.

Web Ex allows you to record directly to your computer, or record to the cloud then download and delete it from the server. The Web Ex paid plan also allows you to choose automatic transcriptions for recordings.

Both of these platforms offer more limited free services, or paid services that you can contract on a monthly basis. If you are conducting interviews over a time-limited basis, paying for a month or two might be worthwhile in order to access more features. For example, a feature like automatic transcription might make a paid plan a worthwhile investment. Be sure to check for student or educator discounts.

Platforms that Allow You to Delete Records from Company Servers

Commercial platforms such as Adobe Connect record to their servers but allow you to download the recording and delete it from the server. Adobe Connect is enterprise-level, with no option for a free or individual plan. However, many educational institutions have a contract, so you might find that you can get access through your university.

Another type of platform allows for more than videoconferencing. You could post materials for focus group members to review and discuss, have extended interactions in a longitudinal study, and have asynchronous forums with participants in Mighty Networks. It allows you to choose the Mighty Networks meeting tools, or to embed Zoom meetings within your Mighty Networks set-up. The meeting features are only available in the paid plans. According to their tech support, once you delete any recordings there are no persistent records.

Platforms that Only Record to the Cloud

All of the Microsoft products, including Teams and **Skype**, record to the cloud. From the information I have, it appears that Skype and Teams users cannot opt to record directly to their hard drives. Once recorded, you can delete the files from the cloud. Skype is offered in a free or business version. Teams and business Skype are part of Office 365, so purchasing them might involve a long-term contract. Additional limitations in Teams:

- Whiteboards and shared notes are not currently captured in meeting recordings.
- When you view a meeting recording, you'll see no more than four people's video streams at once.

---------- SPOT CHECK ----------

- What do you need to flesh out in your research design in order to select the appropriate ICTs?
- Based on your plans so far, what tools and setting(s) fit your proposed research?
- If you are planning to collect data from participants, what features will be most important, given your participants and research purpose?
- If you are planning to collect extant data, what aspects of the setting will be important to observe?

SUMMARY OF KEY CONCEPTS

This chapter explored and categorized communication features common to various software programs, applications, platforms, or social networking sites. The capability for different types of exchange including non-verbal communication was discussed. Given these options, a primary question to consider is this: What kind(s) of data do you want to collect? Will verbal, text, or visual data best help you answer the research questions?

The technologies may be new, but none of the many modes of online communication is wholly unique to the online environment. Whether face-to-face or online, communication typically mixes verbal and non-verbal, written and symbolic visual modes. The key difference online is that a strategic choice must be made. If we want to be able to see the research participant, then arrangements must be made to use the technology that allows for that visual exchange. The researcher must be sure that the participant has access to a computer or device with a webcam and knows how to use it. As noted in Chapter 2, the technology may serve as a communication medium, research setting, or research phenomenon.

DISCUSSION QUESTIONS AND EXERCISES

- Identify the communication needs associated with your study.

  o What ICTs or specific features will help you meet the needs of your study?
  o Do you have access to these ICTs, or will you need to purchase or subscribe to use them?
  o Do you have the skills needed to use the ICTs for a research purpose?

- Find three qualitative online research articles and analyze the rationales offered for selecting online data collection methods. How did the researcher describe the reasons for choosing their approach? Did the researcher make a compelling case? How did the basis for selection given by the researcher compare or contrast with reasons discussed in this chapter?

- Formulate three topics for an informal discussion (e.g., the weather, recent holidays, favorite meals). With a classmate or friend, try discussing the topics using different online communication technologies. Select at least one that is synchronous, and one that is near- or asynchronous. Compare and contrast what you learned from each interaction.
- How would your choices vary when planning to communicate with research participants or partners, librarians, or gatekeepers?

SECTION II

BECOMING AN ETHICAL

ONLINE RESEARCHER

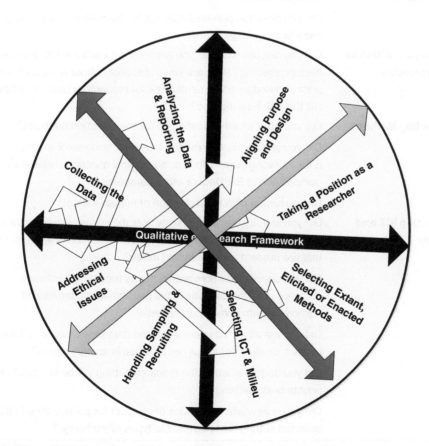

Figure II.1   Ethical considerations within the Qualitative e-Research Framework

The entire process of research – from designing the study through completion of the final report and publication of results – is fraught with ethical dilemmas. For online researchers, much of the process is carried out on your own computer, in your own home or office, where no one else can see. How do we behave? It is incumbent upon us to take an ethical stance that goes beyond the questions those providing oversight may ask. While the design or proposal may go through an **ethics** or **institutional review board** process, that is only the beginning. We must continue to ask ourselves whether we exemplify high ethical standards throughout every step, every interaction with co-researchers or participants, librarians, or archivists. Some questions to consider at each phase of the Qualitative e-Research Framework are presented in Table II.1.

Table II.1   Ethical issues in relation to the Qualitative e-Research Framework

	Addressing Ethical Issues
Aligning Purpose and Design	Did you explain and address potential ethical dilemmas in the research design?
	Did you describe potential benefits to the individual or public good this study could generate?
Taking a Position as a Researcher	Did you discuss whether you are a known insider in the selected research setting? If so, are you transparent about ways status or prior knowledge add potential risk for researcher bias – and how will this risk be mitigated?
Selecting Methods	Did you offer an ethical rationale for the selection methods?
	Did you address issues related to access and use of extant data, including permissions or any ethical questions related to composition of Big Data or other databases?
	Do you have a plan for protection of human subjects?
Selecting ICT and Milieu	Did you identify and address any specific ethical issues (privacy, protected areas, use of avatars, need for community agreement) that are present in the selected milieu?
	Did you specify minimum requirements regarding hardware, software or technical skills in the recruitment materials and agreement with human participants?
	Did you identify what user-generated data (use of video or images, avatars, profile info) should be included in an agreement?
	Did you decide whether the research setting will be in a public or private online setting?
	Did you review whether codes of conduct for participating in the selected setting limit permissible types of exchange?

	Addressing Ethical Issues
	Did you find out whether permission is needed to access profiles or posted documents or images?
	Did you find out whether collected data will be protected and deleted from the server?
Handling Sampling and Recruiting	Did you plan to locate and select credible research participants or relevant materials?
	Did you verify the identity and age (or other relevant criteria) of research participants recruited online?
	Did you outline what will be included in the consent agreement to encompass all aspects of interview(s), observations, or other research events?
Collecting the Data	Did you determine how participants and their digital identities will be protected during the data collection?
	Did you decide whether data will be collected using open or covert observation? If so, how will identities and personal information be protected?
Analyzing the Data and Reporting	Did you determine how participants and their digital identities will be protected in reports or publications?

4

Designing an Ethical Online Study

HIGHLIGHTS

Addressing ethical issues is a dimension of the Qualitative e-Research Framework. As noted in Chapter 1, this Framework is portrayed as a circle because the elements of research design are interrelated. Nowhere is this truer than in discussions of ethical issues, which influence decisions at every stage of the design and conduct of an online study. It would be wonderful to have straightforward, universal guidelines that clearly delineated right from wrong. Instead, we have some areas of black and white but many shades of gray.

In the 'offline' world, being able to determine place and identify people is a fairly straightforward process. We usually do not have difficulty in distinguishing a human being from another species. We know where we are very specifically now that we have **Global Positioning System** (GPS) software on the smartphones in our pockets to map our exact location. We can tell when we walk into a home or office that we are in someone's private space or that when we visit a park or restaurant we are in a public space. Online, these simple distinctions are not so clearly differentiated. Yet they are important because ethical practices depend on the answers. Very simply, we need permission to do research in a private place, and human participants must give their consent to being a part of the study.

The complex topic of research ethics is beyond the scope of this book. Broad foundations only are offered since detailed explanations can be found in other texts. The focus here is on how these principles can be applied in qualitative online inquiries. The ever-changing nature of technology and the evolving ways it is becoming inseparable from our lives means we are redefining ways that ethical research practices apply when we use ICTs to collect and analyze data – and to disseminate findings. To that end, research ethics principles and concepts are introduced in this chapter. In Chapter 5 the focus will turn to more practical application of ethics principles when conducting qualitative online research. Chapter 6 will invite you to think about your positions and potential biases. Then in Chapters 13 and 14 ethical dimensions associated with **data analysis** and reporting are explored.

OBJECTIVES

After reading and reflecting on this chapter, you will be able to understand design considerations for:

- knowing the foundations for research ethics and accepted Internet research ethics practices
- determining whether a study setting is in a public or private online space
- thinking through the nature of the study and the need to protect human subjects and their avatars or digital identities.

RESEARCH ETHICS AND YOUR STUDY

At its simplest *research ethics* can be defined as the responsibility of the researcher toward others, including society broadly, other scholars, and most importantly, those whose attitudes, behaviors, and experiences we are studying. Central to research ethics is the intention to protect the human subjects who provide data for the study. While following applicable codes and guidelines is essential, researchers also need to develop and exhibit moral judgment about how to interpret guidelines in the particular context of the study.

Ethical issues should be considered at every stage, from initial plans through to dissemination of findings. The research design shows how all of the major parts of the research project work together to accomplish the study's purpose and address the research questions. As such, the researcher should use the design to map out, explain, and justify how ethical issues will be addressed through all stages of the proposed study.

Research should ideally be conducted to generate new knowledge that benefits the common good. Shifts in public policy around research funding, combined with imminent social problems, mean researchers need to state what impact their studies will make. Farley-Ripple suggests that:

> Impact can be understood in multiple ways, which may broadly include academic and societal. Academic impact includes advancing scientific knowledge, methods, or theory within or across fields of study – which can be thought of as occurring within the academy. But societal impact is much broader and transcends the silos of academia. (Farley-Ripple, 2020, p. 2)

Farley-Ripple's (2020) research showed that while impact is demonstrated by use of the findings, use itself is a narrow interpretation, since research can do more than instigate instrumental change. One of Farley-Ripple's participants suggested 'that impact might look more like "planting a seed"' (p. 4) because it will take time to translate results to reality. Another way to look at meaningful impact is: Does the study take beneficial steps toward improving the social good and social justice (Poth, 2021)? Based on expert interviews with scholars and practitioners from multiple disciplines, Mor Barak (2018) defined domains of social good as (1) diversity and social inclusion, (2) environmental justice and sustainability, and (3) peace, harmony, and collaboration (Mor Barak, 2018, p. 144). These domains are matters at the heart of the study. Some practical questions include:

- Whose priorities are reflected in the research problem?
- What assumptions, biases, or expectations influence the research design?
- Who, or what, is included or excluded from research? Why?
- How are cultural norms and ways of knowing respected?
- Who benefits from findings, discoveries, or new knowledge?

Thinking about scholarly or practical impact and contributions toward improvements in society are not aspects of the study that are generally considered in an ethics review, but are nevertheless important. When working to generate findings that are a 'benefit to society and the groups and individuals within it', researchers must exercise vigilance toward maintaining 'high scientific standards in the methods employed in the collection and analysis of data and the impartial assessment and dissemination of findings' (SRA, 2003, p. 13).

─────────────── SPOT CHECK ───────────────

- The priorities for research impact, and the definition of social good might be different in your field of study. How do they vary from the descriptions above?
- How will your study create positive research impact?
- What goals for improving social good drive your research purpose?

INTERNET RESEARCH ETHICS

What are 'Internet research ethics' and how do they vary from ethical principles applicable to other types of research? An entire field of study is emerging to answer these questions. Buchanan (2011, p. 83) described a 'research ethics 2.0' that 'allows us to think holistically and evolutionarily about the meeting of research methods, ethics, and technologies in general, and Internet, or online, technologies in particular'. Burbules (2009) refers to *networked ethics*, advocating a 'rethinking of how one makes ethical judgments in an environment that is structured by a complex, interdependent, and rapidly changing set of relations, as these new technologies are'. The Association of Internet Researchers have been publishing, and updating, guidelines that are respected because they are developed by groups of researchers from various countries and disciplines (franzke, Bechmann, Zimmer, Ess, & The Association of Internet Researchers, 2020). The most recent version will be referenced throughout this chapter, and you are encouraged to download a free copy here: https://aoir.org/reports/ethics3.pdf. Rather than spell out a dichotomy of ethical versus unethical practices, the AoIR guide (franzke et al., 2020) suggests 'a process approach':

> This process approach is first of all reflective and dialogical as it begins with reflection on our own research practices and associated risks and is continuously discussed against the accumulated experience and ethical reflections of researchers in the field and existing studies carried out. (p. 4)

The AoIR approach, then, suggests that you reflect on your study, think about potential risks, discuss any ambiguous issues with other researchers, and look for examples in the literature in your own field or discipline. Many discipline-based associations in fields such as education, sociology, psychology, or business, offer ethical guidelines that can help you ensure that your ethical stance is appropriate. The theories and practices described in this book are offered as food for your own **reflection**, for dialogue with others, and for further reading in the literature.

To think in a holistic way about how to ethically design and conduct qualitative research online, we need to begin with some basics. Where do we derive our sensibilities about research ethics? In this chapter we will begin with a broad overview of ethical theories. Then we will look at the essential documents that spell out ethical research parameters, and we will consider the recommendations specific to online research ethics offered by research institutes and associations. Finally, we provide some interpretations for qualitative e-research specific to the approaches for extant, elicited, and enacted research discussed in this book.

ETHICAL THEORIES

Researchers are, of course, not the only people with an interest in ethics. Questions about right and wrong have been discussed and argued since the earliest records of human interaction. Three major perspectives in classic thought about ethics are **deontological ethics, consequentialism**, and **virtue ethics**.

Deontological ethics build on the philosophies of Immanuel Kant (1785/2008). They are a normative way of viewing morality in terms of duties and principles. The Greek words for 'duty' (*deon*) and 'study' (*logos*) form the word (Alexander & Moore, 2012). Deontologists believe the priority for ethical behavior is in adhering to principles and duties, based on the premise that some choices are morally wrong, no matter how good the consequences (Baggini & Fosi, 2007). The rule-based approach of deontology should guide choices of what we ought to do, in contrast to virtue theories that aim to guide what kind of character we have as persons and how we should be (Alexander & Moore, 2012).

Consequentialism is concerned with the moral rightness of acts. This view holds that whether an act is morally right depends primarily on the consequences of the act, the motive behind the act, or a general rule requiring such acts (Sinnott-Armstrong, 2011). This theory emphasizes the concept that ethical action provides the most good or does the least harm (Baggini & Fosi, 2007). Ethical decisions, then, are based on the consequences of specific actions judged to be moral when the outcome is good for the individual or society (Wiles, 2013, p. 4).

Utilitarianism, a form of consequentialism, builds on the philosophies of John Stuart Mill, who defended his views in his book of that title of 1863. He stated, 'Questions of ultimate ends are not amenable to direct proof. Whatever can be proved to be good, must be so by being shown to be a means to something admitted to be good without proof' (Mill, 1871). Mill's interpretation of the utilitarian tradition is based on his claims about the nature of happiness, the role of happiness in human motivation, and the relationship between happiness and duty. From this view, the aim of each person is predominantly, if not exclusively, the promotion of the individual's own happiness or pleasure (Brink, 2008). Moral behavior is thus guided by the principle that 'actions are right in proportion as they tend to promote happiness' with 'the interest, of every individual, as nearly as possible in harmony with the interest of the whole' (Mill, 1871, p. 14).

Virtue ethics are grounded in ideas from Plato and Aristotle. This theory centers on virtues, or moral character, as the guiding force for ethical decisions. It emerged due to dissatisfaction with limitations of deontology and utilitarianism (Hursthouse, 2012). This approach suggests that ethical actions ought to be consistent with certain ideal virtues that provide for the full development of our humanity (Velasquez, 2012). These virtues enable us to act in ways that demonstrate values such as honesty, courage, compassion, generosity, tolerance, and fairness. Hursthouse (2012) points to the complexity of virtuous behavior:

> A virtue such as honesty ... far from being a single track disposition to do honest actions, or even honest actions for certain reasons, is multi-track. It is concerned with many other actions as well, with emotions and emotional reactions, choices, values, desires, perceptions, attitudes, interests, expectations and sensibilities. To possess a virtue is to be a certain sort of person with a certain complex mindset.

People are best able to practice virtue ethics when they possess *phronesis*, moral or practical wisdom. Moss (2011, p. 205) interprets Aristotle's writings on phronesis:

> Virtue makes the goal right; *phronesis* is responsible only for what contributes to the goal. That is, practical intellect does not tell us what ends to pursue, but only how to pursue them; our ends themselves are set by our ethical characters.

As an example of ways in which these theories overlap, Sinnott-Armstrong (2011) identified two versions as virtue consequentialism and rule consequentialism:

> [V]irtue consequentialism ... holds that whether an act is morally right depends on whether it stems from or expresses a state of character that maximizes good consequences and, hence, is a virtue. ... [R]ule consequentialism ... makes the moral rightness of an act depend on the consequences of a rule. Since a rule is an abstract entity, a rule by itself strictly has no consequences. Still, *obedience rule consequentialists* can ask what would happen if everybody obeyed a rule or what would happen if everybody violated a rule.

These brief descriptions do not, of course, plumb the depths and multiple perspectives on ethical theory. As Wiles (2013, p. 13) observes, these and other ethical frameworks do not provide clear answers to ethical dilemmas that emerge, where we must decide what is right or wrong, but they offer a means for thinking about them and assessing an appropriate and defensible course or action. However, they do introduce a basis for grounding – and defending – our own views on research ethics.

INTERNATIONAL ETHICS CODES AND STATEMENTS

With this backdrop of classical ethical theories, several important documents are recognized internationally because they set forth principles that are foundational to contemporary understandings of ethical research.

The Nuremberg Code

After the World War II atrocities called 'experiments' by the Nazis, the Nuremberg Code was articulated in 1947 to prevent such horrors from occurring in the pretense of research. This code includes ten principles, of which the following are most relevant to non-experimental qualitative research (The Nuremberg Code, 1949):

- The voluntary consent of the human subject is absolutely essential.
- The study should be such as to yield fruitful results for the good of society.
- The study should be so conducted as to avoid all unnecessary physical and mental suffering and injury.
- The degree of risk to be taken should never exceed that determined by the humanitarian importance of the problem to be solved by the study.

human > Risk

The Nuremburg Code continues to be influential, playing a significant role in shaping the content of ethical guidelines published by academic institutions and professional organizations. The Nuremberg Code also influenced federal regulations that were set forth by the US Congress in the National Research Act of 1974. This legislation created a National Commission for the Protection of Human Subjects in Biomedical and Behavioral Research and required the formation of an institutional, or internal, review board by every university or other organization that receives federal funds for research in the United States (Dik, 2007). See the Belmont Report, below.

The Declaration of Helsinki

This statement from the World Medical Association, first issued in 1964 and revised most recently in 2013, was intended to guide medical experimentation (WMA, 2013). It is relevant to the research community at large because of its clear articulation of the rights to privacy of information and the right to voluntarily participate in the research, a process now referred to as *informed consent*. Principles from the Declaration of Helsinki that apply more broadly to non-medical qualitative research include the following:

- Every precaution must be taken to protect the privacy of research subjects and the confidentiality of their personal information.
- Participation by individuals capable of giving informed consent as subjects in medical research must be voluntary. Although it may be appropriate to consult family members or community leaders, no individual capable of giving informed consent may be enrolled in a research study unless he or she freely agrees.
- In medical research involving human subjects capable of giving informed consent, each potential subject must be adequately informed of the aims, methods, and sources of funding, any possible conflicts of interest, institutional affiliations of the

researcher, the anticipated benefits and potential risks of the study .... The potential subject must be informed of the right to refuse to participate in the study or to withdraw consent to participate at any time without reprisal. Special attention should be given to the specific information needs of individual potential subjects as well as to the methods used to deliver the information.

- After ensuring that the potential subject has understood the information, the researcher must then seek the potential subject's freely-given informed consent, preferably in writing. If the consent cannot be expressed in writing, the non-written consent must be formally documented and witnessed.
- For a potential research subject who is incapable of giving informed consent, the researcher must seek informed consent from the legally authorised representative.

The Belmont Report

The **Belmont Report** is a 'statement of basic ethical principles and guidelines that should assist in resolving the ethical problems that surround the conduct of research with human subjects'. It was issued in the US in 1976 by the National Commission for the Protection of Human Subjects of Biomedical and Behavioral Research. Two broad principles emerged from this report. The Belmont Report is respected as central to the Internet research ethics guidelines from the AoIR (franzke et al., 2020). The report clarifies researchers' goal to ensure **minimal risk** or harm by explicating the concepts of beneficence and justice:

- **Beneficence**. Persons are treated in an ethical manner not only by respecting their decisions and protecting them from harm, but also by making efforts to secure their well-being. Such treatment falls under the principle of beneficence. The term 'beneficence' is often understood to cover acts of kindness or charity that go beyond strict obligation. In this document, beneficence is understood in a stronger sense, as an obligation. Two general rules have been formulated as complementary expressions of beneficent actions in this sense: (1) do not harm and (2) maximize possible benefits and minimize possible harms.
- **Justice**. [C]onceptions of justice are relevant to research involving human subjects. For example, the selection of research subjects needs to be scrutinized in order to determine whether some classes (e.g., ... particular racial and ethnic minorities, or persons confined to institutions) are being systematically selected simply because of their easy availability, their compromised position, or their manipulability, rather than for reasons directly related to the problem being studied.

ETHICAL GUIDELINES FROM PROFESSIONAL SOCIETIES

In an effort to promote ethical research practices appropriate within disciplinary expectations, professional associations commonly create ethics guidelines.

These types of guidelines aim to create baseline assumptions about what is expected of researchers in the society's disciplines in order to maintain the integrity and credibility of the field as a whole. As deRoche and deRoche (2010, p. 387) observe:

> Science depends on *trust*. Two concerns ensue: reliability of the scientific knowledge base; and the public good name of research.
>
> First, despite checks and balances in scientific culture (rigorous training, replication, peer review, and critique), one can readily misrepresent methods or findings. Obviously unethical, under cultural proscriptions about lying and the assumption that distortions set back our knowledge base, dishonesty harms us all.
>
> Second, exposure of a lying researcher undermines *public trust* in science and scholarship generally. This sets back future research by reducing the likelihood of funding or the credibility of well-researched policy recommendations. More deeply, it diminishes popular trust in the social system, hence community cohesion.

Naturally, institutions and faculty members whose names will appear on a finished thesis or dissertation do not want to be associated with research that betrays the public trust, nor do reviewers or editors want to enable dissemination of such research.

Depending on the nature and breadth of the particular field, the relevant society may develop guidelines that aim to encompass all possible research types. As an unintended consequence, codes may be designed to cover a very wide range of designs from medical to social behavioral, and from quantitative to qualitative; thus researchers attempting to apply them may find that they are too general or

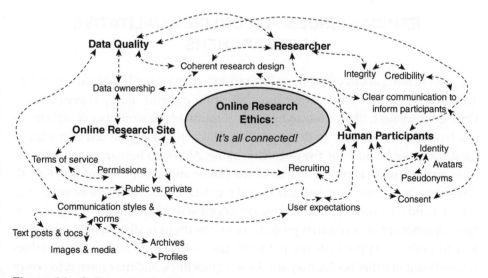

Figure 4.1 Online research ethics map

address topics not relevant to the study at hand (Preissle, 2008, p. 280). Often professional societies' guidelines pinpoint emerging issues and unanswered questions, with the intention of stimulating dialogue and determining new practices acceptable to people and institutions involved with the field the organization serves. While valuable in a larger context, such disagreements can add to the challenges for the new researcher who is looking for a clear sense of what is acceptable in his or her research design.

Several professional guidelines with subject matter relevant to online researchers are referenced in this book; you are encouraged to look for the guidelines that are available from your own academic institution, disciplinary field and/or relevant professional association.

--------------------------------- SPOT CHECK ---------------------------------

Find the ethics guidelines most relevant to your research.

- What is your field of study or discipline? What professional societies serve your field?
- What is your methodology? Often multidisciplinary societies or groups organize around a shared interest in a particular research approach.
- Look at the websites for the most relevant professional society or methodological group, and search for the ethics guidelines.
- Do the guidelines reference the reports, theories, and/or principles described in this chapter?

ETHICAL ISSUES FOR ONLINE QUALITATIVE RESEARCHERS

Decision-making about ethics in online research is anything but linear (see Figure 4.1). It is a complex process that must take into account multiple perspectives. Online researchers, like all researchers, are accountable to a number of stakeholders. Decisions about how to design and conduct ethical online research will, in most cases, not be made by the researcher alone. All researchers are accountable to their research participants as well as to the public and larger community. And all researchers are subject to existing laws and regulations, including those governing Internet and data privacy. Student researchers must work within boundaries set by the instructor for class research projects, or by the thesis or dissertation supervisor and committee. At the institutional level, the institutional review board, ethics review board or other bodies may administer guidelines, and may have veto power over a research proposal that does not meet certain requirements. Beyond the student experience, researchers may be guided by their professions and/or their professional societies which, as we have seen, may have codes of conduct or ethics guidelines for research. Any researcher desiring publication and dissemination of findings will be subject to peer reviewers' and editors' perspectives on publication. Given these levels of approval – before the researcher gets to the point of interacting with participants or collecting data – it is incumbent on the researcher to think carefully about the ethical dimensions of the study, clearly articulate the approach, and compellingly present a rationale.

Much of the scrutiny about research occurs at the proposal stage. This 'anticipatory review' approach may not be well suited to qualitative e-research, which by its exploratory and emergent nature does not always proceed according to plan (Miller et al., 2012). Miller (2012, p. 30) observes that anticipatory review can make ethics approval a 'curiously disconnected facet of a research project's life.' Miller's observation points to the need for consideration of ethics not only at the design stage, but also throughout the study. However, if the proposal is not approved, the inquiry cannot proceed, so it is essential for researchers to make every effort to think carefully in the design stage, anticipate and prepare for ethical dilemmas. This means consulting relevant ethics resources, as well as reviewing published studies or cases that utilized comparable approaches.

However, when online researchers consult various guidelines and regulations, they may find that some expectations and practices used by conventional researchers apply but others do not readily fit. After reading several resources, it may become apparent that some practices are generally agreed upon while for others there is a great deal of controversy. The following section will explore key principles to address at the design stage. Main areas for consideration at the design stage are identified, and varied perspectives and examples highlighted. Chapter 5 will focus on the application of these principles in the conduct of the study.

THINKING ABOUT ETHICAL POSITIONS THAT SUPPORT ONLINE QUALITATIVE RESEARCH DESIGN

The plethora of ethical theories can be narrowed down to four broad positions relevant to framing qualitative online research: deontology, consequentialism, virtue ethics, and ethics of care (see Figure 4.2).

The position advanced by *deontologists* is 'rules-based, based on the premise that some choices are morally wrong in any situation. Researchers' actions are governed by principles such as honesty, justice and respect and judged by intent rather than consequences' (Edwards & Mauthner, 2012, p. 19). From their view the process for conducting the study is important, whether or not the findings are worthwhile. A primary tenet of deontology is respect for the individual; individuals are not seen

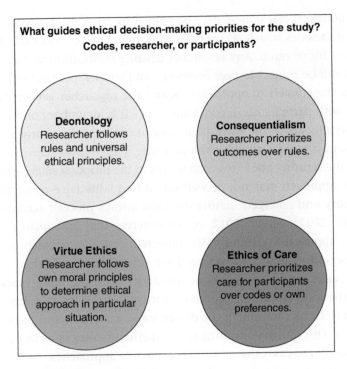

What guides ethical decision-making priorities for the study?
Codes, researcher, or participants?

Deontology
Researcher follows rules and universal ethical principles.

Consequentialism
Researcher prioritizes outcomes over rules.

Virtue Ethics
Researcher follows own moral principles to determine ethical approach in particular situation.

Ethics of Care
Researcher prioritizes care for participants over codes or own preferences.

Figure 4.2 Ethical theories and research

merely as a means to an end. 'Informed consent becomes a way of operationalizing that tenet, through an acknowledgement of an individual's values and choices that are freely made' (Loue, 2000, p. 97).

Researchers using deontological ethics are concerned with following ethical rules, codes, or formally specified guidelines (Berry, 2004). The Belmont Report and professional codes of ethics such as those from the Association of Internet Researchers have their origins in Kantian deontological theory (franzke et al., 2020; Markham & Buchanan, 2012). For Internet researchers, deontological perspectives could be interpreted to mean that priority is given to adapting, updating, and clarifying codes to make sure fellow researchers have appropriate guidelines as needed to protect the rights basic to human beings. According to this thinking, researchers should be required to follow applicable rules. Thus online qualitative researchers are responsible for following the guidelines as closely as possible – even if that means following rules developed to guide conventional research – to the online study. Deontologists would not view participants as merely the means by which they gather data, hence they stand in opposition to *consequentialists*, because they do not believe the ends can ever justify the means.

Consequentialist researchers prioritize the outcomes, such as the potential of research findings to add to the greater common good, over strict adherence to established rules or guidelines (Markham & Buchanan, 2012). Oversubscribing to

deontological ethics

consequentialist

a literal interpretation of the consequentialist view that the ends, important discoveries, can justify the means, could be used to justify deception. A researcher's focus on his or her own research could outweigh concerns about questionable ethical practices. However, since consequentialism seeks to maximize good, involvement of individuals in research without their understanding or permission, or against their will, would be considered clearly unethical (Loue, 2000). Researchers who take a consequentialist or utilitarian perspective sometimes take a pragmatic cost–benefit approach and weigh the value of research outcomes, such as increased knowledge, against the approach taken to achieve it (Edwards & Mauthner, 2012, p. 19). For Internet researchers, this could mean taking a flexible approach to applying established guidelines or principles, believing that the value of the study outweighs adherence to rules the researchers perceive as outdated. They may believe that by doing so they can advance more appropriate ground rules for future Internet researchers – a positive consequence.

Rather than focusing on whether to follow rules or not, *virtue ethics* positions point to the individual researcher's internal compass, personal value system, or moral code to determine what is the right decisions. Researchers adopting this view might agree with Johnsson, Eriksson, Helgesson, & Hansson (2014):

> If ethical conduct implied rule-following, anything less than perfect compliance would be unacceptable. As we have argued in this article however, responsible conduct often runs obliquely to compliance with rules, and even where they intersect, institutionalized distrust may backfire, undermining rather than supporting morality. (p. 40)

Virtue ethics focuses on the 'moral character of the researcher rather than principles, rules or consequences of an act or decision' (Wiles, 2013, p. 15). A researcher grounded in virtue ethics focuses on the development of the character so they are ready to confront ethical dilemmas (Morris & Morris, 2016). Researchers who take a virtue ethics approach take a 'contextual or situational ethical position, with an emphasis on the researcher's moral values and ethical skills in reflexively negotiating ethical dilemmas' (Edwards & Mauthner, 2012, p. 19). This means, according to Edwards and Mauthner (2012), that researchers who take a virtue ethics position rely on their own intuitions, 'including their sensibilities in undertaking dialogue and negotiation with the various parties involved in research' (p. 19). Virtue ethics emphasize the qualities of respectfulness and benevolence, which again argue for the recognition of and respect for an individual's freely made choice and informed consent (Loue, 2000).

Online researchers taking this position trust that the researchers themselves – in consultation with others knowledgeable about the online participants, site, and the types of data – can best determine what they believe to be the most ethical approach. Trevisan and Reilly suggest the need for what they call 'discipline-grounded ethical reflexivity' since researchers need to determine what is best for their own studies, given that guidelines cannot keep up with the changing technologies (Trevisan & Reilly, 2012, p. 2). Similarly, the Association of Internet Researchers Ethical Guidelines (franzke et al., 2020) advocate a context- and case-based approach. This kind of approach emphasizes that ethical judgment must be based on a sensible examination of the unique object and circumstances of a study, its research questions, the data involved, the expected analysis and reporting of results, along with the possible ethical dilemmas arising from the case' (Lomborg, 2013, p. 22). The virtue ethics reliance on dialogue with those involved with the research to determine the most respectful approach, and emphasis on the researcher's own thoughtful consideration about how to avoid risks, may be beneficial in the evolving field of online research where even the best guidelines may be limited in their applicability.

Ethics of care

As a fourth type, positions based on the *ethics of care* privilege the participants. Researchers working from this theory prefer to understand caring for others as a practice. Researchers taking this position would weight care and compassion for participants over the application of rules and would put participants' preferences above their own. From this stance, concerns for the participants would outweigh potential value of the data that could have otherwise been collected or used, and over the potentially valuable outcomes of the research.

Each of these positions has its advantages and drawbacks. Overly rigid adherence to rules and ethics codes may mean researchers lack flexibility to address rapidly changing circumstances in the volatile world of technology usage. But omission of requirements set by rules and codes may mean the study is not approved and cannot move forward, or cannot be published. A virtue ethics approach puts the responsibility on the researcher to practice due diligence, learn about and reflect on the study circumstances and decide how to proceed. While this approach allows for flexibility, it has other drawbacks. Student and novice researchers may lack the experience needed to understand the implications of their choices. It can also allow for moral relativism, where each researcher has a very different interpretation of boundaries and priorities. After all, as we saw earlier in this chapter, international codes evolved after scientists made choices that the broader society deemed unequivocally unethical. On the other hand, taking ethics of care as the guiding principle may, by itself, not offer sufficient guidance for studies where 'participants' who created materials posted, archived, or published are not immediately involved in the study or available for consultation.

Finding Balance and Synthesis

What takes priority in ethical decision-making: rules, principles and codes, outcomes, researchers' moral compass, or participants' preferences? Throughout this book a more balanced, synthesis-based stance is offered that draws on the four major theoretical perspectives introduced in this chapter: deontology, con-sequentialism, virtue ethics, and ethics of care. This approach for designing and conducting ethical qualitative online studies is rooted in respect for all participants and their varied digital representations, the researcher's moral judgment (crucially important in sometimes unpredictable emergent studies), clear understanding of the risks and benefits associated with obtaining the desired outcomes, and obser-vance of the applicable codes and guidelines.

Spanning these diverse stances is the Aristotelian concept of phronesis (Figure 4.3) – the researcher must cultivate the practical wisdom necessary to apply, adapt, and act in an ethical manner. Greeff and Rennie's research found that:

> The participants indicated that it was practical wisdom that saves the researchers in difficult situations, because they can base the situation on past experiences and prior knowledge. One's moral conduct is embedded in the researcher's own value system and backed by their personal and religious beliefs. Researchers have to be able to think on their feet. ... Although they are in touch with their own values, it is also extremely impor-tant to always consider the cultural norms and values of the community. (2016, p. 176)

While approval procedures may occur under watchful eyes, much of the work of a researcher is conducted away from the glare of others' views, so you need to develop a steady moral compass to guide the way as well as the confidence that you can carry out the inquiry in an exemplary manner.

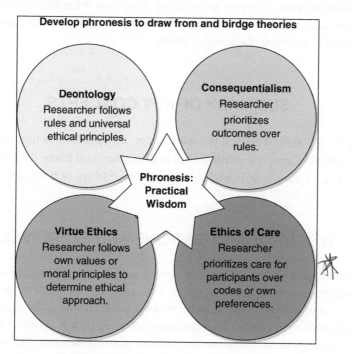

Figure 4.3 Phronesis: Bridging ethical theories

—————————————————— SPOT CHECK ——————————————————

After reading about different ethics theories, what stance do you feel best fits your own study? Why?

—————————————— RESEARCH CAMEO 4.1 ——————————————

Researcher 1 feels this study, using databases of published journal articles as extant data, offers few ethical dilemmas or risks. They will follow guidelines from their institution and research supervisor, so feel at this stage that an ethical approach drawn from deontological theory will be appropriate.

Researcher 2 will study the lived experience of qualitative researchers. They feel drawn to the ethics of care, because they want to work from a respectful stance and avoid situations that could make participants feel uncomfortable.

Researcher 3 will offer a workshop and collect data from those who join. They intend to proceed in a respectful way and avoid risk to participants, but at the same time, to take a pragmatic approach. They value the outcomes, and believe that the outcome of participants' improved publication skills will be worth it even if there is some discomfort along the way.

Researcher 4 will observe a writing group. They think virtue ethics will be a useful guide, since they are not sure what might emerge and want to be prepared to take a moral stand in any situation that arises.

SUMMARY OF KEY CONCEPTS

This chapter introduced ethical theories, codes, and guidelines that offer a variety of ways to think through potential ethical dilemmas and make decisions that will minimize risk to participants and increase the credibility of the study.

DISCUSSION QUESTIONS AND EXERCISES

- Deontological ethics, consequentialism, virtue ethics, and ethics of care are four core ethical perspectives that can be used to frame qualitative online research. They offer different ways to think about a situation where the guidelines are incomplete or in conflict. Pick one perspective and use it to create a rationale for some research. Compare and contrast your rationale with the one created by a peer. Did your peer make a compelling case? Why or why not? What would strengthen the rationale?

- Review at least two studies conducted with data collected online (observation, participant observation, interviews or focus groups) and discuss ethical frameworks in an essay of 3–5 pages.
- After reading the overview of ethical theories, select one to study in more depth. Find at least two sources on the theory and summarize the most essential positions or constructs. How would you apply this theory in an online study? How would the principles influence your choices when interacting with participants or working with extant data?
- Reflect on this quote from Greeff and Rennie (2016) and describe how you can 'become phronimos:'

Becoming phronimos – a person with practical wisdom – was perceived [by research participants] as a dynamic evolving process, which issues, and then looking for the signs of phronesis in their involved the accumulation and assimilation of experiences over time, as well as an openness to learn from the community or from new situations with which they were confronted. (p. 178)

5

Conducting an Ethical Online Study

Avoid focusing on getting procedures right over getting ethics right. (Rallis & Rossman, 2012)

HIGHLIGHTS

Research ethics is a process, not an event. It is not enough to simply ask a participant to sign a form – consent necessitates an ongoing conversation. An ethics committee or **institutional review board approval** of the proposal and authorization to conduct the study implies that once it is accepted, decision-making about ethics is complete. In reality, it has just begun. At every stage of research we need to review plans and directions, and consider whether we are doing the right thing.

In Chapter 4 we explored classical ethics theories as well as some of the ethics guidelines offered by professional associations. In this chapter we look at ways to use these ideas to design and carry out ethical qualitative research online using extant data, elicited, or enacted approaches. In Chapter 6 we will explore ethical and practical implications for the researcher's roles and positions. Discussion of ethics will be woven throughout Chapters 7–12 to emphasize the need to consider ethics at all stages of the inquiry. In Chapters 13 and 14, ethical issues at the reporting stage are considered.

OBJECTIVES

After reading and reflecting on this chapter, you will be able to understand design considerations for:

- communicating ethically with and about participants at all stages of the research process
- applying ethical codes and theories to your research design and plans
- crafting an appropriate consent agreement
- informing participants about the study and verifying consent
- reflecting on your own ethical stance and addressing your own potential conflicts of interest or researcher bias.

Throughout this book we have explored three broad categories of online qualitative research: studies using extant data collected without direct contact with participants, and elicited or enacted styles or research that do involve direct interaction with participants. Ethical practices and expectations vary greatly depending on whether you plan to question or engage with participants. At the same time, even when there are not active participants, you might need to think about the sources represented in the database or social media site. And all researchers need to communicate and collaborate to some extent with stakeholders or gatekeepers, librarians or archivists, research supervisors or editors. In this chapter we explore some ways to navigate potential ethical challenges and develop defensible ways to approach and explain the study to participants and others throughout all stages of the inquiry.

ADAPTING AND APPLYING ETHICS THEORIES AND CODES IN QUALITATIVE ONLINE RESEARCH

No research should be done without a clear expectation of a tangible benefit, whether it is the advancement of a body of knowledge, developing new understanding of human experience, or finding ways to improve individuals, communities, organizations, or society. The researcher must be able to identify the core purpose and articulate the benefits. If the researcher is not clear about why the study is important, it will be difficult to gain buy-in from others, not least participants who typically volunteer time from their busy schedules to share their stories. In other words, before being honest with participants or other stakeholders, you must first be honest with yourself about the proposed research.

In Chapter 4 you learned about ethical theories and codes and were introduced to the idea that online qualitative research calls for a holistic approach. Based on this premise the researcher needs to develop the 'practical wisdom' necessary to find the balance of theoretical and ethical perspectives appropriate for the study.

- Is your work governed by institutional, disciplinary or funding entities with specific requirements or parameters? Is it necessary to follow guidelines and/or to meet research by external parties such as an institutional review board or ethics board? If so, can drawing on constructs from deontological ethics perspectives strengthen the proposal and study?
- Is it a priority for you to act in ways that respect the wishes and rights of the participant, even if that means making changes to the research approach or questions? If so, do you need to learn about and apply ethics of care?
- Will you make your own assessment of the situation and sense of what is right and moral and proceed accordingly? If so, will you draw on thinking about virtue ethics?
- Will you explain potential risks as balanced with beneficial outcomes of the study for the greater good? If so, can drawing on constructs from consequentialist ethics theories strengthen the proposal and study?

As with many ethical dilemmas, there may be competing demands and no easy answers when it comes to defining and applying ethical theory to the research design. The concept of 'practical wisdom' is not easily defined, and researchers must learn from experience. But when research involves participants' trust that their stories and identities will be protected, the onus is on the researcher to think through the options, carefully reflect on decisions, and communicate a rationale that supports the ethical approach the study will take.

Step 1. First, be certain of the purpose and anticipated benefits that justify the study. Next, consider your circumstances. To what extent must your research design fit with established guidelines? What are the ethical implications of those fixed parameters? What other elements – such as your own moral sense and values, the principles of your field or discipline, or your concern for the well-being of participants – influence your ethical decision-making? With whom can you discuss options and questions about the best way to resolve ethical concerns?

FOUR ISSUES THAT MATTER WHEN DESIGNING ETHICAL ONLINE RESEARCH

Simply stated, research that involves participants should be based on freely given informed consent of individuals who have been provided with adequate information on what they will experience in the study, the limits to their participation, potential risks they may incur by taking part in research, and their ability to discontinue participation. These points can be organized into four broad, interrelated categories. After careful evaluation of all steps of the planned study, researchers must explain how they will:

1. Protect human subjects
2. Obtain appropriate informed consent from participants
3. Respect the research site
4. Safeguard participants' identities and data.

The first stage of evaluation is to consider how these four imperatives would apply given the nature of the study. Protection of human subjects, participants' consent, and research site permissions are explored in this chapter; issues related to protecting participants' identities are discussed in Chapter 14.

Three types of data collection approaches were described in Chapter 1: extant, elicited, and enacted. These approaches vary greatly in regard to the relationship the researcher has with the participant, the types of interactions between researcher and participant, and indeed whether there are human subjects. Inquiries built on extant data collected through external (non-participant) observation, posted and/ or archived material, or databases may need to address some or all four of these imperatives. Since elicited and enacted data collection methods entail direct communication with participants, all four must be addressed. Multimodal qualitative studies that utilize a mix of these approaches will also need to evaluate which may apply and at what stage of the study. The typology of qualitative online methods was introduced in Chapter 1. It is expanded in Table 5.1 to include considerations for ethical conduct in various types of studies.

Step 2. Review the research design. Will you collect extant data, elicit data from or enact data with participants? If it will use a mix of extant and elicited/enacted approaches, will the same participants generate data at all stages of the research?

PROTECT HUMAN SUBJECTS

The terminology used in this book is *participants*. In Chapter 1 three metaphors for the researcher's role were introduced: the miner, the traveler, and the gardener (Kvale, 2003; Salmons, 2010). While the miner may view those who provide data as *subjects*, the traveler and the gardener realize that these individuals must take an active role in the study and are more appropriately described as *participants*. Online qualitative researchers need to consider protection not only of known human subjects, but also of the identities and avatars they may have assumed or imagined for their lives in cyberspace or for games. Regardless of what terminology they use, researchers are obligated to make every effort to do no harm to those involved in the study, according to the principle of *beneficence* described in Chapter 4.

At the design stage researchers need to identify who needs to be engaged directly or indirectly, in what way, to collect the data needed to answer the research questions and achieve the purpose of the study, and the real or potential risks involved with participation in the research. The most important of all ethical issues is the protection of human subjects.

By carefully analyzing data needs, expectations, or participants and risk factors early, as a part of the earliest conceptualization of the study, it is possible to anticipate potential risks and develop strategies for minimizing them. At the same time, research rarely unfolds precisely as planned, and researchers need to be prepared for emergent ethical dilemmas that may require researchers to re-evaluate òr renegotiate some aspect of the design.

Defining Human Participants Online

What does the term 'human participant' mean in online research? In some online situations the human participant may be distant from the data where, for example, large-scale collections of records have been organized into databases. However, as suggested in guidelines from the Association of Internet Researchers, since 'all digital information at some point involves individual persons, consideration of principles related to research on human subjects may be necessary even if it is not immediately apparent how and where persons are involved in the research data' (Markham & Buchanan, 2012, p. 4).

The definition for the term *human participant* used in this chapter was drawn from the US Common Code (HHS, 2017), and further explained by the University of Washington Human Subjects Division (2012):

> A human participant is a living individual about whom an investigator conducting research obtains (1) data or samples through intervention or interaction with individual(s), or (2) identifiable private information.
>
> **Living**: means that the subject is alive at the time of the research, according to applicable local and national regulations.
>
> **About whom**: means the data or information relates to the person. Asking individuals what they think about something is almost always about the person.
>
> **Intervention**: includes both physical procedures by which data are gathered, and manipulations of the subject or the subject's environment that are performed for research purposes.

Table 5.1 Consent and the typology of qualitative online methods

Typology of Online Methods		Researcher and Participant	Ethical Considerations
Extant	Studies using existing materials developed without the researcher's influence	No direct contact with individual participants	Could the participant(s) be identified based on the data?
			On what basis (permissions, user agreements) were archives assembled? Was data anonymized or not?
			Is the subject matter sensitive? Is the subject matter protected (such as medical information)?
			Will you use information from users' profiles?
			Will you use information from users' images?
			Will you use data from more than one platform? Do terms of usage vary?
			Do members represent a vulnerable population?
			Do users reveal personal information because they lack digital literacy or awareness of online privacy?
Elicited	Studies using data elicited from participants in response to the researcher's questions or prompts	Interaction between researcher and one or more participants	How will consent be verified: written or verbal assent?
			How will you inform participants before and during the study?
			Have you clarified all expectations for the participant(s), through all the stages of the study?
Enacted	Studies using data generated with participants during the study	Interaction and collaboration involving researcher and one or more participants	Have you discussed use of images, quotations, or other characteristics that could potentially identify the participant?
			Are specific permissions needed from a research site/list/community?

Interaction: includes communication or interpersonal contact between investigator and subject.

Identifiable: the identity of the subject is or may readily be ascertained by the investigator or associated with the information.

Private information: includes information about behavior that occurs in a context in which an individual can reasonably expect that no observation or recording is taking place, and information which has been provided for specific purposes by an individual and which the individual can reasonably expect will not be made public.

For our purposes, the human participant is the person on the other side of the monitor, the 'user' with a mobile device who is typing on the keyboard, chatting on a video call or uploading images or files. When the human directly, or indirectly through digital representations, contributes data to the study we consider this individual a *human participant*. The human may be represented or expressed online by diverse avatars, pseudonyms, or screen names. If you collect posts, profiles, and any other kind of information that either overtly identifies or could be used to identify the individual who wrote them, that individual must be treated as a participant.

Protecting Secondary Participants

LeCompte (2008, p. 805) writes that:

A *secondary participant* is someone who was not initially designated as a primary participant in a study, but about whom information is gathered from persons who are primary participants. Secondary participants are created when individuals provide information about other people whom they know or to whom they are related.

Given the interactive nature of social media and online communication, researchers may encounter circumstances where secondary participants may be present. As Livingstone and Locatelli (2012, p. 70) observe, 'once researchers recognize that identity and interaction are fundamentally social, separating data from primary (consenting) and secondary (involuntary) participants without damage may be difficult.' For example, a researcher who is observing the webinar presentation style of a participant might see the identities and responses of the audience members logged into the event. The researcher observing (consenting) participants' posts on social networking sites might be able to see friends' identities and messages. If the researcher conducts an enacted study using a simulation or role-play, it might occur in a virtual space or game where others (or their avatars) are present. The 'others' may be defined as secondary participants. Henderson et al. (2012, p. 2) describe common circumstances:

A social network site (SNS) by its very nature comprises connections between many users, and many concerns arise because of the number of, and connections between, the various key actors. These include the SNS users participating in an experiment, their friends (who may be mentioned or included in participants' data), other SNS users with whom the participants may have shared data and the operators of the SNS. The researchers themselves may also be considered key actors, as might any other researchers with whom data might be shared. Each of these actors will have different concerns about the SNS data that are generated and collected. A participant might be willing to share some data with a researcher, but not other data. A participant's friend might be completely unwilling to have their data shared.

Given the socially interactive nature of online communication, the presence of participants' friends can complicate consent decisions. As a general rule of thumb, anyone not identifiable is a bystander but not a secondary participant. Anyone who is identifiable needs to be asked for consent. This distinction rests on *personally identifiable information*. For example, in a study using Facebook:

> [T]he co-participant (the person who the recruited participant was talking to) in that chat or message also needed to be 'recruited'. For this task, the participants themselves contacted their friends to ask if they would be willing for their chats to be recorded. Thus, data collection required not only the agreement of a main participant, but also a number of 'secondary' participants. (Ditchfield & Meredith, 2018, p. 9)

In this study, the participants helped the process along, which was beneficial to the researcher because including both sides of the conversation was critical for a full understanding of the question under investigation. If you ascertain that the user may be identifiable, two options are available: you could do as Ditchfield and Meredith did and contact the secondary participant and ask for consent to use the post(s). Alternatively, you could avoid recording or collecting posts from secondary participants and delete any of their comments that may appear in the data. Neither solution is perfect: when a side of a conversation is omitted, the context and meaning may be altered. If the participant has a small, regularly contributing network, soliciting consent may not be an impediment and, indeed, may expand the study. However, if the participant's network is diffuse, it may be difficult to engage irregular contributors and obtain their consent, in which case their posts or comments should not be used.

Step 3. Identify who needs to be engaged directly or indirectly, and in what way, to collect the data needed to answer the research questions and achieve the purpose of the study.

Considering Potential Risks for Online Participants

The primary risks for participants in most qualitative studies involve disclosing the identities of participants, or leaking raw data to the public that contains information the participant shared on the condition of privacy. Depending on the nature of the study, such breaches could result in minor embarrassment or in life- or career-changing implications.

As was discussed in Chapter 3, some technologies are more secure than others. Interviews or observations conducted in seemingly private areas may not be protected if site policies or ownership changes. As will be discussed in Chapter 14, the reporting and publishing process involves risks to participants' privacy when direct quotations or demographic characteristics may make it possible for readers to identify the person.

In any case, the protection of information and identities is the responsibility of the researcher. Whether serious or trivial, intentional or unintentional, disclosure of a participant's identity violates the consent agreement and compromises the researcher's credibility as a scholar.

Step 4. Think through the sensitivity of the research topic and levels of risk to the participant. Determine safeguards needed to minimize or eliminate risks. Discuss risks with participants as part of the informed consent negotiation and agreement.

OBTAIN APPROPRIATE INFORMED CONSENT FROM PARTICIPANTS

The essential tool online researchers have to protect participants and ensure integrity of the study is a robust informed consent process. Informed consent describes the actual agreement as well as the process researchers engage in to ensure that individuals are informed about the study before they voluntarily agree to participate. The UK Economic and Social Research Council (ESRC) states that freely given informed consent entails (ESRC, 2021):

- giving sufficient and appropriate information about the research, to allow participants to make a meaningful choice about whether or not to take part
- ensuring that there is no explicit or implicit coercion, so prospective participants can make an informed and free decision on their possible involvement.

In brief, *informed consent* consists of three components: adequate information, voluntariness of participation, and competence to sign the agreement (EC, 2013).

It is important to parse words here because each is significant.

Adequate information. To state the obvious: if participants were not informed, they did not authentically consent. About what exactly do researchers need to inform participants? It is beneficial to the researcher, as well as the participant when they both understand and agree to expectations for the type, timing, setting, and duration of the interaction. Participants should also know how resulting data and findings will be used.

Participants should be informed of any foreseeable risk or discomfort, including that harm, loss, or damages that could occur, including physical, psychological, social, economic, and/or legal risks (Owens, 2010). The potential harms for participants in social sciences and the humanities are, in general, more subtle than those associated with medical or other types of research. Harms may be of a psychological nature and/or linked to how cultures and/or ethnicities are represented in the community (Romare & Collste, 2015). Risks related to technology-oriented types of research studies are largely informational, primarily from the inappropriate or inadvertent disclosure of information and not from the research interventions themselves (HHS, 2017, p. 7152).

Participants should also be informed about any benefits from making a contribution to scientific knowledge; tangible benefits for the participants (i.e., food, money, and medical/mental health services); insight, training, learning, role modeling, empowerment, and future opportunities; psychosocial benefits (i.e., altruism, favorable attention, and increased self-esteem); kinship benefits (i.e., closeness to people or reduction of alienation); and community benefits (i.e., policies and public documentation) (Owens, 2010, p. 603).

Voluntariness of participation and competence to agree. Potential participants must freely and voluntarily agree to the conditions and expectations of the study. Research participants should be made aware of their right to refuse participation for whatever reason they wish and withdraw from the study without penalty or repercussions (BSA, 2002, p. 3). Researchers should clarify the point at which it will not be feasible to withdraw because of analysis and/or publication. (This is a requirement for those researchers under the aegis of the European Commission.)

Individuals must be free to choose to participate without substantial influence, coercion or control by others, including the researcher. Researchers need to demonstrate that they will treat individual participants as autonomous agents who can decide for themselves whether and to what extent they wish their personal information and interactions to be studied (Stern, 2009). Voluntary consent also means the signatory is capable of providing consent, and is of legal age, and if not, parental consent was acquired.

Voluntary consent implies two additional concepts. One is that the individual is capable of providing consent, being of legal age and competent to make such decisions. Another is that the individual chooses to participate without substantial influence, coercion or control by others, including the researcher. Researchers need to demonstrate that they will treat individual participants as autonomous agents who can decide for themselves whether and to what extent they wish their personal information and interactions to be studied (Stern, 2009).

Certainly, many components of a consent agreement for an online study are comparable to agreements for studies carried out face-to-face. People are people, and deserve the same respect whether they talk in an office or chat on social media. However, a consent agreement for online research additionally answers questions specific to characteristics of the online setting or communications technology. For example, a study that involves collecting images or artifacts must address ownership and permissions not needed in text-only data collection. If the researcher intends to use a webcam, avatars, or other special tools or applications, the expectations should be clearly spelled out in the agreement discussion and form.

The informed consent form or letter documents the agreement of researcher and participant and formalizes study participation. A signature on the consent agreement 'serves as a proxy indicator of the participant's trust in the researcher' (Rallis & Rossman, 2012, p. 64). When a written form is impractical, 'verbal' informed consent can be allowed, meaning prospective participants indicate their willingness to participate in the research aloud, but they do not sign a consent form (Anderson & Corneli, 2018).

The consent agreement should answer fundamental questions for potential participants, with special attention to information needed by participants in online studies. If changes emerge after the initial agreement, participants must be informed and agree to continue. See Table 5.2 for recommended questions to adapt as appropriate to the study.

─────────────── RESEARCH CAMEO 5.1 ───────────────

Researcher 1 is designing a study using extant data. They plan to analyze Big Data from journal databases as well as mission statements and editorials from selected journals to understand how and where qualitative research is published. Since they are using peer reviewed journal databases, they will not need consent agreements.

Researcher 2 is designing a study that involves eliciting data through one-to-one and group online interviews with qualitative researchers who have successfully published their studies. They will need consent agreements from all participants.

Researcher 3 is designing a study that will involve generating data with aspiring and successful qualitative researchers in a workshop setting. They will need consent agreements from all participants that will spell out what aspects of the workshop experience will be recorded for the purpose of this study.

Researcher 4 is designing a study that will include observations of social media posts from a writing group, analysis of extant data from journal archives, and online interviews with selected authors and editors. They will not need consent agreements for the extant data collected from journal archives. They expect to make an agreement with group members and will only collect data from members who agree to participate. They will need agreements with the interview participants.

Table 5.2 Questions to ask in the consent agreement

Questions	Additional Questions to ask in Agreement for Online Research
• Who is conducting the study: identity of researcher(s)? Is there an affiliation with an institution, agency, or a funder?	• Can you include links to a website or blog that contains credible information about the researcher and the study? Can you include links to any affiliated institution or agency, including contact information for the research supervisor if the researcher is a student?
• How can researchers be contacted at any time to answer pertinent questions about the research and the participant's rights?	
• What is the purpose of the study?	
• What rights does the participant have to withdraw from the study at any time without penalty?	
• Will interactions with the researcher be recorded?	• Will interactions with the researcher be recorded, saved, or archived online? Will the researcher download any recordings, interview chat records or posts and delete them from commercial servers?
• What are the rights of the participant in terms of reviewing transcripts, images, or media collected or generated, and correcting information provided?	• How will participants be able to review transcripts or recordings – will you send links or attached documents? Does the participant have the ability to access materials in this way?
	• How will participants communicate any corrections? By email? Are participants expected to make changes on documents and return them? If these approaches require technology skills the participant does not have, are there alternative ways to convey any requested changes?
• What does the study entail in terms of duration, time commitment, and types of interactions (one-to-one with researcher or as part of a group)?	• What does the study entail in terms of duration, time commitment, and types of interactions (one-to-one with researcher or as part of a group)? If in a group, how will the individual's identity be protected?
	• What types of technologies will be used for communications with the researcher, data collection activities, and/or as the setting for the study?
• How will the researcher ensure protection of confidentiality and anonymity of the data?	• How will the researcher ensure protection of confidentiality and anonymity of data collected online?
• How will the data be used?	
• Where will findings be published?	
• What procedures will be used in cases of incidental findings?	
• What are the risks or potential risks associated with participation?	
• What are potential benefits associated with participation?	

The Process of Informing Prospective Online Research Participants

At its simplest, the researcher informs individuals who meet inclusion criteria about the study, invites them to contribute, and asks them to sign the consent agreement. However, in research as in life, the simplest approach may or may not be possible. When communicating online, additional factors may apply. Southerton and Taylor (2020) point out that:

> Notice-and-consent practices require the informed consent of participants based on information provided by the data collector about the way the data will be collected, stored, and disseminated. Crucially, it is the 'informed' dimension of consent that becomes key to this framework, the assumption being that individuals evaluate, in a rational manner, and, based on the given information, make an *informed choice* whether they wish to participate in the collection of data. Once 'informed,' individuals are believed to be able to consent to data collection and dissemination based on their evaluation of risks and benefits. (p. 2)

The onus is on the researcher to ensure that potential participants understand the information given about the study and the roles the researcher and participant will take. Anyone who has clicked through user agreements for software is aware that sending or posting lengthy documents will not be an effective way to truly inform participants of your expectations and their rights. Some individuals may quickly scroll through, sign, and ostensibly provide consent without truly understanding the study's purpose, procedures, risks, benefits, and their rights.

The question you will need to answer, based on the nature of the study, degree of risk, and expectations for participants is: How can you satisfy your institutional requirements for legalistic agreements, while recognizing that such paperwork rarely translates into authentic informational accuracy for potential participants? Louise Couceiro (Couceiro, 2020a, 2020b) shared information using the diagrams shown in Figures 5.1 and 5.2. These clear, engaging visuals provided information in a way that child participants and their parents could easily grasp. What would work for your study?

Being a Credible Researcher

Participants will contribute richer data when they believe that the researcher is trustworthy and is acting ethically. To convey a respectful attitude, researchers need to inform participants about themselves. Can participants trust that you will honor the agreement? Can they trust that you will be respectful and

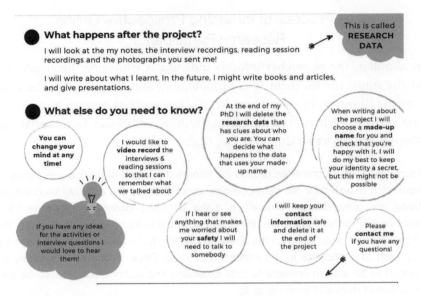

Figure 5.1 Examples of participant information in Louise Couceiro's online study

observe stated parameters for what data will be collected and how it will be used? Attention to how you are viewed by participants is essential, especially when conducting research in communities and cultures different than your own. Gray et al. point out that:

> How we reach a decision to trust another person varies a great deal between individuals and between cultural groups. Whilst traditional research ethics guidelines place a lot of emphasis on informed consent, indigenous guidelines put much greater emphasis on interdependence and trust. (2016, p. 28)

Reflecting on these questions is essential, especially for new researchers who are not experienced, and cannot point to an academic position or a list of publications to establish credibility.

Crafting Viable Consent Materials

Thoughtful, accessible messages will ensure that would-be participants understand what they are agreeing to do by participating in the study. McKee and Porter (2009, p. 17) suggest that researchers consult persons being studied, and other researchers who may have conducted similar studies, to devise appealing announcements. It will help to take into account the perspective of the reader. Is the material too 'academic'; does it contain jargon? Is it written more for the internal audience of an ethics board or committee than in the everyday language of the prospective participant? Is it too long and dense?

The online attention span is short so important information about the study must be presented succinctly. Additionally, in some settings participants may simply be accessing the study information using a mobile device, perhaps one with a small screen. Expecting the reader to download, sign and return a document may be unrealistic. To ensure that all materials describing the study, including all of the implications of the consent agreement, are understood, the researcher may want to provide the information in multiple formats:

> Understanding may be improved by providing potential subjects with several options to hear, view or read the consent form at their own pace. If done interactively, subjects can be given immediate feedback about their level of understanding of study procedures, risks, and so on, thereby theoretically increasing their overall comprehension. (Rowbotham et al., 2013, p. 1)

Rather than simply uploading the types of consent agreement information pages and forms used in a face-to-face study, the creative researcher can use the visual, interactive ways of communicating online to inform and engage potential participants. How does the target population typically communicate online? How can you use the types of communication they use in order to reach them in ways they will appreciate? Explain the study, participation requirements, and expectations in clear terms understandable to the target population using online tools. Links to an electronic consent form or other means to verify agreement can be included (more below on verification of the agreement). For example:

- **Media**. Create a short, friendly video to inform participants who are deciding whether to volunteer. Introduce yourself, and discuss why this inquiry is important. In studies where participants may be involved for a period of time, create additional videos to inform participants about the progress of the study and share preliminary findings.
- **Graphics and infographics**. Minimize text and present key information related to study participation visually (See Figure 5.1, an example from Louise Couceiro's study with children.).
- **Researcher site**. Create a simple website, blog, or page on a social networking site. Link to your institution, funding agency, or other relevant affiliation.
- **Quiz or game**. Create an interactive site that provides and allows the users to click through to the next item once they have read or viewed each segment of information (e.g. time commitment, risks, rights).
- **Questionnaire.** Combine information-sharing with the consent agreement. Create an opening section for the questionnaire that includes required information about rights and requirements and questions that allow participants to easily verify agreement. Collect demographic or background information (e.g. years or types of experience with the phenomenon) that can be used for assigning participants to groups. Online researchers can use free survey software to create questionnaires

that combine study information and electronic consent forms. These tools allow participants to quickly answer yes/no questions or to write in comments about their preferences. See the example at www.surveymonkey.com/s/RP7W5VY. You can adapt the questions and options to fit your own study.

Tips for Successfully Informing Participants Online

Written materials should be provided in the language best understood by the participant and be written at a reading level that can be understood by the participant. In studies involving diverse participants, translations into other languages can be posted.

Use alternative mechanisms to convey the information, as appropriate, if the participant has hearing or vision impairments, literacy or reading limitations. If the researcher is concerned that participants will not fully grasp the information in written form, share an audio or video recording, or use visual ways of getting across key points about the study and expectations for participation.

Verifying Consent

Researchers typically need to follow institutional or other requirements to verify the consent agreement. For example, in some legal jurisdictions electronic signatures are not valid and the only choice is to have a hard copy of a signed form returned via surface mail.

Some institutions accept verbal consent (Anderson & Corneli, 2018). If allowable, the researcher can explain the expectations and requirements of the study, as well as the participant's rights, and answer any questions. The researcher can conclude the consent discussion with a statement such as 'by continuing with this interview/focus group/observation you signify your agreement with the requirements of the study.' This verbal exchange is recorded so the researcher can verify agreement. If desired, the researcher can provide a written summary of the agreement for the participant's reference. A verbal approach is advantageous when written agreements can be long and somewhat intimidating to some participants, and a conversational approach is friendlier. It also sets the stage for further conversations, should the needs of the study change.

Researchers are responsible for discerning whether potential participants have the capacity to give consent. Capacity to consent includes the caveat that participants are of legal age. If the participant is under the age of consent (usually 18 years of age) or cannot legally sign for other reasons, an appropriate individual, such as a parent or guardian, must typically sign for them.

SPOT CHECK

- Think about potential participants for your proposed study. What would be the most effective way to inform them about the study? What would be the most effective way to verify consent?

Consent for Using Data Collected in Online Observations Conducted in Conjunction with Online Interviews

Observation occurs when a researcher conducts an interview in a physical place, whether or not it is an intentional part of the study. The researcher can see the participant, and can observe such matters as age, race, ability, attire, and comportment. The researcher may see the pictures on the participant's desk, books on the shelf, and other features or artifacts in the environment. Such informal observations may provide details about personal tastes, family or sexual orientation, hobbies or social memberships that may or may not be relevant to the study. If such observations were noted, would the researcher ask for the participant's agreement to use that information as data?

This question is even more intriguing online, where researchers may choose to conduct interviews using video or web conferencing options that allow them to see the participant(s). They may purposefully choose to use these tools in order to observe the participant during the interview. Interviewers may thus be able to see facial expressions, to sense emotional responses and other non-verbal cues. They may also set up the interview in a way that allows participants to share views of the environment or artifacts. However, unlike the kinds of informal observations that may happen in the course of a face-to-face interview, in online interviews these require conscious design and technology choices, for example, whether to use videoconferencing tools that allow visual as well as audio exchange. The decision to combine observations with interviews should be agreed upon with participants and described in the consent agreement.

While some researchers may feel that it is laborious to carry out the steps involved with negotiating, obtaining consent before the study, and updating the agreement as needed, from a positive perspective informed consent is a valuable part of the study. Discussions between the researcher and participant can help to build rapport and establish a shared commitment to the study. Next, consider how to accomplish an authentic, productive consent process when conducting qualitative research online.

————————————— RESEARCH CAMEO 5.2 —————————————

Researcher 1 is designing a study using extant data. Since they are using peer reviewed journal databases, they will not need to inform anyone or obtain consent agreements.

Researcher 2 is designing a study that involves eliciting data through one-to-one and group online interviews with qualitative researchers who have successfully published their studies. They plan to observe the non-verbal cues during inter-views, and include that visual data as well as the verbal responses. They will need consent agreements from all participants. They will create a visual infographic depicting the stages of the study from preparation for the interview, the interview, potential follow-up questions, member checking, through to any needed discus-sions about presentations or publications. They will create a simple blog about the study and include basic information about timing for each stage and any logistical information participants might need. They will also verbally review the expecta-tions at the beginning of each interview to make sure any participants' questions have been fully answered.

Researcher 3 is designing a study that will involve generating data with aspir-ing and successful qualitative researchers in a workshop setting. They will need consent agreements from all participants that will spell out what aspects of the workshop experience will be recorded for the purpose of this study. Researcher 3 is offering this free workshop in exchange for the opportunity to learn from the experiences of workshop participants. In addition to written information about this approach, they will record a short video participants can watch to fully understand the expectations. In addition, Researcher 3 will verbally review the expectations and answer any questions at the beginning of the first workshop session.

Researcher 4 is designing a study that will include observations of a writing group, an analysis of extant data from journal archives, and online interviews with selected authors and editors. Researcher 4 will create a detailed information sheet for group and interview participants and update it as the study proceeds.

Informed Consent (or Not) in Qualitative Research Using Extant Online Data

While the need for informed consent agreement when the researcher is directly eliciting data is generally accepted, the requirement for consent agree-ment in extant data collection online is less clearly defined. When researchers want to observe online interactions and/or collect user-generated posts, docu-ments, images, or media, a different set of ethical issues are present. With ever-changing technologies and shifting public attitudes on privacy there can be no one-size-fits-all answer. In this section a number of perspectives are outlined, together with a discussion of differentiating factors and key questions researchers should review when deciding which approach most closely aligns with the study at hand.

The first distinction is between two ways of observing behaviors and activities online; each has its own ethical implications. While language may vary in different research traditions, the following definitions are suggested to clarify the role of the researcher in observational studies:

- **Unobtrusive observation** to collect extant data containing no personally identifiable information or look for patterns in such posts on websites, blogs, or microblogs, or in interactions on discussion groups. In this form of observation the researcher does not ask questions, make posts or otherwise get involved in interactions with the online community, group, or social networking site. Members of the group being observed do not know observation is occurring.
- **Open observation** to collect data using observational methods in settings where participants are aware of the study and have given consent.
- **Participant observation** to collect data that includes extant and elicited types of data as well as the researchers' own field notes on reflections, experiences, or interactions with other participants. The researcher is a participant in the study. Involvement may include posting to forums, blogs, or walls in online communities or social networking sites. Participant observers can conduct formal or informal interviews with other participants.

In other words, when researchers become involved in the site or group, their actions change the method from 'observation' to 'participant observation'. While posting questions on a social media wall to the group or chatting with an individual may not seem to rise to the level of an *interview*, from an ethical standpoint it does. When researchers collect data based on responses to their prompts or questions, the study needs to follow the same kinds of expectations *vis-à-vis* consent.

In open observation the researcher is identified and people in the group, community or social networking site are aware that the researcher is present and collecting data. In covert observation the researcher is present without the knowledge of the group or community. In some cases the moderator or group leader may have agreed to the presence of the researcher, but the individuals communicating on the site are not aware that their posts are being collected as data.

An important differentiation – if a fuzzy one – is between public and private online settings where data may be collected. When differentiating public from private on the Internet, a continuum can help clarify degrees instead of an either–or determination. The public–private Internet continuum in Figure 5.2 expands on and illustrates this suggestion (Salmons, 2010, 2012, 2015). It presents criteria that can be used when trying to distinguish between public and private research settings in order to make the best ethical design decisions.

At one end of the continuum is the free and open Internet, where no registration, membership or log-in is required. These websites or blogs can be defined as 'public' when they are online spaces where governmental agencies, companies, organizations, or individuals post information available for anyone to view or read. The archives are open so readers can follow stories over a period of time. Freely disseminating information to the public is the purpose of such sites. Researchers collecting extant data do not interact with any writer. This kind of extant data collection seems comparable to conventional document analysis and can follow similar approaches. Documents and materials on these websites can be viewed as authored materials, and referenced using the appropriate academic citations. As with any ethical decision, the appropriate disciplinary and/or institutional guidelines should be consulted at the design stage.

It is less clear what the ethical research approach should be in the 'gray area' as indicated in the public–private Internet continuum in Figure 5.2. Such environments are those that allow anyone to read or view material but require some type of registration to contribute, post, or comment. These might include blogs, magazine, news, or e-commerce sites that offer free content and encourage participation or feedback by consumers. Because the public can read any posts one might assume that people who make comments expect wide readership. These sites are in the gray area because in some cases sensitive subject matter may be discussed and, while **pseudonymization** may be used, typically a reply to the person making a post may be relayed by email. This means personally identifiable information is conveyed. Also in the gray area are

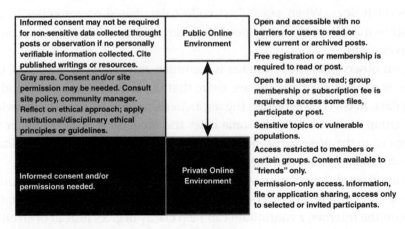

Figure 5.2 The public–private Internet continuum

sites that are free but require membership and approval of the owner of the content before visitors can access the material. Such online communication includes most subscription email lists and social networking sites.

—————————————— RESEARCH CAMEO 5.3 ——————————————

Researcher 1 is designing a study using extant data. Since they are using peer-reviewed journal databases, they will not need to inform anyone or obtain consent agreements. It will be legitimate for Researcher 1 to cite sources from the journals.

Researcher 3 is designing a study that will involve generating data with aspiring and successful qualitative researchers in a workshop setting. They will need consent agreements from all participants that will spell out what aspects of the workshop experience will be recorded for the purpose of this study. Researcher 3 plans to openly observe the workshop participants and will note this fact in the consent agreement. They will give participants the option of engaging anonymously if sensitive issues are being discussed that they would rather not be included in the data.

Positions on Consent for Use of Extant Data

Four main perspectives have emerged in the research community about ethical behavior in strictly observational or document analysis studies where the researcher *does not* directly interact with people who make online posts.

The people who make posts researchers collect for data are human participants

From this perspective, researchers using posted material should consider the person who made the post as a human participant, and proceed accordingly. As Stommel and Rijk (2021) note, awareness of posting things publicly is not the same as consenting with research. Ethical research behavior, from the human participant perspective, would entail contacting the person who made the post, and proceeding with an informed consent protocol.

Decisions about ethical use of extant data are situational

From this perspective it is not possible to make general definitions or specify clear boundaries between what is public or private online, so the researcher needs to look at the nature of the proposed study, sensitivity of the issues and

potential risks, and the online context. The researcher must weigh risks, benefits, and options, and decide what is best for the specific study.

The AoIR Ethics Guidelines (Markham & Buchanan, 2012) fit this perspective.
They point out that:

> [It] is strongly arguable that postings to both synchronous and asynchronous discus-
> sion groups ... do not automatically count as public activity. When constructing research
> using discussion groups, any requirement for consent by participants obviously needs
> to be tempered by a consideration of the nature of the research, the intrusiveness and
> privacy implications of the data collected, analysed and reported, and possible harm
> caused by the research. (p. 3)

> Individual and cultural definitions and expectations of privacy are ambiguous, contested,
> and changing. People may operate in public spaces but maintain strong perceptions or
> expectations of privacy. Or, they may acknowledge that the substance of their commu-
> nication is public, but that the specific context in which it appears implies restrictions
> on how that information is – or ought to be – used by other parties. (pp. 6–7)

Another situational factor relates to the digital literacy of the user (McKee &
Porter, 2009; Salmons, 2014). Are users posting personal information because
they are unaware of or unable to use privacy settings? Does the user realize that
anyone can read the posts? In a survey for a study about the future of the Internet,
Oostveen et al. (2012) found a dichotomy between the increased awareness and
concerns about privacy expressed by some social media users and, at the same
time, a seeming lack of awareness by others of potential implications of their
online interactions:

> As the Internet becomes more integral to the way we live our daily lives, end users are
> becoming increasingly aware of the dangers of making too much information available
> publicly. Careers and personal lives can be severely affected by not considering what
> information (including multimedia – photos, videos etc.) is disclosed online. For most
> users, the main concern is the extent to which information was becoming public, and
> some are now allowing less of their content to be published openly. ... But while atti-
> tudes towards privacy are changing significantly, for many the level of privacy concern
> is decreasing. Privacy is heavily compromised by a lack of awareness as much as by
> technical or cost issues. (Oostveen et al., 2012, p. 44)

In a NatCen report based on qualitative interviews and focus groups with social
media users, similar findings emerged. Users reported their 'difficulty staying up
to date with dense and frequently evolving terms and conditions' (Beninger et al.,
2014, p. 2). More recent studies continue to uncover the same issues and attitudes,
especially with younger social media users. Pangrazio and Selwyn (2018) studied
younger users aged 13 to 17. While these users were wary of being tracked, they
did not understand basic facts about data posted online:

Several young people were uncertain about what the term 'personal data' referred to, with some assuming that these only related to mobile phone use. Similar uncertainties emerged in regard to how social media data are generated and how these are reused and repurposed. For example, [one participant] assumed that geo-locational data were only generated when he opened the Google maps app on his phone. Other participants were not sure what happened to images and texts once 'sent' assuming that these 'disappeared.' (Pangrazio & Selwyn, 2018, p. 5)

Given these factors, the onus is on the researcher to avoid taking advantage of those who unwittingly post revealing information. This might mean making contact with the user and asking for consent or taking extra steps to ensure that no identifiable information is inadvertently gathered or if gathered, is not included in publications.

Researchers should reflect on questions such as: What risks to the observed subjects may be associated with the study? Would participants be unhappy to learn that their posts are being collected for research purposes? Would the credibility of the study be jeopardized by collecting data without obtaining permission from the group or moderator, and/or consent from participants (Salmons, 2015)? What harm might result from asking for consent, or through the process of asking for consent? What harm may result if consent is not obtained (Markham & Buchanan, 2012)?

Posts are a form of informal writing

From this perspective, social media or blog posts, archives of online community exchanges, or documents publicly accessed online without special permissions, registration, or log-ins may be comparable to articles, newsletters, or other informal writing. Researchers collecting such data *without* interacting with any writer may make a case that the study is comparable to a document analysis study. A blog or post can be seen as a textual artifact or a cultural product (Lomborg, 2013, pp. 21–22). Accordingly, proper attribution is accomplished by citing the source (Salmons, 2015).

Waldron (2013) and Bruckman (2002) exemplify this view and suggest that it is ethical for researchers to 'lurk' unannounced, quote, and analyze online information if the following four criteria are met:

- It is officially and publicly archived.
- No password is required for archive access.
- No site policy prohibits it.
- The topic of discussion is not highly sensitive.

Ethical behavior of researchers involves choosing open-access sites for the data collection, identifying any sensitive issues that may be off-limits, and examining site use policies to make sure the research activities are not excluded. The researcher attributes the material to the writer, giving him or her credit using the referencing protocol laid out by the academic document format. More about how to address this type of research in writings and publications is discussed in Chapter 14.

Databases comprised of a large number of posts or records are not handled the same way as individual human participants

In some large datasets or databases, no personally identifiable information is available, so obtaining consent is not possible. Additional permissions may be needed to use the data from these sources for your study.

Researchers using such databases want to be sure ethical practices were used to collect the data. The AoIR Guidelines (Markham & Buchanan, 2012, p. 7) raise an important question:

> Whether one is dealing with a human subject is different from the question about whether information is linked to individuals: Can we assume a person is wholly removed from large data pools? For example, a data set containing thousands of tweets or an aggregation of surfing behaviors collected from a bot is perhaps far removed from the persons who engaged in these activities. In these scenarios, it is possible to forget that there was ever a person somewhere in the process that could be directly or indirectly impacted by the research.

The 2020 AoIR Guidelines discuss dilemmas specific to Big Data research:

> Consent is manifestly impracticable in the case of Big Data projects, however, resulting in a serious ethical dilemma. Researchers have taken different steps to mitigate risk against research subjects in such cases (Bechmann & Kim, 2020). Some researchers are trying to obtain first-degree informed consent, others are focusing on deleting names and other highly identifiable information from the dataset when storing and processing the data. Most commonly, researchers pseudonymize their data separating keys from the actual dataset and also make sure to justify both any questions using/processing sensitive data and/or how risk in this process has been dealt with (e.g. storage, aggregation of data, publication of aggregates). (franzke et al., 2020, p. 10)

> Scrutiny may be needed to ensure that 'anonymized' data sets have indeed stripped out any personally identifiable information. If the database is searchable and contains enough personal information and metadata that may enable users to be identified, researchers will need to think carefully about using it (BPS, 2013; Markham & Buchanan, 2012).

These four perspectives are summarized in Table 5.3.

Table 5.3 Perspectives on consent and types of extant data

Perspective 1	Perspective 2	Perspective 3	Perspective 4
People who post online are human participants who must agree to use of their writings or images as data	Online posts and exchanges are so varied that each situation must be evaluated, and a general rule cannot apply	People who post online on publicly accessible sites are writers whose work should be cited	In 'Big Data', databases and archive data have already been anonymized so there are no known participants. Without contact information it is not possible to obtain consent.
Always obtain informed consent	Evaluate sensitivity of topic, perceptions of privacy, expectations of users and other factors then decide whether consent is needed	Informed consent is not needed; respect intellectual property by citing the writer with proper attribution Other permissions may be needed to use the data, and/or to publish findings based on the data	Informed consent cannot be obtained because there are no names associated with the data Other permissions may be needed to use the data, and/or to publish findings based on the data

To some extent, the selection of the appropriate perspective may be determined by the prerogative of the researcher, the type of research, and/or the type of data. The perspective may be influenced by other factors. Students or researchers in academic environments may need to follow the institution's guidelines. Researchers may choose to follow disciplinary guidelines established by the professional association or scholarly society. Researchers may also need to follow the requirements and observe the parameters established by the research setting. Finally, you must determine what you feel is ethical behavior, given the circumstances of the study.

———————————————— SPOT CHECK ————————————————

- Based on your understanding of the Internet, social media, archives, and sites you visit, what ethical dilemmas do you find challenging when thinking about collecting extant data?
- If you plan to collect extant data, which of the four perspectives on informed consent makes sense for your proposed study?
- As an Internet user, how would you feel about having your posts collected by a researcher?

————————————— RESEARCH CAMEO 5.4 —————————————

Researcher 2 is designing a study that involves eliciting data through one-to-one and group online interviews with consenting participants. However, to understand some of the issues and dilemmas academic writers face, they plan to conduct unobtrusive observation of social media posts to hashtags such as #acwri or observations of open discussions on social networking sites. They do not intend to collect data in these settings, simply to gain some background on the issues, challenges, and topics being discussed.

Researcher 4 is designing a study that will include an analysis of observations of a writing group, extant data from journal archives, and online interviews with selected authors and editors. They intend to gain agreement from a writing group, including the moderator and members, before collecting data. They do not plan to collect data from members who choose not to participate in the study. They foresee the possibility of secondary participants who engage in conversation with consenting members. They will handle this on a case by case basis, either asking for permission to use the quote or paraphrasing it in a way that would not link it back to the non-consenting group member.

 ## RESPECT FOR THE ONLINE RESEARCH SETTING

The organization or case purposefully selected as the site where the researcher can study the problem is the *setting*. Traditionally the research setting is 'the physical, social, and cultural site in which the researcher conducts the study' (Bhattacharya, 2008, pp. 787–788). The research setting could be in the controlled environment of the laboratory, or in the environment where the phenomenon naturally occurs.

In the online *research setting* data is collected, and the setting can be virtually anywhere in the online universe. Those using extant data may download or **scrape** posts or documents, media, or images from social media sites, websites or blogs, online communities, messaging, or email. Researchers using elicitation or enacted approaches may choose web conferencing, videoconferencing, virtual worlds, games or other interactive applications or sites. These technologies serve as the virtual place where researchers meet participants for interviews, focus groups, simulations, or other activities that allow for data to be collected or generated. Researchers who want to carry out the study online must choose the milieu carefully and respect applicable boundaries and expectations. The selection of information and communications technologies for the study is discussed in Chapter 3. Here, we are looking specifically at ethical issues associated with the research milieu.

Stommell and de Rijk observed, based on a study of articles that used online data, that:

> Legally, terms and conditions stand for a contract between platform and user. When users are active on a platform, it is implied that they agree to the terms and conditions of that platform. ... An analysis of users' and researchers' attitudes toward research of social media data (Golder et al., 2017) revealed that users' agreement with the terms and conditions of platforms was thought insufficient as a replacement of informed consent. The Golder et al. study also showed that although some users felt that a study's importance could trump individual privacy concerns, others argued that users' privacy interests should always take precedence over the researchers' goals. Additionally, some users in this study thought that researchers needed to gain permission from administrators *as well as* individual users, while others specifically opposed the possibility that list owners give permission on behalf of the users without user involvement in the process. (Stommel & Rijk, 2021, p. 16)

Depending on the type of research and characteristics of the setting, online researchers may find that they need to:

- Obtain permission from the site to carry out research activities but *do not* obtain consent from users
- Obtain permission from the site *and* obtain consent from users who serve as research participants
- Obtain consent from participants but do not need permission from the site.

Features of social media or social networking sites include discussion walls, threads, and forum or comment areas. The nature and operations of such features are largely determined by the commercial entities that own and run them. Owners' goals are driven by the desire for advertising exposure, traffic, and revenue. Technology companies are in competition to increase and retain users by encouraging frequent visits and posts. The types of posts, including length, use of text, images or media, are controlled by the platform. Therefore these online spaces are not neutral; they are places where interactions are monitored and the posts are owned by the company that provides the platform. Some sites have clearly spelled out guidelines or ways to obtain or purchase the right to use the live stream or archived posts as data.

A first step in screening a potential research setting involves looking at what the owners or users say about it. Does the site, group, list, or community have posted policies, guidelines, 'frequently asked questions' or 'about us' areas that spell out norms or rules? If such guidelines exist, do they explicitly prohibit research activities? If the group exists within a larger social media platform, do terms of service describe any parameters in relation to privacy of content and/or how it is shared with third parties? When such sites require registration for log-in but no fee, users typically assume anything posted will be read by people who do not actively participate in the group. When a subscription is required or membership fee is paid, researchers may assume that users expect some level of privacy and confidentiality (Markham & Buchanan, 2012).

Groups that form on social networking platforms have their own cultures and norms, and often have individuals whose job it is to make sure that usage agreements are observed. Community managers, moderators or facilitators are an important resource in membership-oriented sites. Sometimes these individuals are paid staff and in other cases they are the founders or active members of the community who voluntarily take the role of moderator. Contacting the manager is an important first step. It may be necessary to obtain written permission from the community manager or moderator before proceeding with research activities.

Gatekeepers who support the goals of the study may be helpful in a variety of ways. They can provide insights into the formal and informal expectations of group members. Gatekeepers may be able to link the researcher to useful archives or records of relevant discussions from the past. Or they may help the researcher recruit interview participants.

Ethics Tip: When you plan to collect extant data from posted comments, discussion, images, or media, first review any posted terms of membership or terms for the group. Observe how group members interact and try to gauge the culture and norms in terms of personal disclosure and privacy. If possible, discuss research goals with the moderator and/or members and act accordingly in terms of the expectation for consent or for disclosure of your identity as a researcher. The appropriate ethical approach to data collection will depend on the type of site or group, the nature of the study and/or the sensitivity of the conversation. Researchers must decide whether to remain anonymous or to possibly disrupt or change the course of events by announcing research intentions. The AoIR guidelines (Markham & Buchanan, 2012, p. 4) note that:

> The greater the vulnerability of the community/author/participant, the greater the obligation of the researcher to protect the community/author/participant.

The AoIR guidelines (Markham & Buchanan, 2012, pp. 11, 18) suggest some key questions to consider when making decisions about how to ethically go about collecting data, from whom, in a specific social media or online space:

- How do the terms of service articulate privacy of content and/or how it is shared with third parties?
- Does the author consider personal network of connections sensitive information?
- How is profile or location information used or stored by the researcher?

Online interviews and other interactive ways of enacting data collection are typically conducted in what is clearly a 'private online environment' where the interviewer and interviewee(s) are the only people who can access the conversation. They are both aware that they are engaging in online interactions for purposeful data collection. In this type of research, informed consent is unquestionably required.

RESEARCH CAMEO 5.5

Researcher 1 is designing a study using extant data using journal databases. They will be working within their university library system. They will familiarize themselves with any library regulations and adhere to them.

Researcher 2 is designing a study that involves eliciting data through one-to-one and group online interviews. They will conduct the study using a videoconference platform and they will make sure that they have selected an online setting that is accessible and easy to use, and created a setting conducive to interviews.

Researcher 3 is designing a study that will involve generating data with aspiring and successful qualitative researchers in a workshop setting. They are considering the option of offering this workshop under the aegis of an organization that serves academic writers. They will meet with staff or volunteers from the organization to make sure that plans for data collection are acceptable.

Researcher 4 is designing a study that will include observations of a writing group, analysis of extant data from journal archives, and online interviews with selected authors and editors. The setting for the group will be in a members-only space in a social networking platform. They will review guidelines for users before selecting a platform and negotiate consent before collecting data.

SUMMARY OF KEY CONCEPTS

Chapter 4 introduced ethical theories, codes and guidelines that offer a variety of ways to think through potential ethical dilemmas and make decisions that will minimize risk to participants and increase credibility of the study. The present chapter described how to put theory into practice. Given that no single approach can apply to all online qualitative studies, the focus here is on assessing the nature of the study, types of data and how it will be collected.

This assessment includes the researcher's reflexive consideration of roles, positions, and avoidance of bias or conflicts of interest. The researcher must cultivate and apply practical wisdom to make the best decisions.

Considerations for Ethical Qualitative Online Research

To what extent: do the nature of the site, types of communication and demographics of users ICT align with the purpose of the study?

EXTANT METHODS

Collect data without interacting directly w/ participants

ELICITED OR ENACTED METHODS

Interact directly w/ human participants

Documents, media archives & records

Observation, scraping in social media, forum or community

Participant Observation

Interviews or Events to Generate Data

- Is it accessible to the public, "members" or "friends"?
- Is there an owner, host or moderator?
- Are topics sensitive, e.g. health, sexuality, addiction?
- Do users post with names, avatars or pseudonyms?
- Are participants children, youth, vulnerable population?
- Do visual images, pictures, media or locative technologies contain identifiable information?
- Are there terms of use or conduct?
- Are exchanges, conversations current?
- For archived materials: under what agreement or assumption were posts originally made?
- For datasets: under what arrangement were data assembled?

[Plus]

- If the owner, host or moderator agrees to the study--are members aware that you are collecting data?
- How are members informed, do they consent? Can they opt out? How is the researcher introduced, how represented?
- Is any aspect of the group or community off-limits to the researcher?
- What are the norms, what is the culture of the community?
- How can the researcher communicate in an acceptable, respectable way?
- Can the research protect data collected from any 1-1 "private" communications with members?

[Plus]

- How are participants informed, how do they consent affirm consent?
- Does the SNS, forum or community allow for 1-1 or 1-group interactions?
- Are communications options synchronous, near-synchronous or asynchronous?
- Is communication by audio, text and/or visual exchange?
- Can visual images, pictures and media be shared and/or generated during the interview?
- Can recordings be downloaded from commercial server and deleted?

Figure 5.3 Ethical questions related to online research type

While ethical research practice is multidimensional, four main areas were identified to help researchers think through specific issues for the study. Researchers need to assess their studies in relation to these main questions:

- **How to protect human subjects?** Have you considered all potential risks or harms to participants and taken steps to mitigate them? Have you been transparent about any risks in discussions with participants before initiating the study? Have you observed relevant parameters set by your institution or discipline, as well as legal or regulatory requirements?
- **How to obtain appropriate informed consent from participants?** Have you adequately informed participants about the voluntary nature and expectations for their involvement in the study? Is the information considered public, or authored so you can simply cite it?
- **How to respect the research site?** Have any other permissions, such as access to the research site, members or users, documents or archives, been obtained?
- **How to safeguard data and protect participants' identities?** Have you designed a study that will allow you to shield privacy, identity, anonymity and confidentiality of participants? Is privacy respected for bystanders or secondary participants? Have you considered issues of participants' identity protection when collecting locational, visual, or audio data? At the data management and analysis stage, can you keep data from being accessed or viewed by others? At the reporting and publishing stage, how can you protect the identity of those who contribute data?

The diagram in Figure 5.3 summarizes ethical considerations for different types of online studies.

DISCUSSION QUESTIONS AND EXERCISES

- Four perspectives offer different ways to think about a situation where the guidelines are incomplete or in conflict. Pick one perspective and create a rationale from a deontological, consequentialist, or virtue ethics stance.
- Compare and contrast your rationale with the one created by a peer. Did your peer make a compelling case? Why or why not? What would strengthen the rationale?
- Create a checklist for ethical online research that articulates your own standards of values and ethics before you start collecting and analyzing data. Justify your choices using principles from one or more ethical theories.
- Read the research cameos for Chapter 5.

  o   How can these researchers address all the potential issues in the pre-research consent agreement process?

(Continued)

○ Create an infographic or other visual you could use to communicate with participants in one of these hypothetical studies.

○ Record a two minute video that explains expectations for one of these hypothetical studies.

- Review at least two studies conducted with data collected online (observation, participant observation, interviews, or focus groups) and discuss ethical decision-making in an essay of 3–5 pages. Do you agree with the approaches taken by the researchers? Why or why not?

6

Researchers' Roles and Positions

Ethics review and guidelines are insufficient to ensure morally responsible research.
(Johnsson, Eriksson, Helgesson, & Hansson, 2014)

HIGHLIGHTS

In Chapters 1–5 we have explored the researcher roles and responsibilities at the design stage. These include being the primary decision-maker, or as a member of a research team. There are many choices to make at the design stage, so the role of decision-maker is significant. Ethical stances and protocols must be devised that establish expectations for research approaches and modes of interaction with any human participants. Researchers must fine-tune their goals, since multiple researchers studying the exact same questions can carry out dramatically varied studies based on the methodology, and methods, or technology. The proposal for a study of resilience factors for youth at risk would look quite different if the researcher planned a grounded theory study using archived records from an agency, versus a case study with online observations and interviews, versus a participatory study using an online game. Nevertheless, design decisions only take us so far. At some point we must get out there and conduct the study! At that point, the clean, clear, plan meets messy realities. As researchers, we must meet new obligations to ourselves and others. In Chapter 6 we transition from decision-making in the abstract to roles and responsibilities needed to carry out the study.

OBJECTIVES

After reading and reflecting on this chapter, you will be able to:

- identify ways to apply self-awareness, transparency, and people skills when in the role of an online researcher
- analyze the relationships between self-awareness, transparency, people skills, and researcher credibility when working online
- differentiate insider and outsider positions in online research
- determine and reflect on your roles, positions, and relationship to the study.

SELF-AWARENESS + TRANSPARENCY + PEOPLE SKILLS = RESEARCH CREDIBILITY

Chapters 4 and 5 focused on the formal side of ethics, including theory and the agreements essential to a comprehensive research proposal. Designing and planning research that is appropriately aligned with defined purpose, problems, and questions requires knowledge and skills. But there is also a personal side. As researchers we need what some might call 'soft' or 'people' skills. These dimensions are not ancillary, they form the foundation for our work as qualitative researchers. In some ways these intangible skill sets are more difficult to learn from a book (even this one!). However, the first important step is to recognize and appreciate ways that who we are, and how we act as researchers can either further or obstruct the progress of the study.

- **Self-awareness**: Research is about inquiry – asking questions and analyzing answers. To build self-awareness throughout the process, you may need to flip the inquiry and question your own ways of thinking, and limitations. You need to be aware of your comfort zones and responses to uncomfortable situations. Johnnson et al. state that 'neglecting the moral competence of researchers paves the way for disaster' (2014, p. 42). What is your *moral competence*? How do your own views about yourself, your role, and your position(s) as a researcher affect how you view the participant or other data sources? How do your knowledge and opinions about the research problem (from first-hand experience or the literature) affect the ways you problematize the research and interpret potential outcomes? Researchers build moral competence and exercise self-awareness by being both reflective and reflexive.
- **Transparency**: Others associated with the research project need to feel that you are being open and truthful about your motivations and research practices. Honesty and openness are essential to any research project. Being transparent might also mean openness about power differences between researcher and participant and the opportunities and limitations for power sharing.

- **People and cultural skills**: It is rare for researchers to work alone. Relationships and information technology are increasingly intertwined. As Hargrove (2001, p. 114) predicted at the early beginnings of pervasive Internet use: 'The so-called information revolution is, in reality, more a relationships revolution.' For online researchers, people skills are even more important since most communication is computer-mediated and may lack the warmth provided when we can shake hands, hug, or simply have eye contact. Communities, cultures, and norms might not be readily obvious from the ways individuals engage with posts or writings.

Having people skills means being able to build respectful relationships with those from diverse cultures, disciplines, and abilities. Miller framed it this way: 'For me, the process of engaging with communities involves personal education, experiencing life and culture from a different perspective, and gaining insight via a different paradigm, as well as undertaking this formal thing we call research' (Miller, 2013, p. 829). In their research with an Aboriginal community, they realized the need to 'recognize that one type of knowledge is not wrong and the other right, they are not mutually exclusive' (p. 832).

Qualitative researchers need people skills, whether or not they are interacting with participants, because access to archives or databases also relies on trust and clear communication. With participants, people skills are needed from the beginning, with discussion group moderators, online community owners, and other gatekeepers, before you are able to reach individual members with recruitment messages.

We need to collaborate with supervisors, funders, editors, fellow researchers, co-authors and others. Complex studies often mean collaboration is necessary with those who have skills we lack, such as data analytics, foreign languages, or cultural competencies. In essence, success in online qualitative research is predicated on communication and people skills.

Self-awareness, transparency, and people skills are interrelated. If we are self-aware, it is easier to be honest with others. If we are honest and transparent, it is easier to come across to others as genuine and trustworthy. Very simply, if people do not trust us, they will not fully cooperate with the study. If readers do not trust us, they will not find the study credible.

These factors must be at the center of our efforts when we communicate electronically. Some might be additionally challenging because we may or may not have the opportunity for the kind of informal conversation that is possible when we are physically present. We do not have casual time over a cup of coffee that allows us to connect person-to-person. That might mean others who are already unfamiliar with the research process or suspicious of what they perceive as intrusive behaviors, will have little patience for actions that confirm negative attitudes. It is even more important in such circumstances to do exactly what we say we are going to do, when and how we have agreed to proceed. When working online, keep in mind that just as you can search for others, they can search for you! Will they find supporting background information about you, your institution, and the problems that you intend to study that boosts your credibility? The simple things like being on time and being prepared can go a long way towards building confidence.

If we do not act with integrity, we can jeopardize the field of scientific research writ large, because the public will not see empirical research to be of value. While good scholarly research rarely makes the front page, unethical or improper research makes headlines. Today's wary public needs not only trustworthy findings, they need clear explanations of what we are doing, and why. They need to see the good ideas we discover put into practice to improve the lives of individuals and the health of the planet. They need us to answer two basic questions: how do I know you are telling the truth, and what difference can this truth make in my life? To respond, we need to start with some soul-searching and commit to being the best researcher we can be.

―――――――――――― RESEARCH CAMEO 6.1 ――――――――――――

Researcher 1 is designing a study using extant data. They plan to analyze Big Data from journal databases and related writings. People skills will be important when interacting with librarians, research supervisors, and other stakeholders. They are more concerned with the need for self-awareness and cultural competence. They do not want to overlook indigenous scholarship or writings from emerging researchers.

Researcher 2 is designing a study that involves eliciting data through one-to-one and group online interviews. They know that people skills will be essential in this study in order to establish rapport with interviewees and to convey to them the importance of their contributions to the research. They know that self-awareness, and self-control, will be needed in order to respond appropriately and respectfully to participants.

Researcher 3 is designing a study that will involve generating data with aspiring and successful qualitative researchers in a workshop setting. In addition to the skills Researcher 2 has identified, they will need to be transparent about the dual purpose of the workshop: to help the writers who join, and to collect data. They will need to be self-aware about how they juggle these priorities.

Researcher 4 is designing a study that will include an analysis of observations of a writing group, extant data from journal archives, and online interviews. Similar to Researcher 3's considerations, they will need to balance multiple priorities, some with and some without participants.

SELF-AWARENESS, REFLEXIVITY, AND ETHICAL RESEARCH PRACTICE

Researchers' work receives some degree of oversight and an expectation of accountability, regardless of whether the researcher is a student, academic researcher, or an independent or professional researcher. Regardless of how tight the scrutiny, the moment comes when the researcher is alone with the participant, alone with the data, alone on the computer. And in that moment the researcher needs to answer to the questions: What is the right thing to do? What is ethical behavior, and will I act ethically in this situation? Each of us will answer these questions in our own way. We may be guided by research guidelines from our institutions or professional society, ethics theory, beliefs, a moral compass, and/or a sense of integrity.

Guillemin and Gillam (2004) distinguish between two major dimensions of ethics in qualitative research: procedural ethics, which usually involves seeking approval from a relevant ethics committee to undertake research involving humans; and 'ethics in practice' or the everyday ethical issues that arise in the doing of research (p. 263). 'These are issues about the ethical obligations a researcher has toward a research participant in terms of interacting with him or her in a humane, non-exploitative way while at the same time being mindful of one's role as a researcher' (Guillemin & Gillam, 2004, p. 270). Going a step farther, researchers have 'ethical obligations' to research partners and other stakeholders. The researcher using extant Big Data or archives has 'ethical obligations' to fulfil by abiding by any agreements made for access and use of the data. Taking the time to think carefully about your own ethical stance towards both the procedures and practice of ethics is an important responsibility of a researcher.

REFLECTION AND REFLEXIVITY

Researchers exercise self-awareness by being both reflective and reflexive. 'Reflexivity is commonly viewed as the process of a continual internal dialogue and critical self-evaluation of researcher's positionality as well as active acknowledgement and explicit recognition that this position may affect the research process and outcome' (Berger, 2013, p. 220). While reflection and reflexivity have some similarities, the terms are not synonymous. Hibbert, Coupland, and MacIntosh explain the relationship between reflection and reflexivity:

> First, *reflection* suggests a mirror image which affords the opportunity to engage in an observation or examination of our ways of doing. When we experience reflection, we become observers of our own practice. *Reflexivity*, however, suggests a complexification of thinking and experience, or thinking about experience. Thus, we regard reflexivity as a process of exposing or questioning our ways of doing. (2010, p. 48)

To be mindful of these behind-the-scenes research activities, Rallis and Rossman (2012) suggest that as researchers we should strive to become moral practitioners. They suggest that 'morally compelling moments demand a reflexivity we call research praxis, informed action, back and forth between reasoning and action thinking about the doing through a moral lens' (p. 61). Reflexivity is essential to the ethical research praxis because it allows the researcher to check that the approach to the study is actually embodying his or her principles (Guillemin & Gillam, 2004, p. 270).

Reflexivity is important in online qualitative research because with all the unknowns and potential for changes in the technology or inputs of participants we cannot see, we need to add the critical element that goes beyond simply being self-aware. We need to be agile, so what we realize while the research is being designed or conducted translates into better work as researchers.

HOW-TO STEPS

How do researchers reflect on their research? Reflective practice is individualized and may involve taking notes or journaling, to document ideas and observations, successes and obstacles at each stage of the study. Journals can be of the analog variety, with sketches, drawings, and writing. Or you can create an electronic journal, using note taking applications that allow you to sync and access it from across computers and smartphones.

Some researchers go a step farther to open up and share their thinking. They create a research blog that is either public, or private with password-protected access. The reflective blog approach allows others, such as a dissertation supervisor or research collaborators, access to one's progress and developments. LaBanca described using this approach. He listened to the viewpoints of his 'auditors,' which helped him stay objective and aware of his position (LaBanca, 2011). The blog, together with comments, generated a chronological record of the study's evolution, which LaBanca reported as very valuable to his own evolution as a researcher.

Small groups of researchers using similar methods or studying similar problems find it valuable to share observations, reflective and reflexive thinking. They can offer mutual critiques, help solve problems, or give the encouragement and moral support researchers so often need. Depending on geographic proximity, they meet for coffee (or something stronger) on a regular basis, or exchange in an online group.

As the research progresses to the dissemination stage, groups might transition to a focus on writing and publishing. These writing circles offer a safe place to explore ideas with trusted colleagues. They discuss goals, review options and share information about journals or publishers, provide friendly reviews of drafts, and lessons learned along the way. Group members might decide to publish together, co-authoring or co-editing books or articles.

Reflexivity is not a step to ignore. Whether you set aside time for a purely personal process of re-examination of the research process and your role in it or collaborate with others in a reflexive process, find the approach that works for you.

TAKING A POSITION AS A RESEARCHER

Self-awareness, transparency, and people skills intersect when the researcher establishes their position in relation to the study. Qualitative researchers who interact with participants value the closeness and contact these methods allow. Qualitative researchers who use extant data value access to posts and discussions that exhibit robust interactions or detailed knowledge of the subject. In both cases some knowledge of online groups, sites or the topic being studied can enable access that other researchers might not have. How close is too close? At what point does the degree of intimacy with the organization, group or participant, or the familiarity with the research problem jeopardize the researcher's ability to carry out the study with integrity? When does the researcher's closeness to the study invite unwanted criticisms about conflicts of interest? When does the researcher's knowledge of the research problem mean it is hard to be objective and avoid bias that taints the findings? The researcher should know from the earliest design stage where he or she stands in relation to the study and be transparent about this position to participants, collaborators or others involved in the study as well as to the reader.

Researchers must be able to explain whether, or to what extent, they take an outside or inside position – and how that position adds value to the study. Dodgson explains:

> As readers of qualitative research need to understand who is doing the research in ways that go beyond their name and professional affiliations to include the researcher's positionality in relation to what is being studied ... the researchers' position as an insider or outsider and/or whether they have shared the experiences with the study participants is especially important when considering both similarities and differences between the researcher and the participants (Berger, 2015; Teh & Lek, 2018). Therefore, the researcher must be cognizant of these similarities and differences, and make them known to readers. (2019, p. 220)

Robert Stake (1995) defines the outsider position as etic. Researchers working from an etic position identify research problems or questions from the literature. Stake (1995) defines the insider position as emic. Researchers working from an emic position draw on their own knowledge of issues and problems to iden-tify research questions. VanDeVen (2007, pp. 269–270) contrasts the outside researcher as a 'detached, impartial onlooker who gathers data' with the inside researcher who is a 'participant immersed in the actions and experiences within the system being studied'. VanDeVen (2007) describes the value found in com-plementarity of knowledge gained from research that uses the insider perspective to provide a concrete grounding in the research problem in a particular context or situation together with research from an outside perspective that uses empiri-cal evidence to build a broader understanding of the scope of the problem.

Some methodologies inherently call for an insider or outsider role for the researcher. Researchers are necessarily insiders when they conduct autoethnogra-phies, participant observations or action research. Some insiders contribute data in the form of reflective journal entries or field notes to complement data col-lected from participants. Researchers are typically outsiders when they conduct research using observations or archival or historical records analysis.

INSIDER (EMIC) AND OUTSIDER (ETIC) E-RESEARCH POSITIONS

In online research positionality needs a somewhat different interpretation than in other kinds of research. Some degree of insider knowledge may be needed to access research settings or to understand the situation, culture, and type of experi-ence being studied in an online setting. An insider who understands the norms of the group may have an easier time recruiting participants or gaining permission to use archives and posted data. Insiders who understand the styles and modes of communication can develop rapport and trust with virtual research participants.

At the same time, if studying a community where the researcher is a mem-ber, he or she might be recognized by others, which could mean others either contribute more, or less. Such a researcher must guard against having too much familiarity with the online setting and challenge pre-existing assumptions to probe more deeply and uncover difficulties or conflicts he or she might pre-fer to ignore. The outsider can bring broader, objective understandings of the research problem into the study. Depending on the topic of the research or the nature of the discussion thread or community, the researcher as objective social scientist may have more credibility than another member of the group. To take the research problem discussed in the research cameos used throughout this book, might a human resources professional who introduces the study in the context of improving company policies receive more thoughtful responses than a researcher who is simply a fellow member of the social networking site? Alternatively, might such an etic researcher look for ways to gain emic insights by joining or participating in the online group, social media, or online community – which would raise ethical questions?

As with many areas of qualitative research, polar options are not always adequate and many studies can be conducted from a full range of positions. In a discussion of an online ethnographic study, Paechter draws on Labaree's earlier work and observes:

> Labaree (2002) suggests that, while the mainly outsider researcher has to 'go native' in order to understand the local culture, insiders have, by corollary, to 'go observation-alist', distancing themselves introspectively from phenomena. Insider positioning also necessitates the observation of oneself and one's relation to the research process; in this way, research makes outsiders of us all. (Paechter, 2013, p. 75)

This quote suggests that in some situations the researcher may vacillate between insider and outsider perspectives at different stages of the study. The researcher may have some degree of inside knowledge, access or experience while conducting the study from an emic stance. The insider may begin with questions that emerged from experience, then generate new areas of inquiry after consulting the literature. Importantly, researchers should understand where they are positioned within the research space and aim at achieving high methodological transparency (Finefter-Rosenbluh, 2017, p. 9).

The Qualitative e-Research Framework offers a way to think about the complex and potentially fluid nature of the researcher's position with an etic–emic continuum. As shown in Figure 6.1, a continuum illustrates nuanced options more comprehensively than does an either/or model.

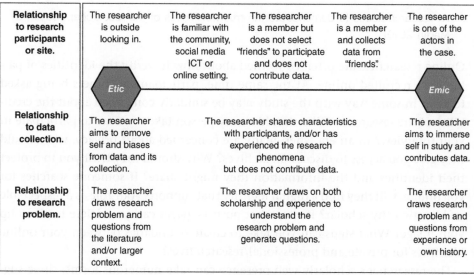

c.2010-2021 Vision2 Lead

Figure 6.1 An etic–emic continuum of e-research positions

--------------------- SPOT CHECK ---------------------

- In your own words, describe the differences between etic and emic positions.
- When you think about the target demographic for your study, in what ways is your position etic or emic?
- Are your insider positions obvious (first language, age, race, gender) or not visible (disability, sexual orientation, economic class)? How would you communicate positions that may not be visible?

--------------------- RESEARCH CAMEO 6.2 ---------------------

Researcher 1 is designing a study using extant data. Given the nature of the study, they are coming from an outsider position.

Researcher 2 is designing a study that involves eliciting data through one-to-one and group online interviews. While they share some characteristics as a qualitative researcher, they will approach the study as an outsider.

Researchers 3 and *4* will both interact with writing groups, and they both intend to approach the study as insiders, relying on shared experiences as fellow qualitative researchers and academic writers.

BUILDING CREDIBILITY AS A RESEARCHER

All research needs to demonstrate the trustworthiness of the researcher. (Bulpitt & Martin, 2010)

Online researchers are often concerned about how to verify the identities of participants recruited online. At the same time, participants or others being asked to assist in some way with the study may be similarly concerned about the credibility of the researcher. Why should a busy person take the time to participate in your interview? In an era when many are concerned about privacy, why should they give you access to discussion archives? Why should they trust you to protect their identities and the information they might share? If someone searches for you online, will they find a digital identity that supports your role as a respectable and trustworthy scholar? If not, what posts or pages can you delete to clean up your image? What steps can you take to create boundaries between your online identities for private and professional/research lives?

The researcher's scholarly web presence can take numerous forms; three suggestions are described broadly here. The first step is to create a statement that introduces the researcher and the study. Think from the position of a potential participant or site host: what would inspire trust in the researcher and interest in his or her work? This statement should include the researcher's academic and professional credentials and affiliations. Student researchers may want to identify their academic institutions, and (with permission) their professor or dissertation supervisor.

One benefit of such a statement is consistency of language and message, so potential participants or partners begin from the same common understanding about the nature of the study. In addition to written statements, the researcher can create a video clip or audio version. Once crafted, the statement can be summarized when post length is limited and linked to a fuller description posted elsewhere.

Researchers can create a space where this fuller description is posted, including the researcher's introduction, study information and possibly a recruitment message. Free blog or website services are ideal for this purpose. A link can also be posted on others' sites, blogs, friendship walls, or communities. Unlike the reflective blog used to describe observations of the research process for readers who are colleagues or stakeholders, a research information blog or site should be public. It should be accessible to potential or current participants, gatekeepers of spaces or sites, and other allies or stakeholders.

Personal touches can help to increase interest and build presence with site visitors. Links to the researcher's academic institution or other publications can convey integrity and authenticity of the study. Be sure to provide means for contact, such as a link to an email or messaging address, preferably one associated with the educational institution to reinforce academic credibility. Avoid using the researcher's physical address or phone number to avoid privacy violations for the researcher.

As the study unfolds, use this online space to keep participants and other interested parties abreast of your progress and emerging discoveries. Link to relevant publications and practical resources that provide value and establish your reputation. Links to the researcher's academic institution or other publications can convey authenticity of the researcher. Provide a means for contact distinct from your personal email, ideally an educational institution email address. If not a part of an institution, use a free email service to set up a channel dedicated to communications associated with the study.

Another way to develop credibility and reputation as a researcher is by using the networking possibilities of the digital milieu: the researcher can offer a webinar or host an online event or discussion on issues related to the study. Events offer an opportunity to interact with individuals who are interested in the subject of inquiry and may be helpful not only with the study underway but also in publishing and disseminating the findings.

BECOMING A CREDIBLE, ETHICAL, REFLECTIVE ONLINE RESEARCHER

Many writers referenced here discussed qualitative research generally – but their points are, if anything, even truer for online researchers. Self-awareness, transparency, and people skills are essential to build credibility for you as a researcher and for your study. No matter how well developed the research design may be, changes will occur as the online study unfolds. The researcher's position may also change as familiarity with the research phenomenon and participants grows. As the researcher becomes more engaged in the study, it may become more difficult to retain an objective stance, whether in the data collection or analysis stage. Reflexivity allows for monitoring and self-correction as needed.

In many situations you might only know key players in the research project virtually, so being able to communicate and collaborate effectively will be essential to success. To do so, you need to present yourself in a way that engenders trust and believability. You cannot get through any type of research single-handedly, and most often you are asking very busy people to give precious time to your project. You need to present yourself as someone who is responsive, responsible, and has the kind of contagious enthusiasm that motivates others to get involved. If you aren't excited about the project, and able to succinctly explain why it is important, why should anyone else care?

─────── RESEARCH CAMEO 6.3 ───────

Researcher 1 is designing a study using extant data. Their challenge for building credibility will come later in the research process when they are writing, presenting, and/or publishing results.

Researcher 2 is designing a study that involves eliciting data through one-to-one and group online interviews. They will create a research blog to share their research journey. They will discuss their motivations for conducting the study, link to their academic institution and relevant affiliations. If they have publications, or online posts participants can view, they will share links.

Researchers 3 and 4 will rely on shared experiences as fellow qualitative researchers and academic writers. They will select anecdotes and stories that illustrate ways they succeeded or failed and how they learned from the experience.

SUMMARY OF KEY CONCEPTS

Building on prior chapters' foundations in ethical theory and practice, Chapter 6 brings abstract ideas into practical focus. This chapter extends research ethics into the personal domain, asking you to think about who you are, and how you find your inner compass in order to commit to acting from a place of moral responsibility. It described the need to be self-aware, using reflection and reflexivity throughout the stages of the study. Transparency, that is, making motivations and plans clear and available for all stakeholders, helps them gain trust in the researcher and the project. Positionality, that is, the degree to which you are an insider or outsider, is an example that asks you to be both self-aware and transparent. Using well-developed people skills, the researcher is able to communicate and collaborate, online or face-to-face.

DISCUSSION QUESTIONS AND EXERCISES

- Discuss the kinds of agreements and ground rules you would need to feel comfortable sharing reflections with a group. Do you need different agreements and ground rules when the group is online?
- Rallis and Rossman (2012) suggest that researchers should become *moral practitioners*. They suggest that 'morally compelling moments demand a reflexivity we call *research praxis*, informed action, back and forth between reasoning and action thinking about the doing through a moral lens' (p. 61). What does being a 'moral practitioner' mean to you?
- Look at the theories outlined in Chapter 4. Which ones guide your actions and behaviors as a researcher? If you draw on other sources of guidance, explain what they are and why they are important.
- Compare and contrast an analog versus digital journal for recording reflective and reflexive observations. Try both, and think through the pros and cons of each, given the nature of your research project and your own writing preferences.
- Using your own research concept or a hypothetical one, compare and contrast approaches for conducting the study as an insider or an outsider.
- Outline approaches for communicating a sample project design to a) a research supervisor, editor, or funder, b) a co-researcher, c) a gatekeeper you hope will allow you to conduct research in their community, and d) potential research participants.

SECTION III

PREPARING TO COLLECT DATA ONLINE

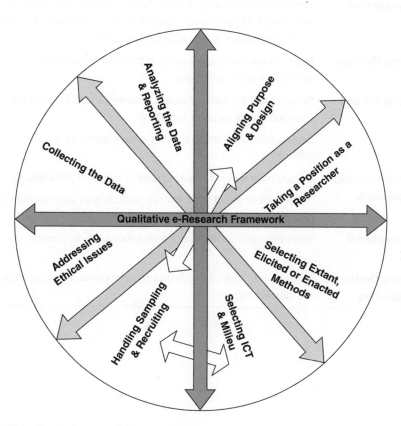

Figure III.1   Preparing to collect data online

Before you are ready to carry out a study that involves participants, you need to decide what kind of characteristics they need to exemplify, and then recruit people who can fulfil those requirements. These are the steps and rationales described in the sampling and recruiting plans. (Similar issues are present in studies with extant data, handled in Section IV.) Before you can move forward with your interactions, you need to decide what ICTs you will use to communicate about the study and to collect data. These parts of the process are covered in Section III.

Let's plan these activities in the context of all the dimensions of the Qualitative e-Research Framework. Some key questions are outlined in Table III.1.

Table III.1 Data collection issues in relation to the Qualitative e-Research Framework

	Collecting the Data
Aligning Purpose and Design	How do participant characteristics relate to the purpose of the study?
Taking a Position as a Researcher	How does your position in relation to the study and potential settings influence your choices for the sample population, the recruitment of participants known or unknown to you, and to the ways you prepare to use ICTs in the study?
Selecting Methods	How can you align your research preparation with the methods you will use for data collection?
Selecting ICT and Milieu	Do you have the skills needed to manage the ICT during the intended data collection activities?
	Do you have a contingency plan in case there are technical difficulties?
Handling Sampling and Recruiting	Do you have a plan to locate credible research participants?
	Are you clear about what you will discuss with participants during recruiting and screening processes?
Handling Ethical Issues	What potential conflicts of interest should be disclosed?
Analyzing the Data and Reporting	How will you protect the data and participants' identities during the recruitment stage?

7

Creating a Sampling Plan

HIGHLIGHTS

Steps and activities associated with extant, elicited, or enacted data collection are the same and different. This chapter focuses on aspects common to all types; Chapters 10, 11, and 12 respectively focus on the particular characteristics of methods to collect and generate extant, elicited, and enacted data online.

The design and conduct of studies using extant methods are distinguished from those using elicited or enacted methods by a critical factor: as a researcher using extant methods you do not interact with human participants. However, this does not mean that you do not interact with others. You will most likely need to negotiate with librarians, site hosts, group moderators, or others whose agreement or permission is needed to access archives, records, or datasets. All must determine a sampling strategy – whether for selecting people or materials.

OBJECTIVES

After reading and reflecting on this chapter, you will be able to:

- refine the research purpose, and define types of sources needed to study it
- compare and contrast approaches to sampling and selecting participants or materials
- develop a sampling plan
- communicate your plan to partners, gatekeepers, and potential participants.

Every researcher must make a variety of conceptual and practical decisions about how to design and conduct the proposed study. Every researcher must consider ways theoretical stances and principles influence approaches to data collection and analysis. Because all aspects of the research design are interrelated, each design decision a researcher makes has implications for the entire study. Ripple effects of each decision impact other areas of the research design and may have subtle or radical effects on the outcomes of the study. Researchers must assess and balance risks and opportunities and determine what is to be gained or lost with each choice. Nowhere are researchers' choices more critical than in determining how they will identify and select extant materials or the individuals who will contribute relevant thoughts and experiences as research participants.

Online sampling for online research is a relatively new area without established conventions. General approaches to sampling for qualitative research can be adapted to structure and organize the process. This chapter provides an overview of key issues in qualitative research sampling in general and a discussion of significant issues in sampling specific to online research. The chapter recommends ways the online researcher can creatively address common expectations reviewers of a research proposal may hold for online sampling and in the process strengthen the research design.

METHODS AND STRATEGIES FOR SAMPLING

Sampling is the systematic process for determining who or what can serve the purpose of the study. Some researchers need to locate individuals who can and will provide honest, robust information about themselves and/or the phenomena of interest, and fully engage as a participant or co-researcher. Other researchers need to decide what particular documents, records, datasets, images or media to analyze. No one can study every possible perspective on their topic, so choices must be made. On what basis will the researcher make the decision to include some kinds of people or materials and not others? These strategic and critically important decisions fall within the topic of sampling.

The term 'sampling' originated in quantitative research methodology where researchers look for participants who are a 'sample' of a larger population. In what is sometimes called **probability sampling**, members of the research population are chosen at random and have a known probability of selection. Quantitative researchers are concerned with minimizing bias in the group, so the sample represents groups in their proportion to the population at large, thereby producing a statistically representative sample (Koerber & McMichael, 2008). This enables the researcher to test hypotheses and make generalizations from a small population to the whole population (Wilmot, 2005, p. 3).

The goals of qualitative research do not include producing a statistically representative sample or drawing statistical inference, so non-probability sampling methods can be used. Qualitative studies tend to entail a deeper, more detailed exploration with a smaller number of research participants. Even researchers using qualitative methods to study large datasets generally avoid probability sampling. Qualitative researchers have other goals and means for ensuring rigorous sampling appropriate to the study, including triangulation and cross-checking, discussed in Chapters 8 and 9.

Qualitative researchers often use what is broadly defined as **purposive** or **purposeful sampling** because the sample is intentionally selected according to the purpose of the study (Coyne, 1997). Mason (2002) suggests that there are two kinds of purposes the sample should satisfy: the empirical purpose, which is to provide data needed to address the research questions; and the theoretical purpose, which is to generate ideas that advance your understanding of, prove, or develop a theory.

To align with empirical purposes the researcher seeks participants or materials because they typify a circumstance or possess a characteristic that may have salience to the subject matter of the study (Ritchie & Lewis, 2003, p. 82). To align with theoretical purposes, the researcher seeks participants or materials on the basis of how their charac'teristics or experiences relate to theoretical positions and the explanation or account the researcher is developing (Mason, 2002). Benoot et al (2016), describing purposeful sampling of extant data, observed that:

> One of the core arguments supporting a purposeful sampling approach is that it is not meant to be comprehensive in terms of screening all potentially relevant papers, mainly because the interest of the authors is not in seeking a single 'correct' answer, but rather in examining the complexity of different conceptualizations. (p. 2)

According to Miles and Huberman, the researcher wants to see different instances of theoretical principles, at different moments, in different places, with different people or sources so the qualitative researcher's concern is with the *conditions* under which the construct or theory operates, not with the generalization of the findings to other settings (Miles & Huberman, 2014, p. 29). In grounded theory studies, the theoretical purposes for sampling take priority. In grounded theory, the data provide the basis for describing the theory, whereas in other studies, the theory provides the basis for explaining the data. When grounded theory researchers see a new phenomenon in the data, they purposely look for new research participants who can confirm it or raise relevant questions about it (Charmaz, 2014; Koerber & McMichael, 2008). Note that the terminology is not consistent across the literature. Here, we are defining purposive sampling broadly, to encompass a number of types, including theoretical. Others distinguish purposive and theoretical as two different categories.

Sampling decisions may be motivated by empirical or theoretical goals, sometimes in the same study.

TYPES OF PURPOSIVE SAMPLING

What type of sampling aligns with your purpose? When you make those decisions, you are developing a sampling strategy. The sampling strategy is one of the most critical parts of the research design. You could study the same problem in disparate ways, depending on who or what provides data. Do you want to discover how a group of similar sources represent a subject? Or to find out how a diverse group of sources represent a subject? Let's explore the options, then see how they might be used in an online study.

Differentiating Among Qualitative Sampling Types

A number of types are presented in Table 7.1. Certainly, some kinds relate more to studies with human participants than others, but the principles generally apply to the sampling strategy for extant data. With this premise in mind, we will use the term *sources* to refer to participants or to materials.

Unless you are selecting an entire population, known as a *census*, you will need a way to determine which sources fit your study. Sampling types fall into two broad categories. The first describes the way sources are found. The second describes characteristics of the sources. We will assume that for most qualitative studies a combination of types will be used, perhaps one or more from each category.

SPOT CHECK

Based on the sampling types in the Table 7.1, identify two possible ones that might work.

- Compare and contrast the implications for your study.
- Which would work better? Why?
- Could you combine more than one type of sampling for your study?

The Sampling Type Relates to the Way Sources are Found

Convenience, opportunistic, and *emergent* types allow you to use available sources. This option can be associated with insider status, because you might be able to find participants from acquaintances of people in your network. (See Chapters 1

Table 7.1 Qualitative approaches to sampling

Type	Description of Approach	Advantages
Combination or mixed purposeful	More than one sampling approach is used to address different aspects of the research design or purpose.	Triangulation, flexibility, meets multiple interests and needs (Patton, 2014).
Convenience	The researcher selects sources readily available and easy to access.	Saves time, money, and effort, but has the lowest credibility; yields information-poor cases (Patton, 2014).
Criterion	Sources are chosen because they meet a predetermined set of criteria (Patton, 2014).	Useful for quality assurance (Miles & Huberman, 1994); enables the researcher to focus on participants or materials aligned with identified characteristics or themes of the study.
Critical case	The researcher selects cases seen as 'critical' to an understanding of the subject of inquiry (Patton, 2014).	Permits logical generalization and maximum application of information to other cases; what is true of the critical cases is likely to be true of all other cases (Patton, 2014).
Deviant or extreme	Sources are chosen because they are unusual or uniquely manifest the phenomenon (Miles & Huberman, 1994; Ritchie & Lewis, 2003).	Researchers can learn from highly unusual manifestations of the phenomenon of interest, such as outstanding success/notable failures, top of the class/dropouts, exotic events, or crises (Patton, 2014).
Emergent	Participants are chosen as opportunities arise during the study (Patton, 2014).	Useful in fieldwork or when there can be no a priori specification of the sample; it cannot be drawn in advance (Lincoln & Guba, 1985, p. 201).
Heterogeneous	A deliberate strategy to include participants who have widely different experiences of the phenomena of interest (Ritchie & Lewis, 2003).	(See *maximum variation*.)
Homogeneous	Participants are chosen to give a detailed picture of a particular phenomenon or experience they have in common (Patton, 2014; Ritchie & Lewis, 2003).	Focuses the study on common characteristics, reduces variation, and simplifies analysis (Miles & Huberman, 1994).

(Continued)

Table 7.1 (Continued)

Type	Description of Approach	Advantages
Intensity	Select participants who manifest the phenomenon intensely but not extremely (Patton, 2014).	Although similar to deviant or extreme, intensity sampling allows the researcher to focus on participants that strongly manifest or have deeply experienced the phenomena of interest rather than participants who are unusual (Ritchie & Lewis, 2003).
Maximum variation	Purposefully picking a wide range of variation on dimensions of interest … documents unique or diverse variations that have emerged in adapting to different conditions. Identifies important common patterns that cut across variations (Patton, 2014).	Researcher can document unique or diverse variations and identify important common patterns in the data (Creswell, 1998; Patton, 2014).
Nominated	Potential participants are recommended by other participants or by knowledgeable experts (Roper & Shapira, 2000).	Researcher's choices can be confirmed by input or recommendations from a third party.
Opportunistic	The researcher takes advantage of opportunities that arise to find sources (Ritchie & Lewis, 2003).	(See *convenience* and *emergent* sampling.)
Politically important	Sources are chosen because they connect with politically sensitive issues in the study (Miles & Huberman, 1994).	Attract desired attention or avoid undesired attention to politically sensitive studies or findings (Miles & Huberman, 1994).
Snowball, chain or respondent-driven sampling	Snowball sampling relies on 'vertical/deep social networking.' It usually starts with a multiple (though relatively small) number of initial contacts and then uses these to establish links with other research participants and thus build up sampling momentum and sample size (Geddes et al., 2018)	Snowball sampling can be used to access hard-to-reach populations or individuals and groups often 'hidden' to outsiders.

Type	Description of Approach	Advantages
Stratified purposive	A hybrid approach used to select sources in subgroups.	Illustrates characteristics of particular subgroups of interest; facilitates comparisons. May be used in studies that begin with one sampling approach and add another to focus the sample (Patton, 2014). Often used in Big Data studies to create categories within large sets of data, such as different time frames (Winskell, Singleton, & Sabben, 2018).
Theoretical sampling	Selection of participants based on the emerging findings to ensure adequate representation of theoretical concepts (Moser & Korstjens, 2018, p.10).	Grounded theory researchers conduct interviews with an initial sample of participants selected using criterion sampling. In analysis of this initial set of data, they identify categories of experience or perspectives. To gain insight into these categories they select additional research participants on the basis of how participants' characteristics or experiences help them to explicate the data (Charmaz, 2014).
Theory-based sampling	Finding manifestations of a theoretical construct of interest so as to elaborate and examine the construct (Patton, 2002).	To get to the theoretical construct, 'we need to see different instances of it, at different moments, in different places, with different people. The prime concern is with the conditions under which the construct or theory operates, not with the generalization of the findings to other settings' (Miles & Huberman, 1994, p. 29).
Total population or census	The researcher studies an entire population of people or an entire set of sources with a common experience or characteristic.	Appropriate for studies of a publicly experienced phenomena, event, or crisis or situations where a small group constitutes the 'total' population.
Typical case sampling	Illustrates or highlights what is typical, normal, or average (Creswell, 1998; Miles & Huberman, 1994).	What is 'typical' must be known or based on specific shared characteristics.
Volunteer	The researcher studies people who volunteer to be a part of the research.	Useful when the researcher is studying a common experience or phenomenon.

and 6 for more about insiders, outsiders, and positionality.) Availability is not a factor to take lightly in online studies, where access can be an obstacle.

For example, a study of staff in the university you attend could be described as a convenience or opportunistic sample. If, once you started collecting data, you found that staff at another campus were willing to participate, you could include an emergent group as well.

Extant data can also be convenient or emergent. You might decide to use documents or datasets you can access conveniently without special permissions. Don't be surprised if new sources or ideas emerge once you start reviewing and analyzing what you've found. For example, I used historical records archived in the graduate library as sources for part or my Master's research that I was able to access because I was on the staff of the university. After reading correspondence, I wanted to see the story from the other writer. To follow these emergent threads I had to request permission and make special arrangements with the foundation archive that housed these letters.

Nominated or *snowball* sampling are different methods with a common feature: both have a role for someone other than the researcher. If you are using nominated sampling (also known as referral), someone with knowledge or acquaintance with potential participants refers them to you. Snowball sampling uses participant-to-participant referrals. For example, if you wanted to study the experiences of Indigenous university students, you could ask a program leader or advisor who works with them to refer or nominate students who might be willing to participate in the study. Once you have found willing students, you could ask participants to share study information with their friends, using a snowball technique.

Nominated or snowball approaches are particularly useful in online research and are discussed in more detail in Chapter 8.

The Sampling Type Relates to the Characteristics of Sources

Start with criterion-based sampling because it is helpful to begin by establishing a set of criteria. What are the characteristics of the sources you want to include, and what are the characteristics you want to exclude? Once you have a draft of your inclusion and exclusion criteria, you can refine your choices using other sampling types. You might decide that you want to group sources by common criteria and use a stratified purposive approach. For example, if your inclusion criteria spell out an age range of 20 to 40, you could create subgroups for participants from age 20 to 30, and for 30 to 40. Similarly, your inclusion criteria for extant documents could include a time frame of 1990 to 2010, with a subgroup of 1990 to 2000, and a second subgroup from 2000 to 2010.

If you are looking for diverse sources, choose a *heterogeneous* or *maximum variation* approach. For example, if you are studying victims of online bullying, you could decide you want a wide, global range of examples from different ages, gender, races, or cultures, in workplace or social contexts. The one common criterion relates to the experience as a victim of online bullying.

Alternatively, when you are looking for similar sources, choose *homogeneous* sources. Again, for a study about victims of online bullying, you could choose only sources that describe experiences of youth from one racial group, in one country. These sources share all inclusion criteria.

A study using *volunteer* participants will most likely be heterogenous, unless the recruitment process outlines specific criteria for participation or recruitment is limited to a group that shares common characteristics.

Critical case, extreme, or *intensity* types are selected when you want very specific sources that fully exemplify the issues or problems under investigation. Using the same example of research about online bullying, you could decide that you want sources that describe physical harm experienced by the victim. While 'physical harm from online bullying' could be described as criteria, using the descriptor of *critical case, extreme*, or *intensity* highlights the degree to which this experience is central to your strategy. If the study about online bullying relates to a campaign or policy-making, 'physical harm from online bullying' could also be described as *politically important*.

In a study designed to develop or test theory, *theory-based* or *theoretical sampling* is used to locate examples of the constructs of interest, or participants with insights that could illuminate an emerging theory. Let's use the Research Cameos to work through this decision-making process.

─────────────── RESEARCH CAMEO 7.1 ───────────────

Researcher 1 is designing a study using extant data. They plan to analyze Big Data from journal databases as well as mission statements and editorials from selected journals to understand how and where qualitative research is published. They begin with criterion-based sampling. The inclusion criteria will be implemented as key word searches that include 'qualitative,' and terms that describe methodologies that are typically qualitative such as 'ethnography,' and 'phenomenology.' Researcher 1 could decide that given the specificity of these criteria, they will aim for a *heterogeneous* set of sources. These could include those from discipline-specific journals, such as *Business & Society* or *British Journalism Review*, as well as research-oriented journals that cover all types of research, such as *Research Ethics* or *Methodological Innovations*. They will also look at databases for journals specific to qualitative research, such as *Qualitative Inquiry*.

Researcher 2 is designing a study that involves eliciting data through one-to-one and group online interviews with qualitative researchers who have successfully

(Continued)

published their studies. They will start with a convenience sample of participants they know from professional networking circles. After the initial set of interviews, they might use a snowball approach, asking participants to get the word out about the study to their circles of friends and colleagues.

Researcher 3 is designing a study that will involve generating data with aspiring and successful qualitative researchers in a workshop setting. They will create a plan based on a nominated approach. They intend to ask people who supervise doctoral students or early-career researchers to refer individuals who might benefit from the workshop, and who would be willing to commit to the process.

Researcher 4 is designing a study that will include observations of social media posts from a writing group, analysis of extant data from journal archives, and online interviews with selected authors and editors. The first stage will involve finding an online writing group that will allow a researcher to observe. Given the specificity of the requirement, they will use a critical case strategy. They will use a criterion-based strategy for finding specific articles that are exemplars for types of qualitative publications. They want to interview diverse writers and editors, so will use a maximum variation strategy.

SAMPLE FRAMES

Fundamental to the sampling strategy is the choice of a **sample frame**. This refers to a list or grouping of people from which the sample is selected. There are two broad types of frames:

- *Existing sample frames.* Existing frames usually consist of records previously organized or constructed for administrative purposes. They could include membership lists for organizations or associations or lists of students or program participants (Ritchie & Lewis, 2003; Wilmot, 2005). An existing sample frame could include libraries, archives, or databases or other sets of media or documents assembled based on specific criteria.
- *Constructed or generated sample frames.* Where an existing frame or list is not available, researchers may have to create their own. In some cases, researchers can construct a frame from partially adequate or incomplete existing frames.

Constructing a sample frame online is possible but adds more layers of information or identity the researcher must verify. Thus, it may be time-consuming. **Existing sample frames** are preferable, and fortunately the Internet is a boon to the online researcher. With the advent of online communities and social networking sites, and the movement of professional associations and clubs to the Internet, many potential sample frames exist online. In some cases faculty, employee, or membership lists may be posted on a website or published in a directory. Someone else has already aggregated pools of individuals based on some shared characteristics and has verified their identities.

By using existing frames researchers avoid a time-consuming recruitment process of filtering out potential participants who will not or cannot contribute to the success of the study. What groups or affiliations would attract and engage the target sample population, and what appropriate means can be utilized to communicate the study's call for participation? Or what institution, governmental or non-governmental agency or community has collected materials relevant to the study? Who can grant use of the list or access to the materials?

SAMPLE SIZE

Sampling procedures for qualitative research do not follow standardized guidelines, and guidelines for sample size are no exception. There is little agreement in the field about what constitutes an appropriate number of participants, with 'it depends' typically preceding the fuzzy answers given. There is even less clear guidance on the number of material sources, since some qualitative researchers use Big Data and others study a limited number of cases.

One perspective asks researchers to consider data needs in the context of the research purpose and methodology: 'The adequacy of the sample is not determined solely on the basis of the number of sources but the appropriateness of the data' (O'Reilly & Parker, 2012, p. 6). Another points to the sufficiency of the criteria used to select human participants: 'With a purposive non-random sample the number of people interviewed is less important than the criteria used to select them' (Wilmot, 2005, p. 4). Yet another view suggests that researchers interview 'as many subjects as necessary to find out what [they] need to know' (Kvale, 2007, p. 43). Although the literature does not offer a straightforward protocol for determining the number of participants, key questions will help the researcher think through the most appropriate sample size:

- *Heterogeneity or homogeneity of the population:* If the population is diverse in nature, a larger sample will be needed; the more homogeneous the sample population, the smaller the sample can be.
- *Number of selection criteria:* The more different criteria, the larger the sample (Ritchie & Lewis, 2003).
- *Multiple samples within one study:* If it is necessary to have more than one sample within a study for reasons of comparison or control, then a larger sample will be needed (Ritchie et al., 2003).
- *Emerging factors in data:* Unexpected generalizations may lead the researcher to seek out new research participants who can add to or contradict the data (Silverman & Marvasti, 2008). Researchers using snowball, chain, or nominated sampling expect this to occur. Researchers using other sampling strategies need to decide whether or not they are open to an increase of sample size while the study is in progress or whether they prefer to make a note of the emerging factors for consideration in a follow-up or future study.

- *Saturation or redundancy:* Saturation or redundancy occurs when the researcher begins to hear the same or similar responses from participants, or see the same themes in material sources. 'If the purpose is to maximize information, the sampling is terminated when no new information is coming from the new sampled units; thus redundancy is the primary criterion' (Lincoln & Guba, 1985, p. 202).
- *Interview style.* For researchers using elicited or enacted approaches with human participants, additional questions should be considered. The intensity, and therefore the length, of the interview or research event will also impact the design of the qualitative sampling strategy and the decision of sample size. Longer interactions may provide more data than shorter interactions. Depending on the nature of the study, think about whether to conduct a larger number of short interactions or a smaller number of longer interactions. In a study that entails more than one interview, or involves multiple types of data collection such as questionnaires and observations as well as interviews, a relatively small sample is appropriate.

Like the storied Goldilocks, the interview researcher needs a sample size that is not too big – in other words, so big 'that it is difficult to extract thick, rich data' (Onwuegbuzie & Leech, 2007, p. 6). At the same time, the sample should not be too small, thus taking the risk of missing key constituencies or lacking enough diversity to show important influences. Look at other similar studies to find both examples and support for decisions about sample size. Weigh all factors and determine what size is just right for your proposed study.

─────────────── RESEARCH CAMEO 7.2 ───────────────

Researcher 1 will use an existing sample frame, that is, the journal databases.

Researcher 2 will use an existing sample frame, that is, their professional network. They are planning for a sample size of 20 participants.

Researchers 3 and **4** will construct their sample frames. Researcher 3 will aim for a sample of 10 participants, since they will interact with them multiple times. Researcher 4, given that they will have multiple forms of data, plans for a sample of 4 to 6 for the interview stage.

DEVELOPING A SAMPLING PLAN FOR ONLINE RESEARCH

Your decisions should be articulated in a systematic and well-defined sampling plan (Lee & Lings, 2008, p. 213). This kind of plan lays out the approach(es) to be used and explains how they align with the research purpose and questions, epistemology, and methodology. To begin, you will need to define your purpose and determine which type(s) of sampling fit.

How do I Create a Sampling Plan?

Start your purposive sampling plan with a clearly defined purpose. Reflect on the purpose, and if necessary, refine it given the options and examples you have studied in this chapter. These interrelated questions will help you think through the type(s) of sampling most appropriate to your study:

Criteria

- What criteria are essential for all sources to meet? Are there criteria that only some should meet?
- How much detail on the sample criteria should be developed in advance of the study? Should some criteria be developed while the study is underway? Might an initial review of some data offer you a better sense of the research problem, or raise new questions to be explored? Might you decide that the inclusion criteria are too loose, or too restrictive?

Population

- What is the target population?
- What kinds of people can help the researcher achieve the purpose of study?
- What is it about this population that interests me (Mason, 2002)?
- Am I interested in people as individuals, groups, collectives, or communities? Will I define them or rely on members' definition of whether or not they comprise a group or community?
- How should I classify people for the purpose of the study? By characteristics such as age, sex, class, ethnicity, occupation, social class? By specific life experiences, feelings, perceptions, behaviors? By levels or types of online participation?
- Who should be excluded from the sample? On what basis?

Materials

- What particular types of materials are most relevant to the study? Written, multimedia, video, or audio files? Digital artifacts? User-generated or created by business, governmental or institutional bodies? Big Data? Screenshots? Downloads?
- Am I interested in compilations of materials, sets of records? Will I assemble the materials or chose compilations or sets put together by others?
- What materials should be excluded? On what basis?

Other considerations

- Should the sampling strategy take a planned or an iterative approach to determining sample size and selecting participants or materials before or during the study?
- How much diversity is needed to represent the variations known to exist within this population (Koerber & McMichael, 2008)?
- 'What relationship do I want to establish, or do I assume exists, between the sample or selection I am making, and a wider population' (Mason, 2002, p. 123)?

- What time parameters should be set?
- What era of the experience or life stage is relevant to the inquiry?
- What is the time frame of the posts or online discussion?

SPOT CHECK

- How would you answer these questions for your sampling plan?
- What questions are unanswered? How will you learn more so you can decide the best sampling strategy for your study?

COMMUNICATING YOUR PLAN

Researchers do not act alone. To succeed, your efforts require others' cooperation. You could need permission to conduct your study in a particular site, help distributing recruitment messages to members of a group of potential participants, or access to a private archive. When communicating the study's purpose to others whose cooperation is needed, clear, succinct messages may mean the difference between whether or not they will click on a website button or respond to text or email. Keep in mind that the ways you describe the research design and sample for an academic audience may be stylistically quite different from the ways you will communicate to potential participants.

Translate any jargon or 'academese' into plain language that is quickly understandable. In addition to clear inclusion/exclusion criteria, it is important to spell out what it is the researcher expects. Will a participant be asked to discuss potentially sensitive subjects or not? Point out whether hot-button issues such as marital/relationship/family/sexual history are or are not going to be discussed. If access to documents is being requested, specify the ways financial or personal information will be excluded from the data. Specify the time required or time frame for the study.

Ethics Tip: Be open and disclose unknown factors that could result in changes in expectations or in scheduling.

SUMMARY OF KEY CONCEPTS

This chapter reviewed options for sampling in qualitative online studies. Whether determining criteria for choosing human participants or for selecting materials to review, decisions about sampling must align with the purpose of the study as well as the methodology. Before the researcher seeks out sources, a sampling plan is needed. Qualitative researchers use non-probability sampling. Although a combination of sampling approaches can be used in online research, developing specific criteria will help the researcher locate and verify potential interviewees. Thus, criterion-based sampling is recommended as a component of the online sampling plan.

DISCUSSION QUESTIONS AND EXERCISES

- Use the questions in this chapter to map out the approach that best fits your study.
- Outline at least two ways you can share your sampling plan.
- Use your academic library to find articles or other resources that go into greater depth on the sampling strategies you have selected.
- In an essay of 3–5 pages describe a rationale for your sampling strategy and plan.

    o   Why is this plan the best fit?
    o   What are the potential obstacles for implementing this plan for an online study?

8

Recruiting, Finding, and Selecting Participants Online

HIGHLIGHTS

This chapter builds on Chapter 7, which offered guidance on developing your sampling plan. Once you have a sampling plan, you are ready to implement it. In Chapter 8 we will explore issues and options relevant to researchers using *elicited* or *enacted* methods. See Chapter 10 for guidance about finding sources and collecting extant data.

We cannot ask questions or interact with participants unless we have consenting individuals who are willing to respond. Think through the characteristics you are looking for in each person who participates, as well as the characteristics of the group as a whole. With this foundation, you will be ready to decide how best to recruit them for your online study.

OBJECTIVES

After reading and reflecting on this chapter, you will be able to:

- understand recruitment options
- find and use existing sample frames

(Continued)

- research and construct a sample frame
- evaluate whether a commercial service will work for your study
- align a recruitment strategy with your sampling plan
- develop a recruitment message and approach for sharing with potential participants.

RECRUITING AND SELECTING HUMAN PARTICIPANTS

The sampling plan is essential to this next step, developing a recruitment strategy. If as a researcher you are unclear about what you want, it will be challenging to build the relationships needed to gain entrée to an existing sample frame or to develop your own.

How will you find the right people who have the ability, experience, and willingness to serve as research participants? If research interviews are, as the saying goes, 'conversations with a purpose,' then recruiting is the systematic process for determining who fits the purpose of the study. The qualitative interview or research event is meant to generate descriptions of a particular experience and/or context in-depth, with as much nuance and complexity as possible. The researcher needs to locate individuals who can and will provide honest, robust information about themselves and/or the phenomenon of interest and participate fully.

OPPORTUNITIES AND CONSTRAINTS FOR ONLINE RECRUITING

On the one hand, you have fertile ground for reaching the right participants for your study from a global pool of possible participants when you recruit online. On the other hand, you have to address factors unique to communication in the virtual milieu. Online, you are competing with well-funded advertising campaigns and platforms that vie for users' attention. You are also competing with false and misleading entreaties from bots and spammers (Godinho, Schell, & Cunningham, 2020). The persistence and pervasiveness of these aggressive players can make life difficult for the honest, humble researcher.

Given the complexities, approaches previously used to recruit participants have limited relevance. New thinking is needed when you use the Internet to locate, recruit, and ultimately select appropriate participants. Here are a few challenging questions specific to online recruitment:

- How will you verify the identity and age (or other demographic criteria) of research participants recruited online?
- How will you assess whether the potential participants have access to the communications technology you intend to use, and the capability and willingness to use it as a research participant?
- How will you motivate potential participants to volunteer or accept an invitation, and complete all requirements of the study?
- How will you select and navigate settings where you can recruit participants?
- Will response to a recruitment message inadvertently disclose personal or health issues given data may be collected by the site or search engine?
- What permissions are needed to post recruitment messages to specific groups?
- How can you counter potential communication gaps or breakdowns that are more prevalent in online communication?
- How will you present a credible and trustworthy identity to differentiate your messages from disinformation from fraudulent players?

No two researchers will answer these questions in the same way. You will need to customize your tactics based on the nature of your topic, including degree of sensitivity, and the characteristics of your target demographic group. Considerations and recommendations are offered here.

WHAT CHARACTERISTICS SHOULD PARTICIPANTS HAVE?

As mentioned in Chapter 7, criterion-based sampling is a good starting point, whether or not you want to combine it with other types of sampling. When you answer the question, *'what characteristics should participants have?'* you are taking the first steps in defining inclusion criteria. You will want to decide whether all participants need to meet all criteria, or whether you have some categories or priorities for a stratified sampling approach. For example, you might decide that all participants need to have a high school education, but that some might be in the workforce and some might be job-hunting. Or you could decide that all participants need to have a high school education and be employed at least 20 hours a week. You can define the criteria broadly or narrowly to best meet the purpose of your study.

Clear delineations of the inclusion and exclusion criteria will be a boon to online recruiting, especially when you need to explain to a moderator or gatekeeper why permission should be granted to promote your study to an online community or e-mail list. By stating criteria, you create additional factors that can be independently verified by other sources besides the research participant's own statements. Depending on the nature of your study and the prevalence of people with the desired experience, you might need to expand or narrow your criteria:

Demographic criteria?

Do you want participants of particular ages, races, abilities, cultures, or do you want a heterogenous sample?

Experience or expertise?

Are you looking for particular levels of knowledge or types of knowledge about the problem or phenomenon you want to study?

Sensitive information?

Will the participant be asked to discuss potentially sensitive information or not? If hot-button issues such as financial information or marital/relationship/family information are not going to be discussed, then emphasize those exclusions in the initial recruitment messages and through the screening process. If sensitive matters will be discussed, reassure them of privacy and safety precautions. (See Chapters 5 and 6 for more about protecting participants.)

Time commitment?

The time period for the study should be defined as closely as possible in advance. If the research calls for advance preparation, multiple interactions, and/or follow-up during data analysis, state those requirements up front. It makes sense that the more you view the interactions with participants as knowledge-generating events, the more time you and they will need to build trust, relationships, and understanding of the study's focus. In online research, a participant may drop out by simply closing the interview window or deleting the e-mail. In this digital milieu, specify expectations from the beginning of the relationship to ensure persistence.

Technology access and skills?

Next, you need to specify technology access and skills involved in research participation. Participant access is a fundamental question that influences any research design. Researchers who intend to interview people in person are concerned with geographic access to the desired meeting place and access for people with disabilities or other restrictions. Researchers consider possible effects of the setting on participants' responses – will they be intimidated or influenced by the room arrangement or by associations with the institution, power, or authority reflected in the meeting space? Answer these questions to identify technology access and skills issues relevant to your study:

- What combination of online communication tools do you intend to use for preparation, interviews, or other data collection events, and any follow-up communication?
- Will routine communication such as arranging times to meet or discussing the next steps of the study be carried out through e-mail, text messaging, or telephone?
- Will research participants require a microphone, a web camera, or other specialized hardware or software? What can you provide? Will you need to find funds to subsidize participants' acquisition of technology? If participants do not have their own hardware, can you arrange for participation from a computer lab or another setting?
- Will potential participants who fit the sample demographic have access to the online tools you intend to use?
- Will they feel comfortable responding to questions in the selected online meeting space?
- Will it be necessary to schedule a preliminary online meeting to introduce the ICT or specific features to the participants?
- Will it be necessary to arrange for someone else to assist the participant? For example, might an adult need to assist a child, or senior center volunteer assist the elderly participant? If so, should that assistant sign some kind of consent form or agreement to ensure confidentiality of the participant's responses?

Digital literacy, technology adoption, and census studies mapping rates of Internet access by people in various demographic categories and geographic areas provide researchers with useful background information on the target sample population. In addition, you can look for signs of an online presence for the target population. Are there websites on topics of interest to this population? Are online communities or social networking sites by and for them up-to-date and active? This kind of broad exploration may help you answer the general questions; specific questions will need to be posed to individuals as part of the initial discussion of needs and requirements for participation in the study.

———————————————— SPOT CHECK ————————————————

Recruiting is a challenge for online researchers, but it also offers an opportunity to shape your study.

- How can you build on and implement the sampling plan you sketched out in Chapter 7?
- Do you have clear answers to these questions about participant characteristics and inclusion criteria?

RESEARCH CAMEO 8.1

When recruiting for the cameo studies about publishing qualitative studies, the researcher will have a simpler time spelling out what they seek, such as defining specific parameters. In these examples you can see that even studies about the same topic might require different kinds of participant characteristics.

Researcher 1 is designing a study using extant data, so this chapter is not applicable.

Researcher 2 is designing a study that involves eliciting data through one-to-one and group online interviews with qualitative researchers who have successfully published their studies.

o   *Inclusion:* Academic writers with a doctoral degree and 3–5 publications in peer-reviewed scholarly journals.

o   *Exclusion:* Student writers with no publications in peer-reviewed scholarly journals.

In addition to clear inclusion/exclusion criteria, it is important for Researcher 2 to spell out what they expect from participants. Are they looking for specific expertise or experience? Using the same example, we could offer more specific criteria:

o   *Inclusion:* Academic writers who have published qualitative research based on organizational ethnography in the business sector.

o   *Exclusion:* Academic writers who have published qualitative ethnographic research about individuals, the public sector, or NGOs.

Researcher 3 is designing a study that will involve generating data with aspiring and successful qualitative researchers by conducting a workshop and collecting data from consenting participants.

o   *Inclusion:* Doctoral students in the dissertation or thesis stage, or early-career researchers who completed their degrees within the last five years.

o   *Inclusion:* Doctoral students or early-career researchers who can commit to attending all sessions of the free workshop and complete a written publication plan.

o   *Exclusion:* Doctoral students or early-career researchers whose research is quantitative or mixed methods.

Researcher 4 is designing a study that will include observations of an online academic writing group and interviews with selected authors and editors. This case is a bit different, because the researcher must first locate a writing group willing to allow observations. They will select participants from that group for interviews. While observing the group, they could look for potential interviewees using these criteria:

o   *Inclusion:* Writing group members who post at least twice each week about their publishing journey.

o   *Inclusion:* Writing group members who contribute reviews and comments to other members.

o   *Exclusion:* Writing group members whose research is quantitative or mixed methods.

COMMUNICATING WITH POTENTIAL PARTICIPANTS

When communicating the study's purpose, clear, succinct messages may mean the difference between whether or not people will click on a website button or respond to a text or e-mail recruitment notice. Keep in mind that the ways you describe the research design and sample for an academic audience may be stylistically quite different from the ways you will communicate recruitment messages. Translate any jargon or 'academese' into plain language understandable to your target audience. Unless you have access to a convenience sample, you will most likely be seeking assistance from others who might refer, suggest, or introduce potential participants. You might be looking for others to distribute a call for participation to their respective networks. Think through how you communicate, as well as the content of your messages. (See Chapter 12 for suggestions about visual communications.)

ENSURING THAT PARTICIPANTS ARE CREDIBLE

Strategies to verify potential research participants' identities and ensure that they authentically meet the study criteria are important to any recruitment plan but critical when you intend to reach out in public online environments. Researchers who have access to private, members-only online spaces have less concern for identity and consenting age of potential participants and can proceed in a similar style to that used by any researcher. Using Researcher 2 as an example, if they promote this study to an online group that is part of a university writing center, they can be assured that group members are students who want to publish academic writing. However, if they promote the study on social media, they will need a way to verify respondents. Let's explore some options.

Two suggested approaches for locating credible research participants online are: *nomination* and *existing sample frames.* The first relies on verification by membership in a group, organization, or reliable administrative list and the second relies on verification of identity by another person who knows the potential participant. Nomination or existing sample frame approaches can be combined or used together with other tactics as needed to meet the purpose of the study. A third approach, *open recruitment,* will mean advertising for volunteers. While open recruitment is free, you need to develop your own method for verification of ages and authentic identities, and cross-checking of participant information for duplicates, similarities and inconsistencies (Godinho et al., 2020). By using nomination or existing frames, researchers avoid the grueling recruitment process necessary to filter out potential participants who will not or cannot contribute to the success of the study.

---------------------------------- SPOT CHECK ----------------------------------

You want to be sure you are collecting data from knowledgeable, authentic participants.

- What are your concerns, given the nature of your study and population?
- How can you address these concerns?
- Who can you turn to for advice or suggestions about how best to address credibility issues for your study?

PARTICIPANTS DRAWN FROM EXISTING SAMPLE FRAMES

The sample frame, a list or grouping of people from which the sample is selected, is fundamental to any sampling strategy. As discussed in Chapter 7, some researchers construct sample frames while others rely on existing frames.

Existing Sample Frames

Existing sample frames can serve the online researcher because they are aggregate pools of individuals who have often verified their identities (and perhaps even credit card numbers) to qualify as part of the group. You might be a member of a group, or have access to a group, so you can use a convenience sample to meet your participant needs.

Some lists that can serve as sample frames, such as email lists, reach people with a common interest, but do not verify the identities of subscribers. For example, an email list about teaching elementary school might reach teachers, as well as students, parents, or others who want to keep up-to-date about teaching practices. On the other hand, professional associations and societies that serve people with the same occupation, medical condition, hobby, or interest might target more specific members. When people have to pay to join a group, you can assume that they share key characteristics with other members.

With the advent of online communities and social media, and the movement of associations and clubs to the Internet, many potential sample frames exist online. Researchers have had mixed success with simple posts to recruit volunteers, and the problems associated with open recruiting can present obstacles. Depending on the type of study you want to conduct, paid advertising on social media sites or relevant platforms can be used to recruit participants. While expensive, researchers have been able to find hard-to-reach populations with ads (Schwinn, Hopkins, Schinke, & Liu, 2017; van Gelder et al., 2019; Wozney, Turner, Rose-Davis, & McGrath, 2019).

In some cases, faculty, employee, or membership lists may be posted on a website or published in a directory. Sometimes such lists are behind a paywall or accessible to other members or staff. Gaining agreement to allow you to recruit their members involves negotiation with the gatekeepers, including group moderators, or membership coordinators.

Key questions for using existing sample frames include:

- What groups or affiliations would attract and engage the target sample population for your study?
- Are their member lists public or private?
- What appropriate means can you utilize to communicate the study's call for participation to group members?

Commercial Services and Panels

Commercial services have emerged to help connect researchers and participants. These services find individuals with many backgrounds who are willing to be called on for research projects – for a fee. Some of these individuals see research participation as a source of income, while others are motivated because they enjoy the process. Typically these services are designed to support survey research, however, qualitative researchers are using them in a variety of ways. Since the product offerings continue to change and expand, look at current options to see whether they might serve your purpose.

These are fee-based services, however, if they will work for your study you might find that given 'time is money,' the cost is a worthwhile investment in timely completion of your study. Generally, once your application is accepted, they can connect you with participants very quickly. The service also takes care of some of the consent agreement requirements. These are real advantages that can make it possible to move into data collection more quickly. There are potential disadvantages to using these services: you need to check whether the diversity of participants and types of research they are willing to complete fit your study. Some services are limited to surveys.

Companies that make survey software often offer recruitment services. Market research firms offer services focused specifically on business topics. The large player in the field is Amazon's Mechanical Turk, or MTurk. Advantages for using this service include a large and diverse participant pool, ease of use, quick responses, reasonable costs, and flexible design options (Aguinis, Villamor, & Ramani, 2020, p. 825). MTurk participants are willing to:

- write essays for open-ended qualitative research
- participate in video interviews
- engage with other participants in interactive games and group-based social experiments
- participate in longitudinal studies, including studies that require intensive, daily tracking
- complete a wide variety of social and behavioral experiments, including those that measure reaction times (Litman & Robinson, 2020, p. 1)

Given that recruitment can be one of the most time-consuming and challenging parts of the qualitative research process, it is worth exploring whether MTurk or another service might serve your purpose. As Cheung et al. observe, 'There is not a one-size-fits-all answer to whether MTurk is appropriate for a research study. The quality of the data is not defined by the data source per se, but rather the decisions researchers make during the stages of study design, data collection, and data analysis' (Cheung, Burns, Sinclair, & Sliter, 2017). Once you have your design and have defined inclusion criteria, you can look at MTurk and other available services and see whether they can provide suitable participants. If the answer is yes, look at whether they can provide, in a timely and cost-effective manner, individuals who are willing to be a part of the type of study you want to conduct.

CONSTRUCTING A SAMPLE FRAME

Constructing a sample frame online is another possibility. It will entail creating your own list of potential participants. Doing so can add more layers of information or identities you must verify. Depending on your situation, constructing a new sample frame online may be a way to organize your list of accessible participants or it might be too time-consuming to be practical.

Participants are Nominated or Referred by Trustworthy Third Party

Can someone else recommend potential participants who meet sampling criteria? In the act of nomination, the identity of the potential participant is verified. A nomination from a known person or organization deflects the question, 'How do you know the participant is who he or she says?' Online nomination could be accomplished with a request to colleagues, program directors, or others in a position to know individuals who meet the sample criteria. For example, Researcher 2 could ask staff at a school or youth program to refer working parents. Researcher 2 could ask a moderator of an online discussion group to refer active members who might be willing to participate. Or Researcher 2 could create a recruitment message and ask friends and colleagues to suggest working parents they know who might be interested. Researcher 2 makes contact and invites the nominee to participate.

Nomination can be meshed with a snowball or chain approach. Research participants whose identities and credibility have been established may be asked to nominate others who share characteristics or experiences. For example, Researcher 2 could create a recruitment message and ask friends and colleagues to share it with working parents they know. Those contacts can choose to contact Researcher 2 if interested. The referee is not necessarily informed whether the contact has volunteered to participate.

A crucial element of successful nomination, referrals, or snowball sampling is trust. You need to trust that the referee knows the needed characteristics of the people they suggest. Streeton, Cooke, and Campbell (2004) noted the importance of trust when asking for a nomination:

> Trust and networking, and the role of the professional relationship, have an impact on the nature, strength, and numbers of further nominations in this type of recruitment and retention. Researchers rely on the truth and fidelity of information received from their contacts, and perhaps more importantly, contacts must feel they can trust the fidelity of the researchers. (p. 45)

The use of nominations, referrals, or snowball sampling does add more steps for the researcher, who must explain the study and ask for assistance from others. However, other steps can be passed over when the researcher has verifiable evidence that the potential participant is who they say they are.

SPOT CHECK

- What would the ideal sample frame look like for your study? Does it exist, or must you create one?
- What types of recruitment would work for your study? Why?

ENSURING THAT RESEARCHERS ARE CREDIBLE

As noted in earlier chapters, we live in an interview society, a society where nearly every purchase is followed by a request for participation in a follow-up questionnaire.

Our telephones buzz with a stream of polling requests. At the same time, people who participate online in social media and other communities are increasingly wary about their privacy. They wonder, who wants my information and why? How will this information be used? Why should I spend my precious time giving you my information? These conditions may lead to reluctance to participate in research studies.

While as researchers we are concerned with the credibility of participants, potential participants are equally concerned with *our* credibility. Discussing online research with hard-to-reach populations, Kaufman and Tzanetakis observe that 'credibility can be conceptualized as an investment of time and resources to build a trustworthy relationship between the researcher and participants' (2020, p. 934). They describe the commitment needed to establish and maintain this relationship.

A thoughtfully crafted web presence is one way to address this issue by introducing ourselves and our research interests in a way that builds positive impressions with potential participants.

The researcher's web presence can take numerous forms; two are described broadly here as (a) statements and images posted on others' sites, blogs, friendship walls, or communities, or (b) statements and images posted on the researcher's own site, blog, or social media page.

What options will work best for you?

Introduce Yourself: Embrace Your Identity as a Researcher

The first step is to create a statement that introduces you as a researcher. Think from the position of a potential participant: What would inspire someone to trust me as a researcher, and what would generate interest in my work? This statement should include the researcher's academic and professional credentials and affiliations. Student researchers may want to identify their academic institutions and (with permission) their professor or dissertation supervisor. However, the simple statement 'I am a doctoral student conducting research for a dissertation' is not usually adequate to appeal to potential participants. The introduction should point to the new knowledge the study aims to contribute to build a sense of importance for study participation.

To build this sense of importance, a very specific recruitment message should be used to better reach the target population. The researcher can fruitfully use this message to appeal to potential participants who meet inclusion criteria or ask for nominations of research participants.

The statement should explain your approaches and expectations on the matters discussed in this chapter. A succinct but comprehensive statement may include some or all of the following elements, with additional details posted on a blog, website, or information sheet.

- *Purpose of the study*: Summarize the research questions, reasons for conducting the study, and your plans for disseminating and/or applying the results. Are you conducting dissertation or thesis research? If so, note the institution. Such academic purposes assure potential participants of some level of faculty oversight of the study. Are you assessing needs for programs or services? Creating the basis for a larger survey research project? How will you disseminate the findings? What aspects of your goals will draw in potential participants and motivate them to contribute?
- *Ethics and privacy*: Offer assurances about ethical conduct of the study, confidentiality, protection of privacy, and private data storage. Indicate appropriate ethics, institutional, or other review board approvals granted for the study. If the study anticipates an international sample, indicate how you will address multiple sets of requirements.
- *Criteria*: State key sampling criteria, including characteristics, scope, and focus of the desired sample.
- *Expectations*: List the time frame for the study, time commitment, and technology tools needed for participation. All steps of the study should be spelled out, particularly when the researcher wants more than one interview, the opportunity to send follow-up questions by e-mail, review of the interview transcript after the interview, or additional data collection steps such as a questionnaire or observation of the participant's interactions in an online community.
- *Screening and selection process*: Provide sample size information and explain how the researcher will choose participants.
- *Incentive for participation*: Discuss reasons target population members should participate. Appeal to their sense of altruism and point out that they will be creating new solutions to a problem, improving understanding of an issue, or adding to the body of knowledge on a topic. Mention any other incentives for completion of all data collection steps, such as a gift card or perhaps an executive summary of findings, or invitation to a webinar on the findings.

--------------------------------- RESEARCH CAMEO 8.2 ---------------------------------

Researcher 2 wants to avoid giving the impression that they will be judgmental about struggles and feelings of failure potential participants might have about falling short on meeting publication goals. They want to convey openness to a range of academic writing competence and success.

This is a sample recruitment message Researcher 2 could use:

Hi! I am Janet Salmons, thanks for your interest in my research about publishing qualitative research in scholarly journals.

I hope to have a chance to talk with you about your goals for getting your research published.

(Continued)

Lots of academic writers want the career boost from getting work published but find this process to be challenging and time-consuming. I have been through this experience myself!

Now I want to build on my experience and produce research that will help us understand how to navigate past the obstacles.

I am interested in talking with doctoral students who are completing their thesis or dissertation, or new researchers who have graduated in the last five years.

I am not interested in confidential information or reviews you have received on your writing – and you'll have a chance to review any interview notes before I publish anything.

If you are interested, please click the link for a short questionnaire and agreement and let me know how to reach you to take the next step.

Here are notes on the cameo message:

Hi! I am Janet Salmons, thanks for your interest in my research about publishing qualitative research in scholarly journals. *Make a personal connection. If appropriate given the nature of the study, show your face. Avoid a detailed explanation of your academic project or doctoral research.*

I hope to have a chance to talk with you about your goals for getting your research published. *Very short description of the study and how you want to interact. This statement signals an interview study, so 'talk with you' fits.*

Lots of academic writers want the career boost from getting work published but find this process to be challenging and time-consuming. *Get more specific about the target group of potential participants and the topic you are studying.*

I have been through this experience myself! Now I want to build on my experience and produce research that will help us understand how to navigate past the obstacles. *Establish your credibility as a researcher.*

I am interested in talking with doctoral students who are completing their thesis or dissertation, or new researchers who have graduated in the last five years. *Get more specific about inclusion criteria.*

I am not interested in confidential information or reviews you have received on your writing – and you'll have a chance to review any interview notes before I publish anything. *Mention exclusion criteria, especially when you can use them to allay fears. Communicate an unbiased view.*

If you are interested, please click the link for a short questionnaire and agreement and let me know how to reach you to take the next step. *Give them an easy way to contact you and agree to participate. In addition to linking a recruitment message to the email address you are using for the study, participant application, and/or consent form; you can link it to an information sheet with more detailed information about the study.*

Once crafted, the statement can become the basis for communication with potential participants or those who can help with recruitment. When a brief, restricted-length post is needed on a social media site, e-mail list, or online community, the short message can include a link to the full statement. A benefit of such a statement is consistency of language and message so that all potential nominators or research participants begin from the same common understanding of the researcher's identity and the nature of the study. In the case of a heterogeneous or extreme case sample, the researcher may refine some elements of the statement to appeal to diverse audiences.

SPOT CHECK

- How will you present yourself to potential and consenting participants? Use the sample message as a template and craft your own message. Try recording it.

Create a Research Information Hub

You might need to share more information than will fit in a short statement. Create a research information hub where your introduction, statement about the study, and recruitment message can be posted online: a website, blog, or other virtual space. Free blog or website services are ideal for this purpose. In addition to text-based descriptions of the call for participation, you can create a video clip or audio version of the recruitment message. These personal touches can help increase interest and build presence with site visitors. Links to your academic institution or other publications can convey integrity and authenticity of the study. Be sure to provide means for contact, such as a link to an e-mail or messaging address, preferably one associated with the educational institution to reinforce academic credibility. Avoid using your physical address or phone number, which could lead to privacy violations for the researcher.

GETTING OUT THE RECRUITMENT MESSAGE

Locating the right people and recruiting them to participate in a study is a challenge for any researcher. One way to think about recruitment messages is that some are designed to '"pull in" online users with an interest in the phenomenon or topic central to the study, and any strategy to target online users who are actively trying to complete tasks for cash incentives or rewards on the web' (Antoun, Zhang, Conrad, & Schober, 2016, p. 2). If you are trying to pull in people who already know about your topic, such as members of a related group, less effort is needed for background explanations. If you are appealing to people who are looking for incentives, make sure to set it up so they cannot be rewarded unless all parts of the study are completed.

Alternatively, you can use a push strategy, meaning you are trying to share the recruitment message to online users engaged in other, unrelated online activities (Antoun et al., 2016). If you are pushing into a space where users' characteristics are unknown or into a public space, more attention will be needed to the context and purpose of the study. Keep in mind that online posts will reach a very general audience. Where can you find potential participants who meet specific sampling criteria?

You can share a recruitment statement or link to your recruitment site through e-mail or online community discussion lists. If relevant to the topics of the list, you can initiate a conversation about the nature and importance of the study.

Listservs may accept posts only from group members or consider messages posted from someone outside the group to be spam. In addition, because some Listserv participants receive messages in a daily or weekly 'digest' format rather than in real time, or have configured their mail system to send Listserv messages to a separate mailbox to be reviewed at a later point in time, recruitment messages via Listserv may have a slower response and a lower response rate than paid advertisements (Dworkin, Hessel, Gliske, & Rudi, 2016, p. 551).

You want to avoid sending or receiving unwanted messages, so if you want to post to a list where you are not a subscriber, contact the moderator or active members and request their assistance.

Similarly, you can interact with others in online discussions or social media. By interacting informally with members of the target population you can gain insights that may help in determining sampling and recruitment strategies best suited to the study. If you want to post your recruitment message, a best practice is to approach the moderator of the list or discussion group directly and respect any norms or guidelines.

Another way to find participants is by using the networking possibilities of the digital milieu. You can offer a webinar, workshop or host an online event or discussion on issues related to the study. By doing so, you create an opportunity to interact with individuals who are interested in the subject of inquiry and to attract potential participants or people who can nominate participants.

The public–private continuum is helpful for thinking through ways to match recruitment activities with the setting where you are trying to reach potential participants (Figure 8.1). As you can see in the Figure, additional permissions and safeguards are needed when recruiting participants in open, public online spaces.

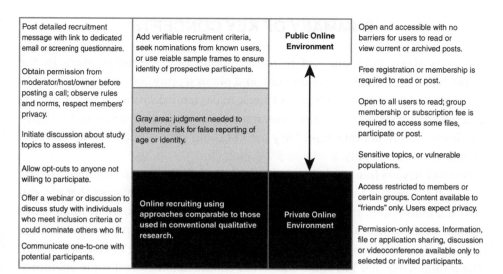

Figure 8.1 Permissions and safeguards needed for recruiting participants in open, public, online spaces

─────────────── RESEARCH CAMEO 8.3 ───────────────

Researcher 1 is designing a study using extant data, so this chapter is not applicable.

Researcher 2 will look for volunteers who respond to a promotional post they will include on their social media pages. However, they are not confident that enough participants will respond, so they are planning to use a commercial panel. They will review Mechanical Turk and other options to find one that can help recruit participants willing to engage through a video interview.

Researcher 3 is designing a study that will involve generating data with aspiring and successful qualitative researchers by conducting a workshop and collecting data from consenting participants. They have partnered with a university writing center that will allow them to offer the online workshop for doctoral students and early career faculty and will assist in recruiting participants. Since they will enroll verified members of the university community, credibility issues will not be a concern. They will share findings with the university writing center, making the project a win–win.

Researcher 4 is designing a study that will include observations of an online academic writing group and interviews with selected authors and editors. Researcher 4 is looking for active writing groups with a blog or social media presence, and contacting moderators or organizers to find one willing to participate. They are also contacting qualitative methodologists to ask whether they would be willing to make a referral to a formal or informal writing group. They have created a video recruitment message, noting clear boundaries about the data they will and will not collect. They are open to the possibility of sharing findings or related resources with the group.

SUMMARY OF KEY CONCEPTS

Decisions about sampling and recruiting strategies are essential steps in the research design, proposal development, and planning process. Although researchers using extant data collection also must make hard decisions about sampling and selecting sources (see Chapter 10), researchers using elicited or enacted methods have a more delicate task. They are choosing people with whom they will communicate personally.

You will have before you a human being – not simply an information-rich data source. If the process was successful, trust and rapport will develop so that you can gain the information needed to answer the research questions, in an interchange characterized by mutual respect. Sampling and recruiting are complex and sensitive processes for any interview researcher, regardless of experience or research design. The online researcher has some additional considerations – and some additional options. Nomination and existing sample frames offer ready verification of the identities of participants recruited online.

DISCUSSION QUESTIONS AND EXERCISES

- Locate articles describing studies using types of online data collection you intend to adopt.

  o   What kind of sampling and recruiting did each use? Do you feel the researcher made the best choice? Why or why not? What would you recommend?

  o   Identify two tips for recruiting participants online.

- Create a researcher blog with an introduction and recruitment message. Share the link with at least three colleagues, peers, or fellow classmates.

  o   What feedback do they offer that can help you develop a credible presence as an online researcher?

  o   What suggestions do they have for making the recruitment message more appealing?

- Outline the steps for a study using two different types of recruitment. Discuss advantages and disadvantages for each.

- Explore Amazon's Mechanical Turk and other commercial services. Look at the costs and other requirements for using the service(s). Also, look for at least one study based on data collected from a sample selected in this way. Based on your research, would a commercial service be appropriate for your study?

9

Preparing to Interact with Participants Online

HIGHLIGHTS

Collecting data begins with preparation. Chapters 7 and 8 covered two important areas of preparation that must be addressed in a research plan or proposal for online studies. In Chapter 3 you looked at the decision-making involved with choosing the right information and communications technologies (ICTs); this chapter lays out ways to get ready to use them when collecting data with elicited or enacted methods. Since the preparation described in this chapter is relevant to a wide range of styles, from interviews to creative methods, we will use the term *interacting with participants*. If you are planning to collect extant data, you might learn skills that will help you to communicate effectively with collaborative partners, co-authors, gatekeepers, and others.

OBJECTIVES

After reading and reflecting on this chapter, you will be able to:

- outline specific preparations needed based on technologies to be used in the study
- identify and develop skills and practices for synchronous, near-synchronous, and/ or asynchronous communications
- develop a plan for interacting with participants in online studies using elicited or enacted methods.

GET READY TO COLLECT DATA ONLINE!

Once you have discerned the research purpose, designed the study, considered ethical issues, obtained approval, planned for sampling, and recruited sample participants, it is time to move to the practical steps of planning and preparing to interact with participants. Preceding chapters have shown that online researchers can and should draw principles from relevant qualitative research methods and methodologies and adapt them as appropriate for use in their research. Research preparation is no exception. In addition to general steps researchers take before interacting with participants, online researchers need to learn the technologies they intend to use. Even if you are familiar with the ICTs you selected for data collection, you will have added responsibilities when using them as a researcher.

The selection of tools and platforms to use for data collection may depend on a variety of considerations. As discussed in previous chapters, besides the obvious practical matters of cost and access, technology selection may also be influenced by the research design and sampling and recruiting plans.

When online interactions are conducted to investigate face-to-face phenomena, as noted in Chapter 3, the online environment is the communications medium, not the subject of investigation. Such a researcher may have limited opportunities to introduce unfamiliar technologies, and the participant may have limited interest in learning new ICTs. In this type of study, access to and comfort with the ICT might be the critical factors for success.

A different set of factors may influence technology choices for online interactions to investigate online behaviors, events, transactions, or experiences. You may want to use the same ICTs the participants are using in the circumstances being studied. Would a researcher who wants to understand the ways facilitators stimulate discussion in online meetings want to carry out the interview in the same meeting space? Might you find conducting interactions in a variety of spaces beneficial, or might it be impractical? Given that each type of communications medium needs a slightly different preparation, researchers may prefer to offer a limited selection from which to choose so every interaction does not require additional preparation.

COMMUNICATIONS TECHNOLOGIES AND RESEARCH PREPARATION

Considerations for ICT Selection

In synchronous interactions, researchers and participants communicate in real time. In near-synchronous interactions, researchers and participants post questions and answers with the expectation that a response will be posted as soon as the other logs on next. In asynchronous interactions, there is a gap in time between question, answer, follow-up, and response.

Learning the ICT (and Avoiding a Crisis)

Practice interactions are essential for the online researcher, who must be confident and fluent in the selected technology tools before interacting with research participants. Communicating in the medium should come naturally by the time the first interaction with a participant occurs. Don't ignore this step, even when you are familiar with the ICT. The ideal practice partner is candid and generous with constructive feedback. Consider rehearsing with fellow researchers (or fellow students), friends, or colleagues. Such practice is even more essential. The online interviewer also may ask for impressions conveyed by written and visual communications. Another suggestion is to ask a colleague or more experienced researcher to observe a practice interview or interview recording and offer suggestions.

Record the practice interview and listen to it. Were your explanations of the study expectations and/or any background information concise and clear? Were questions asked in a supportive but neutral tone? Did you avoid emotional reactions to responses that participants might interpret as judgmental or disrespectful? Researchers may benefit from practicing both roles: interviewer as well as interviewee. By taking the research participant's side, the researcher may gain new insights about how to proceed.

If possible, arrange a time when you can meet, using the selected technology. A brief online planning session and orientation to the software will reduce the pressure on both researcher and participant in the interview. This planning session can be used to reiterate expectations spelled out in the recruitment statement (Chapter 8), to discuss the informed consent process (Chapters 4 and 5), and/or to answer any remaining questions, in addition to practicing communication with the selected technology. Such informal dialogue is valuable for building the trust and relationship needed for productive and open dialogue in the interview.

It is important to anticipate types of technical problems and either learn to fix them, work around them, or find alternatives that could be quickly made available. Implications of last-minute changes must be considered. For example, if it is necessary to switch from Voice over Internet Protocol (VoIP) to telephone, do you have the participant's phone number and alternate contact information? Given the importance of the recording, do you have a backup option if there is a problem? To avoid last-minute stress, pre-research communications should include an assessment of the research participants' experience and comfort level with the selected technology or technologies. Make available clear log-in or call-in procedures and provide any technical support service phone numbers or links to live-chat help.

SPOT CHECK

Think about the kinds of communications you will need to carry out in the process of your study. They could include other stakeholders in addition to research participants. Now think about what ICTs you would prefer to use. How can you practice using these technologies so that you are fully comfortable with them before you need to use them in productive research-oriented interactions?

PREPARATION VARIES BY ICT CHARACTERISTICS

Some ICTs require researchers to actively manage various communication, shared screen, and recording features when collecting data. Others, such as text chat, are simple to operate. Look closely at the ICTs you plan to use, and list all the features you plan to use. Some steps common to all online interactions and some specific to particular ICTs are outlined here.

Preparing for any Online Interaction with Participants

- Confirm time frame, anticipated length for the session.
- Confirm online setting for the session.
- Schedule time as needed to rehearse, practice with the ICT prior to formal data collection.
- Schedule data collection event.
- Establish protocols for the data collection event, including basic logistics. These may include agreement on signals to indicate need for more time to answer or time for a break. Protocols may also include discussion expectations for level of focus expected during the interview.

PREPARING FOR A SYNCHRONOUS OR NEAR-SYNCHRONOUS TEXT-BASED INTERACTION

You can text chat with participants for a variety of reasons. You can collect data in a written interview, answer questions, arrange for other research interactions, or follow up on a research event. Written forms of data collection have a practical advantage: no transcription is needed. While some chats might be informal or in-the-moment, it is useful to think about how and why you use this technology.

Synchronicity and Synchronous/Near-Synchronous Text-Based Interactions

Synchronous or near-synchronous text-based interactions can be conducted in a chat or instant message application. Texting can use free-standing applications or features of a social networking site. When used for an interview, the interviewer posts main questions first, then posts follow-ups and probes based on the participant's written responses. Synchronous or near-synchronous text-based interactions can also occur as part of multichannel communications in a virtual environment or on a videoconferencing platform. In such interactions, other audio and/or visual elements may complement the written exchange.

When both parties are engaged in a live exchange, fully focused on the question–response interaction, synchronicity is achieved (Dennis, Fuller, & Valacich, 2008). (See Chapter 3 for more about synchronous communications.) In other cases, the interview may be ostensibly synchronous but the participant is not devoting full attention to it. While a pause in response might indicate participant reflection on the question, a time lag can also mean the participant is engaged in some other activity. A key risk is participant distraction, which can cause lost momentum or a premature termination of the interview. Multitasking participants may engage in several synchronous events, without truly focusing attention on any one conversation. While the interviewer is thinking about, then typing, the next question, the participant may find other, more fast-paced activities to engage his or her attention. An interview that the researcher intends as 'synchronous' can become 'near synchronous.' Or participants could simply close the window and be gone! When discussing the interview protocol, consider asking the participant to signal you when he or she needs a break or needs to respond to another conversation.

The continuum in Figure 9.1 can help you think through the preparations you need to complete depending on the style of interaction.

Preparation Helps Ensure the Interaction is Meaningful

Preparation is essential to keep the dialogue moving. Preparation entails decision-making about the level of structure versus spontaneity desired. For more structured interactions, the researcher may type out main questions and frequently used probes to be quickly cut and pasted into the messaging window. Even for less-structured interactions, definitions of terms or clarifications of concepts related to the research phenomenon may be written out beforehand.

At another level, preparation starts at the research agreement and consent stage, which can include discussion of the researcher's expectations for focused

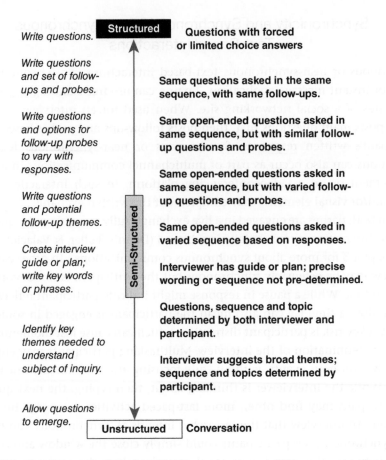

Write questions.

Structured

**Questions with forced
or limited choice answers**

Write questions
and set of follow-
ups and probes.

**Same questions asked in the same
sequence, with same follow-ups.**

Write questions
and options for
follow-up probes
to vary with
responses.

**Same open-ended questions asked in
same sequence, but with similar follow-
up questions and probes.**

**Same open-ended questions asked in
same sequence, but with varied follow-
up questions and probes.**

Write questions
and potential
follow-up themes.

Semi-Structured

**Same open-ended questions asked in
varied sequence based on responses.**

Create interview
guide or plan;
write key words
or phrases.

**Interviewer has guide or plan; precise
wording or sequence not pre-determined.**

**Questions, sequence and topic
determined by both interviewer and
participant.**

Identify key
themes needed to
understand
subject of inquiry.

**Interviewer suggests broad themes;
sequence and topics determined by
participant.**

Allow questions
to emerge.

Unstructured | **Conversation**

Figure 9.1 Continuum of e-interview structures

synchronicity during the interview, or for a less-restrictive time frame between question and response.

To avoid lengthy chat sessions that carry the risk of distractions, text-based interactions can be conducted in near-synchronous episodes. Instead of one significant interview, consider arranging for multiple short sessions. Plan to post initial main questions before the participant logs in for the interview to allow time for reflection on the research problem. Or questions could, for example, be posted every morning for a time-limited series of interactions, with the expectation that at some point during the day the participant will answer. Mobile, on-location access makes it possible for participants to check in and report on observations or experiences as they happen. For example, the interviewer and participant could log in for a couple of short questions on a daily or weekly basis, allowing data collection at strategic times relevant to the purpose of the study.

Emoticons in Text Chats with Participants

Whether the researcher and participant are using full-sized or tiny virtual keyboards, the process of posing and responding to questions is slowed by the act of writing those questions and responses. To hurry along the typing of a conversation, texters use various shortcuts. Electronic paralinguistic expressions such as *lol*, meaning 'laugh(ing) out loud,' or *ttyl*, meaning 'talk to you later,' have evolved as part of a large system of shorthand that has emerged as a kind of visual, digital shorthand. Text users allow emoticons to build social presence and substitute for social cues. These visual symbols can also soften difficult messages (Amaghlobeli, 2012) or convey an impression of conscientiousness and likeability (Krishnan & Hunt, 2021). In speech, non-verbal signals such as intonation can provide nuance or clarify the intended meaning better than the verbal context can, and, similarly, emoticons can radically alter the meaning of the message.

Like facial expressions or gestures, emoticons do not all have universally shared meanings. When an interviewer conducts a text-message interview with an interviewee from another cultural background or communication style, the interviewer must pay careful attention to the use of emoticons. Emoticon use varies by age and gender, with greater popularity with women and younger users (Amaghlobeli, 2012; Oleszkiewicz et al., 2017). It cannot be assumed that emoticons will be interpreted in the manner the interviewer intended (Aldunate & González-Ibáñez, 2017; Krishnan & Hunt, 2021). Miscommunication can occur during a text interview when a participant is more competent or comfortable with the use of emoticons or text abbreviations than the interviewer is (O'Connor, 2019). In preparing for an interview, think about whether and how you will use emoticons. If you decide to use them, will you determine some kind of consistent meaning you associate with each one? Preparation also entails decisions about whether or to what extent to use non-text elements, including shared files or links to images or media. (See Chapters 11and 12 for more about visual research options.)

Tips to Overcome Limitations

Even with the use of shortcuts, keep in mind that online interactions are slow. In one study, researchers reported that text-based synchronous interactions took about twice the length of in-person interactions and produced far fewer words.

A 120-minute online interview produced about seven pages of text. A 90-minute face-to-face interview produced 30 to 40 pages of text. The exchange of questions and responses was clearly influenced by the reading, reflection and typing skills of the respondents. (Davis, Bolding, Hart, Sherr, & Elford, 2004, p. 947)

To adapt, they resorted to short, closed-ended questions that allowed for simple question-and-answer sequences (Davis et al., 2004).

To prepare for a text-based interview, do the following:

- In absence of face-to-face introductions, decide whether you want to share images, a recorded introduction, or other information about yourself and the study. You might decide to create a research website that participants can visit to learn more.
- Select a text interview technology with which participants are familiar; discuss platform choice as part of the consent agreement. Provide any instructions or tech support information the participant may need.
- Familiarize yourself with communications options in that setting; review archiving function for saving the transcript.
- Make sure you and the participant agree on the expectations for the exchange, using the time–response continuum.
- Familiarize yourself with electronic paralinguistic expressions, emoticons, or other communications shortcuts or slang used by the target population. Decide how you will use these shortcuts to save time and keep the conversation moving.
- Articulate a greater number of questions that elicit shorter responses; break big questions into a series of sub-questions.
- Write out questions or key phrases in advance so you can cut and paste them into the text window to save time and keep the interview flowing.
- Provide any background information in advance so you can move quickly into a dynamic exchange.
- Determine what protocols are needed for the interview and how you will communicate them to the participants.
- Choose at least one person who is not a research participant with whom to practice an interview. After the practice session, make any needed adjustments to wording of questions, use of emoticons, and timing.

PREPARING FOR AN ASYNCHRONOUS TEXT-BASED INTERACTION

Asynchronous interactions can be carried out by email, or by posting in a private forum or blog. Again, you might decide to collect data with an email interview, or connect asynchronously to make plans, answer questions, or follow-up another research activity. In any case, thinking through the ways you communicate will mean you can use any exchange to build trust, rapport, and commitment to the study.

Like the interactions described earlier, asynchronous communications primarily take the form of writing, with the potential for shared images or links to other media. Many of the issues with texting are relevant to this type of interview, with one big exception: while text-chat interactions require close attention to fast timing, the timing in asynchronous interactions is more relaxed. The researcher can be much more flexible and allow for an iterative process in this type of interview.

The interviewer can read and reread the participant's response and think carefully about the next question. Indeed, the main attribute cited in favor of asynchronous interactions is the opportunity for reflection by researcher and participant between question, response, and the next question (Hawkins, 2018). In either synchronous or asynchronous text-based interactions, the researcher needs to design the study carefully and prepare for the interactions.

Structured or unstructured interactions are possible using written exchanges, each with distinct advantages. In a structured interview style, researchers can interview more than one participant at a time because questions can be sent individually to several participants at once (Meho, 2006). In less-structured interactions, participants can more freely discuss general themes, perhaps contributing unexpected perspectives.

The researcher needs to be clear about expectations and gain agreement from participants. The overall time frame for the study should be spelled out, as well as the turnaround time for responses. Do you want participants to respond within 24 hours, or within a week? What should participants expect from you in terms of feedback, probes, or follow-up questions, and within what time frame? The longer the interview, the larger the number of expected iterations and the greater the risk that participants will lose interest or become distracted and not provide complete data.

To prepare for an email interview, do the following:

- In the absence of face-to-face introductions, decide whether you want to share images, a recorded introduction, or other information about yourself and the study. You can link to your research statement, blog, or website so participants can visit to learn more.
- Set up a separate email account to ensure privacy. If you are associated with an institution, use your academic email address.
- Develop an interview schedule and guide. More-structured interactions may be laid out with main questions to be asked at specific intervals, such as each week. A less-structured interview should offer an outline of the themes or topics to be explored within a defined time frame.
- In addition to the informed consent agreement, create a procedural agreement with expectations for length of the interview and turnaround time for responses.
- Enlist at least one person who is not a research participant with whom to practice the interview (or a partial interview). Refine questions and approach as needed.

PREPARING FOR A VIDEO INTERACTION

Not long ago, studios with costly setups were the only way to meet via videoconference. However, desktop and mobile options are common now using low-cost or free online services. These informal video calls or video chats can be carried out almost anywhere.

Movement toward greater access and flexibility for videoconferencing is advantageous for interview researchers with small budgets. Many text-messaging and chat services now allow users to plug in a web camera; other services offer two-way audio, video, and chat in free Internet calls.

Additionally, facilities, including videoconference/integrated classrooms, offices, and meeting rooms, offer high-quality options for research purposes. Multiple cameras and assistance from trained technicians mean videoconferencing facilities enable either close-up or room visibility, can accommodate groups, and allow for complex interactions or the presence of observers. Many businesses, governmental agencies, and educational institutions have invested in such videoconferencing systems. If you need more than the kind of service you can access on your own computer or device, rentals are available at commercial sites such as those that provide office and business services.

Depending on whether the technology is a videoconference facility or video call on a cell phone's tiny screen, the researcher will need to decide whether a close-up, waist-up, or wider picture of the person in the room will work best.

Prepare to interact by video:

- Experiment with setup and camera positioning options.
- Review other features, such as text chat or areas for presenting visuals, and determine whether or how to use them.
- Decide how you want to present yourself. Just as in a face-to-face live interview, the background, your attire, and style all convey messages.
- Carefully review questions or interview guide, or position on the screen, so you can minimize the need to look down at notes. Make the best 'virtual eye contact' possible.
- Discuss options and parameters for the participant's web camera. Is it acceptable for the participant to turn the camera off and use audio only?
- If using a facility where others (e.g., technicians, camera operators) will be present, determine policies for confidentiality. Depending on the setting, technical personnel, and policies, you may decide to ask more sensitive questions in another way.
- Enlist at least one person who is not a research participant with whom to practice the interview (or a partial interview). Refine questions and approach as needed.

PREPARING TO INTERACT IN A WEB CONFERENCING MEETING SPACE

'Videoconferencing' and 'web conferencing' might seem synonymous, but there are some distinctions. Here, we use the term *videoconferencing* to refer to a platform where the primary interaction is with communicants on camera. Online meeting or *web conferencing* platforms integrate text chat, audio, and videoconferencing functions with various combinations of tools that may include shared screens, applications, and/or whiteboards. The entire interaction is captured and archived, thus providing an audiovisual data record for the researcher to review and analyze. The robust and interactive potential of a web conferencing platform make them ideal for visual elicitation or for participatory enacted research.

When people log in to an online meeting space, they typically see a screen divided into different areas, with space for text chat, various toolbars for drawing and writing, and icons linking to other services. The central workspace can be used to share written or visual details about the study using PowerPoint slides, diagrams, photographs, or other visual elements. Depending on the level of access the researcher sets, the participant has access to some or all of the tools that allow for content sharing or generation.

Some web conferencing platforms are marketed for online meetings in business or for instructional purposes. Some are fee-based enterprise or subscription services, so it might be possible that you could gain access through your academic institution. Some services often offer free or low-cost versions for personal use.

Multimedia Elicitation or Enacted Research Events

To plan for data collection in an online meeting space, review the various communication features to determine which to use to convey questions, and what options to make available to participants. See the points provided earlier in this chapter to prepare for using the text and videoconference applications in the interview. See Chapters 11 and 12 for more about the visual research potential for interactions in a web conferencing space. Think about how visual, verbal, and/or text options could be used in your research.

Elicitation: Interviews on a web conferencing platform

Elicitation in a web conferencing platform can be more flexible than in an online interaction that relies on spoken words. Questions, discussion themes, and/or diagrams, images, or media clips for elicitation can be presented on PowerPoint slides or other documents that can be shared from your own screen.

Preparation for structured or semi-structured interactions in a web conferencing space entails outlining questions in advance. By preparing question prompts, you are able to focus on the conversation, without the need to cut and paste from another document or type during the interview. Interview questions or themes can be presented one by one by advancing through the slides or pages. It is also possible to move back and forth through the pre-set questions if changing the sequence is desirable. You can speak and explain the questions, and the interviewee can also read or view the prompts. Because the medium is flexible, additional questions, follow-ups, and/or probes can be either spoken or written during the interview.

For less-structured interactions, themes for discussion can be written, drawn, uploaded, or linked to on your shared screen during the interview. You can speak and write the question or pose a question related to a visual element presented on the shared screen.

Enacted research on a web conferencing platform

Three other components found in most online meeting platforms can also be beneficial for creative activities and/or collaboration with enacted methods: the shared whiteboard, shared applications, and the web tour. The whiteboard allows the researcher and/or participant to draw on the screen. The whiteboard can be used to generate or build on existing models, visual maps, or diagrams. In studies that relate to software or other technologies, shared applications allow the participant, for example, to demonstrate how he or she would solve a particular problem. The web tour option can be used to view websites or media that may illustrate some aspect of the research phenomenon.

All elements the researcher intends to share must be selected and tested in advance of the interview. Any intellectual property issues, such as permissions for use of images or media, should be obtained before finalizing the interview plans.

Get Ready to Use Web Conferencing Tools

The main issue that is both an advantage and a disadvantage of the meeting space is the diversity of tools, which some researchers may find overwhelming. With a little practice, researchers can overcome this potential challenge. Highly engaged participants may be less likely to exit out of the interview prematurely. Diverse options for communication make the online meeting environment an ideal choice for the interviewer who wants to cultivate answers from and with participants as the metaphorical gardener or explore answers by traveling through the interview with the participant.

Once the tools, process, and approach have been selected, preparation steps include the following:

- Review the interactive features of the platform. Which of them can be used in the course of the interaction? For example, could you ask participants to draw or diagram answers to some questions?
- Check audio features. If the space allows for only one speaker at a time, determine protocols for turn-taking in conversation and conduct a preliminary run-through.
- Check recording/archiving features. You may want to set up an external voice recorder as a backup to ensure audio capture.
- Select or develop relevant diagrams, illustrations, examples, photographs, visual maps, and so on that can be used to show, rather than ask or tell, the participant what you want to discuss.

- Platforms allow for the use of media, such as video clips. If you are incorporating media, make sure you can easily access, run, and close out of the media element, and return to the main discussion area.
- Enlist at least one person who is not a research participant with whom to practice the research interaction. Record and review the practice session. Refine questions and approach as needed.

PREPARING TO INTERVIEW IN AN IMMERSIVE VIRTUAL ENVIRONMENT

While not as common as the other technologies discussed here, virtual reality technology is growing. The capability to create realistic, life-like social experiences, make these technologies popular for training purposes (Taylor, Valladares, Siepser, & Yantis, 2020). They can also be adapted for enacted research.

Some types of virtual reality allow researchers and participants to interact within a game or 3-D environment. These might use a web interface or a gaming unit. Others involve participants who use VR displays in a laboratory setting.

Virtual reality technology includes multiple components such as head-mounted displays (HMDs) used in combination with tracking systems. The HMDs enable changing head position to be reflected in a three-dimensional visual landscape. (O'Connor, 2019, p. 523)

O'Connor's data collection for a study about e-learning included:

... two video cameras, one roaming alongside a learner and one on a tripod in the corner of the VR space, to document all user activity. Learners also wore a wireless lapel mic for audio capture. Learners often narrated their experience – often ranging from 20 to 30 minutes – providing a running commentary of their experience. Researchers documented all VR interactions, taking field notes throughout the experience. After learners completed the experience, or chose to stop, we conducted semi-structured interviews with them, which lasted approximately 15–30 minutes. (O'Connor, 2019, p. 524)

Preparing to interact with participants in virtual reality or a game can include creating (or updating) an avatar that represents you as a researcher. Williams (2007) calls the avatar a 'graphical pseudo-presence.' The avatar 'explicitly communicates a wealth of information upon the observer's online identity. The choice of pseudonym for the day and the dress and stature of the avatar chosen impact on how the observed react to the observer' (p. 11). Researchers need to decide how to present themselves as avatars, based on the focus and the setting of the study. Researchers can embody their online identity any way they see fit (Dunn & Guadagno, 2012), to appear in a way that others in the game or virtual world will accept.

Preparation, then, includes learning the social norms of participants' culture(s) and deciding whether to appear as a new or experienced member of that culture – or as an outsider.

Preparation for Research in a Virtual Reality or Game

Steps for creation of a virtual reality space or simulation is beyond the scope of this book. However, gamification is showing early results for engaging participants and in particular, for encouraging them to complete an online form or questionnaire. Respondents found gamified surveys to be more interesting, fun, enjoyable, satisfying, and easy to fill out than a conventional web survey (Keusch, 2020). In their discussion of the potential, Keusch points to Adamou's (2019) taxonomy of types of research gamification:

> She mainly distinguishes between research games (or 'hard gamification') and gamified surveys (or 'soft gamification'). Research games are defined as full-fledged games created for a research purpose that include all ingredients of a game (i.e., goals, autonomy opportunities, rules, and feedback), and data are collected as participants move through the game, take actions, make decisions, and answer questions embedded in the game. She identified six types of research games that are not mutually exclusive in how they can be implemented: (1) avatar-based research games (i.e., participants create avatars and make choices for this avatar), (2) role-play research games (i.e., participants have to make decisions for a predefined character, e.g., the CEO of a company), (3) narrative-based research games (i.e., participants navigate through a narrated storyline relevant to the research context), (4) text-based research games (i.e., only text is used to convey the game and interact with participants), (5) simulation-based research games (i.e., participants go through simulated scenarios, e.g., building an ideal home), and (6) questions as mini-games (i.e., stylizing an individual question as a full game). (Keusch, 2020, p. 4)

For researchers working within a game or other VR platform, these steps will be helpful:

- Test your 'image' with colleagues or friends to assess whether you convey the persona you intend to present to research participants. Enlist at least one person who is not a research participant with whom to practice the interview or research interaction. Refine questions and approach as needed.
- Familiarize yourself with the selected virtual world or game's functions and norms, including movement, teleporting, and sharing items with other avatars.
- Decide where and how to conduct the interview and/or interaction. If you create a space within a game or web-based environment, consider making it private and requiring permission to enter (make sure space is large enough so that audio exchanges are out of range of others who could eavesdrop).
- Make sure the participant has all information needed, including meeting place.

- Offer to meet in advance so both researcher and participant are familiar with the VR or game setting and features.
- Decide whether to use text chat or audio features for dialogue.
- If you are using text chat, see the suggestions for text-based interactions.
- If using VoIP or telephone, check audio operations. Arrange for audio recording.

——————— RESEARCH CAMEO 9.1 ———————

Researcher 1 is designing a study using extant data, so they are not preparing to interact with participants. Still, they will be interacting with others so are looking at ways to improve online communication skills. They realize that the informal, casual communications they are accustomed to using with friends will not be appropriate when discussing access to databases.

Researcher 2 is designing a study that involves eliciting data through one-to-one and group online interviews. They plan to conduct interviews on a videoconference platform. While they have participated in video calls and chats, they have not been responsible for managing the platform for serious matters. They have not led groups on a videoconference platform. They are scheduling at least two 1–1 and small group pre-interview practice sessions. While they typically have a 'just do it' attitude about technology, they plan to watch tutorials on the platform to ensure they know all the features and are able to address any problems.

Researcher 3 is designing a study that will involve generating data with aspiring and successful qualitative researchers by conducting an online workshop and collecting data from consenting participants. As noted in Chapter 8, they were able to partner with a university writing program for this study. However, this means they will need to use the university's web conferencing and e-learning platform. They are not familiar with this platform, so will take advantage of the tutorials and help sessions offered by the IT department.

Researcher 4 is designing a study that will include observations of an online academic writing group and email interviews with selected authors and editors. Their study will involve primarily text-based communications. They do not need to learn new technology to move forward.

GETTING READY TO INTERACT WITH PARTICIPANTS

The online researcher using elicitation or enacted approaches has three kinds of preparations to make:

- preparing questions, discussion themes, or creative activities a propos the empirical and theoretical basis of the study
- preparing for the use of selected technology

- personal preparation needed to serve as guide and facilitator of the interview or research event – as the person behind the monitor in a human-to-human conversation with a purpose.

Defining Roles

Earlier sections have explored researchers' roles in terms of the miner who excavates information, the gardener who cultivates exchange, or the traveler who journeys with the participant (see Chapters 3 and 4). Researchers need to have clear intentions in mind. They also need to consider how participants perceive these intentions. Rubin and Rubin (2012) point out that people relate to one another through culturally understood roles in which obligations and responsibilities are known to both parties. In establishing an acceptable role as researcher, it is important to decide how you want to present yourself and how much of your own experience you want to share. In the online interaction, unless a full videoconferencing system is used, your visual image may be limited and, as a result, may seem even more significant. What image do you want to convey as it relates to your role in this study?

Epoche, Self-Reflection, and Preparing to Listen

As the researcher, it is important to approach each interaction with a clear and fresh perspective; this is what phenomenological researchers call **epoche** (Moustakas, 1994). Whatever methodological tradition guides the study, starting with an open mind is important for data collection through interview research.

Moustakas (1994) points out that epoche is 'preparation for deriving new knowledge' by listening without expectations for any particular outcome (p. 85). 'In the epoche, we set aside our prejudgments, biases, and preconceived ideas about things' (p. 85). It is, of course, impossible to pretend that researchers have no biases and can listen to answers without sifting through their own experiences and cultural lenses (Berger, 2013). Researchers need to continually examine their own understandings, biases, and reactions (Jacobson & Mustafa, 2019). Moustakas calls this being 'transparent to ourselves' (p. 86).

The attitude of epoche emerges when you are self-aware and set aside time to mentally refresh before beginning an interaction with one or more participants. The attitude of epoche emerges when the researcher has a sense of deep respect and appreciation for each participant's unique contribution. When online researchers are confident about the intended direction for the research event and the smooth application of the ICTs, they enter ready to listen deeply, openly, and respectfully to each participant. With ongoing self-reflection and a mindset of epoche, each new interaction is a fresh experience. The researcher who has made a conscious effort to set preconceived notions aside may hear or observe subtle or profound nuances that might otherwise be overlooked.

—————————————— RESEARCH CAMEO 9.2 ——————————————

Researcher 1 is designing a study using extant data, so they are not preparing to interact with participants.

Researcher 2 is designing a study that involves eliciting data through one-to-one and group online interviews. As a new researcher, they want to feel confident in the role. They also want to feel capable of conducting interviews in a way that does not reveal emotions or reactions that could intimidate participants. They plan to schedule several practice interviews, for content as well as technology. They will ask friends or fellow students to be painfully honest, and to make constructive criticisms.

Researcher 3 is designing a study that will involve generating data with aspiring and successful qualitative researchers by conducting an online workshop and collecting data from consenting participants. Like Researcher 2, they plan to ask friends or fellow students to attend a demo class and give candid feedback on pacing, flow, and level of **interactivity**.

Researcher 4 will conduct email interviews. They will craft the questions ahead of time, and ask friends or fellow students to tell them whether these questions are clear and jargon-free, and invite substantive responses.

SUMMARY OF KEY CONCEPTS

Preparing for online research with participants involves personal, theoretical, and technical steps. Exchanges throughout the process – whether routine or substantive – should be seen as meaningful aspects of the overall research relationship. The relationship begins when you describe the study, clarify expectations, and negotiate informed consent agreements (see Chapters 5 and 6). The process of planning for the interview or other research event offers important opportunities to communicate and build trust, which are foundational to successful research.

Although new tools for communication will undoubtedly appear, the basic distinctions of synchronous and asynchronous, visual, and text-based interactions will likely persist. Decisions about the ICT and means of communication are closely interwoven with the research purpose, methodology, and theoretical framework. There is no simple recipe for how to mix them; finding the right synergy will be part of the learning and new knowledge that result from the study.

DISCUSSION QUESTIONS AND EXERCISES

- Identify an ICT you are interested in using for an online study with participants. Discuss the specific options and features available for communicating, how you would use them, and steps you would take to prepare.
- Locate an article that describes qualitative research conducted with the ICT you want to use. (Keep in mind that you might need to look in journals that serve other fields or disciplines.) Based on what you learned from the article, what new steps should you add to your plans?
- Create a planning timeline and checklist for an online interview that uses the ICT you chose in the above assignment.
- Discuss the concept of epoche. What could you do to clear your mind in readiness for an online interaction with a participant?
- Look at the Research Cameos for Chapter 9. Did these researchers miss any steps for preparation? What would you advise them?

SECTION IV

COLLECTING QUALITATIVE DATA ONLINE

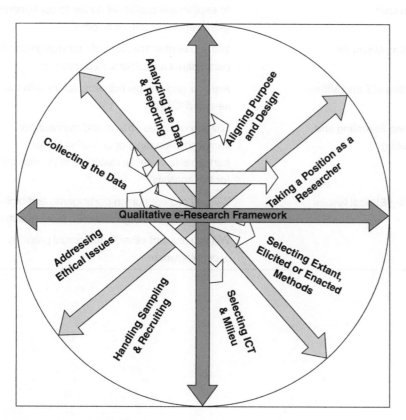

Figure IV.1   Collecting qualitative data online

When the design stage is complete and the approvals have been won, when the participants, sites, and/or materials have been found and permissions granted, the time comes to collect the data. In this part of the book the design and conduct of studies using extant, elicited, or enacted methods are discussed. Once again, it is important to consider these activities in the context of all the dimensions of the Qualitative e-Research Framework. Some key questions are outlined in Table IV.1.

Table IV.1 Analysis and reporting issues in relation to the Qualitative e-Research Framework

	Analyzing the Data and Reporting
Aligning Purpose and Design	How do you plan to work within methodological traditions and paradigms when retrieving and reviewing materials, conducting the interviews, observations or research events?
	How do you plan to maintain a focus on the research problem during the data collection stage?
Taking a Position as a Researcher	Are you clear about your position? Do you need to explain any positional issues to participants, gatekeepers, or site managers?
Selecting Methods	Will you explain the rationale for design choices to participants and others, as appropriate?
Selecting ICT and Milieu	Are you, and any participants, adept with the selected ICTs?
Handling Sampling and Recruiting	Will you describe criteria and methods for sampling, recruiting, or selecting human participants or online materials to provide context for the analysis?
Handling Ethical Issues	Will you protect human participants and digital identities by avoiding traceable direct quotations?
	Will you respect others' intellectual property and avoid plagiarism?

10

Finding and Collecting Extant Data Online

HIGHLIGHTS

In today's world, an extensive array of extant data is available for researchers to examine. Not only do we have data being created every minute of the day by Internet users, governments, businesses, and cultural institutions, we also have historical documents being scanned and uploaded into libraries and archives. Of course large datasets, or Big Data, add sample sizes qualitative researchers have never before been able to analyze. Extant data analysis can stand alone or be used with other qualitative (multimodal) or quantitative (mixed methods) research.

OBJECTIVES

After reading and reflecting on this chapter, you will be able to:

- distinguish between types of extant data
- plan a sampling plan
- explain modes of collecting extant data
- explain modes of analysis for extant data
- consider how decisions made about the type of data collection relate to other design decisions for the online study.

IN PERSPECTIVE: DOCUMENTS IN RESEARCH

Not that long ago, the term 'documents' referred to pieces of paper and 'archives' referred to the places where these paper documents were saved and protected. Researchers with an interest in documents conducted their reading of often fragile materials in the library or archive center. I conducted some research of this kind for my master's degree thesis (Cocke & Salmons, 1993; Salmons, 1992). I reviewed documents in the Cornell University archive which I could access as part of the University staff. Boxes were brought up one by one and I could dig through and read correspondence, notes, and look at photographs about the professor whose work from half a century earlier I was studying. Given my interest in culture and policy, I also visited the Rockefeller Foundation archive center to read the other side of the correspondence exchange between the professor and his grants officer to learn about the funding decisions around the project central to my study. To access the Rockefeller Foundation archives required an application, and only a limited number of scholars were given permission in a given time frame because archive staff were needed to retrieve the specific documents on request. The archivists wore white gloves to protect carefully preserved documents.

For this thesis project the document analysis component was used to provide a historical context and foundation for an action research case study that included other types of data collected through participant observation in a contemporary program. Using the language of this book – which I had not yet articulated – the study combined extant and enacted methods.

Fast-forward to today. To do the research I conducted previously I would still need to visit the archive center to access the correspondence, memos, and other original artifacts. However, many of the records have been digitized (see http://dimes.rockarch.org). As with the Rockefeller Foundation archives example, many but not all documents from the pre-Internet era have been scanned and secured in electronic archives. As with my experience, some archives are available for access by almost anyone while others are private and require permission for access.

Why Use Extant Data?

The widespread use of the Internet and the volume of material from the past and the present available online have increased the interest in varied forms of document or materials analysis research. Three main reasons motivate researchers to use extant data:

1. when data is readily available to answer the question
2. when it is advantageous to avoid researcher effects, that is, there is no influence of a researcher, who might be perceived as an outsider or intruder
3. when participants are not available.

Sometimes extant data collection is necessary because participants are not available for other types of interactions. For example, this team of Brazilian researchers intended to conduct their study in person because they planned to study at-risk youth who emerged from homelessness due to the development of a work cooperative. After the COVID-19 pandemic made in-person research impossible, they could not find a way to reach the participant group. The group simply had no online footprint or contact information. To continue the study, they analyzed existing materials that had been written about this youth cooperative. They described their dilemma:

> Before the COVID-19 pandemic, our planned research methods relied on interviews, observations and ethnography with at-risk young adults in a project that helped them move out of homelessness. In other words, we needed to collect information through our direct contact with our research participants. However, after the first cases of the disease in Brazil, our university suspended all field research that required the contact or circulation of individuals. With this new reality, we pondered over our possibilities of remote work. We began reading and revising the previous literature written about the Cooperative, which is abundant, as well as searching for images, videos and past projects online. At the same time, we analysed articles, documents, videos and webinars about remote research. (Goldstein, 2020; Goldstein, Vasques, & Santos, 2020, pp. 114, 118)

Types of Extant Data

Types of materials are organized here into three broad categories:

1. *Historical materials.* Materials from the pre-Internet era are scanned into digital formats and posted online. News or magazine articles, letters, diaries, oral histories, maps, census or government records, photographs, speech, radio or film clips are just some of the kinds of materials now available electronically. Scanned documents are often not searchable so text mining or word searches might not work. Extensive collections of historical materials can be accessed from libraries, museums, national or foundation archives, historical societies, and other sites. Some collections require permission, others are open to anyone. Historical materials can also be privately held: families have pictures, writings, and other treasures from past generations.
2. *Contemporary materials.* Materials we will classify as *contemporary* are those created in the digital age. Materials created in the twenty-first century are likely to have an electronic version, even if they were also released in print. For example, a business

researcher can find annual reports that were distributed as print brochures but also posted on the company's website. While you can find contemporary materials in a library and other archives, you can also find them open access, on the public web.

3. *Emergent materials*. Materials we will describe as *emergent* are those being created by users every minute of the day when Internet users log on and post. This wide range of materials includes uploaded documents or media, posted comments and questions for online discussion forums, groups, games, communities, blogs and/or social media. Karamshuk, Shaw, Brownlie, and Sastry (2017, p. 33) observed:

> Social media has created vast amounts of potential qualitative research material – in the form of the observations and utterances of its population of users – that social scientists cannot ignore. Unlike the responses to survey questions, such material is not elicited as part of the research process, nor is its volume limited by the constraints and practicalities of the sample survey.

These vast amounts of data are popularly known as Big Data. Yes, qualitative researchers can use Big Data! There is even a signifier: *Big Qual*. Brower, Jones, Osborne-Lampkin, Hu, and Park-Gaghan (2019, p. 2) define Big Qual as: 'data sets containing either primary or secondary qualitative data from at least 100 participants.' Giaxoglou categorizes large or Big Data by their sources (Giaxoglou, 2017, p. #8957):

1. Public Data: data typically held by governments, governmental organizations, and local communities.
2. Private Data: data held by private firms, non-profit organizations, and individuals that cannot readily be imputed from public sources (website browsing and mobile phone usage).
3. Data Exhaust: ambient data that are passively collected, non-core data with limited or zero value to the original data-collection partner – but can be combined for new meanings. It includes tracking for searches and information-seeking behavior, which can be used to infer people's questions, needs, desires, or intentions.
4. Community Data: distillation of unstructured data – especially text – into dynamic networks that capture social trends. Typical community data include consumer reviews on products, voting buttons (such as, 'I find this review useful') and Twitter feeds. These community data can then be distilled for meaning to infer patterns in social structure.
5. Self-Quantification Data: revealed by the individual through quantifying personal actions and behaviors. A common form of self-quantification data is that obtained through wearable devices or smartphones that monitor exercise and movement, data which are then uploaded and can then be tracked and aggregated.
6. Image data: aerial and satellite images, video, photographs, and artifacts.

What types of data, from what sources, will fit your study? Consider the possibilities and create a sampling strategy to guide your selection.

SPOT CHECK

What type(s) of extant data interest you? The term extant data covers a wide range of possible types and forms of data, from many kinds of sources. Use the three main categories – historical, contemporary, and emergent – to help you narrow down the choices suitable for your study. Whether your study relies on extant materials for data, as part of your literature review, or simply as background information, an understanding of what is available on your topic of study will be beneficial.

RESEARCH CAMEO 10.1

Researchers 1 and 4 will make use of extant data.

Researcher 1 plans to search and export lists of references from journal databases as the first stage, then sort by keywords for methodologies, methods, and publication dates. Given that they plan to look at trends over a period of time, they will encompass both historical and contemporary data. They will be reviewing records from scholarly journals originally published in print, then scanned in or digitized, as well as journals published in the digital era. While some journals are open access, they will use private databases, available through an academic library. Researcher 1 is enrolled at a university where they can utilize this private database.

Researcher 4 plans to observe a writing group's social media interactions, and their online meetings. They categorize this work as being primarily emergent because they will study a group that is currently active. The group is private, members only, so their writings and conversations are not accessible to the public. They do share tips and resources with each other on social media, but writings and support-related interactions are private.

CREATING A SAMPLING STRATEGY

A sampling strategy for materials has some similarities with a sampling strategy for human participants. (See Chapter 7 for more about sampling.) In both situations you need to determine whether a homogeneous or heterogeneous collection is appropriate to the study. Is it important to use a variety of materials from different perspectives and perhaps different media or is it preferable to compare similar materials that adhere to a common format or content? In both situations you need to develop inclusion and exclusion criteria.

Inclusion Criteria

Without inclusion and exclusion criteria, you might find that you collect large amounts of materials that might not be directly relevant to your study. Initial questions are:

- What types of materials are needed to answer the research question and fulfill the purpose of the study?
  - o Visual, verbal or aural, multimedia, and/or written?
  - o Historical, contemporary, and/or emergent?

- What keywords, hashtags, or other identifiers should I use to organize my search?
  - o Online materials are organized, even though they do not necessarily follow a consistent system. Hashtags can help you find relevant social media posts. You can then pare down the collection by imposing additional parameters, such as time frames or original writings versus links or reposts.
  - o Keywords are familiar to anyone who has used an online library database. If the document does not have author-supplied keywords, using word search or 'find' features, you can quickly sort large quantities of materials to find those most relevant. Note that some scanned documents might not be searchable.

- Do I have access to these materials, or will permission be needed? From whom?
  - o Some materials are open access, free and open to the public, while others require subscription, membership or association with an institution (such as a university). Some, which contain sensitive or confidential information (such as proprietary, medical, or financial records), have limited access and require permission for access and for use in research.
  - o Social media sites are commercially owned and have varied policies governing access to data. If log-ins are required, review any terms of membership or user guidelines first before you plan to collect extant data from posted comments, discussions, images, or media on social media or other interactive sites. If you want to study an online group or community, where possible, discuss research goals with the moderator and/or members and act accordingly. (See Chapter 5 for a discussion of ethical issues involved with user-generated data in research.)

What is available that meets my inclusion criteria?

Once the desired types of materials have been identified it is essential to conduct a preliminary scan to determine whether they are indeed available and complete. This important first step should be carried out before the research proposal is finalized because even though it would seem every kind of topic would be covered in documents available online, that is not always the case.

To contribute to the study, materials need to be authentic, and directed toward the purpose of the study. The following issues, identified by Guthrie (2010, p. 101) about documents generally, are adapted to address particular issues when assessing the adequacy and value to the study of materials found online.

1. **Incomplete records**. This may be due to the fact that 'filing and archiving are low status activities.' There may be gaps in the records that have been scanned and/or uploaded.

2. **Biased data**. 'While bias is not necessarily deliberate, available data is usually collected for organisational and not scientific purposes.' The purpose of the researcher is not the purpose of the organization and materials may be presented in a way that showcases success and that obscures challenges, shortcomings, or conflict.

3. **Intentional incompleteness**. Materials, especially those posted on the public web, may omit financial or other information critical to understanding the entire story. 'Written records, such as minutes of meetings, might contain little of the background discussion of issues or the different views that were considered. Decision makers looking to their future might only file material that they think will reflect well on them and destroy anything questionable.'

─────────────── RESEARCH CAMEO 10.2 ───────────────

Researchers 1 and 4 will make use of extant data.

Researcher 1 Given the purpose of the study, even though articles include images and diagrams, they are outside the scope of their current research. They might want to study changes in the use of diagrams and visualizations in a future inquiry, so while they will exclude visual data now, they will make notes when they encounter interesting exemplars.

Researcher 4 Given that it is a writing group, they expect the data to be primarily in text form. However, they will collect outlines, visual maps, diagrams or other ways they organize their work.

EXTANT DATA COLLECTION

We will explore two types of online extant data collection: *materials analysis* and *unobtrusive observation*. While the terms 'document analysis' or 'Big Data analysis' have been commonly used to describe the review of written texts, here the term 'materials analysis' is used in acknowledgment of the diverse visual media as well as written materials available to review online. As defined in Chapter 5, in unobtrusive observation, sometimes called 'non-reactive' research, the researcher collects data without interacting with participants.

Collecting Online Materials

Let's look at two basic ways you can collect extant data: manual downloading or web scraping. There are other forms of data collection that are not simple to use by individual researchers, such as access to the back-end software of the social media or other site. 'With this kind of access, full sets of data – metadata, user-provided content, network structures – are directly available. Most researchers with this kind of access to data work either in the research labs of the service providers themselves or in research projects that are collaborating with the service providers' (Prandner & Seymer, 2020, p. 2).

You are familiar with downloading, you do it every day! If you are using libraries or archives, you will most likely use those familiar skills to download materials you locate in relation to topics or key words. Downloading extant materials is a technique to use when selecting specific items, collections, or lists. If you are collecting large sets of data, these manual approaches are impractical. and you might want to use web scraping. 'Web scraping describes a set of techniques that are used to automate the collection of data from the web' (Munzert & Nyhuis, 2020, p. 389). You might find that manual downloading, non-automated forms of data collection may not result in what is considered Big Data, but 'they may well produce quantities of data that are too large to manage effectively with traditional qualitative methods' (Munzert & Nyhuis, 2020, p. 389). Munzert and Nyhuis explain:

> Automating the data-collection process requires researchers to use software that will scan, filter, and collect select data from the web or other searchable texts. For instance, web scraping uses software to read the underlying HTML and CSS markup of a webpage, looking for tags or strings of text that match certain patterns, then 'mines' or 'scrapes' the text from the matching tags and strings, saving them in separate files or spreadsheet columns for later analysis. (2020, pp. 390–391)

For example, if you are using an archive for letters and diaries from the 1918 flu epidemic, once you find ones that fit your inclusion criteria, you can simply download them and organize them on your computer. However, if you are looking for posts and media from the 2020 COVID-19 pandemic, you might find that a simple download is inadequate. Even if you limit your search to a particular topic, such as *parenting during the 2020 COVID-19 pandemic,* you might find the collection of materials is of a scale larger than you can manage with conventional qualitative data management and analysis techniques. Daniel Turner suggests that even off-the-shelf data analysis software programs can help qualitative researchers extend their reach and understanding of the scope and characteristics of the research problem:

> Qualitative research could use larger data sources if a tool could at least speed up the work of a human researcher. While we aim in qualitative research to focus on the small, often this means focusing on a very small population group or geographical area. With faster coding tools we could design qualitative research with the same resources that samples more diverse populations to see how universal or variable trends are. (Turner, 2020)

Analytic techniques for this kind of research are beyond the scope of this book; however, some simple tools can help. For example, Google Sheets has an open-source add-in that helps you download, organize, and archive Tweets. N-Capture is a browser extension that allows you to download any online source and save it to your NVivo data analysis package. This checklist, adapted from the SAGE Research Methods *Research Project Planner* (2021), suggests key questions that will be useful when considering how to use Big Data or other datasets in your research:

- Can you access the dataset(s) in readily available downloadable form?
- Have you arranged access when you have to go through a registration/permission process?
- Have you gone through the dataset and satisfied yourself that it contains information on the topic or problem that you plan to study? Does it fit your inclusion criteria?
- Have you examined the sampling basis of the surveys or other processes used to generate the data so that you understand:
  - the sample design
  - the nature of the population(s) from which the sample(s) were drawn
  - the nature of the sampling frame employed and the extent to which it covers the sample of interest
  - the achieved proportion of cases actually yielding data and any issues this poses for interpretation of the dataset.
- Are there good metadata descriptions available for the datasets you wish to use?

UNOBTRUSIVE OBSERVATION CONDUCTED ONLINE

The researcher using these methods is a passive observer rather than co-discussant. Typically, this kind of observer takes an etic role, that is, an outsider perspective, while a participant observer takes an emic, or insider, perspective. (See Chapter 2 for more on participant observation.) Online settings allow observational researchers to be the 'fly on the wall' (Whiteman, 2007, p. 4). Unobtrusive observations are related to materials analysis because the observer can collect data by downloading or copying relevant materials from an online discussion, group, or community. Importantly, the observer also makes field notes to record what is taking place as well as the researcher's perceptions of relationships and events.

Bowen (2009, p. 31) suggests that 'unobtrusive' and 'non-reactive' methods mean those being studied are 'unaffected by the research process'. He suggests that an event may proceed differently because those involved know it is being observed. Hine points out that observations can be preferable to interviews when research focuses on sensitive areas, or particularly vulnerable groups, since it can be a considerable imposition to ask respondents to recite their situation for the researchers' benefit (Hine, 2011, p. 3).

An unanswered question for online researchers relates to the potential impact of a 'cyberspace effect' combined with the 'Hawthorne effect' (Sharpe, Kool, Whittaker, & Ameratunga, 2019). Does knowing they are being researched in cyberspace make people more open and willing to communicate, or does it make them more secretive? Does the known presence of an observer (or an interviewer) cause people to modify their behaviors or positions in reaction to being under scrutiny? Might they withhold socially unacceptable views; act the way they think researchers want them to act; become self-conscious about their posts being collected; or just modify activities to accommodate the presence of a researcher in the online discussion space (Burles & Bally, 2018; Hennell, Limmer, & Piacentini, 2020)?

Challenges for the online researcher may include the nature of dynamic websites which configure the website based upon earlier interaction and make it questionable whether it is possible for an observer to log in multiple times and see the same site set-up (Nørskov & Rask, 2011). In other words, based on searches or clicks, the site may only present the range of information or activities that correspond to the previous visit's preferences.

Planning an Online Observation

When planning to conduct an observation, first consider what purpose it will serve. What site will best fit the needs of the study and serve as the field of observation? Are the possible options public sites, private member-only sites, or is it unclear whether users expect the content they post to be accessed by others or not? What are the norms, user agreements, or other guidelines for those who participate on the site generally or in the specific discussion? (See Chapter 3 for more on selection of the online research setting.) What user characteristics are appropriate for the study? Are there special factors in terms of at-risk or vulnerable populations, or sensitive topics that require additional steps or ethical considerations? (See Chapters 4 and 5 for more about research ethics.)

Will the observation serve as a preliminary foundation for a study that will include other kinds of data? In this case, the researcher aims to build familiarity with the topics being discussed or the ways users interact in the online setting. The researcher may be looking for intriguing examples or unusual behaviors to discuss with participants in future interviews. Alternatively, are the observations to be conducted after other data have been collected in order to gain a context for participants' comments or to better understand situations or points they discussed in an interview?

Another option: will the observation be conducted in conjunction with a search for documents and visual materials to download and analyze? In this case researcher discussions and exchanges being observed may help to provide a sense of the importance or priority for any reports or articles posted in the social networking site or community. The researcher may want to look for community users' understandings, agreement, or disagreement with the documents in question.

In these two circumstances the researcher may have specific questions or concerns to explore through the observation that will reinforce or counter what is learned through other data. These questions may be used to construct a guide or system used to organize examples, quotes or notes recorded based on the observation. This guide forms a structure for the observation that allows for some consistency between sites, or between dates of visits to the same site.

In a third broad type, the observations are the main source of data to be collected for the study. This researcher will most likely give more attention as needed to observe behaviors, activities, or content creation over a period of time. The observation could use both structured and unstructured approaches. The observation could be structured to correspond with dimensions of the research question, with types of participants or sites, or the frequency of certain kinds of activities or posts. For example, Stiver et al. (2015) used the literature review to facilitate development of a list of keywords relevant to their social media research (e.g. community and crowdfunding, Spacehive). They found that 'use of these keywords helped pinpoint the number of fields involved in civic crowdfunding research (e.g. economics, urban planning, new media) and hone in on dominant themes, debates, platforms, and projects' (Stiver et al., 2015, p. 254). Unstructured observation could aim to uncover the subtle nuances of meaning in the behavior of social actors (Nørskov & Rask, 2011).

Mulhall (2003) considers the conventional view that structured observations fit a positivist paradigm while unstructured observations fit an interpretivist paradigm:

> 'Structured observers' are attempting to remain objective and not contaminate the data with their own preconceptions, whereas 'unstructured observers' carrying with them the tenets of the naturalistic paradigm would contend that it is impossible to separate researcher from 'researched'. (Mulhall, 2003, p. 307)

She points out the limitation of this binary view when considering face-to-face observations and the kinds of roles researchers take. In an online environment where there may be a large volume of activity and a fast pace of diverse posting by users, some degree of structure may be useful, particularly for a new researcher. Here we are thinking about the roles of observers in light of several criteria. In this chapter the focus is on unobtrusive observations where the researcher does not participate or interact with those creating posts or records. Where possible the researcher obtains permission from or agreement with group owners or moderators. The researcher respects the norms, terms of use, and any other parameters existing for the site or group.

Decisions about the level of structure, discussed elsewhere in relation to research with participants, are also relevant here. Are you looking for very specific activities or exemplars, or are you open to a wide range of possibilities? See Figure 10.1 for a depiction of options.

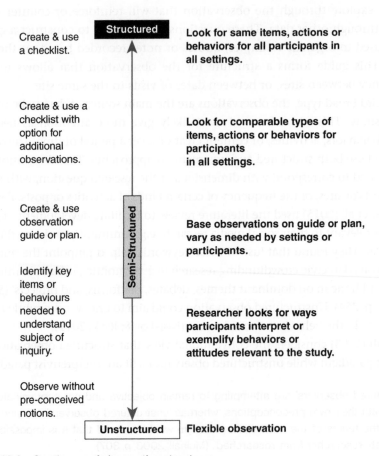

Figure 10.1 Continuum of observation structures

—————————————————— RESEARCH CAMEO 10.3 ——————————————————

Researcher 4 wants to observe an online writing group as part of their data collection. While they negotiated permission and consent, they do not plan to interact with the group members during their meetings. They are considering two options, either structured or unstructured:

1. **Conduct a structured observation**. They identify specific time frames for the observation. They draw key themes from the literature and align them with what is learned from a preliminary scan of the community. They construct an observation guide so they can track discussions and posts during the planned time frames. They intend to identify interview questions based on this observation and then to conduct the second stage of the study with group members willing to meet one-to-one.

2. **Conduct an unstructured observation**. They observe the group with an open mind, recording data specific to the research questions. They plan to keep an open mind to any topic discussed in the group.

FIELD NOTES IN AN ONLINE OBSERVATION

Face-to-face researchers in the field need to make choices about where to focus their field notes, to distinguish between descriptions of people and actions and dialog as a representation of something that was said. Online researchers do not face that dichotomy since dialog in the form of posts is typically conducted in writing and the researcher can view features of the setting and the dialog simultaneously. Hine (2011) notes another advantage for online researchers: rich data is available for almost any social researcher with the added advantage of being ready transcribed. Written exchanges and materials related to the research purpose and questions can be downloaded or copied directly into a computer-assisted qualitative data analysis software (CAQDAS) program. (See the companion website for links to resources and CAQDAS programs.)

Even so, it is necessary to keep field notes. While the descriptions of the people and setting may be recorded using posted materials or screenshots, the observer's comments are essential and must be written by the researcher. Merriam (2009, p. 131) recommends that reflected comments include:

> the researcher's feelings, reactions, initial interpretations, speculations, and hunches. These comments are over and above factual descriptions of what is going on; their comments or thoughts about the setting, people, and activities. In raising questions about what is observed or speculating as to what it all means, the researcher is actually engaging in preliminary data analysis. The joint collection and analysis of data is essential in qualitative research.

In addition to written comments, researchers may want to sketch impressions or create diagrams to illustrate relationships between users, emerging themes and concepts, and/or technology features of the research setting.

A field journal can be constructed to manage both the directly quoted material and the researcher's reflections using a cross-platform note-taking application (such as Evernote™ or OneNote™). It is important to set up a system to organize and code observations from the beginning of the study. Labels or tags should include basic information such as the time and place of the observation as well as any important descriptors of events or activities. A consistent approach will make the analysis stage proceed more simply.

TRIANGULATION: USING EXTANT DATA IN MULTIMETHOD STUDIES

Many researchers find, as I did, that extant data is valuable as a complement to other types of data. By combining types of data, gaps or missing content can be countered. As noted, Big Data is increasingly used in combination with data collected from participants.

Triangulation, the practice of using multiple sources of data to enhance the credibility of a research study, is particularly valuable in online studies with extant data (Hastings, 2010). Importantly, a concern raised by Hine (2011) can be addressed. She pointed out that with 'unobtrusive use of Internet-derived data researchers lack access to how Internet users might interpret and make use of online information or what, ultimately, their browsing, hyperlinking and social networking mean to them' (p. 3). By triangulating with elicited methods such as interviews, researchers can ask the 'how' and 'why' questions needed to gain insights apparent in extant data (see Table 10.1). By combining qualitative methods, researchers can generate alternative explanations for what may appear as trends in data collected from posts and online discussions.

Table 10.1 Variations in multimethod online qualitative studies: Combining extant and elicited methods

1. Unstructured interview:	2. Semi-structured interview:	3. Online observation:	4. Online materials review:	5. Unstructured interview:
Build trust and foundation on topic and discuss observation strategy.	Ask same main questions to all participants, with varied follow-ups and probes.	Researcher observes how participant interacts in online group.	Researcher reviews participant's posted images and videos on the research topic.	Ask questions to gain insights and explanations based on interviews, materials, and observation.
Desktop videoconference	Web conference meeting room	Social networking site	Social networking site	Web conference meeting room

Table 10.2 Variations in multimethod online qualitative studies: Moving from a broad to narrow focus

1. Unobtrusive observations:	2. Online materials review:	3. Plan interviews: Contact key	4. Semi-structured interview:
Observe interactions over a period of time to learn about issues. Identify key players.	Researcher reviews well-linked texts, images, and videos from group members.	players and request consent from 1–1 or group interview.	Conduct interviews; ask for explanation of posts/discussion on SNS.
Social networking site	Social networking site	Social networking site messaging or email	ICT selected by participant(s)

There are numerous ways researchers can mix online interviews with analysis of materials and online observations. Conceptually they can move from the broad to the narrow, or the narrow to the broad. When beginning in a new area of inquiry, broad exploration can be used to gain some sense of the dimensions of the topic, scope, and priorities of those involved. Once clarity is gained by unobtrusively observing those engaged in discussion of the issue and reviewing materials posted publicly, specific questions may emerge that can be answered with other methods. Or, starting from a specific question, multiple perspectives and angles may be discovered by unobtrusively observing those engaged in discussion of the issue and reviewing materials that broaden the inquiry.

Another way to think about the mix of qualitative approaches is a move between structured and unstructured inquiry. The first stage can use an unstructured style to explore the topic. This wide-open view can serve as the basis for more structured interview questions or observation criteria in a second stage. Or, a more structured style of interview and precise observation can become the basis for a wider-ranging, unstructured second stage of the study.

The researcher may use unobtrusive observations and/or review of publicly available documents to do some background research on participants, their employers, schools, interests or other details. This research can be a formal part of the study, and included in the informed consent agreement, or a more informal scan of publicly available information. In such studies, findings from the observations may become the basis for more specific, personalized interview questions. Alternatively, the participant may discuss online involvement or experiences in the interview, which the researcher wants to view in order to gain a better understanding. In such case the interview may precede the observations. (See Chapter 8 for more about structured and unstructured online interviews.) The key to integration of methods is to establish a credible rationale for what you are trying to do and how it achieves the purpose of the study.

BIG QUAL

Some researchers use Big Qual in conjunction with other qualitative methods or as part of mixed methods studies that combine qualitative and quantitative methods. While Big Data can show the scope and breadth of the issues at hand, by combining such research with qualitative approaches the stories behind the numbers can emerge. As Moeller observed:

> Data must be evaluated by those who have the math skills, but also by those who understand the content of what is being evaluated. Great visualizations of data, for example, can make something so seemingly self-evident, that complicating factors can be overlooked and additional questions are never asked. That's another reason why the 'human instinct' is needed – and at both the front end, and the back end of working with Big Data. (Moeller, 2013)

Multimethod qualitative studies researchers use Big Data analytics to identify the scope and dimensions of a problem and use what is learned to craft questions to explore with participants. You could conduct research with human participants and once you have identified key themes, look to Big Data Analytics to verify whether your findings fit with a larger population or set of records. It also could allow for secondary analysis: qualitative research generates huge amounts of deep detailed data that is typically only used to answer a small set of research questions. Using Machine Learning tools to explore existing qualitative datasets with new research questions could help to get increased value from archived and/or multiple sets of data. Brower noted that Big Qual studies generally involve teams of researchers. While it is possible for solo researchers to carry out Big Qual research, the involvement of data scientists is common in larger projects.

─────────── SPOT CHECK ───────────

Before you can make an informed decision about what kind of extant data fits your study, do a preliminary scan. What kinds of materials do you have access to through your university or local community? What groups are engaged with the topic, and how do they operate? What time frame interests you – and what digital resources are available? Taking the time to scout out potential sources will save time and frustration.

USING EXTANT SOURCES IN YOUR STUDY: BIG QUAL, DOCUMENTS, OR MATERIALS

Using extant data can be as simple as downloading documents or photographs from an archive, or so complex that you need specialized tools and skills, and a team of researchers who know how to use them. With the high-level descriptions offered in this chapter, you have a place to start your decision-making, and directions to take for further reading.

Once you have determined that adequate and appropriate materials are available, it is time to confirm how they fit the study. Will they be utilized alone or in conjunction with other methods? Bowen (2009, p. 30) suggests five ways that extant materials can be used in qualitative studies:

1. To 'provide data on the context within which research participants operate', with text providing context.
2. To 'suggest some questions that need to be asked [in interviews] and situations that need to be observed as part of the research.'
3. To 'provide supplementary research data. Information and insights derived from documents can be valuable additions to a knowledge base.' This kind of data offers a means of tracking change and development. For example, a researcher could examine periodic and final reports to get a clear picture of how an organization or a program fared over time.
4. To 'provide a means of tracking change and development.'
5. To 'verify findings or corroborate evidence from other sources' including other data you collect using different qualitative methods.

SUMMARY OF KEY CONCEPTS

This chapter surveyed types of extant data that can be collected online for a qualitative study, including online observations and user-generated materials. An overview was provided for ways these methods could be used on their own or in conjunction with other methods. This chapter describes a large, and rapidly changing area of research by providing some frameworks to help you decide what is of potential value to your study, and what is do-able given available time and skills.

DISCUSSION QUESTIONS AND EXERCISES

- Identify ethical risks or issues in (a) collecting user-generated materials; (b) collecting documents from institutional or publication websites; or (c) conducting unobtrusive observation.
- Conduct a practice online observation.
  - Create an observation guide. Address the criteria using data from at least two different SNSs, public comment areas for online publications, or product reviews.
  - Discuss how, as a researcher, you experienced these observations.
  - Based on the practice observations and debrief, provide guidelines for researchers using your preferred style(s).
- Locate two articles that use different forms of extant data collected online. Compare and contrast their approaches for using extant data.
- Visit a publicly accessible archive such as one of the following.:
  - The Martin Luther King, Jr. Research & Education Institute: https://kinginstitute.stanford.edu/
  - The Internet Archive: https://archive.org/
  - The Library of Congress: www.loc.gov/collections/
  - British Library: http://searcharchives.bl.uk/primo_library/libweb/action/search.do?dscnt=1&dstmp=1599249660458&vid=IAMS_VU2&fromLogin=true
  - Archives Portal Europe: www.archivesportaleurope.net/
- Review usage guidelines and find out whether permissions are needed to use the sources for research purposes. Using keywords relevant to your research interest, scan the archive for materials. How would you move forward if you wanted to use these sources in your study?
- Look for Big Data or datasets relevant to your research interest. Use the checklist in this chapter (page XX) to analyze the dataset. How would you move forward if you wanted to use these sources in your study?

11

Eliciting Data Online

HIGHLIGHTS

In Chapter 10 you were introduced to the type of online qualitative research that is data-driven. That is, the researcher works with source materials generated for some other purpose or observes activities that occur independent of the researcher. The form and nature of such writings, images, or media was determined by the individual who posted them. They were not created in response to the researcher; indeed the researcher who uses extant data collection has no direct contact with participants, who may or may not even know they have contributed data to a study. By contrast, the researcher who *elicits* data from participants has extensive, in-depth, and sometimes very personal contact with them. At the most basic level, researchers elicit responses by asking questions. Participants who are knowledgeable about the phenomena central to the study consent to contribute answers. Of course, no research unfolds in quite that simple a way, especially when communication occurs electronically. In this chapter you will explore the diverse options online researchers have to elicit data from participants, and design considerations for using such methods to collect data. In Chapter 12 you will continue to look at approaches that actively engage consenting participants to generate data online.

OBJECTIVES

After reading and reflecting on this chapter, you will be able to:

- distinguish between types of elicitation with individuals or groups
- analyze ways each type might be employed to achieve the study purpose
- understand the role(s) and position(s) of the researcher in planning and conducting research with consenting participants
- consider how decisions made about the type of data collection relate to other design decisions for the online study.

WHAT DOES IT MEAN TO ELICIT DATA?

Researchers determine a research problem, purpose and question(s) that guide design decisions. To understand the research problem and address the research question they look for participants who have experienced, have observed, or understand the problem. The challenge for any qualitative researcher is to find ways to engage each participant, develop trust and rapport, so the participant is willing and able to share his or her perspectives and perceptions of the phenomenon under investigation. The challenge for the online researcher is to find ways to carry out these steps online. What ICT is appropriate for researcher–participant communications? How can the online researcher develop trust and rapport using the selected ICTs? What options are possible for posing questions and receiving responses from participants online?

Qualitative researchers use various methods to elicit data, including verbal interviews (one-to-one or group) or written exchanges (such as questionnaires, diaries, or journals). Interviews may include visual exchanges as well. Visual elicitation online is discussed in this chapter, while approaches to generating visual data are discussed in Chapter 12.

ONLINE INTERVIEWS

Critical differences in interview methods center on distinctions between planning and spontaneity, and on roles and expectations of the interviewer, interviewee, and their interactions during the interview. Stylistic choices are influenced by researchers' epistemic views of knowledge and whether they believe knowledge exists apart from or is created during and through the interview process. Accordingly, researchers look at the interview as a way to obtain information or answers from *respondents* or *interviewees* or to construct knowledge with *research participants*.

Interview Style and Structure

Structure is a pivotal methodological concern that influences the method of interview data collection. In this context, *structure* refers generally to the extent to which the questions, order, and process are planned ahead of the interview and the extent of consistency from one interview to another.

Some interviews are carefully planned in advance, while others are more spontaneous to allow the conversation to shift depending on the experiences the participant wishes to discuss. Some interview studies are designed so that the same kinds of questions are asked of all participants in order to generate a corpus of comparable responses that can be analyzed to determine common experiences across the group. Other interview studies aim to collect a wide range of unique perspectives.

Will you try to obtain the same types of answers from multiple interviewees or to make each interview a unique narrative event? The nature of online communication varies greatly depending on the ICT; some technologies lend themselves to more natural, conversational exchanges, while others require some planning.

Questioning and Prompting

The term *questions* itself takes on different meanings depending on the research design. For some studies specific open-ended questions are posed to participants; for others the researcher uses more informal prompts and a conversational style to encourage participants to simply talk rather than give an answer.

Interview researchers collect data from and with participants by:

1. **Asking questions**

    -   Structured: All questions are articulated in advance.
    -   Semi-structured: Main questions are articulated in advance; follow-up questions are determined during the interview when more details are needed.
    -   Unstructured: Broad questions or prompts, with specific framing of questions determined during the interview. You could also invite the participant(s) to identify the questions they want to answer or topics they want to discuss within the framework you provide.

2. **Using prompts**

    -   Verbal prompts: Suggesting a direction, following up on a question. For example, 'Tell me more ...' or 'Then what happened?'

- Non-verbal prompts: Facial expressions or movements. For example, nodding the head, smiling, making eye contact.
- Visual prompts: Using images, media, diagrams, or artifacts to prompt a response.

One factor in selecting the interview style and structure relates to timing between question and response (see Figure 11.1). A conventional live interview typically occurs at the *synchronicity* end of the continuum. The interviewer and participant(s) are in the same place at the same time and generally the research exchange is the only thing happening. In contrast, online interviews, even when using synchronous technology tools, occur in settings with other potential distractions. Still, the synchronous interview is most comparable to natural speech interactions since there is little lag time between the question and response. At the other end of the continuum is the asynchronous elicitation. Here, the participant has time to think about the answer or perhaps gather photographs or artifacts to share in the response. When is it important to have a real-time response versus time to reflect on the question and respond later?

While every interview researcher must make these decisions, the online researcher has additional considerations that relate to the kind of technology and setting chosen as the communications medium. The nature of online communication varies greatly depending on the ICT; some technologies mimic face-to-face dialogue, while others require some planning. For example, desktop videoconferencing or video chat lends itself to natural, conversational exchanges. Others, such as web conferencing, require some planning to set up the space and create written or visual materials used to elicit responses. Written exchanges may combine predetermined questions that can be cut and pasted into a chat window and informal questions that emerge from within the interview.

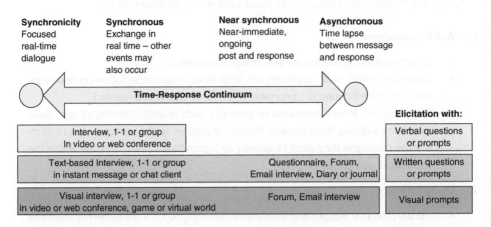

Figure 11.1 Elicitation in varied time–response relationships

Let's explore these options, so you can evaluate which will work best for your research with individuals or small groups.

TYPOLOGY OF E-INTERVIEW STRUCTURES

The typology of e-interview structures (Figure 11.2; see also Salmons, 2010, 2012, 2015, 2016) illustrates the relationships between the level of structure and flexibility in interview research. On one end of the spectrum, **structured interviews** use predetermined questions in a planned order when interviewers query respondents. At the other end of the spectrum, few or no questions are framed in advance, and *unstructured* conversational interviews occur between researchers and participants. Between these extremes, there are many variations, generally termed *semi-structured* interviews: interviews with a basic structure but varying

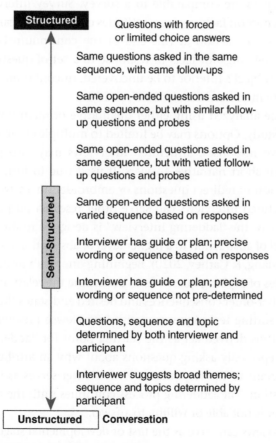

Figure 11.2 Typology of e-interview structures

degrees of flexibility in planning and exchange, and in the ways in which the main questions are followed up.

Structured, unstructured, and semi-structured interview styles are not usually applied in a rigid manner. You may choose to organize an entire interview within a similar level of structure, or design an interview with planned, responsive, and participant-generated questions and interactions. In research where more than one interview is conducted, a variety of levels of structure could be used across the study. Depending on the responses offered, researchers may need to shift into a more structured approach when the interviewee is straying too far off-topic, or to a more conversational approach when it is apparent that the interviewee has important stories on points the interviewer had not thought to include in the script. To reflect these realities, structure is considered on a continuum.

Structured Online Interviews

Structured interviews are comparable to a survey. Survey interviews usually ask respondents to report on facts or assess attitudes on a product, candidate, or event. The metaphor for interaction at this end of the continuum is excavation; the *miner* dispassionately digs for facts in response to a set of questions. 'Knowledge is waiting in the subject's interior to be uncovered, uncontaminated by the miner who conducts the interview' (Kvale, 2007, p. 19).

The data can be analyzed using either qualitative or quantitative analysis in a mixed methods study. Options may be limited to multiple choice, yes/no, or three to five alternative responses. Structured interviews may also pose open-ended questions to elicit short narrative answers. If used true to form, respondents do not have the option to redirect questions or embroider on answers.

However, structured interviews can serve other research purposes. One type of structured interview, the 'laddering interview,' is designed to move the discussion from a lower level of abstraction to a higher level of abstraction (Gruber et al., 2008; Kumar, Follen, Huang, & Cathey, 2020). Beginning one attribute at a time, the interviewer asks a series of probing questions to determine the relationship between the attribute and higher-order consequences and desired end-states (Kumar et al., 2020). Interviewers use sorting techniques to derive interviewee preferences and develop criteria. Criteria thus derived act as the starting point for 'laddering' probes, with the interviewer repeatedly asking questions about why an attribute, consequence, or value is important to the respondent. Each answer serves as the starting point for the next question. The laddering process continues until the respondent either repeats answers or is not able or willing to answer.

Structured interviews can serve as the first or developmental stage. Structured questions can be used to gain background information such as demographics, time, or level of experience with the issue being studied, general points of view, or preferences. As an initial stage, structured interviews can help the researcher generate items for exploration using other methods. The structured interview may be followed with a survey in a quantitative or mixed-methods study, or with observations and/or less structured interviews in a qualitative study.

Responses can be used to craft more specific questions for a less structured interview in the next stage of the study. Or responses to structured interview questions can help the researcher determine what extant materials to review or observations to conduct.

To prepare for structured interviews, the researcher articulates all questions in advance. Because an interviewer using a structured is meant to be as neutral as possible, the researcher may recruit and train others to implement the interview.

When selecting the ICT appropriate for structured interviewing consider these points:

- What ICT will allow the researcher to either read verbatim the questions and response options, or to cut and paste prepared questions in writing?

    o   Which will be preferable to participants?
    o   What will make it easy for participants to see or hear the questions and quickly respond?

- Will the structured interview be accompanied by observation?

    o   If interviewing the participant on a video- or web conference platform, will you look for the same kinds of non-verbal cues with each participant? Will you observe the same kinds of elements in homes or offices visible to the camera?
    o   If observing the participant, will the researcher look for the same kinds of posts, records, or activities for each participant?

Verbal or written interactions in an interview or questionnaire?

In online interviews, structured questions can be posed verbally or in writing. In a fully structured interview, is there a reason to conduct it in a verbal, synchronous way (given the need to coordinate schedules to do so)? Verbal interviews are conducted synchronously using videoconference or web conference tools. They may use VoIP, with or without the webcam. In a verbal interview, the interviewer is meant to be as neutral as possible without using follow-up questions or prompts. While we think of a verbal interview as being synchronous, it is possible to record spoken questions for participants to answer in an application designed for this purpose. Participants could either record their responses or put them into writing.

In a structured written interview, questions are posed in a text chat for asynchronous or near synchronous interview. Questionnaires are a form of structured, asynchronous, written interview. Written questions are answered with written answers.

To ask for responses in writing, a link to a simple online questionnaire can be sent to participants on receipt of the consent agreement, or the links can be embedded, for example:

By clicking this link to proceed with the questionnaire, you verify that you are voluntarily consenting to participating in this study. For more on the study, see my research site at www.janetstudy.com. Once you have completed the questionnaire I will contact you to arrange a one-to-one interview.

Thank you for completing the consent agreement. To begin the study, click this link to www.janetstudy.com and complete the questionnaire. Once you have completed the questionnaire I will contact you to arrange a one-to-one interview.

To collect narrative responses a similar approach can be used in a forum where threads can be made private, accessible to only the participant with a log-in identity and password. Initial structured questions can also be sent to the participant via email or posted in a private text chat application.

Semi-Structured Interviews

Semi-structured interviews endeavor to balance the organization and framework of the structured approach with the spontaneity and flexibility of the unstructured interview. The researcher prepares questions and/or discussion topics in advance and generates follow-up questions during the interview. A metaphor for the semi-structured interviewer is the *gardener*. The gardener realizes that harvest is not possible without planting the seed. At the same time, many seeds can be sown without results if contextual conditions of weather, soil, and care are not in balance. The researcher–gardener realizes that the question seeds the participant's thought process. With reflective listening and encouragement, the answer will emerge. With it, both the researcher's and the participant's understanding will grow.

In more structured *standardized open-ended interviews*, interviewers may ask the same open-ended questions in the same sequence but with varied follow-up questions and probes. They also may ask a consistent set of questions but vary the sequence based on responses. In more flexible *guided open-ended interviews*, researchers create themes or develop an 'interview guide' of topics to discuss, but do not develop a precise wording or sequence in advance of the interview (Kvale, 2007).

In *responsive interviewing*, a flexible approach defined by Rubin and Rubin (2012), the main initial questions are set and the researcher is prepared to ask follow-up and probing questions based on the responses. **Responsive interviewing** is based on trust and mutual respect in the relationship between interviewer and interviewee (Rubin & Rubin, 2012). Another semi-structured approach recommends a three-interview series (Seidman, 2019). In Seidman's phenomenological approach, there is an overarching structure to the series, with a specific theme for each respective interview. Within the series of 'focused life history,' 'details of experience,' and 'reflection on the meaning' interviews, a semi-structured approach is used (2019, pp. 17–19).

In online interviews, semi-structured questions can be posed verbally or in writing, using any degree (or combination of degrees) on the time–response continuum (see Figure 11.1). When choosing the ICT to use for the interview, some considerations include:

- What technology allows the researcher to deliver the main questions so that participants can easily see or hear them? What technology allows for timely delivery of follow-up and probing questions?
- To what extent are synchronous spoken or written exchanges used for all or some of the interview? Are researcher and participant frequent text-chat communicators who are able to think and type quickly enough to make a less structured interview work smoothly? Or might they find that trying to think of questions or follow-ups, and type them, is too slow a process? In which case, would a verbal exchange, such as a video chat, be preferable?
- If visuals will be used to prompt discussion, will they be used in the same way across all interviews (more structured) or will different images or visual exchanges be used in different ways for each respective interview? (For more on visual methods in interviews, see Chapter 9.)
- If a virtual world or game is used as a setting, will time be needed to navigate to different settings or to show various features that could create a gap between question and response?
- Will the semi-structured interview be accompanied by some data collection by observation? If so:
  - Will the same ICT be used for the interviews and for observations?
  - To what extent will observations be consistent from one participant to the next? Will the same ICTs be used with all participants?
  - What kinds of non-verbal cues will the researcher look for during the interview?
  - What kinds of posts, records or activities will the researcher observe to learn about each participant? Or will the researcher follow up particular responses by looking for related posts and materials after the interview?

Unstructured Interviews

At the other end of the continuum, unstructured interviews are used to collect data through what is essentially a conversation between the researcher and participant. In the unstructured interview, questions emerge from the context and events occurring in the circumstances of the interview. The unstructured interview may be a planned discussion in a selected interview setting. Or it can be naturalistic, meaning it occurs on site where the participant lives or works, occurring in conjunction with other field or participant observations. Data collected from unstructured interviews are different for each person interviewed and may be different for the same person interviewed on multiple occasions (Patton, 2015). Researchers 'travel with' their participants and adapt to directions the participant chooses to take.

While in online interviews unstructured questions can be posed verbally or in writing, the nature of this kind of interview lends itself to synchronicity and synchronous approaches. These kinds of ICTs allow the researcher to offer prompts and follow the participant's lead in generating a rich dialogue on the problem under investigation. Considerations include:

- Can you use an ICT that allows for natural dialogue, such as video- or web conferencing, so the conversation can easily flow and change course as needed?
- If you want to conduct an asynchronous unstructured interview, how will you retain focus on the research purpose between communications?
- Should parameters be set to keep the conversation on topics closely related to the research problem?

────────────────── RESEARCH CAMEO 11.1 ──────────────────

Approaches Using Elicited Data from Interviews

Researcher 2 plans to elicit data from consenting participants using multiple types of synchronous and asynchronous interviews to understand their experiences and plans for publishing qualitative research.

Semi-structured questions: For a synchronous interview on a videoconferencing platform, they articulate main questions, and will develop follow-up and probing questions depending on the answers:

- Briefly describe your qualitative research.
- What are your publishing goals?
- What will help you meet these goals?
- What obstacles will you need to overcome?
- Who do you communicate to help you meet your goals?

Unstructured questions: Tell me why it is important to publish your qualitative study?

Structured questions: They articulate questions and will post them to each participant by text message at 6 pm each day for one week. For this near-synchronous exchange they craft the following questions:

- Did you work on writing you hope to publish, or take other actions to move your publication process forward?
- In a few words, how do you feel about progress made today toward meeting your goals?
- What steps will you take tomorrow?

PREPARING THE QUESTIONS AND/OR PROMPTS

Thoughtful questioning and meaningful interactions are central to any interview. Whether the interview is structured, semi-structured, or unstructured, the interviewer must think in advance about how the participants can contribute data that helps achieve the purpose of the study.

Researchers planning for structured or semi-structured interviews will articulate all or most of the **main interview questions** in advance and plan the sequence for asking them. Open-ended questions – those that cannot be answered with a simple yes or no – solicit participants' stories, thoughts, and feelings.

Methodologists suggest a number of strategies for scripting questions. Weiss (1994, p. 73) observes that 'any question is a good question if it directs the respondent to material needed by the study in a way that makes it easy for the respondent to provide the material.' Kvale (2007, p. 57) describes *thematic* questions that relate to the 'what' of the interview and *dynamic* questions that pertain to the 'how' of an interview. Dynamic questioning refers to building rapport needed to keep the conversation flowing.

A challenge for researchers is to go beyond the main questions and encourage interviewees to dig deeper. How far does the researcher want the participant to go with one particular question? If the interviewee has a great deal to say on one topic, is it worth potentially sacrificing breadth and leaving some questions unasked? If not, how will the interviewer guide the participant to the next question? Rubin and Rubin (2012) spell out a number of kinds of **probes** that encourage the participant to continue the line of comments or that redirect the participant into a new direction. The simplest probes, such as 'tell me more' or 'how did you feel when that happened?', help to keep the conversation flowing. To be more strategic, Rubin and Rubin (2012, pp. 139–140) identified three types of probes:

- *Attention probes* ('Okay, I understand', etc.) let the interviewee know you are listening.
- *Conversation management probes* keep the conversation focused on the research topic and help regulate the desired level of depth. Researchers use such probes to confirm answers, ask for better definition or clarification if the researcher cannot follow the thread of the comments.
- *Credibility probes* ask participants to share relevant evidence in support of their own claims.

Verbal probes are complemented with non-verbal probes – the eye contact or timing patterns researchers use to show participants that they are interested in hearing them continue.

The sequence of main questions may be predetermined or arranged as the interview proceeds. Although sub-questions, **follow-up questions** or probes can be outlined in advance, the researcher typically refines or adds to the planned list as needed based on interviewee responses.

In less structured interviews researchers may want to be more spontaneous than is possible when questions are formulated in advance. To be more flexible, such researchers may develop an *interview guide*, a kind of 'cheat sheet' to remind them of the key points to cover. Guides can be very detailed or simply list or outline the subject areas to be covered and key words the researcher wants to make sure to use when posing the question. Researchers can modify Moustakas's (1994, p. 116) suggested list of questions to fit their own research designs:

- What dimensions, incidents, and people connected with the experience stand out for you?
- How did the experience affect you? What changes do you associate with the experience?
- How did the experience affect significant others in your life?
- What feelings were generated by the experience?
- What thoughts stood out or are memorable?
- Have you shared all that is significant with reference to the experience?
- Researchers at the unstructured end of the continuum approach the interview with the larger purpose for the inquiry in mind; they develop specific topics and articulate questions as the interview unfolds.

Whether the interviewer spells out each question or maps out key topics, if the interview is to be conducted online, the nature of the technology will influence the options for conveying the question, and receiving and responding to the answer. Will the participant be typing responses using text on a mobile device or chat software on a computer? Will the participant be speaking? Will the participant and interviewer be able to see each other's natural visage or an invented persona? Will they be able to observe and respond to visual examples or media? (See Chapter 12 for more about online visual methods.) Each is a distinctively different communication experience. This means selection of interview technology relates specifically to the kind of planning the interviewer needs to do in advance of the interview.

These strategies work with one-to-one individual interviews and with small-group interviews. In more structured group interviews, plan to ask all participants the same questions. In a semi-structured group interview you might decide to ask different questions to each participant. In an unstructured interview, allow members to suggest topics or question each other. If you are planning to conduct a group interview, think about whether you want all the participants to respond to questions in turn, or whether you will invite interaction among interviewees.

PLANNING TO CONDUCT AN INTERVIEW

The moment comes when imagining, training, practicing, and rehearsing are through. The athlete stands poised at the end of a diving board with an Olympic audience's attention, the actor takes the stage, the nervous lover pulls a ring from his pocket – and it is time for action. Similarly, the researcher moves from intellectual exploration of literature and theory to the moment when the very real research participant is there, anticipating a question that will launch the interview. At that moment, the researcher must begin to actualize the purpose of the study and, as Denzin (2001) describes it, 'bring the world into play' (p. 25). The way the researcher proceeds is guided by design decisions and interview structure and approach – and by the researcher's own relational style.

Interview research success depends on the interviewer's personal and professional, affective and cognitive skills. Clandinin and Connelly (2000) observe that the 'way an interviewer acts, questions, and responds in an interview shapes the relationship and therefore the ways participants respond and give accounts of their experience' (p. 110). A skilled interviewer balances content and process, and active or neutral stances when collecting data through interviews. Each interview research approach associates slightly different expectations for the interviewer. Regardless of methodological approach, the core activity is the same for any interviewer: to engage in dialogue with the research participant with the purpose of data collection. And regardless of epistemological or methodological stance, the interviewer is responsible for the interview and must take this role seriously.

It is essential to be prepared to conduct the interview using the selected ICT. Eliciting descriptions of experiences and perceptions of interviewees is the goal of the research interview, and while online interviews share characteristics with those conducted face-to-face, there are unique aspects with implications for the researcher.

Researchers are wise to see all communications with consenting participants as opportunities for building the relationship, comfort with the process, and trust in the interviewer. Planning steps, including discussion of the study as well as logistical arrangements, offer a chance to build rapport. Synchronous, near-synchronous, and asynchronous communications can be used strategically at different points of the study. Early-stage discussions with participants will offer a realistic view on the participant's ability to communicate online. To avoid last-minute stress, assess each research participant's experience and comfort level with the selected technology or technologies. If necessary, offer to log in at a different time for a quick test.

Some preparation steps are outlined here:

- Confirm time frame, anticipated length for interview.
- Confirm online setting for the interview and provide log-in information.
- Provide any technical support service phone numbers or links to live chat help.
- Provide alternate communication options in case there is a problem logging in or accessing the interview ICT. (Telephone or text message number, for example.)
- When you are arranging for a video interview, make sure to confirm that the participant has webcam access in the setting you were trying to view. Miguel Montiel encountered this issue when he tried to conduct video interviews that required participants to show how they carried out specific tasks in their kitchens:

  > There were technical challenges because some of them had desktops to connect to the videoconference, but realized they needed to be in the kitchen. They had to switch to their phones, find a way to prop it up or ask someone to assist. These are things you can't control when you are not in the same location as the participant(s). (Montiel, 2020)

- Establish protocols for the interview, including basic logistics. These may include agreement on signals to indicate need for more time to answer or time for a break. Protocols may also include discussion expectations for level of focus expected during the interview.

—————————————— RESEARCH CAMEO 11.2 ——————————————

Planning for the Interviews

Researcher 2 plans to elicit data from consenting participants using multiple types of synchronous and asynchronous interviews to understand their experiences and plans for publishing qualitative research. They have prepared main questions for the semi-structured interviews, questions to be spoken in a videoconference setting using audio and web cameras. They have written out the questions to be posed in the text messaging application the participant is accustomed to using. They have checked to make sure that the participants have the technical capability to participate in both kinds of interactions.

LEARNING THE ICT

Are you familiar with each ICT to be used in the study? Communicating in the medium should come naturally by the time the first interaction with a participant occurs. Some ICTs require you to actively manage various communication and recording features during the interview. Others, like text chat, are simple to manage. Some researchers may conduct interviews in a videoconferencing facility with technicians who manage the equipment. Researchers must be fully aware of the features – and hazards – of selected interview technologies.

It is important to anticipate the possibility of technical problems and to learn to fix them, work around them, or find alternatives that could be quickly made available. Implications of last-minute changes must be considered. For example, if it is necessary to switch from VoIP to telephone, do you have the participant's phone number and alternative contact information? Given the importance for the interview recording, do you have a back-up option if there is a problem?

Practice interviews are essential, *whether or not you are familiar with the ICT*. The ideal practice partner is candid and generous with constructive feedback. Consider rehearsing with fellow researchers (or fellow students), friends, or colleagues. Another suggestion is to ask a colleague or more experienced interviewer to observe a practice interview or interview recording and offer suggestions. Researchers may benefit from practicing both roles: interviewer as well as interviewee. By taking the research participant's side the researcher may gain new insights about how to proceed.

Record the practice interview and listen to it. Were your explanations of the study expectations and/or any background information concise and clear? Were questions asked in a supportive but neutral tone? Did you avoid emotional reactions to responses that participants might interpret as judgmental or disrespectful?

Recording Practice Sessions and Interviews

One of the benefits of online interviewing is the ability to easily record, save, and archive the interaction for close viewing later. This frees the researcher to focus on questions and responses in the moment. Before thinking about the practical steps, the researcher needs to answer two important questions: did the participant agree to be recorded and can you protect the data?

Ethical researchers protect the data and make sure it is only used for the purposes stated in the consent agreement. Researchers are required to destroy the data after a period of time, typically seven years. This principle applies to recordings or other images associated with documenting the interview.

Did the participant agree to be recorded and what restrictions did they place on its use?

Before you record audio or video of the interview, make sure the participant understands what is involved in making the recording and how it will be used. Who will have access to the recording in addition to the researcher? Intentions should be evident to the participant in the consent agreement. (See Chapter 4 for more on informed consent.)

Make sure that the participant has agreed to allow you to use visual images, since a participant who expects to be anonymous will not want identifiable pictures included in any documentation of the research. In such cases the participant may agree to participate in a video call or videoconference with the agreement that the recording is for the researcher's use only. You might want to add a statement in the informed consent agreement such as:

> I grant permission for the interview session to be recorded and saved for purpose of review by the researcher. [If others, such as research assistants, will view the recording then note here.]

If you want to be able to use the recordings as examples when reporting on the study you may want to offer participants a couple of options, such as:

> I grant permission for audio or video clips or stills from the interview session to be used in academic presentations or documentation of this study.

> I agree to allow audio and visual clips including images, video or still, in reports or presentations about this study that will be accessible to the public.

I agree to allow audio clips only in reports or presentations about this study.

I do not permit the researcher to use images, video or audio from the interview.

───────────── RESEARCH CAMEO 11.3 ─────────────

Agreement on the Use of Recordings

Researcher 2 plans to use a videoconference platform, with webcams on. However, this data is for their own use only, since the participant will be visible and recognizable. They have clarified the researcher-only review of recordings. They have also verified that the text messaging data will not be shared in any way that could reveal the participants' identities.

CONDUCTING A RESEARCH INTERVIEW

For simplicity's sake, four interview stages are defined here as *opening*, *questioning and guiding*, *closing*, and *following up*. While steps taken within these stages may vary depending on the purpose, structure, or approach of the interview, principles discussed here apply in most cases. You can adapt them to fit the style and communication technology used in the study.

Opening the Interview

The introduction allows you to build on pre-interview communication and set the style and pace. Three main tasks should be accomplished: reintroducing the study and its purpose, establishing protocols, and developing rapport. Remind the participant of the research parameters discussed during the recruitment and preparation stage and acknowledged in the consent agreement. Recognize the significance of the participant's perspective of the study and show appreciation for potential contributions to new understandings and knowledge. Discuss protocols, expectations, and ground rules including confidentiality, recording, or note taking during the interview, timing, or breaks.

Rapport means 'an understanding, one established on a basis of respect and trust between an interviewer and respondent' (Gray, 2004, p. 22). It also means 'establishing a safe and comfortable environment for sharing the interviewee's personal experiences and attitudes as they actually occurred' (DiCicco-Bloom & Crabtree, 2006, p. 316). Beginning the interview with some informal conversation or a simple 'How are you?' check-in with the research participant can help set the stage.

Inviting the participant to ask for clarification on any issues related to interview participation before beginning formal questioning can help clear away unresolved matters that could distract the participant. A reliable formula for building rapport and a perception of safety does not exist. Personal qualities, social identities, characteristics, and/or chemistry make one person seem trustworthy and another not.

One point to consider when using webcams in interviews is whether it is acceptable to you for participants to turn the camera off for the entire interview or at some point. Obviously, if the camera goes off you can no longer collect data about the setting or non-verbal cues. On the other hand, if the participant is uncomfortable with the camera then you can continue your verbal exchange without it. Checking with the participants can ensure that they've made a choice versus simply had a technical issue. That is what happened with Bea Gardner in her online interviews:

> I left it up to the participants if they wanted to turn camera on or not but always had mine on, so they could see me nodding etc to show active listening. But on occasions when their camera was off, I had to work out if this was intentional or not and tactfully ask that. In all cases it was accidental, and participants were not familiar with the platform and thought the camera was on – so that was something I hadn't been expecting to have to navigate that I ended up having to do several times. (Gardner, 2020)

Questioning and Guiding

You can ask research participants direct or indirect questions, suggest themes for discussion, or otherwise guide the conversation. Research questions and the purpose of the study typically inform the questions, including both content and types of questions or conversation themes. Usually, interviews include several approaches to allow researchers to collect data of the depth and breadth needed to answer the research questions.

Ritchie and Lewis (2003) describe questioning as a process of 'mapping.' To open a new topic, 'ground-mapping questions' help the researcher identify relevant issues and generate multiple dimensions of the subject of inquiry. To focus the participant more narrowly on particular topics or concepts raised in response to ground-mapping questions, 'dimension-mapping questions' are posed. 'Perspective-mapping questions' are used to encourage interviewees to look at issues from different perspectives, to gain more richness and context. Probes for the purpose of 'content mining' explore detail and allow the interviewer to 'obtain a full description of phenomena, understanding what underpins the participant's attitude or behavior' (Ritchie & Lewis, 2003, p. 150).

Patton looks at the process a little differently. He distinguishes between five kinds of questions, including background and demographic questions, as well as the following (Patton, 2014):

- *Opinion and values questions*: What is your opinion of _____?
- *Feeling questions*: How do you feel about _____?
- *Knowledge questions*: What do you know about _____?
- *Sensory questions*: What do you experience when you are in the _____ situation?

Patton (2002, p. 372) suggests detail-oriented follow-up questions:

- *When* did that happen?
- *Who* else was involved?
- *Where* were you during that time?
- *What* was your involvement in that situation?
- *How* did that come about?
- *Where* did that happen?

Rubin and Rubin (2012) describe using 'open the locks,' 'tree and branch,' or 'river and channel' styles. An 'open the locks' interview aims to create a broad picture, usually as the basis for additional interviews. One or two broad, open-ended questions are asked with the intention of unlocking a flood of responses. They suggest that the 'tree and branch' style is best for exploring multiple themes, with a focus on breadth. The researcher divides the research problem (trunk) into parts, each covered by a main question (branch). When exploring one theme in depth, the researcher uses a 'river and channel' approach. The researcher starts with a topic and follows it wherever it goes.

Closing the Interview

Closure of the interview provides a transition from the interactive event of the interview back to everyday life. Depending on the nature and subject of the interview, an emotional 'cooldown' may be needed. Ritchie and Lewis (2003) suggest that shortly before the end of the agreed-on time frame, the researcher should signal the approaching close of the interview. One way is by introducing questions with phrases such as, 'For the final question. ...' Another is by closing with a summative or reflective question such as, 'Is there anything we have not discussed that you would like to share before we end?' Gray (2004) says, 'It is worth noting that interviewees often make some of their most interesting and valuable points once they think that the interview is over' (p. 226). The closing phase of the interview is a time when any remaining expectations for interviewees can be discussed, including post-interview follow-up.

Post-Interview Follow-Up

As you segue from closing the interview into data analysis, the post-interview follow-up is essential and should be seen as an opportunity for potentially valuable interaction with the research participant. After the interview, while it is fresh in your mind, reflect on what you heard and create research memos. Make notes on key ideas; where relevant, refine questions for subsequent interviews.

Once transcription is complete, member-checking is the final step. Share recordings or transcripts, and verify data with participants and ask for clarification on missing, incomplete, or confusing statements. This step offers participants one more chance to add illuminating details and closes the circle, completing the interview contract they accepted in the consent agreement. This step strengthens the study through data triangulation – the use of a variety of data sources in a study.

--------------------------------- RESEARCH CAMEO 11.4 ---------------------------------

Conducting the Interview

Researcher 2 plans to use a videoconference platform, with webcams on. They have practiced using the platform, and stuck a note in an obvious place as a reminder to start recording. They have positioned the webcam to promote the best eye contact and minimized distractions in the background. Even though they have core questions, they are prepared to ask them in a conversational way. They will have the guide on hand but will not read the questions. They have practiced conducting the interview and asked for feedback from their colleague. Do I seem friendly but professional? Do I seem interested in your response? Do I avoid facial expressions that convey approval or disapproval of your responses? After a couple of practice interviews they are confident about conducting the interview.

CAN YOU PROTECT THE DATA?

Videoconference applications, web conference platforms, and/or VoIP lines typically have the capability to record the event. When you look at products to use for recording online interviews, it is essential to assess the level of control afforded by the recording tools you want to use.

Some services associated with Internet backup or archives allow you to record directly to your own computer, and others allow you to download the file and then delete it from the server. Choose one of these options because if you are unable to delete the file from the server you are unable to verify to participants protection of the data. (See Chapter 3 for more on the selection of the platform.) You do not want your data on the cloud. Data could be accessed intentionally or unintentionally by others and shared publicly without your permission. If this is the case it would be preferable to use a different camera or device that allows you to retain the file and verifiably delete it when the study is complete. Additional questions to consider are:

- Can you allow participants to review the recording?
- Will you have the ability to restrict access to the recording?
- Can you be sure that no one else can forward, copy or share the recording?
- Will you be able to completely erase recorded files?

On a practical level some kinds of audio and video recordings can be imported into data analysis software, such as NVivo, HyperResearch or Atlas.ti. If you are planning to use one of these tools, make sure the format your recording can produce will be accessible to your data analysis software.

SUMMARY OF KEY CONCEPTS

This chapter introduced the steps needed to organize, plan, and conduct an online interview. The relationship between interview structure and types of ICT was discussed. Numerous types, approaches, and styles of interview questioning exist; explaining all of them is beyond the scope of this book. The principles common to most include the use of main, follow-up, and probing questions. Researchers working at the most structured end of the continuum may state all in advance of the interview. Semi-structured interview researchers may state ground-mapping questions to use with all interviews (perhaps varying wording or sequence) and develop some follow-up dimension-mapping and/ or perspective-widening questions to use, depending on answers and interview flow. In some cases, they may share the ground-mapping questions with interviewees prior to the interview to allow time for reflection. Researchers using less-structured interview styles may create a guide, outline, or list of ground-mapping, dimension-mapping, and/or perspective-widening topics and create key phrases or descriptors. Such researchers may familiarize themselves with types of probes but articulate probing questions during the interview based on responses. In an unstructured interview, the researcher could discuss a ground-mapping, dimension-mapping, and/or perspective-widening framework in the context of the study and identify themes for discussion.

DISCUSSION QUESTIONS AND EXERCISES

- Compare and contrast the ethical risks or issues involved in eliciting data in a video-conference versus text messaging application.
- Compare and contrast the ethical risks or issues involved in eliciting data or in collecting extant data.
- Choose a topic of interest and develop at least three different interview plans using varied styles and levels of structure. Choose one plan and explain how it will be implemented. Provide a rationale to support why this plan is appropriate to the purpose of the study.
- Conduct a practice online interview. Address the topic using questions from at least two different approaches. Discuss how, as a researcher, you experienced these styles. Ask your practice partner for his or her perspective on the experience of different styles. Based on the practice interview and debrief, provide guidelines for researchers using your preferred style(s).

12

Using Enacted Methods Online

Every expansive era in the history of mankind has coincided with the operation of factors ... to eliminate distance between peoples and classes previously hemmed off from one another. It remains for the most part to secure the intellectual and emotional significance of this physical annihilation of space. (John Dewey, 1916)

HIGHLIGHTS

Three types of online data collection were introduced in Chapter 1. The first describes ways to collect and study *extant* posts, records, media, or documents. The second describes ways researchers *elicit* data by posing questions or encouraging responses from one or more participants. Throughout the discussion of these types, ways to adapt conventional methods to an online environment have been compared and contrasted with ways digital approaches can take advantage of the collaborative, mobile, visually rich nature of online communications. While intrepid research- ers are increasingly making use of the capabilities of ICTs to engage deeply with participants, there are many opportunities for researchers to innovate.

The focus of this chapter is on promising methods for data collection associated with the third type, *enacted* data collection. As defined in this book, using *enacted* data collection methods means constructing a situation that allows for data to emerge in response to various kinds of prompts. The emphasis is on enacted digital approaches that involve highly interactive research events. Types of enacted data collection discussed include the use of arts-based and creative research, games, and simulations.

OBJECTIVES

After reading and reflecting on this chapter, you will be able to:

- identify ways to design studies that use enacted approaches to data collection
- distinguish between types of enacted data collection
- evaluate ways each type might be employed to achieve the study's purpose
- analyze online data collection options for visual, aural, or multimedia data
- understand the role of the position and role of the researcher in planning and conducting enacted research with consenting participants
- consider how decisions made about the type of data collection relate to other design decisions for the online study.

UNDERSTANDING ENACTED RESEARCH

Enacted approaches online are characterized as those that:

- While making use of extant data, are studies involving human participants
- Engage participants as collaborative co-researchers
- Typically involve more than one interaction with participants
- Utilize the visual, multimedia capabilities of technology
- Can include activities across the time–response continuum.

While studies described in Chapter 11 can draw on established traditions of interview or focus group research, enacted studies can be described as emerging methods. Researchers using them are often in uncharted territories, trying new approaches with few models or examples from published literature to follow. This chapter, rather than offering how-to steps, presents design options and frameworks that can help guide your decision-making as you develop your own strategy for collecting data.

The Setting Is Important in Enacted Data Collection

In methods defined here as *enacted*, research information and communications technologies (ICTs) serve as the *setting* for the research event. The primacy of ICTs as a *setting* for the study reflects the need to choose a place to conduct data collection that includes the specific features needed, such as the capability to share visual or multimedia materials.

You will select or create an online environment, community, or forum as the research setting. You might want a virtual setting that mimics a real-world one to study behaviors that could not otherwise be easily observed. You might want a virtual setting to study how users react to a particular online environment, platform, software, or applications. Or you might want to observe how users behave in online situations or navigate ICT features. In such studies the ICT is part of the research *phenomenon* as well as the place where you meet participants.

The research setting is the space where participants carry out tasks, including activities or actions the researcher prompts participants to do or demonstrate, act or re-enact. Tasks are defined to align with the methodology, purpose, and questions central to the study and are embedded into the online setting. The setting includes implicit or explicit prompts or instructions that invite participants to respond to programmed or open choices or to communicate with other participants. Within the online setting participants might contribute ideas, make choices, select options, navigate the environment, or solve problems presented to them. Researchers may collect data by observing participants in the research event, by recording the choices made or paths taken, by questioning them during or after the event, and/or by collecting diaries or journals participants use to describe their experiences.

ICTs also provide the *medium* for communication, because in enacted research researcher–participant and/or participant–participant interactions are central to the study. What communications features exist within the ICT you have created or selected for the study? Will you also use email or text messaging? Thinking through all of the expectations at the design stage will make it easier for participants to comply.

Researchers using *enacted* data collection construct a situation that allows for data to emerge or be generated in response to various kinds of verbal, written or visually communicated prompts or tasks. Such situations are referred to here as *research events*. This term is used broadly to encompass formal, structured qualitative experiments as well as less structured collaborative activities.

In enacted research events the data may emerge in various ways and represent various types of written, visual, verbal and/or multimedia data. Data may be captured or collected within the research settings, or external to the setting in journals or forums established for this purpose. Visual, verbal, written, and/or multimedia data can be collected from:

- Participants' recorded behaviors, choices, actions or reactions, logs or archives of posts or chats captured by the software used for the research setting.
- Participants' reflections or journal entries in the form of narratives, drawings or links to online materials they selected during the research event.
- Researcher's observations (participant or naturalistic) of the events captured in notes, images or screenshots.
- Researcher's collection of digital artifacts.
- Interviews or questionnaires conducted during or after the research event.

Implications for Recruiting and Informing Participants

Participants in enacted studies need to make a more significant time commitment, and be willing to play along, try new activities, or complete actions between research events. The requirements should be spelled out from the initial recruitment phase. Make an effort to estimate the time needed if incentives are offered, clarify whether they are available for completion of a study stage, or at the culmination of the study. Will partial incentives be offered to those who do not fulfill all requirements of the study?

_____ RESEARCH CAMEO 12.1 _____

Researchers 3 and 4 are using enacted methods.

Researcher 3 plans to offer a publishing workshop online and collect data from the writers who participate.

Researcher 4 plans to observe the writing group's social media interactions, and their online meetings. They will also interview the researchers about their experiences.

MULTIMODAL DIGITAL LITERACIES: FOUNDATIONS FOR ENACTED RESEARCH

Anyone you are likely to recruit for an online study possesses some level of digital literacy. You could design a study that only requires the ability to send or receive email or text messages. Or you could design a study that uses one or more interactive platforms, digital photographs or video captures, scanned images, or other options. What kinds of thinking will be involved, beyond the capability to use the computer or device? Let's take a moment to look at how conceptions of literacy have changed, and how multimodal digital *literacy* contrasts with digital skills, so you can think about what literacies you will need to conduct the study, and what literacies participants will need in order to contribute.

From Local to Global, Page to Screen

ICT advances have made it possible to connect across boundaries in more ways, more immediately. In related or parallel developments, increasingly globalized economies and global cultures have emerged. In this multilingual world, conversations are not limited to words; it also occurs through still and moving pictures, drawn or captured images, icons, and emoticons. The visual element is one part of the proverbial literacy picture. The term **visual literacy**, coined by John Debes (1968), can be defined as the ability to decode and interpret (make meaning from) visual messages and also to encode and compose meaningful visual communications. It includes the ability to visualize internally, communicate visually, and read and interpret images (Bamford, 2003). In addition, visual literacy 'encompasses the ability to be an informed critic of visual information, able to ethically judge accuracy, validity, and worth' (Metros, 2008, p. 103).

Words and images are easily meshed electronically; in an online world we need to go a step beyond visual literacy. Howard Rheingold, the thought leader who originated the concept and term, *virtual community* (Rheingold, 2000) defines *digital literacy* as an active process:

> Participatory culture, in which citizens feel and exercise the agency of being co-creators of their culture and not just passive consumers of culture created by others, depends on widespread literacies of participation. You can't participate without knowing how ... I use the word 'literacies' to encompass the social element as well as the individual ability to encode and decode in a medium. (Rheingold, 2012, p. 53)

Of course, today we communicate online wherever we are, so Barden (2019) adds the need for mobile literacy. His definition is:

> The use and interpretation of written or symbolic representation in texts and practices mediated by mobile digital technologies ... Mobile literacies are characterised by inter-activity, autonomy, spontaneity and creativity when working to make meaning on the move. (Barden, 2019, pp. 23, 28)

Barden discusses mobile literacy as more than simply having the skills to use a mobile device and access the Internet on the go. He describes what he learned from interviewing someone who 'learns and writes through a combination of modes: text, voice, image and touch. He moves rapidly between apps to do so, with a kind of agility' (2019, p. 7).

Kress, a pioneer in thinking about the implications of all of these kinds of changes, describes the fundamental shift from words to pictures as interrelated with a shift from print to digital:

> There is, on one hand, the broad move from the centuries-long dominance of writing to the new dominance of the image and, on the other hand, the move from the dominance of the medium of the book to the dominance of the medium of the screen. (Kress, 2003, p. 1)

Kress points out that even when the screen contains text, it is inherently visual as a result of the layout of the online page and use of colors, fonts, and other elements. He also includes gesture and sound in the mix; when we move from communicating in written words to using video or even animated GIFs, movement is part of the message (Kress, 2010). Kress calls this type of communication *multimodality* (Kress, 2003, 2005, 2010; Kress & Selander, 2012). Literacies are different from digital skills and competencies. Literacies relate to knowledge and comprehension, while skills are the ability to apply this knowledge and competence is seen as the proven ability to use these sets of knowledge and skills for one's development (Iordache, Mariën, & Baelden, 2017). All are needed to conduct enacted research online. Developing these multimodal, digital, mobile skills and literacies is essential for the twenty-first century researcher and participants in order to critically evaluate diverse types of information in interactive settings. The first step is to assess your current status, and your expectations for participants. Think about these questions in relation to your study:

- Will you and participants need to interact using mobile devices, away from homes or offices?
- Will you and participants need to interact in groups, or in social settings online?
- Will you and participants communicate using multiple communication modes?

Of course these principles are complicated in practice. For example, The Keep Talking project, an action research project about wellbeing bridging the university and local community, the transition to online from face-to-face during the COVID-19 pandemic presented new challenges. Initially, the research team made one-to-one telephone calls, which was time-consuming and limited the community interaction central to the study.

> For Keep Talking, video calls negated the time-consuming elements of telephone interviews and allowed for the group to connect through the screen. Although four people initially indicated a preference for group video calls, nine responded to the first call for participants and 15 to the second, indicating that the need to connect with other members of the group was strong. However, each video call shone a spotlight on those with outdated hardware, poorer bandwidth or low levels of IT literacy and confidence (Beaunoyer et al., 2020), causing frustrations within the group and threatening to fracture research relationships which had thrived during face-to-face contact. Equally, the need to mute microphones and the ability to see only a few people on the screen at any one time was contradictory to the inclusive principles underpinning Keep Talking.
>
> Despite the difficulties experienced with video calls, the group and project team were keen to continue finding ways of creating connections between the group. All community researchers had some access to a basic smartphone and so using more accessible digital technologies to strengthen group cohesion and wellbeing became the focus of the project. The group were already communicating via a WhatsApp group. During the first month of lockdown, this became the social space for the group

to have informal conversations, in the same way they would over a hot drink or lunch during our face-to-face meetings ... The WhatsApp group became a strong and constant support network for members, a place not only to share their creative outputs but to also offer support and encouragement, especially where people were feeling isolated or anxious. (Gratton, 2020; Gratton et al., 2020)

─────────────── SPOT CHECK ───────────────

Where are your strengths? What literacies will you need to develop to conduct your study?

ENACTED APPROACHES FOR THE ONLINE ENVIRONMENT

The enacted methods outlined in this chapter are intended as a springboard for your thinking. Don't be limited by the frameworks and suggestions offered here! Use them in your own creative ways. You might decide that you want to add some enacted elements to an interview study or create a fully formed enacted inquiry.

─────────────── SPOT CHECK ───────────────

What creative, engaged approaches do you plan to use? Why? What rationale will you use to explain why the methods you have chosen are the best fit, given the purpose of the study?

Visual and Arts-Based Methods

Visual research has long been essential to inquiries in fields such as sociology, ethnography, and anthropology. The specialized disciplines of visual sociology and visual anthropology are grounded in the idea that valid scientific insight in society can be acquired by observing, analyzing, and theorizing its visual manifestations: behavior of people and material products of culture (Pauwels, 2011, p. 3).

Visual research methodologies, according to Banks (2007), have traditionally encompassed two main strands. The first strand points to ways researchers use visual images to capture observations in the field or graphically describe field data. Photography (still or moving images) or graphics (drawings, diagrams, or maps) have commonly been used to document research phenomena. The second classic approach to visual research revolves around collecting and studying images created by research participants or others in the participants' culture. This approach is used when researchers want to understand the significance or function of artifacts, or artistic or creative expressions.

Typology of Online Visual Interview Methods

The wide public use of digital cameras, web cameras, camera applications or mobile devices, and compact video cameras offers simple, accessible ways to take photographs or videos. Gestural and stylus-oriented graphics programs allow for images to be drawn. GPS programs allow for documentation of locations, and Geographic Information System and other mapping software programs can be used to generate maps. Any of these visual elements can be readily shared between researchers and participants online.

Four main types of visually oriented interactions are available to researchers and participants online (see Figure 12.1). First, they can *transmit* visual images. Researchers and participants can send each other image or media files, links to images posted on a server or website, or images captured in the moment. Second, in addition to sharing images, they can *view* visual representations of phenomena together. Researchers and participants can view photos, graphics, artifacts, or media during the research event. Third, researchers and participants can immerse themselves in a virtual environment to *navigate* through visually rich games, software applications, videos, or virtual environments. Finally, they can *generate* visual images. With the *collaborative image*, the researcher and the subjects work together to represent the phenomena of interest by creating new images or adding to pre-existing ones (Banks, 2007, p. 7). Participants who generate the visual material have another opportunity to reflect on and experience the research phenomenon by re-creating or reimagining it, and then by explaining the image to the researcher during the interview (Rose, 2016). Drawing or creating diagrams allows participants to use visual and spatial thinking and to show relationships between people or concepts.

To be inclusive and culturally sensitive, we can use technology to encourage the participants' authentic voices and be open to the possibility of uncovering and making new kinds of knowledge. The shift to using these types of data collection online seems like a natural stage of evolution from visual elicitation as previously practiced in interview research. Presenting interviewees with a single graphic or photographic image could constrain their thinking. Interviewees may be inclined to suggest only modifications to the diagram or image, rather than offering new conceptualizations. In other words, simply presenting an image to elicit responses can constrain the more creative and collaborative part of the process. By using a

Typology of Online Visual Methods

Researchers can do the following online:	In order to engage research participants through:
Transmit visual images. Image or media files, links to images posted on a server or website, or images captured in the moment are sent to the other party before, during, or after an interview or research event. **View** visual representations of phenomena together: Researchers can view photos, graphics, artifacts, or media before, during, or after an interview. **Navigate** in a visual virtual environment. Observe and experience websites, software applications, games, or 3-D virtual environments. **Generate** visual images. Access shared tools that allow researchers and/or participants to create drawings, diagrams or visual maps, snapshots or videos.	**Visual communication** describes the use of images to communicate abstract ideas, relationships between concepts or data, or examples of research phenomena. **Visual elicitation** refers to the process of using visual stimuli to draw out a verbal or a visual response. Stimuli can include photographs, media, graphics, drawings or artwork, diagrams, maps or mindmaps, The scenery or events in a virtual environment navigated by researcher and participant, the images or media generated during the research may stimulate response. **Visual collaboration** refers to a collaborative approach used to generate new thinking or creative responses by visually representing lived experiences related to the research phenomenon or problem. Researchers and participants can create, edit, or embellish images together during the interview or research event.

Figure 12.1 Typology of online visual methods

variety of collaborative and participant-generated visual approaches, the researcher can build understandings of concepts, feelings, and relationships not sufficiently explained verbally.

How can researchers make strategic use of these four types of visual exchanges in data collection activities? In earlier chapters we explored the use of ICTs as the medium, setting, or phenomenon (see Figure 2.4) and that model applies here as well (see Figure 12.2). Visual exchanges can serve the purpose of communication medium, to enrich the otherwise word-intensive process of data collection through in-depth interviews or documents. They are valuable because, due to the nature of the research problem or the characteristics of the participants (age, verbal literacy, first language or learning style), words alone may not be adequate.

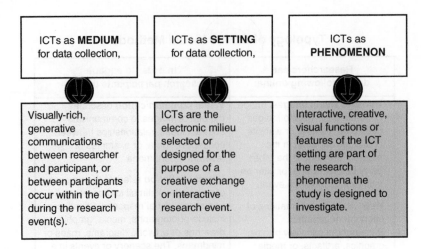

Figure 12.2 Choices for ICTs in enacted methods

Visual Communication

The world told is a different world to the world shown. (Kress, 2003)

Visual communication describes the use of images to reveal abstract concepts, relationships between concepts or data, or examples of research phenomena. A visual representation of the research phenomenon through pictures, media or graphics can convey details it would take many words to explain. Visual representations of some aspect of the research phenomena can be generated by the researcher, by the participant, or obtained from other sources.

One way to think about using visual methods as a communication medium is to distinguish between whether you want to use visuals to serve as the stimulus or response. When researchers ask questions or introduce themes, they hope to stimulate a fruitful response from the participants. While interviews generally use a verbal stimulus to produce a verbal response, visual communication allows for a wider range of possibilities. A question posed verbally can be answered by the participant who draws a diagram or shares a photograph. A visual representation of the question can be answered with a visual, text and/or a verbal response.

The setting can be a factor in visually rich online exchanges. Montiel discovered that the need for visual communication of certain activities meant online webcam access had to be negotiated, leading to technical problems he had not anticipated. The shift also had positive implications for richer discussions. For example, video interviews allow researchers to see the participants' own homes or offices. Montiel (2020) intended for participants to meet at the university to demonstrate a step-by-step process of making tea, for a sustainable design study. With the original plan, they would have been in a laboratory setting with standard implements. He found the video interview worked better 'because in this way people were making tea at their houses with the objects that they usually use in an environment that they are familiar with.' In that comfortable setting, participants discussed other aspects that would not have been captured in a laboratory setting (Montiel, 2020).

In another example, Chávez and her team discovered when they shifted research online, visual communication worked within the research project as well as externally to share their thinking more fully with stakeholders and decision-makers. Chávez, Castro-Reyes, and Echeverry (2020) designed a systematization of experiences (SOE) study, a participatory action research approach that originated in Latin America. 'SOE is based on groups' and communities' ability to create knowledge based on their experience, with or without external aid. Dialogue is the foundation of the research method' (Chávez et al., 2020, p. 112). To continue the dialogue after shifting online due to the COVID-19 pandemic, they invited participants to a virtual meeting in Microsoft Teams and conducted focus groups. They shared applications and whiteboards to collaboratively create timelines. They created spreadsheets in real time and color-coded them, for preliminary classification of responses. They used an application to produce word clouds to visualize discussions, and created infographics that could be shared with participants, used in organizations, and conveyed to stakeholders and decision-makers.

RESEARCH CAMEO 12.2

Researcher 3 plans to offer a publishing workshop online and collect data from the writers who participate. They will offer the workshop in three online sessions. They plan to use visual communication to help the students understand different pathways for getting books or articles published.

Researcher 4 is conducting a multimodal study, including observations of an online writing group and their related posts to social media, plus conduct email interviews with several group members. Like Researcher 3, they want to succinctly communicate steps and editors' expectations associated with the complex process of getting published. They believe a flow-chart would be easier for interviewees to understand than a lengthy written document.

SPOT CHECK

How would you define *visual communication*? In the context of your study, what concepts would you communicate visually, versus verbally or in writing?

VISUAL ELICITATION: 'WHAT DO THESE IMAGES, MEDIA, OR ARTIFACTS MEAN?'

Studies using enacted data collection often incorporate elicitation, in particular, visual, graphic, or film/video elicitation. The general term *visual elicitation* is used here to encompass the introduction of any kind of visual material into the interview or research event, including photographs, videos, drawings, artwork, diagrams, or graphics. Visual representations of some aspect of the research phenomenon can be generated by the researcher, by the participant, or obtained from extant or other sources. *Elicitation* in this context refers to interviews or research events that use visuals to elicit responses and stimulate discussion about participants' experiences of the research phenomenon. When you elicit data by questioning participants, you expect them to recall their experiences and be able to represent them in responses. You hope that their explanations are full and that they have not excluded details they've forgotten or are reluctant to share. With visual elicitation, participants are asked open-ended questions about visuals that depict some aspect of the phenomenon being studied. By sharing photographs or video, researchers and participants can visit other time periods or spaces that would be difficult for them to enter physically (Näykki & Järvelä, 2008). Prompting a participant with 'tell me about this photograph,' for example, shifts the locus of meaning away from descriptive representations of objects, places, people, or interactions. Instead, images gain significance through the way that participants engage and interpret them. Pink (2021) suggests that the researcher and participant can 'create a "bridge" between participants' different experiences of reality. The image becomes a common frame of reference for both parties – researcher and participant. As you can see in Figure 12.3, the use of visual stimuli can be structured, semi-structured, or unstructured.

When the subject matter is of a sensitive nature, the researcher and participant(s) can both turn to the visual image 'as a kind of neutral third party' (Banks, 2007, p. 65). Sometimes fictional vignettes or problematized scenarios shared through media can open a safe space for discussion of sensitive issues.

Participant-generated writing and/or photography provides topics for discussion in the online interview. For example, Waight (2020) adapted photovoice methods to an online study.

> After being briefed by email, participants were asked to take photographs over a one-week period using their own smartphone camera. They were instructed to photograph anything that seemed relevant to their writing experiences and many images contained no direct link to writing at all. To provide guidance on an appropriate number of images, five was suggested as a minimum and emphasized that they didn't have to take photographs every day. By suggesting a low number, it was hoped participants would consider this manageable. As a result, participants took between five

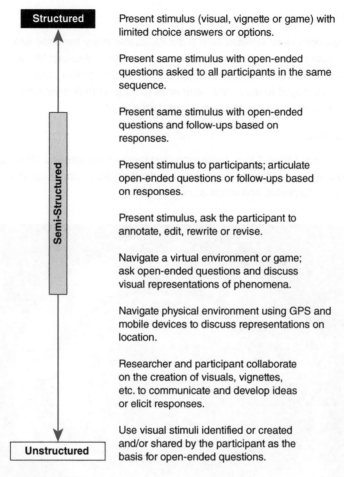

Structured

Present stimulus (visual, vignette or game) with limited choice answers or options.

Present same stimulus with open-ended questions asked to all participants in the same sequence.

Present same stimulus with open-ended questions and follow-ups based on responses.

Present stimulus to participants; articulate open-ended questions or follow-ups based on responses.

Present stimulus, ask the participant to annotate, edit, rewrite or revise.

Navigate a virtual environment or game; ask open-ended questions and discuss visual representations of phenomena.

Navigate physical environment using GPS and mobile devices to discuss representations on location.

Researcher and participant collaborate on the creation of visuals, vignettes, etc. to communicate and develop ideas or elicit responses.

Use visual stimuli identified or created and/or shared by the participant as the basis for open-ended questions.

Unstructured

Figure 12.3   Photo elicitation in a videoconference interview

and fourteen images. Images were emailed to the author before an online video interview took place in which participants were asked to use these images as prompts to discuss their experiences. (Waight, 2020, p. 99)

In another example, Clarke built a study around an ongoing project on Instagram, a project that demonstrated her skills and knowledge, and established credibility for the study (Clarke, 2020). Clarke and Watson (2020) used an online diary and photo elicitation mix of methods, inviting participants to share photos of their crafts alongside their diaries 'to capture the richness of narratives and experiences of participants' (p. 31) (see an example in Figure 12.4). Given that diaries were shared online in Instagram, participants understood that these were not private diaries (Clarke & Watson, 2020). Clarke's study offered both semi-structured and unstructured options.

Semi-structured:

> [P]articipants were emailed with a downloadable diary template which included the headings: 'Date', 'Location', 'What I'm crafting', 'Feelings/thoughts', 'Social media', 'Any other thoughts/reflections' and 'Photos of this craft' ... Participants were encouraged to utilize the framework to support their ownership and authorship in recording their experiences and crafts. (p. 31)

Unstructured:

> They were not limited to a single recording method and emailed their diaries, with photos, in diverse formats including handwritten accounts, email diaries, PDFs, videos, audio diaries and stitch diaries. (p. 31)

Figure 12.4   Clarke's research: An example of offline work posted online

—————————————— RESEARCH CAMEO 12.3 ——————————————

Researcher 3 plans to offer a publishing workshop online and collect data from the writers who participate. They will offer the workshop in three online sessions. They will ask students to generate visual maps or diagrams to illustrate the major stages and related obstacles they anticipate.

Researcher 4 constructed a flow-chart of the publication process for asynchronous email interviewees. They asked participants to annotate the chart in response to questions such as: note the places in the process where you feel confident of success, note the places where you are concerned about success, note your timeline and add dates to the chart.

Both researchers will collect these visual assignments as part of the data for their respective studies. They will use the participants' diagrams as a springboard for further questions.

SPOT CHECK

How would you define *visual elicitation*? In the context of your study, are there images or media that could spark conversation in an interview or other research event? Do you have access to images or media, or would you need to create them? Have you included time necessary to find or create images in your own research plans?

GENERATING VISUALS DURING THE RESEARCH EVENT

Visual collaboration refers to a collaborative approach to either stimulate new thinking or create responses in relation to visual representations of the research phenomena. Shared tools or whiteboards allow researchers and/or participants to create drawings, diagrams or visual maps, snapshots or videos as part of the research event. While we are exploring the ability to generate images online, researchers and participants can create or find and share physical drawings, journals, or artifacts. For example, you can see the difference between semi-structured and unstructured visual interactions that shift from visual elicitation illustrated in Figures 12.5 and 12.6. In 12.5, two

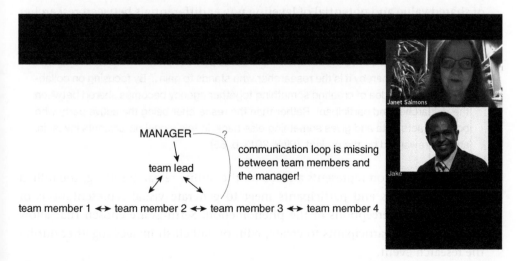

Figure 12.5 Semi-structured visual elicitation on a web conference platform

How do you write your first draft?

Figure 12.6 Options for structure in use of visual stimuli in enacted research events

graphics are offered as a springboard for discussion, after which the participant is asked to use the shared whiteboard to create a graphic describing communication patterns with leaders and team members. In Figure 12.5, they are presented with a broad question and a blank whiteboard.

Participants who generate the visual material can reflect on and experience the research phenomena by re-creating or reimagining it and then by explaining the image to the researcher (Rose, 2012). Drawing or creating diagrams allows participants to use visual and spatial thinking and to explore possible solutions to problems (Buckley & Waring, 2013). In this kind of collaborative method, the researcher and participant are consciously working together to produce visual images and specific types of knowledge through technological procedures and discussions (Pink, 2013, p. 62). Pink further points to the sense of shared value and potential of leveling power differentials between researcher and participant:

> [T]he relationship between researcher and participants is often characterized as one of inequalities whereby it is the researcher who stands to gain ... By focusing on collaboration and the idea of creating something together agency becomes shared between the researcher and participant. Rather than the researcher being the active party who both extracts data and gives something else back, in this model participants invest in, and are rewarded by, the project. (Pink, 2013, p. 65)

Visual collaboration represents a focus on the online research setting, the milieu where researchers and participants meet to generate visual representations of experiences or perceptions of the phenomenon. Settings are chosen that allow researchers and participants to create, edit, or embellish images together during the research event.

Multimodal qualitative studies, that is, studies using more than one qualitative method, often mix two online methods such as a review of extant or Big Data and interviews. You can also fruitfully combine digital and analog communications. As the examples below show, online exchanges with children or youth were mixed with research activities involving hard-copy books and journals sent through the post. With this potential for using physical items, materials, or artifacts, this approach could also be useful with participants for whom English is not the first language. Here are two examples:

1. Louise Cuoceiro's research 'explores how children aged seven to 14 in the United Kingdom respond to and engage with collective biographies of women published from 2016 onwards' (Couceiro, 2020a, p. 36). She sent each child hard-copy books by post. She was surprised at how excited participants were to receive the books, and to feel special and important to get something in the mail addressed to them personally. This helped them feel a part of the study, and motivated to read (Couceiro, 2020b).
2. Coleman et al. (2020) conducted a study using an imaginative, speculative methodology with youth participants. The study encompassed online and analog, synchronous and asynchronous, verbal and visual data collection.

> We assembled a multi-modal physical-digital ecology with home-posted-to-home content, Zoom, Microsoft Teams, email. One of the growths from this is the Zine Travels, a scicurious living data-artwork-science-zine (or da(r)ta-science zine) project, whereby we refer to the artistry of creative research within da(r)ta by inserting the 'r' for emphasis.
>
> Zines are typically low-fi, self-published creative works involving original or appropriated content. Each member of the zine project puts a zine into circulation. Once the zine is received, 'being scicurious' data is added by the receiver who makes the next zine page, then it is posted onwards to its next scicurious destination. This was a collaborative effort to untangle questions around identity, curiosity and belonging.
>
> The time-lapses that are part of postal interactions are consistent with our emergent methodology of cultivating breathing spaces. (Coleman et al., 2020, pp. 106, 109)

─────────────── RESEARCH CAMEO 12.4 ───────────────

Researcher 3 plans to offer a publishing workshop online and collect data from the writers who participate. They will offer the workshop in three online sessions. In the third session they want to create a collective visual representation of the

(Continued)

journey from completion of a study to publication of findings in a book or article. They will use the shared whiteboard feature to construct the map, then download it so each member has a copy. Researcher 3 will use this collective drawing in conjunction with individual students' drawings to better understand their perceptions of temporal and success factors, and obstacles.

SPOT CHECK

How would you define *visual collaboration*? In the context of your study, are there images or media that you hope to generate in an interview or other research event? Could participants create diagrams, visual maps, or time-series charts to explain their experiences? Why would these approaches work (or not) with your target participants, using your selected ICTs?

VIGNETTE, SCENARIO OR PROBLEM-BASED ROLE-PLAYS

Vignettes dramatize real events to show key aspects of the problem under investigation. In research they can be employed as elicitation tools to facilitate an exploration of participants' responses to hypothetical situations.

> A vignette is a short descriptor of a person, object, or situation that represents a cluster of key characteristics that can be explored and tested with the study participant. Vignette-based interviewing is a robust method used to explore beliefs, attitudes, and/or judgments, and why decisions are made in relation to particular situations. (Quigley, Michel, & Doyle, 2020)

The researcher presents the vignette in a written, visual, or media format and uses it as the basis for collecting data from a semi-structured or unstructured interview, focus group, or from a questionnaire.

In qualitative studies vignette approaches focus on the meanings participants ascribe to situations, and the decisions they might make to address problems as presented.

Vignettes can be the basis for role-plays where participants and researchers can speak from within various characters. Vignettes in online role-plays improve realism and increase the level of immersion in the situation.

Constructing Vignettes for Elicitation or Role-Play

The design process for vignettes occurs in three broad stages:

1. **Pre-Design Stage**: Researcher becomes familiar with the context and identifies factors of interest. You might decide to work with subject matter experts or with others who are familiar with the population.

2. **Design Stage**: Researcher and/or subject matter expert writes the vignette, being mindful of cues. You will need to think through the best way to present the vignette and devise the questions you want to pose in an interview. If you want to have a role-play with the participant(s), think about the role you will play and how you will handle it.

Finally, you will need to decide what online setting is best for your study, and whether to interact synchronously or asynchronously with participants. It is possible that you will want to use more than one option at different stages. For example in an asynchronous study you could post a video vignette in a private video-sharing site, then pose questions using an online questionnaire or emailed interview. Or you could interact synchronously by meeting participants in a web conferencing space where you can view or read the vignette, then pose questions or role-play possible responses to the situations depicted.

When constructing a vignette-based study you face the design decisions discussed in Chapter 11 in the context of interview questions: to what extent will the same vignette be used in the same way with all participants (more structured approach) or will the same vignettes be used in different ways depending on the participant (semi-structured approach), or will different vignettes be developed for each participant, co-constructed with participants or generated by participants (unstructured approach)? (See Figure 12.7.)

3. **Post-Design Stage**: Researcher and others (including individuals who meet sampling criteria or understand the target population) review the vignette for clarity and fill in missing information. Practice all stages of the study, including presentation of the vignette, elicitation, and/or role-play

─────────────── RESEARCH CAMEO 12.5 ───────────────

Researcher 3 plans to offer a publishing workshop online and collect data from the writers who participate. In one of the sessions, they will use a role-play exercise that will help writers prepare for a proposal discussion with an acquisitions editor. The role-plays will occur on the class web conferencing platform so will be recorded for review and analysis.

ISSUES IN ONLINE VISUAL RESEARCH

Images are not value free. Whether generated by people associated with the study or not, they were created from someone's subjective perspective, and that perspective enters the research discourse. Goldstein and Stanczak discuss these issues as they pertain to photography:

> When looking at a photograph, it is useful to first consider all of the technical choices made by the photographer. All of these results in the content of the image: what's in the frame (or, more accurately, what's before us, since the frame itself may be an important part of the image). However, the more interesting question is often why the photographer made these choices. Were they conscious or unconscious? What did he or she intend that we notice, and why? Do we see something that was perhaps unintended? If we decide that certain intent is present, does it work effectively, or could other choices have been more effective? What makes these questions interesting is that they often have more than one answer, or no answer at all. (Goldstein, 2007, p. 75)

> Eyewitness accounts and photo or video recordings may provide evidence not available in any other form, but they can also introduce judgments that depart from the facts of a matter. Material artifacts are similarly useful and problematic, not because artifacts make judgments but because the variations, arrangements, and modifications that make artifacts meaningful to researchers can reflect both naive and manipulative human agency. (Stanczak, 2007, p. 27)

In the qualitative options discussed in this book, the researcher focuses not on the image per se, but on the participants' explanations of the images. The researcher – and, to some extent, the participant – needs to demonstrate visual literacy skills to decode and interpret visual images. It is important to evaluate, acknowledge, and discuss perspectives, choices, and potential biases represented in images associated with the study. According to Pauwels's (Pauwels, 2020) 'Integrated conceptual framework for visual social research,' reports of the visual aspects of a study need to be related to, and compared and contrasted with, responses to verbal questions or data from documents or observations. In addition to discussion of methodologies and design choices, the researcher should provide an explanation of the broader context (cultural, historical) in which the visual product needs to be considered (Pauwels, 2020).

Ethical Issues

Issues of public versus private settings and related need for informed consent should be handled with the same care as any data collection (see Chapters 5 and 6). Covert research is an unacceptable privacy breach if 'covert research implies the researcher videoing and photographing the behaviour of [research participants] in a secretive rather than collaborative way, for example, using a hidden camera' (Pink, 2021, p. 53). Images should be treated as private data, with appropriate permissions articulated within the consent agreement (Banks, 2007). Permission to publish or disseminate images also must be part of informed consent. Ownership of images created for or during the interview should be spelled out. If images belonging to research participants (e.g., family photographs) are used in the interview, permissions to use them should be discussed and stated in informed consent or a separate agreement. If images are *not* the intellectual property of the researcher or participant, copyright regulations must be observed.

A COMPARISON OF POSSIBLE RESEARCH DESIGNS

Table 12.1 offers a comparison of three enacted research options to study the question, 'How do workers use social media during business hours?' In the first example, the researcher uses visual communication, in the second they elicit and generate visual representations, and in the third option the researcher uses role-plays to generate data.

SUMMARY OF KEY CONCEPTS

Enacted data collection involves a high level of involvement for consenting participants and the researcher. Indeed, enacted research calls upon the participants to serve as co-researchers. Together the researcher and co-researchers seek to understand meanings and significance. Enacted types of data collection may be used in conjunction with extant data and/or elicited data as described in the previous chapters, or in conjunction with quantitative methods such as surveys. Since the process of constructing such situations may entail technical skills, this kind of inquiry might be well suited to collaborative or team research projects.

The evolution of ICTs – with the popularization of myriad Internet-connected handheld devices with cameras, as well as computers with built-in web cameras and varied drawing and diagramming software – has changed online communications. These changes provide researchers with many options for visual research previously limited to well-funded studies with budgets for film or video cameras, technicians, and graphic artists. At the same time, the changes toward more visual communication styles – and greater orientation to the screen versus the page – mean research participants may be more comfortable expressing themselves with pictures. Drawing relevant practices from visual ethnography, sociology, and/or

Table 12.1 Research design comparisons

	Visual Communication: Exchanging Notes and Screenshots	Eliciting and Generating Visual Representations	Role-play Interviews
'How do workers use social media during business hours?'	In a diary and photovoice study, participants record their social media use each day for two weeks using a calendar application on their smartphones. They take screenshots of social media discussions or activities they found appealing. They are asked to take notes about their work and indicate when they felt distracted by social media.	In an exploratory study, the researcher observes discussions on social media sites and groups frequented by participants during business hours, and makes notes about topics being discussed.	A case study based on data generated through role-plays conducted in videoconferences with participants. Using vignettes constructed by the researcher, participants were asked to take the role of worker and then of manager, to discuss implications of social media use for productivity. Data included recordings of the role-plays, and researcher's field notes.
	Each day the researcher sends a text message prompt and reminder, and responds to any questions.	Visual representations of time-social-task relationships were created by the researcher. Using a shared whiteboard in a web conferencing space, participants were asked to annotate the diagram to reflect their own experiences or to draw their own diagrams.	
	At the conclusion of the two-week period, participants complete a short questionnaire, answering open-ended questions about their experiences.		
Data	Written notes by participants. Written responses via text messaging. Visual screen shots. Questionnaire.	Field notes from observations. Annotated visual diagrams. (Verbal) interview responses.	Media recording of interview and role-plays.
Time–Response Pros and Cons	Near-synchronous and asynchronous	Synchronous	Synchronous
	Pros: Short daily exchanges give the researcher insights into participants experiences' work cadence.	Pros: Annotating and discussing diagrams allows for a rich online interaction.	Pros: Combination of structure, with vignettes constructed by the researcher and unstructured conversation allows for broad exploration of their experiences.
	Cons: Reliance on writing and record-keeping by participants.	Cons: Participants need some visual and digital literacy and skills to engage.	Cons: Participants need to feel comfortable with and trust the researcher in order to embrace the roles and engage in candid discussions.

anthropology, contemporary researchers can design studies that build new understandings from verbal, text, and visual data collected in online interviews.

DISCUSSION QUESTIONS AND EXERCISES

- Think of a time when someone successfully used visual approaches to communicate with you. Describe the experience and identify why the message got through to you by visual means. Create a visual, digital story to share with your class or with peers.
- Using a sample research question, create two options for conducting enacted methods online with approaches introduced in this chapter. Create a table using Table 12.1 as a template for your comparative analysis.
- Conduct an online role-play with a peer from your class.

  - Discuss how, as a researcher, you experienced the role(s).
  - Identify the types of data the role-play could generate.
  - Based on the practice role-play and debrief, provide guidelines for researchers using this technique.

- Develop a visual research alternative for a published research study.
- What does 'multimodal literacy' mean to you? How digitally literate are you? What can you do to become more literate?
- Identify ethical risks or issues you might face if using enacted methods online. How will you address them?

SECTION V

WORKING WITH DATA AND REPORTING FINDINGS

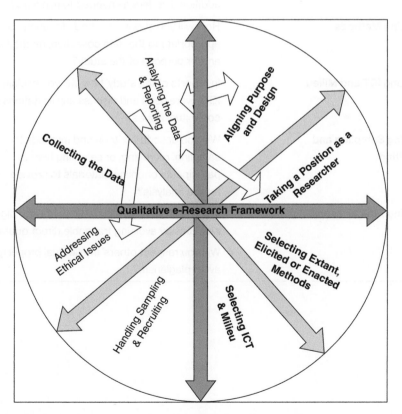

Figure V.1 Working with data and reporting findings in the context of the Qualitative e-Research Framework

Data collected online can, for the most part, be analyzed using the kinds of approaches qualitative researchers use to analyze data collected through other means. Once you have interpreted the findings, you can discuss what you have learned in formal or informal writings to make a contribution to the field and lay foundations for others to build upon. To consider these activities in the context of all the dimensions of the Qualitative e-Research Framework, some key questions are outlined in Table V.1. The full range of data analysis and writing methods are beyond the scope of this book. Additional resources are available in the Appendix.

Table V.1 Analysis and reporting issues in relation to the Qualitative e-Research Framework

	Analyzing the Data and Reporting
Aligning Purpose and Design	How do you plan to arrive at and explain findings within methodological traditions and paradigms described in the research design?
Taking a Position as a Researcher	Are you clear about your position? Will you explain any potential biases? Will you engage additional coders as needed to minimize bias?
Selecting Methods	How will you choose methods for analysis appropriate to the data collection, methodology, and/or purpose of the study?
Selecting ICT and Milieu	In reports of the study, how will you explain how ICTs were used and discuss any limitations or contextual issues?
Handling Sampling and Recruiting	Will you describe criteria and methods for sampling, recruiting, or selecting human participants or online materials to provide context for the analysis?
Handling Ethical Issues	Will you protect human participants and digital identities by avoiding traceable direct quotations? Will you respect others' intellectual property and avoid plagiarism?

13

Organizing, Analyzing, and Interpreting Data

There are no clearly agreed rules or procedures for analyzing qualitative data. (Spencer, Ritchie, & O'Connor, 2003)

HIGHLIGHTS

Once data has been collected online, it can be handled and analyzed in much the same way as data collected through other methods. That said, there is no one-size-fits-all approach for qualitative data analysis that online researchers can apply. Having completed their data collection, online researchers find they have many types of materials to organize, analyze, and interpret that could include visual, audio, multimedia, and text.

With the advent of numerous software packages for qualitative analysis, researchers also must decide which steps of the process to do by hand and which to carry out with the help of technology. Since a comprehensive explanation of this important area of the research process is outside the scope of this chapter, here approaches are compared and essential steps and questions discussed. A list of books dedicated to qualitative data analysis is included in the Appendix, and more resources are available on the book website.

OBJECTIVES

After reading and reflecting on this chapter, you will be able to:

- identify key steps needed to create an analytic strategy
- develop a plan for managing data
- describe stages of the data analysis process
- understand differences in analytic stages as practiced in qualitative methodological traditions
- differentiate between deductive, inductive, and abductive reasoning and explain how they would be used in data analysis and interpretation
- decide whether you want to use a CAQDAS or do manual coding.

PLAN THE ANALYTIC STRATEGY THAT FITS YOUR ONLINE STUDY

There are many options for interpreting and analyzing qualitative data. Articulating the approach and justifying your choices are part of the research design so should be considered from the beginning of your research journey. The analytic strategy should address the following questions:

- What stages will I follow?
- How will I manage and protect digital data?
- When will I begin to analyze the data: during or after data collection?
- Are specific analytic conventions or approaches part of the methodology I have selected? If so, how will I apply them?
- What form(s) of reasoning will I use to interpret the data and find meaning?
- What system will I use for coding? Will I use computer aided qualitative data analysis software (CAQDAS)?
- How will I interpret and analyze different types of data?

You may note that none of these questions is unique to studies using data collected online. Even if you have used technology to conduct your study, you can choose whether and how to use data analysis software tools for analysis. Let's look at each question.

WHAT STAGES WILL I FOLLOW?

Approaches to the analysis of qualitative data are presented here to demonstrate the general flow recommended by respected analysts. The broad stages are as follows:

1. *Managing and protecting the data.* This describes the practical steps of organizing and sorting the different types of data, and familiarization with the scope and substance of what was collected.
2. *Preliminary review and identification of major themes.* Some major themes may be deductively determined, based on the research problem, question, purpose, and the literature in the field. What were you seeking when you designed this study? Other major themes should be inductively determined: regardless of what you were seeking or thought about the research problem, what did you find? What forms of reasoning work best with your data and methodology?
3. *Coding* (two or more rounds). Coding entails close review, reading the data or viewing the images or media and labeling by codes, and adding new codes as they emerge. In essence, coding means naming concepts or keywords in text data, or dimensions or representations in visual or media data.
4. *Deepening understanding of themes, creating categories or typologies.* By naming, labeling and coding important elements you create the ability to summarize, compare, and contrast across the dataset. At this stage, look for relationships between themes. Closely review any outliers or unusual cases that may point to questions for future research.
5. *Interpreting the themes.* So what? How do the pieces fit together to tell the stories that help readers understand what you have discovered? Use abductive reasoning to develop explanations.
6. *Select illustrative thick descriptions.* Select stories or quotations to use in reports or articles. Consider ways to use diagrams, maps, or tables to show themes, sub-themes, and relationships.

──────────────── SPOT CHECK ────────────────

List the major stages of your analytic process. Make notes as you move through this chapter about the choices you will consider for your study, and the steps you will take. Keep in mind that data analysis, especially when it includes multiple forms of data, is beyond the scope of this book, so make notes of questions you have, so you can seek additional source material specific to the knowledge and skills you will need to move forward.

How Will I Manage and Protect Digital Data?

Sometimes it is the small things that trip us up and data management can be one. Pick a system at the outset of your process and stick with it through to the end, otherwise you can waste a lot of time trying to find a specific file or remember the important point you wanted to include. Since online researchers collect digital data, creating a file system is a first step. Create an index for your file system so you can locate items when you need them. Consider using a note-taking software like OneNote or Evernote that allows you to create folders or sections for each participant, source, or type of data. Decide how you will work with media files, images, and photographs – will you file them by media type or by participant or source? Decide on a labeling system and be consistent about using it.

Save a clean copy of written documents or transcriptions before you begin to organize and code them. Make sure ALL original files are backed up on your primary computer and a separate drive and stored in a safe location. If your computer is used by others, set a password on your data files to avoid inadvertent access or damage to the data.

Some online researchers manage all the data electronically. Others prefer printed copies of some materials. You might find that printing out all the transcripts, etc., is too much, but having paper copies of your research memos and the index is helpful when you are trying to manage a large and complex corpus of data. There is no right or wrong system, just the right system for you.

Ethical research practices include protection of the data as you move from collection to analytic stages. In the olden days, that meant keeping records in a locked filing cabinet. Today we need to think in terms of three main places we store digital files:

1. In the cloud, in an online folder or service.
2. On the hard drive of our computer.
3. On a thumb or backup drive.

If you choose to store your data in the cloud, place behind a two-factor authentication or use the best security options available. However, whenever possible, avoid putting your data at risk by leaving it on the cloud.

You might have collected data on a platform that saves copies of your interactions with participants. If you have data on video conferencing or social media platforms, download it to your own hard drive and delete saved copies from the commercial site, otherwise you cannot verify protection of the data because you don't control it. Many video conferencing platforms give you a choice: you can record directly to your hard drive or to the cloud. When you have this option, choose to record to your own computer.

On your own computer, make sure you have anti-malware software installed to reduce the chance of hacking or other data theft. If you share the computer with others, create a password protected space to store your data. Storing data on a thumb or backup drive is handy, especially if you work on more than one computer or need to move from the library, cafe, or field site to your home. However, the mobile nature of these small drives increases the likelihood for misplacing or losing them. If possible, create password protection so others cannot access your data. Thumb drives are also useful when you want to back up your data and your writing without storing it on the cloud. Indeed, a backup thumb drive stored in a safe place can give you peace of mind.

———————————————— SPOT CHECK ————————————————

The digital world is notoriously unstable, so backing up is a habit you want to cultivate. How are you protecting your work, including drafts, academic papers, literature reviews, or presentations you might want to reference?

WHEN WILL I BEGIN TO ANALYZE THE DATA: DURING OR AFTER DATA COLLECTION?

When does analysis start? For some studies it is important to wait until you have finished collecting all of the data, and analyze it all together. In these cases, the researcher wants to be able to look at all of the responses or all of the materials and find common or contrasting themes. For other studies, the analysis process may occur in stages that are interspersed with data collection. Kennedy described these two options:

> There are at least two ways to relate data collection to analysis in the research process. In a *linear-sequential approach*, researchers first collect all data and then start to analyze. This is common in quantitative research but could also be applied in qualitative research, for instance when doing content, thematic, discursive, conversational, or phenomenological analysis after collecting all data. In contrast, an *iterative approach* refers to an interplay between data collection and analysis. Researchers move back and forth between data collection and analysis during this research process. The ongoing data analysis guides researchers to change or add a new data gathering method, to decide which data to collect next and where to find them. The iterative approach is essential, for example, in ethnography and grounded theory, but could be adopted in a range of qualitative research approaches. The two approaches of how to relate data collection and analysis to each other should be understood as ideal types or the opposite ends of a continuum, in which researchers could be more or less close to one of the ends. (Kennedy, 2018, p. 48)

These two approaches are both viable options for online studies. Sometimes an iterative approach is preferable because you want to make sure your data collection strategy is working and be able to check that the data fits your criteria. An iterative approach might fit a multimethod study because you may want to analyze responses to an initial online questionnaire or analyze extant data before articulating interview questions for the next stage of the study. Alternatively, you might adapt a linear approach and analyze all of one type of data, such as all of the images, before analyzing all of another type, such as the text data (see Figure 13.1).

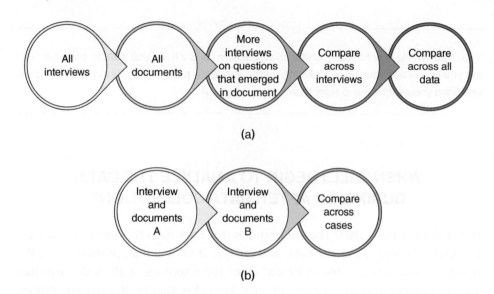

(a)

(b)

Figure 13.1 Sequencing stages of the analysis

─────────────── RESEARCH CAMEO 13.1 ───────────────

Initial Plans for Data Analysis

Researcher 1 plans to conduct the analysis using a linear-sequential approach to begin coding after all data are collected. First, they will code references from journal databases by discipline and location of the lead author's academic institution. They will categorize accordingly, creating two sets of lists. Next, they will code by keywords for methodologies, methods, and publication dates.

Researcher 4 plans an iterative approach. They will begin coding transcripts, observation notes, and visual artifacts while continuing to collect data. After all interviews are completed, they will do a second round of coding of all the data.

─────────────── SPOT CHECK ───────────────

Which cameo most closely resembles your study? Do you favor a linear-sequential or iterative approach to data analysis?

ARE SPECIFIC ANALYTIC CONVENTIONS OR APPROACHES PART OF THE METHODOLOGY I HAVE SELECTED?

The analytic strategy should be grounded in the methodological tradition of the study. The following notes are offered to give you a sense of the variations between major qualitative methodologies in regard to the sequence or adaptation of the six major steps. This question of the timing and sequence of the analysis process may be determined by methodological recommendations.

Case Study

There is not a set process for case study analysis. Researchers can choose a linear or iterative approach. Yin describes four approaches: 1) using the theoretical propositions as a framework, 2) working from the ground up, using a grounded theory approach, 3) developing case descriptions, or 4) examining rival explanations (Yin, 2018).

Some case study researchers make use of the constant comparative method, 'defined by the simple principle of going through data again and again (this is the *constant* bit), comparing each element – phrase, sentence or paragraph – with all of the other elements (this is the *comparative* bit)' (Thomas, 2016, p. 204). They also use pattern matching, explanation building, and time-series analysis strategies.

Researchers who use data collected online to build case studies can learn appropriate ways to analyze data from *Case Study Research* by Robert Yin (2018) or the classic *Art of Case Study Research* by Robert Stake (1995). The updated, more detailed text by Yin offers four different strategies for organizing the case study and five techniques for data analysis. Stake's book offers one example for analyzing data and generating naturalistic generalizations.

Ethnography

Ethnographers collect data in the field, whether that means a remote village or an online community. Analysis is woven throughout the research experience, as the researcher works to make sense of diverse perspectives and sources. Researchers using written materials rely on forms of content analysis. Researchers using participant observations, interviews, and other interactions use an iterative process. Ethnographers look for patterns in what they see and hear from the research site.

Ethnographers see patterns of thought and action repeat in various situations and with various players. The ethnographer begins with a mass of undifferentiated ideas and behaviors, and then collects pieces of information, comparing, contrasting, and sorting gross categories and minutiae until a discernible thought or behavior becomes identifiable. The process requires further sifting and sorting to make a match between categories. The theme or ritualistic activity finally emerges, consisting of a collection of such matches between the model (abstracted from reality) and the ongoing observed reality. (Fetterman, 2020, p. 101)

Grounded Theory

The expectations for grounded theory analysis are very specific: to generate new theoretical principles. Grounded theory researchers build on the understanding of individuals' experiences derived through phenomenological methods to generate theoretical principles (Creswell, 2013; Strauss, 1987). They look at categories discovered in the data and construct explanatory theoretical frameworks, which provide abstract, conceptual understandings of the studied phenomenon. For practical steps see *Constructing Grounded Theory: A Practical Guide Through Qualitative Analysis* by Kathy Charmaz (Charmaz, 2014).

Situational analysis is a style of grounded theory. Situational analysis looks at the social *situation*, while grounded theory looks at social *process*. Situational analysts diagram elements in the research *situation* to capture the complexities and show relationships in the data. In *Situational Analysis: Grounded Theory After the Postmodern Turn*, Clarke, Friese, and Washburn (2018) use examples, illustrations, and clear explanations to promote situational and positional maps as analytic exercises. The situational analysis approach may be useful beyond grounded theory contexts for researchers investigating policies, opinions, or other social science arenas where research participants express distinctive positions on the topic of inquiry.

Thornberg and Charmaz (2014) point out that:

Grounded theory (GT) is a research approach in which data collection and analysis take place simultaneously. Each part informs the other, in order to construct theories of the phenomenon under study. (Thornberg & Charmaz, 2014, p. 153)

Grounded theory researchers begin looking for categories in data as it is collected by using focused or theoretical coding (Charmaz, 2006). This is a process of fragmenting data into conceptual components. Using these components, the researcher can consider how each concept might be related to larger, more inclusive concepts – called categories (Bernard, Wutich, & Ryan, 2017). Using constant comparison, the researcher codes each text, thinking about each theme as it appears and asking whether it was like any other theme that had come before. Grounded theory researchers use both inductive and deductive reasoning. Inductive reasoning helps them isolate patterns to form conceptual categories. Abductive reasoning is used to select or identify a hypothesis that explains a particular empirical case or set of data and is a worthy candidate for further investigation (Thornberg & Charmaz, 2014).

Narrative or Diary

Ollerenshaw and Creswell (2002) discuss two approaches for analyzing and interpreting the stories at the heart of narrative research. One is the problem-solution approach and the other is the three-dimensional space approach (Ollerenshaw & Creswell, 2002). Steps for the problem-solution approach they describe are adapted here for analysis of digital data:

- Record interviews and transcribe them or choose to work with the audio or media file directly. If you are working from written narratives or diaries, save a clean copy before you begin to organize and code.
- Read and reread the transcript, or listen and re listen, to give a sense of the data.
- Color code the transcript for the elements of plot structure (characters, setting, problem, actions, and resolution). If working from an audio or media file, make notes about the place in recording where these elements appear.
- Graphically organize the color-coded transcripts into events representing the setting, problem, physical actions, reactions, thinking, intentions, and emotionally driven goals of the characters and resolution.
- Sequence the events. Rework the sequence until it makes sense. The sequence begins with the characters, setting, and problem. 'The events are sequenced to form an action map that begins with the question and ends with the resolution' (2002, p. 335).

Phenomenology

The phenomenological approach described by Clark Moustakas (1994) also involves three steps: Phenomenological Reduction, Imaginative Variation and Synthesis.

- *Phenomenological Reduction*: At this stage phenomenological researchers talk about 'horizonalizing' the data. 'When we horizonalize, each phenomenon has equal value.' The concept of horizon is of the unlimited and unfolding, which for the researcher means an attitude of continuous seeking for new understanding (p. 95). The researcher does not privilege one type of data over another, looking carefully at each source.
- *Imaginative Variation*: In the next stage, the researcher seeks possible meanings through the use of imagination by varying the frames of reference and approaching the phenomenon from divergent perspectives. Steps include:

Table 13.1 Data analysis and representation by research approaches (Creswell & Poth, 2017)

Data Analysis and Representation	Narrative	Phenomenology	Grounded Theory Study	Ethnography	Case Study
Managing and organizing the data	Create and organize data files.	Create and organize data files.	Create and organize data files.	Create and organize data files.	Create and organize data files.
Reading and memoing emergent ideas	Read through text, make margin notes, and form initial codes.	Read through text, make margin notes, and form initial codes.	Read through text, make margin notes, and form initial codes.	Read through text, make margin notes, and form initial codes.	Read through text, make margin notes, and form initial codes.
Describing and classifying codes into themes	Describe the patterns across the objective set of experiences or source materials. Identify and describe the stories into a chronology.	Describe personal experiences and perceptions of each participant. Describe the essence of the phenomenon.	Describe open coding categories. Select one open coding category to build toward central phenomenon in process.	Describe the social setting, actors, and events; draw a picture of the setting.	Describe the case and its context.
Developing and assessing interpretations	Locate epiphanies within stories. Identify contextual materials.	Develop significant statements. Group statements into meaning units.	Engage in axial coding – causal condition, context, intervening conditions, strategies, and consequences. Develop the theory.	Analyze data for themes and patterned regularities.	Use categorical aggregation to establish themes or patterns.
Representing and visualizing the data	Restory and interpret the larger meaning of the story.	Develop a textural description – 'what happened.' Develop a structural description – 'how the phenomenon was experienced.' Develop the 'essence,' using a composite description.	Engage in selective coding and interrelate the categories to develop a 'story' or propositions or matrix.	Interpret and make sense of the findings – how the culture 'works.'	Use direct interpretation. Develop naturalistic generalizations of what was 'learned.'

    o   Systematic varying of the possible structural meanings that underlie the textural meanings

    o   Recognizing underlying themes or contexts that account for the emergence of the descriptions of the phenomenon

    o   Considering universal structures, such as time, relation to others, that precipitate feelings and thoughts with reference to the phenomenon

    o   Searching for exemplifications that illustrate the themes and facilitate the development of a structural description of the phenomenon.

- *Synthesis*: At this stage, the researcher integrates the textural and structural descriptions to characterize the experience of the phenomenon as a whole. The statements that emerge from this synthesis are the basis for reporting research outcomes and conclusions.

A researcher using a phenomenological approach collects all data before beginning the analysis. In the first stage, all types of data are looked at and given equal weight. In the second stage, the researcher views, reads, and listens to the data for themes, relationships and structures. In the third stage, these themes are synthesized into overarching statements. A researcher using multiple types of digital data can create 'statements' in those same forms, including visual or media presentations, as well as written reports.

Comparing Approaches

The brief descriptions in Table 13.1 provide a sketch of similarities and differences between methodological approaches.

─────────────── RESEARCH CAMEO 13.2 ───────────────

Data Analysis Plans by Methodology

Researcher 1 will use a case study methodology and a linear-sequential approach. They plan to construct cases based on the coding categories of discipline, geographic location, methodology, methods, and dates. They will develop case descriptions, as suggested by Yin (2018). They will construct a time-series analysis with data organized by date, and will conduct keyword cluster analysis to identify methodological and disciplinary trends (Ebrahim et al., 2020). The data, bibliographic entries in journal databases, will be in text form.

Researcher 2 will use a phenomenological methodology. They will collect all interview data, and then begin the stages of Phenomenological Reduction, Imaginative

(Continued)

Variation and Synthesis. For the first stage, they will listen to and view recordings, making notes and memoing. If participants shared any visuals in the interviews, such as pictures of their journals or diagrams of their writing process, they will set those aside. They will make sure they have permission to use non-representational images in publications or presentations. Next, they will transcribe the interviews into text files and moving to the next stage of coding to find themes and contexts that reflect on the phenomenon of writing with group support and exchange.

Researcher 3 will conduct an exploratory qualitative study. Because they are interested in the experiences of writers in an online workshop, they will complete research memos after each class to reflect on the tone, progress, and other observations such as participation levels. They will download or transcribe comments from the classroom discussions, and export student writings into folders established for each individual. They will use a narrative analysis on these text-based documents. While they are not looking for plot and character, they do want to see how the participants' writings evolved over the course of the workshop.

Researcher 4 will conduct an ethnographic study. They will create initial categories when they analyze the data as it is collected and continue to sift the data for new themes and patterns. They will have text-based data from review comments group members made to one another, and email interviews, and will use a content analysis process to gain an understanding of the individuals' experiences and the writing group as a whole.

SPOT CHECK

What methodology are you using to frame your study? Do methodologists offer guidance about data analysis, or leave it up to the researcher to devise a strategy?

WHAT FORM(S) OF REASONING WILL I USE TO INTERPRET THE DATA AND FIND MEANING?

When we conduct qualitative research online we typically gather a lot of data, possibly in more than one form, that we need to work through to find meaning and understand the significance of the study. However, this stage of the inquiry is not a computational endeavor for qualitative researchers. We use an interplay of right- and left-brain activities, and systematic steps are woven together with reflective contemplation. We use both analytic strategies and our own sensemaking to find the connecting threads. We use reasoning to look for insight when we look at the individual story in relation to the big picture.

Researchers can work from deductive, inductive, or abductive perspectives. Which makes the most sense for your study? One way to start is by looking at the original design for this study and in particular the degree of structure imposed on the data collection methods. Researchers who used more structured styles of questioning begin analysis with some classifications that naturally emerge when consistent sets of questions are asked of all participants, or consistent sets of criteria are used in observations. They are using deductive thinking. Other researchers who conducted unstructured interactions have a wide-ranging collection of data they will need to classify. They are using inductive thinking. For example, the first researcher might have asked participants about where they grew up, the occupations of their parents, and favorite playtimes with friends. They begin organizing the data with three broad categories. The second researcher might have simply asked participants 'tell me about your childhood.' The second researcher will need to review the data before identifying themes and categories across the corpus. One is not right or wrong, they are just different. To attend to those differences the researchers will need to apply relevant ways of thinking.

Inductive reasoning means the researcher 'moves from particular instances to conclusions about general principles' (Sage Research Methods, 2021). Data is explored to find regularities, patterns, and themes that lead to generalizations and eventually theory (O'Leary, 2007). The inductive thinker draws more general statements from observed cases (Eriksson & Kovalainen, 2008). When you use inductive reasoning, you seek to find order in chaos, to find the whole from the pieces.

Conversely, **deductive reasoning** is used for research in which a specific explanation is deduced from a general premise, theory, or hypothesis and is then tested (Schutt, 2006). Data is analyzed to see if the premise can be confirmed and the theory substantiated (O'Leary, 2007).

Abductive reasoning is a third form that, along with inductive and deductive reasoning, shows a way you can come to a conclusion. Abductive reasoning is used when the researcher has an insight or makes a guess or an assumption that a connection exists in an incomplete or seemingly unrelated set of observations. Philosopher Charles Sanders Peirce (1839–1914) is credited with the origination of this concept and for applying it to pragmatic thinking.

Don't Be Limited to One Form of Reasoning!

Qualitative analytics are often described as an inductive process, and quantitative analytics as a deductive process. However, qualitative researchers are not limited to inductive reasoning only. Reichertz (2014) points out that: 'These forms of thinking are ... means of connecting and generating ideas. Because they represent the intellectual building blocks of research, they are method neutral' (p. 123). Vogt et al. (2014) observe that purely inductive research would be impossible because that would mean the study is undertaken with no preconceived ideas to direct the researcher's attention when determining what to observe. And surely deductive reasoning can be used in research where the question suggests a premise or is based in a theory. Using the hypothetical example, the first researcher started with a premise that childhood experiences include a sense of place, influences of parents, and play with other children. This premise did not rule out other kinds of experiences, but simply framed the questions to provide a common starting point with all participants. The second researcher started with a more open query, that allowed participants to prioritize the most important kinds of experiences.

Researchers may find that more than one style of thinking is needed at different stages of the analysis:

- At the analytic strategy planning stage, you can deduce a priori codes based on the research questions, definition of the problem, theoretical framework, and/or concepts from the literature.
- At the coding stage, you can use a priori codes as a starting point for deductive reasoning while using inductive reasoning to identify additional codes.
- At the interpreting stage, making sense of concepts and relationships.
- At the meaning-making stage, building understandings from the entire process.

At the coding stage a researcher using a deductive perspective would ask: What premises, categories, and principles are present in the design that I should look for in the data? What concepts or keywords from the research problem statement, research question, theoretical framework, seminal literature interview questions or observation guide should become a priori codes? The researcher working from an inductive mindset would ask: What codes emerge from careful reading of the data, without a set of guiding suppositions? At the meaning-making stage, either researcher could use abductive reasoning and ask: How can I look for connections that reasonably suggest a move from codes to clusters or categories and then to explanations?

—————————————— SPOT CHECK ——————————————

How will you use deductive, inductive, and/or abductive reasoning to analyze and interpret the data you will collect or have collected?

WHAT SYSTEM WILL I USE FOR CODING? WILL I USE COMPUTER AIDED QUALITATIVE DATA ANALYSIS SOFTWARE (CAQDAS)?

A third question relates to the approaches to use for coding generally and use of technology tools in the analysis process.

Coding is an essential part of the analysis process:

> Coding requires the researcher to interact with and to think about the data. It is a systematic way in which to condense extensive data sets into smaller analyzable units through the creation of categories and concepts derived from the data. Coding makes links between different parts of the data that are regarded as having common properties. Coding facilitates the organization, retrieval, and interpretation of data and leads to conclusions on the basis of that interpretation. (Lockyer et al., 2004)

Will software be used in the coding of data or not? Why? Increasingly, researchers are using software for some of these data analysis steps. Data management and storage, text retrieval, and coding are possible with various CAQDAS programs. The analytic stages broadly described in this chapter can be completed manually, or with a CAQDAS. That said, when working with more complex and large-scale types of data, you might find that data analysis software is worth the investment and time needed to acquire and learn these tools. One researcher observed the following:

> I found that switching from paper-based to electronic, software-based research allowed more freedom to play with ideas, because researchers can link and compare patterns within and across documents and the results can be saved, printed, or undone at will. When beginning a project, researchers create new documents or import text, numerical data, and graphics files from compatible software programs. [The software] organizes raw data (interviews, observations, etc.) and links them with memos where researchers might make codes and analytical notes, and then edit and rework ideas as the project progresses. For those involved in multiple projects, it is helpful to keep track of activities from one session to the next. Video images can also be linked to text documents. (Walsh, 2003, p. 253)

Kristi Jackson, co-author of *Qualitative Data Analysis with NVivo* (Jackson & Bazeley, 2019) noted advantages of the updated versions of these tools, including:

> ease of analyzing on-line communication and interaction that occurs on Twitter, Facebook, YouTube, and even email! Users can very easily capture some social media data or link to it (subject, of course, to the restrictions established by the platform). Physical artifacts can be represented via video or images/pictures, along with descriptions of these artifacts such as their size, texture or location. So, even if you can't import something into a Project, you can still find a mode to represent it (like a photograph) and further handle/analyze it. (Salmons, 2019b)

Researcher as Coder

Will you, the researcher, be the only person carrying out stages of the analysis or will others take a part of the process? Some researchers involve others in transcribing recordings or in coding. Sometimes others are involved simply to help the researcher move more quickly through the process. Alternatively, they may have a role in providing inter-rater reliability. What are the expectations for any other research assistants or team members? Does the researcher need to develop an agreement that ensures confidentiality and protection of the participants' identities?

SPOT CHECK

Thinking about using a CAQDAS? Here are a few tips:

- Check to see if your university has a site license available for you to use.
- Download trial versions of software you are considering and look at the tutorials to see whether you find it adequate and workable for the kinds of data you are collecting.
- Learn the software before you are under time pressure to analyze your data. These programs are complex and require some attention to learn.
- Carry out an analysis of extant data or published literature to practice using the CAQDAS before you tackle your data.

HOW WILL I INTERPRET AND ANALYZE DIFFERENT TYPES OF DATA?

There is copious guidance available for working with data in text form. In this section, find some tips and examples for working with visual or video data, and with large datasets.

Visual and Video Data

Your online study could generate visual, aural or multimedia data. Contemporary data analysis software allows you to upload these forms of data so you can review and code them, but how should you proceed? Here are a few key questions and options, with examples that reference the Research Cameos.

- Will you transcribe the audio or video data then analyze the written version? Or will you look at the full range of messages and cues embedded in the original data? Similarly, will images such as drawings, graphics or photographs be described, and the written description subjected to analysis or will the images be analyzed directly? Keep in mind that even if you are working from transcriptions, it may be worthwhile to listen to the original recordings, and/or view any visual data multiple times.

Researcher 2 conducted interviews with individual researchers using video conferencing. They will have recordings that include the writer on camera, responding to questions, and any photographs, diagrams, or other artifacts shared in the interview. Researcher 2 will first review each recording and make note of any non-verbal cues with time stamps so they can associate those responses with the words the participant spoke. Researcher 2 will take screen shots of visual data shared by each participant, and code that data along with the transcripts.

- Did participants generate the visual or media data? Did they explain why it was meaningful to them? If so, will you use their descriptions as the sole basis of analysis, or will you carry out additional analysis?

Researcher 4 conducted observations of a writing group and their related social media posts, then conducted email interviews with selected participants. They captured images group members posted that fit into one or more of three categories:

- o Images members posted of their writing space or office
- o Images members posted of timelines or diagrams of their writing process
- o Images members posted of finished products, such as book covers.

When they downloaded images, they also selected the users' explanations and when managing the data, Researcher 4 was careful to associate the comments and the images.

Researcher 4 began by making notes to denote elements in each image, then to connote initial interpretations. Within the three initial categories, Researcher 4 identified codes to label productive images the writers described in positive terms and codes to label images participants labelled as distractions or problematic.

- Can you use denotation and/or connotation to describe images in a way that provides specificity to your analysis? Ledin and Machin (2018) found the tools identified by Barthes (1977) useful for identifying questions for analysis of photographs or other representational images. The first, *denotation*, means asking what persons, places, and things you see in the image. 'We are not interpreting these photographs. When we ask what a photograph denotes, we are asking who and/or what is depicted. We are identifying the form of expression used and the meaning potentials chosen for this particular instance of communication' (Ledin & Machin, 2018, p. 48). They describe the second, *connotation*, as the ideas, values in wider discourses communicated, including individual elements as well as wider meanings created by the combination of visual elements (p. 49.) Ledin and Machin (2018) also suggest looking at specific elements such as the objects portrayed, colors used, settings and individual people or groups represented.
- How will you analyze multimedia video data? Knoblauch, Tuma and Schnettler (2014) echo the distinctions between denotation and connotation when discussing standardized versus interpretive video analysis:

Standardized video analysis consists of the coding of video segments according to a pre-established coding scheme deduced from (more or less explicit) theoretical assumptions. As a consequence, stretches of video-recorded interactions that vary in length from tens of seconds to several minutes are subsumed under prefixed categories. In sharp contrast, *interpretive video analysis* follows a different methodological premise: it assumes that the actions recorded are guided by meanings that must be understood by the actors themselves. It is only on the basis of the meanings of actions to the actors involved, that is, 'first order constructs', that researchers pursue their questions and create their 'second order constructs'. (2014, p. 426)

Researcher 2 generated videos of each interview. They plan to start with an adaptation of the standardized approach, coding each interview based on the ways each one related to the research question. Researcher 2 selected a platform that provides a transcript of the audio portion of the event; they will code the transcripts. They will also review the transcript and verify whether additional codes or refinements of the coding system are appropriate. Once this standardized coding is complete, they will review each interview again, looking with an interpretive eye towards meanings the participants gave to their experiences. Researcher 2 feels that by using this strategy with the video data, transcripts, and research memos about non-verbal cues, they will have completed a robust analysis.

When researchers collect visual data, they add new analytic steps and potential concerns. These examples provide you with a starting point for further exploration of ways to analyze different types of data.

Large Datasets or Big Data

Depending on the scale of the data, your CAQDAS might be a workable tool. You can use the autocode features to do your initial text analysis and find the major themes and trends. Some CAQDAS have mapping of visualization features that will help you look more closely at the dataset.

Davidson, Edwards, Jamieson, and Weller (2019) suggest a 'breadth-and-depth method' for analyzing extant qualitative data. Whether they are Big Data or simply a quantity of material that cannot be handled with typical qualitative approaches, new ways of thinking are needed. Davidson et al. suggest that it is not enough to simply scale up or do more or a bigger analysis to address larger collections. The methods they describe are iterative, recursive steps that allow you to understand the breadth of the large set of data and the depth appreciated by qualitative researchers.

They suggest a series of steps, discussed here in the context of the data collection strategies described in this book (Davidson et al., 2019, pp. 369–373). We will look at them in relation to the efforts of Researcher 1, whose data were collected qualitative entries from journal databases.

1. Surveying archived datasets to create a new assemblage of data.

Begin by looking at the meta data in the materials you have collected, such as type of data, date of collection, and the socio-demographic characteristics of research participants. Scrutinize these narratives and associated lists of meta data in relation to the inclusion criteria you devised for your study. Develop a precursory understanding of the nature, quality, and suitability of datasets or items for inclusion in the assemblage that will become the new corpus.

Researcher 1 has collected thousands of entries from journal databases. At this step, they will look to verify that the entries fit within the inclusion criteria, and discard those that do not. For example, they will verify that the entries represent qualitative research studies and will exclude editorials, reviews, and other kinds of articles.

2. Recursive surface thematic mapping.

This step entails 'working back and forward between computer-aided surface "thematic" mapping across the corpus and reading of short extracts around samples of "themes" to check their relevance. This is a recursive process likely to involve multiple iterations as readings will sometimes reveal text that is ambiguous in meaning or tangential to the research questions. This would result in elimination of the "theme" and a return to the mapping process' (2019, p. 370).

Researcher 1 will use a CAQDAS to identify keywords and frequently mentioned terms. They will use these to group entries by broad themes, such as methodology, method, and discipline. They will pull out abstracts, as short extracts that can help in further defining and refining themes. Researcher 1 will go back through the computer-aided text analysis to test any new themes for presence across the corpus.

3. Preliminary 'test pit' analysis, remapping, and repetition of preliminary analysis.

In this step, 'key words or "themes" identified by the mapping process can then be sampled for further preliminary examination. In archaeological metaphor terms this is akin to digging shallow test pits, where the digging is only deep enough to show whether anything of interest is present in the data extract being examined. … It is important not to be drawn into wider or deeper reading at this stage since multiple sites must be given this level of preliminary examination in order to justify where to undertake deeper analysis' (2019, p. 371).

Researcher 1 will select one theme, ethnography, for a preliminary analysis. They will pull samples to verify that the text analysis has correctly selected ethnographic studies, rather than bibliographic references in research using other methodology. If, for example, this is the case, they might need to revisit the way they set up the CAQDAS search.

4.   In-depth analysis of the type that is familiar to most qualitative researchers.

Finally, for the next step you will move 'from examining extracts of data to working with whole cases ... The question of "how many is enough" surfaces again for cases to excavate. As with sampling for preliminary analysis, the logic of selection will be shaped by the research questions, the research design, and the different points of further interest thrown up by the thematic analytic "digging"' (2019, p. 372).

As a qualitative researcher, you are selecting cases that will allow you to carry out the thematic coding and interpretation that you can use to answer the research question. You will not necessarily select a strictly representative sample of cases to explore in more depth.

Researcher 1 has decided to review five cases for each of the inclusion criteria: methodology, method, discipline, and national base of the publication. They will try to make sense of the analysis of the corpus as a whole, with more detailed interpretation of these selections, to better understand publication trends for qualitative research as defined in the research problem.

——————————— SPOT CHECK ———————————

What types of data will you, or did you, collect? How will you organize and work with each type? What knowledge and skills will you need to develop to do so?

————————————————————————————————

WHAT DO METHODOLOGISTS SAY ABOUT DATA ANALYSIS?

Interview researchers constructing life histories are looking for different things in the data than are interview researchers constructing new theories. Researchers studying historical letters are looking for something different from researchers who are analyzing posts they downloaded this morning from social media.

Rubin and Rubin (2012), Kvale, and Brinkman (Kvale, 2007; Kvale & Brinkman, 2014) write specifically about analysis of interview data; Ritchie, Lewis, and co-authors (Ritchie & Lewis, 2003; Spencer, Ritchie, O'Connor et al., 2014; Spencer, Ritchie, Ormston et al., 2014) speak more broadly to the analysis of any qualitative data. These respected methodologists describe data analysis as a process that begins with research design and is ongoing throughout the research. The sequence

Table 13.2 Comparative approaches to data analysis

	Rubin and Rubin (2012)	Kvale and Brinkman (Kvale, 2007; Kvale & Brinkman, 2014)	Ritchie and Lewis (2003) (Spencer, Ritchie, O'Connor, et al., 2014; Spencer, Ritchie, Ormston, et al., 2014)
During and immediately after collecting data	Reflection and note-taking are carried out throughout the interview research.	Interviewees may 'discover new relationships'; interviewer condenses, interprets, and sends meaning back for further reply (Kvale, 2007, p. 102).	The 'framework' approach centers on an iterative 'analytic hierarchy' (Spencer et al., 2003, p. 212). The first step is management of the data: familiarization with the data, sorting and synthesizing data to identify initial themes.
	Recognition occurs when the researcher finds concepts, themes, events, or topical markers in the data.	Analysis can focus on meaning, language, or theoretical concepts in the data.	
Describing themes, clusters of themes, and or typologies	Synthesis occurs when the researcher systematically clarifies meanings of concepts and themes.		Construct an initial thematic framework. Group and sort themes by levels of generality. Index or code and sort the data (Spencer, Ritchie, O'Connor, et al., 2014).
	Researchers code to label and designate themes and concepts.		
Interpret and explain findings	Researchers sort by grouping data units with the same code or label.	Allow subject the opportunity to comment on researcher's interpretation.	Create *descriptive accounts*. This is the process of defining elements and dimensions, refining categories, and classifying data (Spencer et al., 2003).
	At the stage of final synthesis, researchers combine concepts to suggest conclusions or recommend policies.	Continue description and interpretation.	Review data extracts and gauge coherence (Spencer, Ritchie, O'Connor, et al., 2014).
			Explanatory accounts refers to the process of developing explanations and applications to wider theory or practice (Spencer et al., 2003).

of steps can vary, depending on the purpose of the study as well as the methodology used to frame the design. While you move through distinct phases, keep in mind that qualitative analysis is recursive and deeply reflective, not linear. Some critical steps described in their books are summarized in Table 13.2.

When researchers collect textual data, they need specific strategies for analysis. *Qualitative Content Analysis in Practice* (Schreier, 2012) and *Qualitative Text Analysis: A Guide to Methods, Practice & Using Software* (Kuckartz, 2014) take you through clearly outlined steps for working with text. Two books by Dr Trena Paulus and co-authors offer guidance: *Doing Qualitative Research in a Digital World* will help you analyze research settings (Paulus & Lester, 2021); and *Looking for Insight, Transformation, and Learning in Online Talk* (Paulus & Wise, 2019) will help you study emergent and social media data.

If you are looking for guidance so you can use a CAQDAS program, the books from Kristi Jackson and Patricia Bazeley *Qualitative Data Analysis with NVivo* (Jackson & Bazeley, 2019) and Christine Silver (see www.qdaservices.co.uk/5lqda-books) will be useful.

DEVELOPING YOUR JUDGMENT AND WELCOMING OTHER VIEWS

In qualitative data analysis there are many situations where your judgment as a researcher is central to the process. In this chapter, we've explored basic approaches to reasoning – but clearly someone is responsible for the intellectual work involved with reasoning. The role of the researcher and ethical phronesis discussed in Chapters 4, 5, and 6 come into play. Practical tactics such as involvement of an additional coder who can surface inconsistent or missing codes, and triangulation across multiple sources, can help. Ravitch (2020) describes the importance of alternative perspectives, that is, perspectives that challenge your own. She offers important guidance:

> Acknowledge that, despite all of the validity strategies employed and your reflexive diligence as a researcher, your interpretations are just that – your interpretations. This does not mean that you have to be apologetic or that you cannot make assertions. It does, however, mean that you need to be transparent and indicate what data support the findings, how they support them, and how you arrived at the key themes and findings. (p. 255)

She outlines considerations for trying to resist misuse of interpretive authority, including:

- Actively engage in structured reflexivity processes and dialogic engagement with other researchers.
- Actively engage in participant validation.
- Stay as close to the data as possible in your interpretations and analytic write-up (findings).
- Acknowledge limitations of the study in the final report/product and describe these in relation to findings.
- Throughout every stage of the research, keep a log/description of your processes, including times when you compose memos, refer back to memos, check in with participants, revise instruments, engage with theory, consult with peers, and so on. These may or may not be documented in a research journal in more detail. If you do not keep a research journal, the act of documenting when you do what with a brief description of it will help you be transparent in your processes as you return to the analysis plan in your text and revise it based on what actually happened methodologically and allow you to think about and reflect on how you are engaging with your data and research design. (Ravitch, 2020, p. 255)

When you map out your analytic strategy, whether for data collected from 10 interviews or 1,000 social media posts, build in time for thinking and reflecting on the process. It is easy to think of data analysis as a computational experience, but for qualitative researchers, it is important to dig into the stories behind the stories.

SUMMARY OF KEY CONCEPTS

A well thought-out analytic strategy will add to the credibility of your study. Qualitative researchers describe many approaches for the analysis of data. Specific attention is needed for different kinds of data: written, visual, or media. Some researchers take a hands-on approach, while others use software to help manage the coding process and generate tables and diagrams. While data analysis is a complex field of study in itself, there are common patterns across methods that move from management to thematic descriptions, to interpretations and explanations. Online researchers confront the same challenges that any qualitative researchers do: finding meaning in the expressions of people who have written about their experiences or perceptions, told or shown researchers about their lives. Analysis is a recursive process. As with the research design, every choice made influences the findings that are generated from the study so determining those choices in advance is not entirely realistic. Discoveries may emerge that take the analysis process in a new direction.

DISCUSSION QUESTIONS AND EXERCISES

- Using your academic library, look for at least one article that addresses each of the key data analysis questions in the context of your field of study and research problem. Create an annotated bibliography and discuss relevant points for your analytic strategy.

  o   What stages will I follow?
  o   How will I manage and protect digital data?
  o   When will I begin to analyze the data: during or after data collection?
  o   Are specific analytic conventions or approaches associated with the methodology I have selected? If so, how will I apply them?
  o   How will I interpret and analyze different types of data?
  o   What form(s) of reasoning will I use to interpret the data and find meaning?
  o   What system will I use for coding? Will I use computer aided qualitative data analysis software (CAQDAS)?

- Using data collected from exercises in Chapter 7, 8, or 9: (a) create an analytic strategy; (b) code the data to identify at least three major themes.
- Read two of the articles listed on the book website. In an essay of 3–5 pages, compare and contrast: (a) their approaches for organizing and analyzing data; and (b) their reasoning styles.
- On the SAGE Research Methods library database, or other sources, locate a dataset for practice. Outline your analytic strategy and main steps for using this dataset in a text or content analysis study, or a multimodal study that uses interview data.

14

Writing, Reporting, and Contributing to the Literature

HIGHLIGHTS

New and emerging online methods will not gain credence unless researchers use them to generate studies that contribute to the literature. The novelty of new approaches may catch readers' attention, but quality research will get published and referenced. It will inspire other scholars to use the methods and extend the inquiry, help practitioners and professionals apply the findings, and make the world a better place.

What characterizes research – and the reports of research – most respected in your field? What will others look for when determining whether your study meets expectations and standards?

In addition to the criteria that apply to all studies, online research will be scrutinized about how and why technology was used. The Qualitative e-Research Framework, introduced in Chapter 1 and discussed throughout the book, can be used to evaluate publication options and organize a self-assessment of your potential publications. The same kinds of questions suggested here can be asked when you review others' research or published studies.

OBJECTIVES

After reading and reflecting on this chapter, you will be able to:

- identify and apply quality standards for qualitative e-research in your field or discipline
- think through the options for reporting on the study including scholarly and informal ways to disseminate it
- use the Qualitative e-Research Framework to self-assess drafts for completeness, before submitting them for publication.

PROCESSES FOR EVALUATING AND REVIEWING RESEARCH ARE CENTRAL TO SCHOLARLY WORK

What distinguishes scholarly writings from other kinds of publications? Peer review. The quality of scholarly research is verified through the process of subjecting writing to the critiques of others who understand the content and methodology of the study or studies being discussed. To reach the point where the completed study can be critiqued by others, we need to put what we have learned into writing and make sure we are making the best representation of our work possible. This means that as researchers we need to evaluate our own work throughout the designing, conducting, and analyzing stages to learn from the process and make adjustments. Mason (2002) suggests that it is essential for researchers to articulate and continuously monitor their own 'internal' working designs to "facilitate the coherent and rigorous development of the project' (p. 25). Reflexivity and memoing allow you to take an active and vital self-evaluative stance toward your study while it is underway. The same scrutiny is needed when looking critically at your own writing.

To be published, the article must meet criteria as articulated by editors and by journals that publish such studies. To publish texts and other books, you need to demonstrate a need and an audience. Researchers in academic settings receive reviews from funders, dissertation supervisors, and others from within (and often across) academic disciplines. Professional socialization and advancement build on an understanding of how your field or discipline defines and evaluates high-quality research.

As part of any review process, when we look at a study based on data collected online, we want to know why and how the researcher made choices about the information and communications technologies (ICTs) in the context of the research questions, methodology, and sampling strategy used for sources. If participants were involved, how did they respond to the process, as well as to the research questions? What would another researcher need to know if choosing a similar approach? What types of data were collected, and were the data adequate and appropriate given the purpose of the study? Ultimately, did the data allow the researcher to construct an analysis and generate conclusions that achieved the purpose of the study?

QUALITY IN QUALITATIVE RESEARCH? CRITERIA FOR EVALUATION AND REVIEW

First, let's look at criteria used to evaluate qualitative research generally, then look at online qualitative research specifically. Tracy (2010) observed, 'Why would qualitative scholars develop criteria even as they critique it? Because criteria, quite simply, are useful. Rules and guidelines help us learn, practice, and perfect' (p. 838). This list melds suggestions from three researchers' efforts to establish standards for qualitative research rigor and contribution (Anderson, 2017, p. 842; Rocco, 2010; Tracy, 2010). Also included are tips from editors that are specific to getting articles published in peer-reviewed journals (Dreyfuss & Ryan, 2018) and tips from editors about publishing qualitative research in particular (Rubel & Villalba, 2009).

1. Coherent design

'Meaningful coherence' (Tracy, 2010) is a pre-requisite of qualitative submissions. This means you need to explain the choices and research design strategies enacted in the research project under discussion, with reference to research context and research questions. Rocco (2010) identified the importance of a well-articulated problem as the core of a good qualitative research paper and Anderson (2017) pressed to go a step further, arguing that evaluation should look at how well a study 'hangs together' around the question being addressed. This requires attention to whether methods and techniques have been used that are consistent with the research questions (Tracy, 2010). The design should be grounded in the relevant literature, including method-ological literature for the method used and the approaches used to collect the data (Rocco, 2010). Editors advising qualitative researchers concur: 'The consensus is that good qualitative manuscripts rely not only on identification of important problems and questions, but also sound design, rigorous implementation, and convincing pre-sentation of results' (Rubel & Villalba, 2009, p. 297).

2. Appropriate sampling strategy

Anderson (2017) points out that good quality qualitative research reports should include an explanation and justification of the choice of research site(s), organizational location(s), contextual setting(s) and recruitment and selection of participants (p. 3). When using documentary or other sources, choose a dataset that supports a conceptualization that incorporates a rich network of concepts and themes with complex, rather than over-simple, connections.

Dreyfuss and Ryan (2018) suggest:

> In describing data collection and the sample, authors should pay particular attention to providing as much detail as space will allow. Given that selecting participants to answer questions is critical to the quality of qualitative research, the audience will be better able to make decisions about the applicability of the results to their own context if they know 'who' is answering the questions even if identities are confidential. (p. 301)

3. Credibility and verification or member-checking

'Credibility refers to the trustworthiness, verisimilitude, and plausibility of the research findings. One of the most important means for achieving credibility in qualitative research is thick description' (Tracy, 2010, pp. 842–843). Verification of data, analytic categories, interpretations, and conclusions with members of groups from whom the data were originally collected has been accepted as an important technique for establishing credibility (Anderson, 2017). Another is triangulation, that is, using multiple sources of data to verify conclusions.

4. Transparency about your position

The acknowledged subjectivity of qualitative methods and the importance of the 'researcher's lens' in qualitative research requires a discussion of the researcher's context, positionality or standpoint, and the ways insider or outsider status can bear on the research process and outcomes. Dreyfuss and Ryan (2018) suggest that 'manuscripts should at least briefly describe this process of examination and disclose biases and assumptions that shape or maybe even compete with the purposes of the study. The demonstrated reflexivity is important' (p. 300).

At the same time, Denzin and Lincoln (2002) point out that texts generated by all researchers, as humans who come to research with their own insider–outsider experiences and notions of the world, are inherently incomplete:

> Positionality recognizes the post-structural, postmodern argument that texts, any texts, are always partial and incomplete; socially, culturally, historically, racially, and sexually located; and can therefore never represent any truth except those truths that exhibit the same characteristics. ... a text that displays honesty or authenticity 'comes clean' about its own stance and about the position. (Denzin & Lincoln, 2002, pp. 333–334)

Yin observes that researchers can choose to optimize what can be gained, regardless of their positions in relation to the study:

People who do qualitative research view the *emic–etic* distinction and the possibility of multiple interpretations of the same event as an opportunity, not a constraint. In fact, a common theme underlying many qualitative studies is to demonstrate how participants' perspectives may diverge dramatically from those held by outsiders. (Yin, 2011, p. 12)

As these researchers and editors note, there is not a right or wrong position, it is simply incumbent on you to make your position clear. In a related point, determine whether the publication wants the writing in first- or third-person. Dreyfuss and Ryan (2018) advise: 'Keep yourself out of your article. It might seem stilted, but call yourselves the authors or the researchers instead of we. Many referees and editors think the first person is inappropriate for scholarly writing' (p. 7). Other editors expect qualitative studies to be discussed from a first-person voice.

5. Ethical study and writing

Researchers and editors are increasingly aware of the practices of ethics or institutional review boards and require evidence of informed consent arrangements before publication can be considered. However, dilemmas may occur when the traditional power relationships of researcher–research subject are reconstructed or unforeseen changes emerge in studies involving documentary sources. Anderson (2017) and Tracy (2010) point out that in qualitative research there may also be 'situational ethics' because each circumstance is different and researchers must repeatedly reflect on, critique, question, and revisit their ethical decisions. Tracy (2010) observes that 'ethics are not just a means, but rather constitute a universal end goal of qualitative quality itself' (p. 846).

6. Rigorous research

A great design is not an asset unless the study is conducted in a way that signifies scholarly rigor. Tracy (2010) lists four key questions:

- Are there enough data to support significant claims?
- Did the researcher spend enough time gathering interesting and significant data?
- Is the context or sample appropriate given the goals of the study?
- Did the researcher use appropriate procedures in terms of field note style, interviewing practices, and analysis procedures?

7. Impact or contribution to the field

Statistical generalizability is not reasonable in qualitative research, but 'thick descriptions' that present findings with categories identified that are clearly defined and supported by sufficient data are expected (Anderson, 2017). Thick descriptions can include rich, direct quotations or the participants' own words, descriptive phrases or experiences that convey a sense of the participants and their environment as the basis for careful interpretation to illustrate in-depth concepts and constructs that are important to the study. Anderson (2017) suggests that thick descriptions can provide the basis for consideration of the potential for application to other times, places, people, and contexts as a useful indicator of rigor.

Tracy (2010) notes that when judging the significance of a study's contribution, researchers and reviewers ask questions such as:

- Does the study extend knowledge?
- Make a theoretical or methodological contribution?
- Improve practice?
- Generate ongoing research?
- Liberate or empower?

No one study will accomplish scholarly, practical, and social impact, but your report should discuss the ways findings will make a difference.

8. Clear writing and presentation

Dreyfuss and Ryan (2018) emphasize the importance of a simple, readable style.

> Use mostly short, declarative sentences in the active voice. Make sure to vary your sentence structure and to write in complete sentences. Omit needless words. Make sure the spelling and grammar are as perfect as possible. If appropriate, include charts, graphs, tables, and images to support the text and summarize your findings. (pp. 8–9)

All of these questions apply to online research as well as more conventional qualitative studies. The Qualitative e-Research Framework helps us think about the additional questions to review when assessing an online study – whether it is our own research or others' writings we are reviewing.

USING THE QUALITATIVE E-RESEARCH FRAMEWORK TO EVALUATE RESEARCH

The Qualitative e-Research Framework includes interrelated categories that serve as the basis for key review questions. The answers to one question can create implications to be addressed in another category. The category listed first, 'Aligning Purpose and Design,' is returned to at each point in the process, to ensure that all decisions are appropriately reflected in the overarching design of the research.

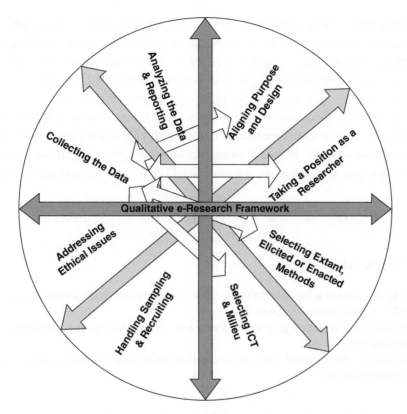

Figure 14.1 Looking for alignment with the Qualitative e-Research Framework

Aligning Purpose and Design

Every qualitative study begins with a central purpose and question. The first challenge is to explain succinctly why the study was conducted and why the results are of interest to the reader. This first step can be one of the most difficult tasks because, as the researcher who has spent considerable time thinking about this project, we are passionate, enthusiastic, and see all of the connections between our extraordinary work and the better world it could bring about. However, we must distill all of those ideas into statements that clearly define the underlying basis of the research. It is essential to show that the topic is relevant and significant to the scholarly discipline and/or to the practitioners who work in the field. In a study that uses online methods, the researcher is tasked with explaining and justifying how and where technology infuses the design. Did the online approach contribute an innovative methodological contribution? How was the study unique and what distinguishes it from those that went before? Build potential readers' interest by showing that this study will look at the phenomenon in a new way or offer a fresh perspective. Why and how is the technology important to the study – and where might it simply serve as a communications channel without adding to the conceptual or practical conduct of the study? How might the online approach make an innovative methodological contribution? Articulating answers to these questions will strengthen your description of the research purpose.

This first step is critical. For one thing, the reader will need go no further without an incentive to continue. Other decisions – described throughout the entire framework – will depend on a clearly defined research problem, question, and purpose. If you are unsure of the precise direction for the study, it will be difficult to build others' interest.

Key questions to ask when reviewing alignment of purpose and design

Does the researcher:

- Succinctly describe the research purpose in a way that someone unfamiliar with the specific phenomenon can understand?
- Articulate how research purpose, theories and epistemologies, methodologies, and methods are aligned?
- Support decisions about the conceptual foundation and research paradigm with scholarly sources?

Taking a Position as a Researcher

Considerations related to the researcher's position should be factored into any review. Factors include the relationship of the researcher to the topic and/or participants. Was the researcher an insider or outsider, or somewhere in between? If the researcher was an insider, did he or she take steps to address undue influence or potential biases? In Chapter 4 the emic–etic, or insider–outsider, concept is treated as a continuum rather than as a duality.

As a reviewer of our own or others' writing, is it evident that the researcher has 'come clean' about the position taken? Did he or she describe use of reflexivity to maintain a position of self-awareness throughout all stages of the study?

Key questions to ask when reviewing the researcher's position

Does the researcher:

- Disclose any conflicts of interest, attitudes or biases that may impair objectivity about the participants or data?
- Describe how any 'insider' knowledge or status may be used online to gain access to sites or communities off-limits to 'outsiders'?

- Make it clear whether he or she is contributing data to the study about his or her own experiences?
- Explain any reflexive practices he or she used?
- Account for any in-process changes made to the study based on ongoing, recursive reflexivity?
- Explain whether changes were covered by the informed consent agreement, and if not, renegotiate the consent agreement and as relevant any review committee's understanding of the research process?

Selecting Extant, Elicited, or Enacted Methods

Hine (2013, p. 127) captures the essence of this stage with one overarching question: 'Is there a methodologically defensible reason why Internet-mediated interaction was deployed?' Given the purpose and design for the study, how does technology serve the study? In Chapter 3, three main reasons were offered for choosing online data collection: as a communications medium, research setting, or research phenomenon. Which of these reasons motivated you to conduct the study online? Clearly explain the interrelationships between aspects of research design and justify the choice of data collection using extant, elicited, and/or enacted methods.

Key questions to ask when reviewing selection of online methods

Does the researcher:

- Explain how the online medium or setting proposed for the study allowed the researcher access to the research phenomenon?
- Describe ways the researcher used features of the selected ICT and/or milieu to remove obstacles between the researcher and phenomenon, and between the researcher and those who have lived experience with the phenomenon?
- Disclose any ways that technology might have limited access to the participants' responses and stories about their experiences or created new obstacles? Describe how the researcher addressed these real or potential problems?
- Disclose any risks to the viability or credibility to the study and describe how they were addressed?
- Explain whether other technology choices or alternatives to stated data collection methods would be more appropriate?

Selecting ICT and Milieu

Some might think that the selection of ICT and/or the online setting would be a simple one, or that it might occur first, based on the researcher's preferences or intentions for types of data to collect. However, selection of the technology to use for communicating with participants or collecting extant data is quite complex. As noted previously, some studies intend to uncover patterns, motivations or characteristics of online behavior while for other studies the Internet is a means for communication about any aspect of life. Does the researcher make it clear on what basis the ICT and milieu were selected? Is the setting appropriate for the study? Are the motivations and justifications for selected technology sufficient?

Key questions to ask when reviewing the selection of ICT and milieu

Does the researcher:

- Make it clear how specific features of the technology relate to the research purpose and questions?
- Describe the type(s) of data to be collected and relate those to ICT choices?
- Spell out minimum requirements for technology access, hardware or software, etc. in the recruitment materials? Or did the researcher offer alternatives if minimum requirements could not be met by potential participants?
- Explain any issues related to participants' access or skills needed to use the selected ICT? Where applicable, explain why the participant's choice of ICT was or was not honored?

Handling Sampling and Recruiting

Deciding on a sampling strategy, locating the right people, and recruiting them to participate in a study are challenges for any researcher. For researchers using extant data, similar decisions must be made in regard to the choice of observation site(s) or choice of datasets, documents, and materials to review. The researcher should be transparent about the processes used in sampling and selecting participants, sites or documents, and discuss any implications in reports of the research. If the participants' or sites' characteristics vary from those originally intended for the study, such modifications should also be discussed and justified.

Key questions to ask when reviewing the sampling and recruiting strategy

Does the researcher:

- Explain how the sampling strategy aligns with the methodology?
- Provide sufficient justification that the sample is appropriate given the goals of the study?
- Demonstrate that ethical recruitment procedures were used to ensure that participants are credible and of legal age to participate? Address any special circumstances such as under-age or at-risk populations?

- Offer information to build participants' trust in the researcher's approach and reliability? Verify commitment to abide by the consent agreement?
- Demonstrate that appropriate permissions were received for observations or use of datasets, archives, or records?

Addressing Ethical Issues

Ethical researchers exhibit a self-consciousness in which they are mindful of their character, actions, and the consequences for others (Tracy, 2010). You should explain how you addressed the following five topics in ways appropriate to the study:

1. Protection of human subjects
2. Obtaining appropriate informed consent from participants
3. Respecting the research site
4. Safeguarding participants' identities and data
5. Conform to expectations for use of existing source materials.

While a detailed description of all agreements and procedures used is not typically included in articles, chapters, or books, the credibility of the study is enhanced when ethical approaches are highlighted.

At the publication stage, the protection of participants' identities is of concern. A hallmark of writing about qualitative research has been the use of quoted material that shows, in participants' own words, the nuances and depth of their experience with the research phenomenon. Previously, it was enough to remove names and other identifiers from the quotations. However, in the digital age this is not enough. Search engines may be able to trace the participant's identity by their word choices or the context of their comments. Researchers using extant methods are particularly vulnerable to unintended disclosure because, even without including names, meta data from original posts may lead a reader to the original material. Those using elicited or enacted methods are not immune, since characteristics of the participant or setting could allow a reader to identify the individual. This presents a dilemma for ethical researchers, especially in studies of sensitive or personal topics where revelation of participants' identities could have negative consequences.

On the topic of protecting anonymity when using quotations in reports of research, the AoIR guidelines (Markham & Buchanan, 2012, p. 10) offer key questions to consider:

- Are individuals adequately protected in pre-publication reports, such as presentations for workshops, conferences, or informal meetings?
- What immediate or future risk might occur by using exact-quoted material in published reports?

To reduce the possibility that participants can be traced, the British Educational Research Association suggests alternatives to using direct quotation:

> Researchers should recognise the entitlement of both institutions and individual participants to privacy, and should accord them their rights to confidentiality and anonymity. This could involve employing 'fictionalising' approaches when reporting, and where using such approaches researchers should fully explain how and why they have done so. (BERA, 2018, p. 21)

Soliciting consent for the use of quotations should include some sense of the extent of and audience for the research dissemination. Participants may find it acceptable for quotations to be used in dissertations or academic journal articles, but not on blogs or in writing for the general public.

Given the nature of the study, the participants, and report style, what additional steps – such as renegotiating consent agreements or creating composite or 'masked' exemplars – may be needed to protect the identities of participants?

Key questions to ask when reviewing ethical issues

Does the researcher:

- Summarize the ethical issues in the study and explain protocols used?
- Explain how any ethically ambiguous issues were addressed?
- Describe how participants were informed about the use of the research findings in publications?
- Demonstrate respect for ethical expectations established by the research site?
- Demonstrate respect for ethical expectations established by the researcher's institution and any guidelines set by professional societies in their field of study or practice?
- Work within any norms, community expectations, or assumptions?
- Write up findings in a way that will respect human and digital identities and preserve anonymity?

Collecting the Data

The Methods section of the academic report, article, or chapter should clearly spell out how online methods were used to collect the data. Any problems confronted should be explained, and mid-study corrections justified.

Key questions to ask when reviewing data collection

Does the researcher:

- Collect the data as spelled out in the research design?
- Use appropriate methods in terms of the selected ICT and online research setting?

- Adapt, as far as possible, to participants' preferences, and their access to and levels of technology literacy?
- Use reflexive, recursive approaches for ongoing monitoring of the data collection process?

Analyzing the Data and Reporting

The phrase 'jumping to conclusions' succinctly speaks to the impression the researcher wants to avoid. The researcher wants to guide the reader through the important process of data analysis and interpretation of results. This is the goal the entire research process aimed toward: being able to state and support results of the study. At this point the researcher situates the findings in the context of the literature in the field or discipline and recommends next steps for future research on the topic.

An academic document such as a thesis or dissertation will include a detailed explanation of the stages of the analysis, in the context of the theory, epistemology, methodology, and methods outlined in the research design or proposal. A document for publication will summarize the analysis process and focus in more detail on the findings. Discussion of the analysis should provide the reader with confidence that the study was conducted ethically, and that all steps were carried out.

Key questions to ask when reviewing data analysis

Does the researcher:

- Introduce the data analysis process and explain major stages?
- Describe analytic steps taken during the study and any changes made in response to preliminary findings or new questions raised?
- Link the data analysis process to the chosen theory, epistemology, methodology, and methods?
- Show how the study supports or refutes previous studies in published literature?
- Point to new questions that emerged in the course of the study and recommend future research?

COMPLETING THE DEGREE, CONTRIBUTING TO THE LITERATURE AND THE WORLD

For some the primary goal of writing up the research report is to fulfill academic requirements. They are writing papers for courses, capstone projects, theses or dissertations. As challenging as these documents are, they have one advantage in common: clear guidelines and requirements, and faculty or supervisors who can give feedback and answer questions. Beyond these types of required documents, researchers must make their own decisions about what to write, and where and how to distribute their reports.

The traditional ways academic researchers have disseminated their work are changing. In addition to scholarly and peer-reviewed journals, researchers are finding ways to share their research with others online. Indeed, some are criticizing the system of academic publishing as being too slow and too narrow. Calls are being made for institutions to note scholars' online presence as an indicator of success, in addition to the traditional expectations for journal publication (Biswas & Kirchherr, 2015). Consider these provocative comments:

> [S]cholars all have an obligation to society to contribute their observations to the wider world. At the moment that's often being done in ramshackle and impoverished ways ... with acres of 'dead-on-arrival' data (that will never be used by anyone else in the world) ... delivered over bizarrely long-winded timescales. From submission to publication in some top economics journals now takes 3.5 years. At the end of such a process any published paper is no more than a tombstone marking where happening debate and knowledge used to be, four or five years earlier. (Dunleavy, 2014)

> Up to 1.5 million peer-reviewed articles are published annually. However, many are ignored even within the scientific community: 82 percent of articles published in humanities are not even cited once. ... We suspect that an average paper in a peer-reviewed journal is read completely at most by no more than 10 people. (Biswas & Kirchherr, 2015)

These and other writers point to the importance of disseminating research in new ways that can reach a larger audience and have more impact. Academic blogs and websites allow researchers to share their work while the studies are underway or after the completion. Academic sites are complemented and reinforced by links to social media where a wide audience of users and readers across disciplines can be cultivated. The availability of easy-to-use software makes it possible for individuals to create their own venues for sharing research in progress and finished studies including links to published work. Researchers also join together through their universities, through professional societies, or through collaboration with others to share their interests. Research blogs can be aimed at various audiences and serve different purposes:

- **Researcher to researcher** blogs and social networking sites sharing and exchanging within and across disciplines. Purposes can include preparing for or reporting on academic conferences, sharing informal or formal essays about research or teaching, offering advice to others in the field as well as disseminating completed research findings.

- **Researcher to participant** blogs can be used to build credibility and 'inform' participants before and during the study. Once the study is completed, researchers can share what they have learned in ways participants might find interesting or be able to apply in their lives, work, or communities.
- **Researcher to audience** blogs focus on sharing findings, results, and practical resources. Since one of the criticisms of academic journals is that they appeal to a narrow, elite audience, some researchers feel it is important to translate findings into usable models and materials. Additionally, researchers who have received funding from public sources may be required to share what they have discovered with the public.

Given these expanded options, researchers have many choices to make when it comes to the decision about how and what to write about the completed research and where to present it. White et al. (2014) suggest four broad types of research output:

- **Comprehensive output** includes substantive reports about the entire study including methods, findings, and implications.
- **Summary findings** include articles, presentations using slides or video that provide a synthesis of key findings.
- **Developmental findings** can be presented during the project to share your emergent findings or ideas.
- **Selective** reports select themes or research elements for particular audiences. They could be presented in the form of presentations, workshops, chapters, or articles.

While the comprehensive type of output may be presented formally, the other options can be aimed at academic, student, professional or practitioner, or general audiences. Whether or not the study as a whole, with all its scholarly foundations and frameworks, is included, it is important to provide a clear explanation for the purpose and approach used to conduct the study as well as the findings that were uncovered.

SUMMARY OF KEY CONCEPTS

Completing the study is not the end of the process! Writing the thesis or dissertation, blog post, article, or book is the next major step. This chapter has presented some ways to plan, organize, and self-assess reports based on the study. These checklists for qualitative research generally and online qualitative research in particular can be used to evaluate your own research, as part of a peer review process, or proposals from your students.

DISCUSSION QUESTIONS AND EXERCISES

- View and discuss the media piece: 'Using the Qualitative e-Research Framework to Assess Design and Research Quality'.
- Read two articles listed on the companion website, and locate a scholarly blog in your field. Compare and contrast the writing styles and approaches for describing research findings.
- Find a qualitative research article in your field of study that utilized online methods. Using the critical questions from this chapter, describe strengths and weaknesses in research quality. What are your recommendations?
- Exchange essays with a classmate, compare, and contrast your writing styles and ways to reach the intended audience.
- Find and review relevant ethical guidelines for suggestions or requirements related to publishing qualitative research.

15

Online Communications and Online Qualitative Research: Trends and Influences

The future often appears strange just before it becomes ordinary. ... Trying to grapple with what comes next is a deep problem. Doing so is partly a matter of science fiction, which consists, after all, of the stories we tell about the future. (Alexander, 2009)

HIGHLIGHTS

Trends in Internet adoption and use mean more 'research' will be 'e-research.' As the use of information and communications technologies (ICTs) becomes ever more pervasive – meshed with and integral to our personal, social, cultural, professional, and civic lives – it will become ever more difficult to separate out and study a discrete 'real' life. As we are more accustomed to online communications, it will be more challenging to conduct qualitative research without some electronic tools.

Other examples demonstrate the fact that for much of the world a digital dualism distinction fades as technology-enabled approaches become widely adapted. Instead of the dualistic view, for example, of 'e-business' versus 'business,' we now see that even small physical stores use social media and online marketing, and some enterprises that started as entirely online operations now have physical storefronts. Instead of 'e-learning' versus 'brick-and-mortar' institutions, we see that online programs often include face-to-face residencies and that classes taught on campuses use online resources and assignments. Instead of digital dualism, we see more of a continuum, without a firm line between what is online and offline. What do these and other trends mean for online researchers who use online tools to study phenomena that often occur online? We need new researchers to contribute methodologically as well as with new findings.

OBJECTIVES

After reading and reflecting on this chapter, you will be able to:

- identify and discuss emerging trends in communications technology usage and implications for qualitative online research
- analyze and generate recommendations for further discussion and development of qualitative online research methodologies, methods, and ethics.

It is hard to predict what ICT, tool, or gadget will next enthrall experienced users and attract new ones. It seems likely that coming generations of ICTs will be faster, with more options for integrating visual media, audio, and text. As devices become smaller, they will go with their owners into more parts of daily personal, social, community, and professional life. More of the important events of life will be experienced in the presence of or recorded on, if not mediated through, some form of communications technology.

The 'anywhere' aspect of new communications goes beyond the mobility factor to include more awareness of physical place even when we operate in a digital world. Global positioning system (GPS) and locative technologies are integrated into smartphones, cameras, and other devices so we can obtain maps of our locations and destinations and see the locations of other individuals and services. We can log into Google Earth and look at the neighborhood from which our participants are virtually connecting to our study.

In addition to changes in ICT tools and communications types, the use of these tools and the ways people think about them are changing. Given the focus here on the use of technology for research purposes, three phenomena that merit consideration are as follows: online collaboration, disintermediation, and online privacy.

ONLINE COLLABORATION AND SOCIAL LITERACIES

The ease of online communication allows individuals or groups to work and learn together in new ways. The 2020 COVID-19 pandemic greatly accelerated this trend. Companies, educational institutions, governmental bodies, and social-sector agencies now work virtually to complete projects and solve complex problems. In these examples, collaboration occurs within an established framework or organizational structure using virtual teams, telecommuting, and mobile or remote offices. Online collaboration, though, extends beyond established organizational applications and disciplinary or geographical boundaries.

Mass collaboration or crowdsourcing occurs when people who do not know each other write, think, or work on projects together. People write collaboratively and edit one another's comments on social media sites or wikis; they design, implement, test, and improve on opensource software. They form social networks of new and old friends who keep in touch in online communities and on social media sites. Individuals and organizations turn to their online networks or to the collective intelligence of the wider web for input on personal or professional decisions or tasks. They turn to these networks of strangers for crowdfunding for personal needs or to support new inventions.

Those creating models for information or new media literacy point to a progression that aligns critical thinking with the social skills to use them in a technological environment. The concept of literacy has changed to refer not simply to a set of skills demonstrated by an individual but also to a level of competence needed to grow a personal and professional network; communicate synchronously or asynchronously with others using text, verbal, and visual modes; derive meaning and build new knowledge; and ethically share cultural productions. When people interact online they are not passive consumers of information; they are often active contributors who intermingle with people known and unknown – adding, editing, and sharing ideas. In the process, they gain skills and attitudes beneficial to online research.

So What?

These trends have implications for qualitative online researchers and their sources or participants. While researchers using more-structured interview approaches may be able to collect data using fairly basic online skills, higher levels of digital literacy will be important for those who want to use the kinds of dynamic, visual approaches discussed in this book. Indeed, even qualitative researchers may find that a data scientist is needed on the team!

According to the Taxonomy of Online Collaboration, a model that depicts stages of the collaborative process, when the level of collaboration increases from simple dialogic transaction to higher synergistic co-creation, digital literacy skills are needed that enable contributors to develop common goals and incorporate multiple inputs into a single output (Salmons, 2019a). The Taxonomy of Online

Collaboration also posits that increased levels of collaboration call for increased levels of trust. Researchers accustomed to an embodied sensibility must find alternative ways to build presence. Researchers who are comfortable with online collaboration will be more capable of building participants' trust.

Similarly, participants who are experienced with online collaboration may find it easier to develop trusting connections with researchers. It is reasonable to expect that people who are at ease collaborating with others 'co-constructing' discussion groups or open-source software might also be willing to co-construct knowledge with researchers. Individuals who share photographs and video clips with Internet friends may be more willing to do so with researchers.

DISINTERMEDIATION AND APOMEDIATION

A companion trend to mass collaboration involves the increased reliance on peers, rather than experts. The term **disintermediation** refers to the removal of the go-between with content producers and content consumers. As Howard Rheingold (2012) observed, there are 'no gatekeepers in participatory culture' (p. 53). Whether the gatekeeper in the pre-digital age was a travel agent or a brokerage firm, today's Internet users want do-it-yourself ways to bypass steps and get things done directly.

Apomediation is distinguished from disintermediation, where the person attempts to find what they want on their own, or think they want, without any help (Dowie & Kaltoft, 2018). Apomediative resources rely on peer-to-peer guidance. Eysenbach (2008) discussed a progression from disintermediation to apomediation:

> Apomediation is a new socio-technological term that ... characterizes the 'third way' for users to identify trustworthy and credible information and services. The first possible approach is to use intermediaries (i.e., middlemen or 'gatekeepers'). Trusted Web portals containing only information vetted by experts can also be seen as an intermediary. The second possibility is to bypass 'middlemen' completely, which is commonly referred to as disintermediation. Apomediaries, such as users and friends ... can help users navigate through the onslaught of information afforded by networked digital media, providing additional credibility cues and supplying further metainformation. (para. 22)

Rather than relying upon traditional hierarchical sources of information, Internet users can help each other navigate to what they consider credible sources, within the vast swathes of information available online (O'Connor, 2009). Consumers use blog and social media sites, or review and comment sections in publications and company websites to convey thoughts, opinions, experiences, or preferences. Companies and content producers understand this power of peer influence.

Although disintermediation and apomediation are occurring in some way in almost every major industry, a poignant illustration is found in the world of print media. Where before editors and publishers served as gatekeepers through editorial processes and professional filtering, today anyone with a cell phone can record videos of unfolding events, and share news and perspectives, from the shortest posts to articles and full-length self-published books.

There is an implicit sense of caveat emptor – let the online buyer, viewer, or reader beware. Without reliable professionals or experts, readers or viewers must utilize their own awareness about the topic at hand to filter the extensive volume of information now available. Indeed, disinformation is a major problem today, because readers rely on bad actors who intentionally take the role of apomediative players and manipulate online discourse. Readers may simply shut out unacceptable information that goes against their own views, or they may suggest or enact changes as needed to correct it.

If the individual's work is considered valuable and reaches its audience, the solo writer's blog or social media account may directly compete for readers with websites of long-established publications. Whether content is accurate, truthful, relevant, or worth reading will be determined by the readers and addressed by mass responses. Disintermediation, apomediation and mass collaboration intersect in this use of information crowdsourcing – in the crowd, terms such as expert and amateur are no longer polar opposites.

Scholars are not immune to these trends. Hine (2013, p. 129) observes that participatory research shifts research away from a process the researcher controls with results the researcher verifies. Boundaries between the researcher and the researched are changing. In a discussion of medical research, O'Connor (2013) observed:

> Apomediated research ... is research in which information about the protocol – for example, its design and conduct – is apomediated, peer-to-peer, between individuals who may appear as both subjects and researchers. By contrast, in intermediated, or traditional medical research, researchers intermediate between subjects and information about the design, conduct, and interpretation of a given research protocol. In the new apomediated world, it is increasingly difficult to tell the difference between the researcher and the subject, begging the question: if regulations are there to protect subjects from researchers, what are regulations for when subject and research seem to be one and the same? (p. 471)

As O'Connor (2013) explains, disintermediation, apomediation, and crowdsourcing combine groups of people together to do their own research on a common problem. O'Connor cited a study conducted by an online group of crowdsourced subjects to test a series of vitamin supplements and observes an increase in these kinds of do-it-yourself approaches to studying health and medical issues – and academic publication of the results (p. 473).

Hine (2013) further observes that the Internet is breaking down the 'boundaries between the consumption and production of research' (p. 129) with open-access journals that are accessible to anyone. Scholars are wrestling with concepts of intellectual property and limits to ownership when research is shared online in an open information commons. While online open access journals retain the peer-review process, research blogs and other sources bypass traditional gatekeepers.

So What?

Several potential implications of this trend apply to online research. On one hand, a culture may emerge where individuals are accustomed to communicating with strangers in very frank, personal, and self-revealing ways. If individuals associate a free and trusting sensibility with their online interactions, such expectations may transfer to the online interviewer. In this milieu of direct communication, potential interviewees may be more willing to participate in research. On the other hand, potential participants may be suspicious of 'expert' researchers and distrustful about the safe keeping of data. We can no longer assume that potential participants will believe that it is beneficial to participate in research. These factors place even more responsibility on the scholarly researcher to be trustworthy and credible, and transparently accountable to high ethical standards. Researchers are more responsible for producing new knowledge and reports understandable to those beyond a specific academic discipline. In a world where casual observations can be so easily distributed, the discipline of empirical research is even more important.

PRIVACY IN ONLINE MILIEUS

The trends selected for discussion here – online collaboration and disintermediation – share a common underlying assumption. If people are going to participate in online collaborative activities as individuals or as part of the crowd, if people are going to read and write online without protective gatekeepers, then they must be willing to disclose information about themselves online. More participation in social media, online communities, multiplayer online games, and virtual worlds is occurring at the same time as increased consternation about privacy of online information. This is an area where commonsense is seemingly missing, since it would seem that privacy concerns would translate into less, not more, sharing of personal information online.

As noted throughout this book, many dilemmas emerge when participants lack the literacies, awareness, and knowledge needed to understand the importance of protecting personal information. Ethical researchers do not take advantage of such circumstances; instead, they look for ways to use these trends in positive ways. We might find that by understanding and appreciating apomediaries and locating the credible peers others trust, we can conduct more impactful inquiries. We might find that consent agreement discussions offer opportunities to help participants understand how to reduce their online vulnerability. You will undoubtedly discover ways that the trends in the communities you study can benefit your own research!

ICT AND SOCIAL TRENDS: IMPLICATIONS FOR RESEARCHERS

These trends and the increasingly pervasive aspects of ICT are important to online researchers for several reasons, in addition to those discussed earlier:

1. Social researchers are interested in studying human behavior and social interactions. If more behaviors and interactions occur online, then it is to be expected that researchers will be interested in studying them. Online researchers have focused on online behaviors; with new tools and broader adoption, researchers can use online interviews to explore behaviors that occur online or offline. The processes used to communicate electronically about any area of life experience, and the significance of such experiences, offer fertile ground for empirical study through online interview research.
2. Sampling possibilities enlarge as more people from diverse demographic groups become accustomed to using ICTs in everyday life. When the total pool of potential participants is larger and more ICT literate, researchers have more sampling options. Researchers can be more specific and particular about selection criteria. Or they can choose to conduct larger mixed-methods studies with varied sampling techniques.
3. The increasing variety of communication types means there are more ways to collect different types of audio, visual, and text-based data. As more people develop personal communication styles through online cultural life and mass collaboration, interview researchers will have more options in terms of type of interview and ways to conduct it.

SUMMARY OF KEY CONCEPTS AND RECOMMENDATIONS FOR FURTHER RESEARCH

Trends in ICT adoption and their potential for qualitative online research were explored in this chapter and throughout the book. But these discussions may raise more questions than they answer! Clearly, research *about* online research is needed. In addition, more work is needed to develop standards and criteria for excellence and integrity in online research.

Methodological and methods issues have been explored throughout this book, and numerous areas deserve more consideration. Each stage of the research process – and each stage of interaction with research participants – deserves more study. Which approaches for interview preparation enable researchers to develop relationships needed to conduct the type of interview that best serves the purpose of the study? How can Big Data and large datasets be used in qualitative research? What approaches motivate participants to stick with the ongoing enacted study – and help them resist the urge to click the window closed when some discomfort arises? Are there benefits to multiple short interactions over a more conventional approach using one longer interview? What level(s) of structure works best with which ICT? How can data best be collected when research is conducted in highly visual environments? What kinds of observation data can and should be collected with consenting or non-consenting online discussants? What other observations or documentation of the participant's online life will be beneficial to the study? How should such data collection be included in consent agreements? These are a few of the many questions the research community will need to answer to fulfill the potential of qualitative online research as a valuable approach for studying human behavior in the digital age.

DISCUSSION QUESTIONS AND EXERCISES

- In an essay of 3–5 pages, discuss trends that could influence online interview research. In your essay, critically review the thinking of at least three futurists. Identify at least one trend the futurists missed.
- Compare and contrast online communication dynamics and effectiveness of two ICTs that have become available in the past year. Could these ICTs be used for data collection? How? Write an analysis of 2–3 pages.
- Building on the preceding assignments and related reading, reflect on the ethical risks for researchers who conduct research with emerging ICTs, and prepare to use your analysis as the basis for leading a small-group discussion.
- What trends will influence how you design, conduct, analyze, and report on your research? How can you optimize your study given these realities?

APPENDIX

Qualitative Research Methods Resources

Do you ...	Then see these suggested resources:
Want to learn more about qualitative research in general?	Saldaña, J. (2014). *Thinking Qualitatively: Methods of Mind* (3rd ed.). Thousand Oaks, CA: SAGE Publications.
	Ravitch, S. (2020). *Qualitative Research*. Thousand Oaks, CA: SAGE Publications.
	Salmons, J. (2019). *Find the Theory in Your Research*. London: SAGE Publications.
	Manen, J. V. (2002). *Researching Lived Experience: Human Science for an Action Sensitive Pedagogy*. London: State University of New York Press.
	Yin, R. K. (2011). *Qualitative Research from Start to Finish*. New York: Guilford Press.
Want to find journals that specialize in publishing online and/or qualitative research?	*Forum: Qualitative Social Research* www.qualitative-research.net/index.php/fqs/index
	International Journal of Qualitative Methods http://ejournals.library.ualberta.ca/index.php/IJQM/index
	New Media & Society http://nms.SAGEpub.com
	Qualitative Inquiry http://qix.SAGEpub.com/
	Qualitative Report www.nova.edu/ssss/QR/
	Qualitative Research in Organizations and Management www.emeraldinsight.com/journal/qrom
	Qualitative Research http://qrj.SAGEpub.com
Want to learn more about online methods?	Paulus, T. M. & Wise, A. F. (2019). *Looking for Insight, Transformation, and Learning in Online Talk*. New York: Routledge.
	Paulus, T. M. & Lester, J. N. (2021). *Doing Qualitative Research in a Digital World*. Thousand Oaks, CA: SAGE Publications.
	Salmons, J. (2019). *Gather Your Data Online*. London: SAGE Publications.

Want to design an ethical study?	Kara, H. (2018). *Research Ethics in the Real World*. Bristol: Policy Press.
	Poth, C. (2021). *Research Ethics*. London: SAGE Publications.
	Salmons, J. (2020). *What Kind of Researcher Are You?* London: SAGE Publications.
Want to become a better collaborative partner?	Lemon, N. & Salmons, J. (2020). *Collaborate to Succeed in Higher Education and Beyond: A Practical Guide for Doctoral Students and Early Career Researchers*. London: Routledge.
	Salmons, J. (2019). *Learning to Collaborate, Collaborating to Learn: Engaging Students in the Classroom and Online*. Sterling: Stylus.
Want to design a case study?	Yin, R. K. (2018). *Case Study Research and Applications* (6th ed.). Thousand Oaks, CA: SAGE Publications.
Want to design a grounded theory study?	Birks, M. & Mills, J. (2014). *Grounded Theory: A Practical Guide*. Thousand Oaks, CA: SAGE Publications.
	Charmaz, K. (2014). *Constructing Grounded Theory: A Practical Guide through Qualitative Analysis* (2nd ed.). Thousand Oaks, CA: SAGE Publications.
Want to design an ethnography?	Gobo, G. (2008). *Doing Ethnography*. Thousand Oaks, CA: SAGE Publications.
	Hine, C. (2013). *The Internet: Understanding Qualitative Research*. Oxford: Oxford University Press.
	Hine, C. (Ed.) (2020). *Ethnography for the Internet: Embedded, Embodied and Everyday*. Abingdon: Routledge.
	Pink, S. (2021). *Doing Visual Ethnography* (4th ed.). London: SAGE Publications.
Want to design a phenomenological study?	Giorgi, A. (2009). *The Descriptive Phenomenological Method in Psychology: A Modified Husserlian Approach*. Pittsburgh: Duquesne University Press.
	Moustakas, C. (1994). *Phenomenological Research Methods*. Thousand Oaks, CA: SAGE Publications.
Want to collect data through interviews?	King, N. & Horrocks, C. (2010). *Interviews in Qualitative Research*. London: SAGE Publications.
	Kvale, S. & Brinkman, S. (2014). *InterViews: Learning the Craft of Qualitative Research Interviewing* (3rd ed.). Thousand Oaks, CA: SAGE Publications.

Rubin, H. J. & Rubin, I. S. (2012). *Qualitative Interviewing: The Art of Hearing Data* (3rd ed.). Thousand Oaks, CA: SAGE Publications.

Seidman, I. (2019). *Interviewing as Qualitative Research: A Guide for Researchers in Education and the Social Sciences* (5th ed.). New York: Teachers College Press.

Want to collect data through focus groups or group interviews?

Hall, J. N. (2020). *Focus Groups: Culturally Responsive Approaches for Qualitative Inquiry and Program Evaluation*. Gorham: Meyers Education Press.

Liamputtong, P. (2011). *Focus Group Methodology: Principles and Practice*. Thousand Oaks, CA: SAGE Publications.

Shamdasani, D. W. S. P. N. (2015). *Focus Groups: Theory and Practice* (3rd ed.). Thousand Oaks, CA: SAGE Publications.

Want to collect data from records, archives or documents?

Boreus, K. & Bergstrom, C. (2017). *Analyzing Text and Discourse*. London: SAGE Publications.

Kuckartz, U. (2014). *Qualitative Text Analysis: A Guide to Methods, Practice & Using Software*. Thousand Oaks, CA: SAGE Publications.

Rapley, T. (2007). *Doing Conversation, Discourse and Document Analysis*. London: SAGE Publications.

Schreier, M. (2012). *Qualitative Content Analysis in Practice*. London: SAGE Publications.

Want to collect data from observations?

Angrosino, M. (2007). *Doing Ethnographic and Observational Research*. London: SAGE Publications.

Gobo, G. (2008). *Doing Ethnography*. Thousand Oaks, CA: SAGE Publications.

Madden, R. (2010). *Being Ethnographic: A Guide to the Theory and Practice of Ethnography*. Thousand Oaks, CA: SAGE Publications.

Want to use visual methods in data collection?

Banks, M. (2007). *Using Visual Data in Qualitative Research*. London: SAGE Publications.

Pink, S. (2021). *Doing Visual Ethnography* (4th ed.). London: SAGE Publications.

Rose, G. (2012). *Visual Methodologies: An Introduction to Researching with Visual Materials*. London: SAGE Publications.

Want to analyze and interpret data?	Bernard, H. R., Wutich, A. & Ryan, G. W. (2017). *Analyzing Qualitative Data. Systematic Approaches*. London: SAGE Publications.
	Miles, M., Huberman, A. M. & Saldaña, J. (2014). *Qualitative Data Analysis: A Methods Sourcebook* (3rd ed.). Thousand Oaks, CA: SAGE Publications.
	Saldaña, J. (2021). *Coding Manual for Qualitative Researchers* (4th ed.). Thousand Oaks, CA: SAGE Publications.
	Vogt, W. P., Vogt, E. R., Gardner, D. C. & Haeffele, L. M. (2014). *Selecting the Right Analysis for Your Data: Quantitative, Qualitative and Mixed Methods*. New York: Guilford Press.
Want to write up the report?	Bloomberg, L. D. & Volpe, M. (2012). *Completing your Qualitative Dissertation: A Roadmap from Beginning to End* (2nd ed.). Thousand Oaks, CA: SAGE Publications.
	Salmons, J. & Kara, H. (2019). *Publishing from your Doctoral Research: Create and Use a Publication Strategy*. London: Routledge.
	Wolcott, H. (2009). *Writing up Qualitative Research*. Thousand Oaks, CA: SAGE Publications.

Glossary

Abductive reasoning A form of reasoning that, along with inductive and deductive reasoning, shows a way to come to a conclusion. Abductive reasoning is used when the researcher has an insight or makes a guess or an assumption that a connection exists in an incomplete or seemingly unrelated set of observations. Philosopher Charles Sanders Peirce (1839–1914) is credited with the origination of this concept and for applying it to pragmatic thinking.

Apomediation Relying on peer-to-peer guidance rather than on experts.

Archival research Archival research uses public records, historical, family, or other documents as data. A data archive is a resource center that acquires, stores, and disseminates data used by researchers for secondary analysis (Corti, 2008). While traditional archival research has been based in libraries and other institutions that housed physical records, as more historical documents are digitized, and records from websites and communities are collected, archival research can now take place online.

Asynchronous communication Communications that involve a delay between message and response, meaning it is not necessary to be online at the same time.

Avatar An avatar is a digital representation chosen or designed by users to represent themselves in virtual worlds or games. The avatar may have humanoid, animal or fantastical characteristics. Users may choose to create realistic avatars that resemble themselves, or avatars that represent imaginary versions of themselves.

Belmont Report The report that spells out essential basis for protection of human subjects regulations.

Beneficence To do no harm and to reduce risks involved in research, a fundamental principle of research ethics.

Blog A blog is a personal online journal where entries are posted chronologically. Users create their own blogs as a way to share thoughts and ideas, and link to other websites and blogs to create families of sites with common interests. Microblogs use the same principle but allow for very short entries. Blogs can be text only or multichannel, with links to images or media. Some are public and others are only seen by subscribers or friend lists. Blogs can be an asynchronous or a near-synchronous form of communication.

Chat See Text, instant messaging and chat

Computer-mediated communication This term refers to human communication that occurs when messages are conveyed by computers.

Consequentialism Ethical framework concerned with moral rightness of acts.

Constructivism The premise of constructivism is that we construct reality based on our perceptions of the world. Subjects construct their own meanings in different ways, even in relation to the same phenomenon (Gray, 2009). The term *interpretivism* is often used synonymously with constructivism. The premise of interpretivism is that we 'interpret' our experiences in the social world.

Data analysis Approach for deriving meaning, findings, or results.

Deductive reasoning Reasoning used for research in which a specific explanation is deduced from a general premise and is then tested (Schutt, 2006).

Deontological ethics Deontological ethics, building on the philosophies of Immanuel Kant (1785/2008), views morality as the responsibility to fulfill duties and to follow principles.

Discourse analysis Discourse analysis is the study of the written or spoken words, pictures or artifacts that constitute communication between individuals or groups. Discourse analysis is both a qualitative methodology that explains how we know the social world, and a set of methods for studying it.

Disintermediation The removal of the go-between with content producers and content consumers.

Document analysis Document analysis entails using content or other analytic methods with existing written sources. Documents can be either primary or secondary sources. Historians and others conventionally regard as primary sources those that were written (or otherwise came into being) by the people directly involved and at a time contemporary or near contemporary with the period being investigated. Primary sources, in other words, form the basic and original material for providing the researcher's raw evidence. Secondary sources, by contrast, are those that discuss the period studied but are brought into being at some time after it, or otherwise somewhat removed from the actual events (Finnegan, 2006, p. 142).

Epistemology A branch of philosophy that considers the criteria for determining what constitutes and does not constitute valid knowledge. In research, epistemology refers to the study of the nature of knowledge or the study of how knowledge is justified (Gray, 2009).

Epoche 'Setting aside prejudgments and opening the research interview with unbiased, receptive presence' (Moustakas, 1994, p. 85).

Existing sample frame Existing lists or collections of information about groups of people such as membership rolls or administrative records.

Follow-up questions Follow-up questions build on interviewee responses to get a clearer or deeper understanding of the interviewee's response.

Forum A form of asynchronous discussion where original comments and responses are organized by topic. Threaded discussion occurs when one user posts a message that is visible to other users, who respond in their own time. Also known as *threaded discussion*.

Global Positioning System (GPS) 'A US-owned utility that provides users with positioning, navigation, and timing services' (GPS.gov). While not a communications medium on its own, GPS can be used in conjunction with other tools in studies where the location is essential.

Human subject A living individual about whom an investigator (whether professional or student) conducting research obtains the following:

- Data through intervention or interaction with the individual, or
- Identifiable private information (Health and Human Services, 2005).
- Documents, written communications, media, or images that include information that would allow the person to be identified

In-depth interview An in-depth interview is a qualitative research technique involving a researcher who guides or questions a participant to elicit information, perspectives, insights, feelings or behaviors, experiences, or phenomena that cannot be observed. The in-depth interview is conducted to collect data that allows the researcher to generate new understandings and new knowledge about the subject of investigation.

Inductive reasoning   Reasoning used for research in which general conclusions are drawn from specific data (Schutt, 2006).

Information and communications technologies (ICTs)   Umbrella term describing communication devices or applications including the following: cellular phones, computer and network hardware and software, satellite systems, as well as the various services and applications associated with them.

Instant messaging   See Text, instant messaging and chat

Institutional review board, research ethics board   Body responsible for verifying that the research design protects human subjects.

Institutional review board approval   The determination of the institutional review board that the research has been reviewed and may be conducted at an institution within the constraints set forth by the board and by other institutional and federal requirements (Health and Human Services, 2005, 2017).

Interactivity   The degree of mutuality and reciprocation present in a communication setting (Kalman et al., 2006).

Interpretivism   Interpretivism is an epistemological viewpoint about exploring the subjective meanings through which people interpret the world, and the different ways in which they construct reality (through language, images, and cultural artifacts) (Sumner, 1995). When using an interpretivist stance researchers aim to understand social events and phenomena from the perspective of the actors themselves, avoiding the imposition of their own preconceptions and definitions (Sumner, 1995).

Main interview questions   Main interview questions are articulated to elicit overall experiences and understandings.

Methodology   The study of, and justification for, methods used to conduct research. The term describes approaches to systematic inquiry developed within a particular paradigm with associated epistemological assumptions (Gray, 2009). Methodologies emerge from academic disciplines in the social and physical sciences, and, while considerable cross-disciplinary exchange occurs, choices generally place the study into a disciplinary context.

Methods   The practical steps used to conduct the study (Anfara & Mertz, 2006; Carter & Little, 2007).

Minimal risk The probability and magnitude of harm or discomfort anticipated in the research are not greater in and of themselves than those ordinarily encountered in daily life or during the performance of routine physical or psychological examinations or tests (Health and Human Services, 2005).

Mixed methods Studies that combine qualitative and quantitative methods for data collection and/or analysis.

Multimethod/multimodal A research design that combines more than one method of qualitative data collection and analysis.

Narrative research Narrative research is a broad term encompassing the interdisciplinary study of the activities involved in generating and analyzing stories of life experiences (e.g., life histories, narrative interviews, journals, diaries, memoirs, autobiographies, and biographies) and reporting that kind of research (Schwandt, 2007, p. 204).

Non-verbal communication Aspects of communication that convey messages without words. Types of non-verbal communication include the following:

- Chronemics is the use of pacing and timing of speech and length of silence before response in conversation.
- Paralinguistic communication describes variations in volume, pitch, or quality of voice.
- Kinesic communication includes eye contact and gaze, facial expressions, body movements, gestures, or postures.
- Proxemic communication is the use of interpersonal space to communicate attitudes.

Observation Collecting data by watching, recording, or taking notes about participants' actions and behaviors.

In *unobtrusive* observation the researcher collects extant data containing no personally identifiable information or looks for patterns in such posts on websites, blogs or microblogs, or in interactions on discussion groups. In this form of observation the researcher does not ask questions, make posts or otherwise involve themselves in interactions with the online community, group, or social networking site. Members of the group being observed do not know observation is occurring.

In *open* observation the researcher collects data using observational methods in settings where participants are aware of the study and have given consent.

In *participant* observation the researcher collects data, including extant and elicited data, as well as his or her own field notes on reflections, experiences, or interactions with other participants. The researcher is a participant in the study. Involvement may include posting to forums, blogs, or walls in online communities or social networking sites. Participant observers can conduct formal or informal interviews with other participants.

Online interviews For the purpose of this book 'online interviews' refer to interviews conducted with computer-mediated communication. Scholarly interviews are conducted in accordance with ethical research guidelines; verifiable research participants provide informed consent before participating in any interview.

Online questionnaires Questions delivered in a written form on an interactive website. Formal online surveys, popular with quantitative researchers, are beyond the scope of this book. However, online questionnaires or surveys can be used to screen participants or solicit demographic or other basic background information from research participants.

Personal data According to the EU's GDPR, personal data includes any information relating to an identified or identifiable natural person ('data subject'); an identifiable natural person is one who can be identified, directly or indirectly, in particular by reference to an identifier such as a name, an identification number, location data, an online identifier or to one or more factors specific to the physical, physiological, genetic, mental, economic, cultural, or social identity of that natural person. (European Union, 2018)

Phenomenological research Research method used to investigate the meaning, structure, and essence of human experience (Patton, 2002).

Positivism A belief, shared by most scientists, that there is a reality that exists apart from our perceptions of it, that can be understood through observation, and that follows general laws (Schutt, 2006). The positivist tradition's view of social reality as 'knowable' relies on a concept of validity in terms of measurement (Hesse-Biber & Leavy, 2006).

Postpositivism A set of 'orienting sensibilities' rather than a particular kind of interviewing (Holstein & Gubrium, 2003). These sensibilities include new ways to look at theory as 'stories linked to the perspectives and interests of their storytellers' (Fontana & Frey, 2003; Gubrium & Holstein, 2003, p. 5).

Pragmatism A worldview that draws on both objective and subjective knowledge (Creswell & Clark, 2007).

Probability sampling A sampling method that relies on random selection so that the probability of selection of population elements is known (Schutt, 2006).

Probes Probes encourage the interviewee to provide detail to flesh out and expand on the answer.

- *Continuation* probes encourage the interviewee to keep going with the current response.
- *Elaboration* probes ask for more explanation on a particular point.

- *Attention* probes (such as 'Okay, I understand') let the interviewee know you are listening.
- *Clarification* probes ask for better definition or explanation if the researcher is confused or could not follow the thread of the story.
- *Steering* probes intend to get the story back on topic. (Rubin & Rubin, 2012)

Pseudonymization (or **Anonymizing**) 'Pseudonymization' means the processing of personal data in such a manner that the personal data can no longer be attributed to a specific data subject without the use of additional information, provided that such additional information is kept separately and is subject to technical and organisational measures to ensure that the personal data are not attributed to an identified or identifiable natural person (European Union, 2018).

Purposive or purposeful sampling A non-probability sampling method in which participants or cases are selected for a purpose, usually as related to ability to answer central questions of the study.

Qualitative e-research An umbrella term used to describe methodological traditions for using information and communications technologies to study perceptions, experiences, or behaviors through their verbal or visual expressions, actions or writings.

Qualitative research An umbrella term used to describe ways of studying perceptions, experiences or behaviors through their verbal or visual expressions, actions or writings.

Quantitative research Methods of inquiry that analyze numeric representations of the world; the systematic and mathematical techniques used to collect and analyze data (Gray, 2009). Survey and questionnaire data are often analyzed in quantitative units (Yoshikawa et al., 2008).

Quasi-experimental research A research approach that uses elements of the experimental design, such as use of a control group, but without the ability to randomly select the sample (Gray, 2009).

Reflection suggests a mirror image which affords the opportunity to engage in an observation or examination of our ways of doing. When we experience reflection, we become observers of our own practice.

Reflexivity 'Reflexivity is commonly viewed as the process of a continual internal dialogue and critical self-evaluation of researcher's positionality as well as active acknowledgement and explicit recognition that this position may affect the research process and outcome' (Berger, 2013, p. 220).

Research design The research design justifies the logic, structure, and the principles of the research methodology and methods in a comprehensive plan that describes all elements of the study coherently and argues for scholarly and scientific merit.

Responsive interview   Rubin and Rubin (2012) use this term to describe their approach, which is characterized by a flexible design. They acknowledge the human feelings and common interests that allow interpersonal relationships to form between interviewer and interviewee. Responsive interviews aim for depth of understanding through ongoing self-reflection.

Sample   The subjects or participants selected for the study.

Sample frame (or **Sampling frame**)   A sample or sampling frame defines the members of the *population* who are eligible to be included in a given *sample* – in the sense of drawing a boundary or frame around those cases that are acceptable for inclusion in the study (Morgan, 2008, p. 801). Existing sample frames represent records previously collected for another purpose outside the research process, such as membership lists. Constructed or generated sample frames are developed by the researcher, based on a set of inclusion criteria.

Sampling   Procedure for selecting cases or participants to study.

Scientific method   The scientific method describes formal step-by-step research procedures: (1) come up with a *theory*; (2) use that theory to deduce more specific propositions or *hypotheses*; (3) gather data – often through experimental design; (4) analyze the data; and (5) draw conclusions that may or may not support the hypothesis (O'Leary, 2007, p. 239).

Skype   An IP telephony service provider that offers free calling between computers and low-cost calling to regular telephones that are not connected to the Internet. Included in the free service is a softphone.

Structured interview   Interviewers ask fixed-choice questions and record responses based on a coding scheme. All interviews ask the same questions in the same order, and interviewers are trained to maintain a consistent, neutral approach to questioning and responding to all participants.

Survey   An investigation into one or more variables in a population that may involve collection of qualitative and/or quantitative data (Gray, 2009). Data may be analyzed with qualitative or quantitative methods.

Synchronous communication   Communications that occur in real time, meaning it is necessary for all parties to be online at the same time.

Text messaging, instant messaging, and chat   People can communicate online by exchanging short written messages. The term *text message* is used when people write back and forth over mobile phones or devices, while *instant messaging* or *chat* refers to the same kind of communication on computers. Chat or messaging may require registration and/or log-in to enter and post; it may be private or open to the public. One-to-one, one-to-many, or many-to-many individuals can converse in writing. This kind of communication can reach synchronicity or can be asynchronous or near-synchronous.

Theory   An explanation of a phenomenon that is internally consistent, is supportive of other theories, and gives new insights into the phenomenon. Some qualitative researchers frame the study in theoretical terms while others aim to discover and 'ground' theoretical principles in the data. In quantitative research, theory 'is an interrelated set of constructs (or variables) formed into propositions, or hypotheses, that specify the relationship among variables' (Creswell, 2013, p. 54).

Utilitarianism   Ethical view that actions should provide the most good or do the least harm.

Videoconferencing, video calls or chat   A videoconference is a live session between two or more users who are in different locations. Options include room systems that allow individuals or groups to see each other in an office, meeting room, or studio. Web conferencing, desktop conferencing, and video calls allow users to see each other using a webcam and computer. Typically desktop web conferencing allows viewing participants face-to-face, in contrast to the broader camera range and potential of videoconferencing to show group activities and events, creating a sense of presence.

Virtual worlds   Synchronous, persistent network of people, represented by avatars, facilitated by computers (Bell, 2008).

Virtue ethics   Ethical actions ought to be consistent with certain ideal virtues that provide for the full development of humanity (Velasquez et al., 2014).

Visual literacy   The ability to recognize, draw meaning from, and convey ideas through visible symbols, pictures, or images.

Voice over Internet Protocol (VoIP)   A term that originally described the transmission of real-time voice calls over a data network that uses IP, but currently is used to describe 'anything over IP,' for example, voice, fax, or video (Techdictionary.com, 2015).

Web conferencing meeting spaces   Multiple communication features are integrated into online meeting spaces. These spaces can be used for one-to-one, one-to-many, or many-to-many online gatherings. Web conferencing platforms allow for dialogue through VoIP two-way audio, text chat, polling, shared applications, webcam desktop videoconferencing, and shared whiteboard. In addition to exchange and dialogue, the shared whiteboard allows users to record meeting notes or brainstorms, illustrate, use graphic reporting, draw, or create diagrams together. Full versions allow the meeting to be archived for later viewing and transcription. (Also known as *web conferencing*.)

Webinar A workshop or lecture delivered over the web. Webinars may be a one-way webcast, or there may be interaction between participants and presenters. VoIP audio, shared whiteboard, and shared applications may be used.

Web scraping describes a set of techniques that are used to automate the collection of data from the web. Manually collecting data takes considerable time and inevitably leads to errors. It is therefore often worthwhile to automate the collection of web data. This is the core of web scraping (also known as web harvesting or web crawling). Resources on a server are accessed by a computer program, and the unstructured information is transformed into a structured format—for example, a database. (p. 2)

Whiteboard The equivalent of a blackboard, but on a computer screen. A whiteboard allows one or more users to draw on the screen while others on the network watch, and can be used for instruction the same way a blackboard is used in a classroom (Mallery, 2015).

Wiki A web application designed to allow multiple authors to add, remove, and edit content (infoDev, 2008).

Wireless Generic term for mobile communication services that do not use fixed-line networks for direct access to the subscriber (infoDev, 2008).

References

Adamou, A., d'Aquin, M., Brown, S., Barlow, H., & Allocca, C. (2019). Crowdsourcing Linked Data on listening experiences through reuse and enhancement of library data. *International Journal on Digital Libraries*, 20(1), 61–79. doi:10.1007/s00799-018-0235-0

Aguinis, H., Villamor, I., & Ramani, R. S. (2020). MTurk research: Review and recommendations. *Journal of Management*, 47(4), 823–837. doi:10.1177/0149206320969787

Aldunate, N., & González-Ibáñez, R. (2017). An integrated review of emoticons in computer-mediated communication. *Frontiers in Psychology*, 7(2061). doi:10.3389/fpsyg.2016.02061

Alexander, B. (2009). Apprehending the future: Emerging technologies, from science fiction to campus reality. *Educause Review*, 44(3), 12–29.

Alexander, L., & Moore, M. (2012). Deontological ethics. In E. N. Zalta (Ed.), *The Stanford Encyclopedia of Philosophy*. Stanford: Stanford University Press.

Amaghlobeli, N. (2012). Linguistic features of typographic emoticons in SMS discourse. *Theory and Practice in Language Studies*, 2(2), 348–354.

Anderson, E. E., & Corneli, A. (2018). *100 Questions (and Answers) about Research Ethics*. Retrieved from https://methods.sagepub.com/book/100-questions-and-answers-about-research-ethics. doi:10.4135/9781506348681

Anderson, V. (2017). Editorial: Criteria for evaluating qualitative research. *Human Resource Development Quarterly*, 28(2): 125–133. i

Anfara, V. A., & Mertz, N. T. (Eds.). (2006). *Theoretical Frameworks in Qualitative Research*. Thousand Oaks: Sage.

Antoun, C., Zhang, C., Conrad, F. G., & Schober, M. F. (2016). Comparisons of online recruitment strategies for convenience samples: Craigslist, Google AdWords, Facebook, and Amazon Mechanical Turk. *Field Methods*, 28(3), 231–246.

Baggini, J., & Fosi, P. (2007). *The Ethics Toolkit: A Compendium of Ethical Concepts and Methods*. Malden: Blackwell Publishing.

Bamford, A. (2003). The visual literacy white paper. *Uxbridge: Adobe Systems Inc*. Retrieved from https://aperture.org/wp-content/uploads/2013/05/visual-literacy-wp.pdf

Bampton, R., & Cowton, C. J. (2002). The E-interview. *Forum: Qualitative Social Research*, 3(2). doi.org/10.17169/fqs-3.2.848

Banks, M. (2007). *Using Visual Data in Qualitative Research*. London: Sage.

Barden, O. (2019). Building the mobile hub: Mobile literacies and the construction of a complex academic text. *Literacy*, 53(1), 22–29. doi:10.1111/lit.12137

Barthes, R. (1977). Image, music, text. *Journal of Aesthetics and Art Criticism*, 37(2), 235–236.

Bell, M. (2008). Definition and taxonomy of virtual worlds. Paper presented at New Digital Media (Audiovisual, Games and Music): Economic, Social and Political Impacts, Sao Paulo.

Beninger, K., Fry, A., Jago, N., Lepps, H., Nass, L., & Silvester, H. (2014). *Research Using Social Media: Users' Views*. London: NatCen. Retrieved from: http://www.natcen.ac.uk/media/282288/p0639-research-using-social-media-report-final-190214.pdf

Benoot, C., Hannes, K., & Bilsen, J. (2016). The use of purposeful sampling in a qualitative evidence synthesis: A worked example on sexual adjustment to a cancer trajectory. *BMC Medical Research Methodology*, 16. doi:10.1186/s12874-016-0114-6

BERA (2018). *Ethical Guidelines for Educational Research*. Retrieved from www.bera.ac.uk/publication/ethical-guidelines-for-educational-research-2018.

Berger, R. (2013). Now I see it, now I don't: Researcher's position and reflexivity in qualitative research. *Qualitative Research*, 15(2), 219–234. doi:10.1177/1468794112468475

Bernard, H. R., Wutich, A., & Ryan, G. W. (2017). *Analyzing Qualitative Data. Systematic Approaches*. London: Sage.

Berry, D. M. (2004). Internet research: privacy, ethics and alienation: An open source approach. *Journal of Internet Research*, 14(4), 323–332.

Bhattacharya, H. (2008). Research setting. In L. Given (Ed.), *SAGE Encyclopedia of Qualitative Research Methods*. Thousand Oaks: Sage.

Biswas, A., & Kirchherr, J. (2015). *Citations are not enough: Academic promotion panels must take into account a scholar's presence in popular media*. The Impact Blog (Vol. 2015). London: London School of Economics and Political Science.

Blaikie, N. (2004). Interpretivism. In M. S. Lewis-Beck, A. Bryman, & T. F. Liao (Eds.), *The SAGE Encyclopedia of Social Science Research Methods*. Thousand Oaks: Sage.

Bloomberg, L. D., & Volpe, M. (2012). *Completing your Qualitative Dissertation: A Roadmap from Beginning to End* (2nd ed.). Thousand Oaks: Sage.

Blum, E., Heinonen, T., & White, J.. (2010). Participatory action research studies. In B. A. Thyer (Ed.), *The Handbook of Social Work Research Methods* (2nd ed.) (ch. 25). London: Sage.

Bowen, G. A. (2009). Document analysis as a qualitative research method. *Qualitative Research*, 9(2), 27–40. doi:DOI 10.3316/QRJ0902027

BPS (2013). *Guidelines for Ethical Practice in Psychological Research Online*. Report of the Working Party on Conducting Research on the Internet. Leicester: BPS. Research guidelines and policy documents, 28. [Updated 2021; available at https://www.bps.org.uk/news-and-policy/listing/policies-and-impact/guidelines]

Brink, D. (2008). Mill's moral and political philosophy. In E. N. Zalta (Ed.), *The Stanford Encyclopedia of Philosophy*. Stanford: Stanford University Press.

Brower, R. L., Jones, T. B., Osborne-Lampkin, L. T., Hu, S., & Park-Gaghan, T. J. (2019). Big Qual: Defining and debating qualitative inquiry for large data sets. *International Journal of Qualitative Methods*, 18. doi:10.1177/1609406919880692

Bruckman, A. (2002). Studying the amateur artist: A perspective on disguising data collected in human subjects research on the Internet. *Ethics and Information Technology*, 4(3), 217–217.

BSA (British Sociological Association) (2002). *Statement of Ethical Practice for the British Sociological Association*. Retrieved from www.britsoc.co.uk/media/23902/statementofethicalpractice.pdf (accessed 7 July 2021).

Buchanan, E. (2011). Internet research ethics: Past, present, future. In M. Consalvo & C. Ess (Eds.), *The Handbook of Internet Studies*. New York: Wiley–Blackwell.

Buckley, C. A., & Waring, M. J. (2013). Using diagrams to support the research process: Examples from grounded theory. *Qualitative Research*, 13(2), 148–172. doi:10.1177/1468794112472280

Budd, J. M. (2008). Critical theory. In L. M. Given (Ed.), *The SAGE Encyclopedia of Qualitative Research Methods*. Thousand Oaks: Sage.

Bulpitt, H., & Martin, P. J. (2010). Who am I and what am I doing? Becoming a qualitative research interviewer. *Nurse Researcher*, 17, 3.

Burbules, N. (2009). Privacy and new technologies: The limits of traditional research ethics. In D. Mertens & P. Ginsberg (Eds.), *The Handbook of Social Research Ethics*. Thousand Oaks: Sage.

Burles, M. C., & Bally, J. M. G. (2018). Ethical, practical, and methodological considerations for unobtrusive qualitative research about personal narratives shared on the internet. *International Journal of Qualitative Methods*, 17(1), 1–9.

Carter, S. M., & Little, M. (2007). Justifying knowledge, justifying method, taking action: epistemologies, methodologies, and methods in qualitative research. *Qualitative Health Research*, 17(10), 1316–1328.

Charmaz, K. (2006). *Constructed Grounded Theory: A Practical Guide through Qualitative Analysis*. Thousand Oaks: Sage.

Charmaz, K. (2014). *Constructed Grounded Theory: A Practical Guide through Qualitative Analysis* (2nd ed.). Thousand Oaks: Sage.

Chávez, N. R., Castro-Reyes, S., & Echeverry, L. F. (2020). Challenges of a systematization of experiences study: Learning from a displaced victim assistance programme during the COVID-19 emergency in ethnic territories in Colombia. In H. Kara & S.-m. Khoo (Eds.), *Researching in the Age of COVID-19 Volume 1: Response and Reassessment*. London: Policy Press.

Cheung, J., Burns, D., Sinclair, R., & Sliter, M. (2017). Amazon Mechanical Turk in organizational psychology: An evaluation and practical recommendations. *Journal of Business & Psychology*, 32(4), 347–361. doi:10.1007/s10869-016-9458-5

Christine Griffin, A. B.-H. (2010). Ethnography. In C. Willig & W. Stainton-Rogers (Eds.), *The SAGE Handbook of Qualitative Research in Psychology* (pp. 15–32). London: Sage.

Clandinin, D. J., & Connelly, F. M. (2000). *Narrative Inquiry: Experience and Story in Qualitative Research*. Thousand Oaks: Sage.

Clarke, A., Fries, C., & Washburn, R. S. (2018). *Situational Analysis: Grounded Theory after the Postmodern Turn* (2nd ed.). Thousand Oaks: Sage.

Cocke, D., Newman, H., & Salmons, J. (Eds.) (1993). From the ground up: Grassroots theater in historical and contemporary perspective. *Cornell University*. Retrieved from https://roadside.org/asset/book-ground-grassroots-theater-historical-contemporary-perspective

Corbin, J., & Strauss, A. (2015). *Basics of Qualitative Research: Techniques and Procedures for Developing Grounded Theory*. Thousand Oaks: Sage.

Corti, L. (2008). Data archive. In L. Given (Ed.), *Sage Encyclopedia of Qualitative Research Methods* (pp. 189–191). Thousand Oaks: Sage.

Clarke, N. (2020). [Interview: Online research/Interviewer: J. Salmons.]

Clarke, N., & Watson, D. (2020). Creative diary approaches for participant-centred research. In H. Kara & S.-m. Khoo (Eds.), *Researching in the Age of COVID-19 Volume 3: Creativity and Ethics*. London: Policy Press.

Coleman, K., Healy, S., Wouters, N., Martin, J., Campbell, L., Peck, S., Belton, A., & Hiscock, R. (2020). Scicurious as method: Learning from GLAM young people living in a pandemic about cultivating digital co-research-creation spaces that ignite curiosity and creativity. In H. Kara & S.-m. Khoo (Eds.), *Researching in the Age of COVID-19 Volume 3: Creativity and Ethics*. London: Policy Press.

Corley, K. G., & Gioia, D. A. (2011). Building theory about theory building: What constitutes a theoretical contribution? *Academy of Management Review*, 36(1), 12–32. doi:10.5465/amr.2011.55662499

Couceiro, L. (2020a). Disorientation and new directions: Developing the reader response toolkit. In H. Kara & S.-m. Khoo (Eds.), *Researching in the Age of COVID-19 Volume 1: Response and Reassessment*. London: Policy Press.

Couceiro, L. (2020b). [Interview: Online research.]

Coyne, I. T. (1997). Sampling in qualitative research. Purposeful and theoretical sampling; merging or clear boundaries? *Journal of Advanced Nursing*, 26, 623–630.

Creswell, J. W. (2013). *Qualitative Inquiry and Research Design: Choosing among Five Approaches* (3rd ed.). Thousand Oaks: Sage.

Creswell, J. W., & Clark, V. L. P. (2011). *Designing and Conducting Mixed Methods Research* (2nd ed.). Thousand Oaks: Sage.

Creswell, J. W., & Poth, C. N. (2017). *Qualitative Inquiry and Research Design: Choosing among Five Traditions* (4th ed.). Thousand Oaks: Sage.

Crotty, M. (2004). The foundation of social research: Meaning and perspectives in the research process. In D. Gray (Ed.), *Doing Research in the Real World*. London: Sage.

Daft, R. L., & Lengel, R. H. (1986). Organizational information requirements, media richness and structural design. *Management Science*, 32(5), 554–571.

Daft, R. L., Lengel, R. H., & Trevino, L. K. (1987). Message equivocality, media selection, and manager performance: Implications for information systems. *MIS Quarterly*, 11(3), 354–366.

Data protection in the EU. (2020). Retrieved from https://ec.europa.eu/info/law/law-topic/data-protection/data-protection-eu_en

Davidson, E., Edwards, R., Jamieson, L., & Weller, S. (2019). Big data, qualitative style: A breadth-and-depth method for working with large amounts of secondary qualitative data. *Quality & Quantity*, 53. doi:10.1007/s11135-018-0757-y

Davis, M., Bolding, G., Hart, G., Sherr, L., & Elford, J. (2004). Reflecting on the experience of interviewing online: perspectives from the Internet and HIV study in London. *AIDS Care*, 16(8), 944–952.

Debes, J. (1968). Some foundations of visual literacy. *Audio-Visual Instruction*, 13, 961–964.

Dennis, A. R., Fuller, R. M., & Valacich, J. S. (2008). Media, tasks, and communication processes: A theory of media synchronicity. *Management Information Systems Quarterly*, 32(4), 575–600.

Denzin, N. K. (2001). The reflexive interview and a performative social science. *Qualitative Research*, 1(23), 23–25.

Denzin, N. K. (Ed.) (2014). *Interpretive Autoethnography* (2nd ed.). Thousand Oaks: Sage.

Denzin, N. K., & Lincoln, Y. S. (2002). Emerging criteria for quality in qualitative and interpretive research. In N. K. Denzin & Y. S. Lincoln (Eds.), *The Qualitative Inquiry Reader*. Thousand Oaks: Sage.

Dewey, J. (1916). *Democracy and Education*. New York: Macmillan.

deRoche, J., & deRoche, C. (2010). Ethics. In A. J. Mills, G. Durepos, & E. Wiebe (Eds.), *Encyclopedia of Case Study Research*. Thousand Oaks: Sage.

DiCicco-Bloom, B., & Crabtree, B. F. (2006). The qualitative research interview. *Medical Education*, 40, 314–321.

Dik, B. (2007). Ethical principles in the conduct of research with human participants. In N. J. Salkind & K. Rasmussen (Eds.), *Encyclopedia of Measurement and Statistics*. Thousand Oaks: Sage.

Ditchfield, H., & Meredith, J. (2018). Collecting qualitative data from Facebook: Approaches and methods. In U. Flick (Ed.), *The SAGE Handbook of Qualitative Data Collection*. London: Sage.

Dodgson, J. E. (2019). Reflexivity in qualitative research. *Journal of Human Lactation*, 35(2), 220–222. doi:10.1177/0890334419830990

Dowie, J., & Kaltoft, M. K. (2018). The future of health is self-production and co-creation based on apomediative decision support. *Medical Sciences*, 6(3), 66.

Dreyfuss, S., & Ryan, M. (2018). How to get your article published: Twenty tips from two editors. *Reference & User Services Quarterly*, 58(1), 8–10. doi:10.5860/rusq.58.1.6834

Duesbery, L., & Twyman, T. (2020). *100 Questions (and Answers) about Action Research*. Thousand Oaks: Sage.

Dunleavy, P. (2014). Shorter, better, faster, free: Blogging changes the nature of academic research, not just how it is communicated. In P. Dunleavy (Ed.), LSE Impact Blog (Vol. 2014). London: London School of Economics Impact Blog.

Dunn, R. A., & Guadagno, R. E. (2012). My avatar and me – gender and personality predictors of avatar–self discrepancy. *Computers in Human Behavior*, 28(1), 97–106. doi:http://dx.doi.org/10.1016/j.chb.2011.08.015

Dworkin, J., Hessel, H., Gliske, K., & Rudi, J. H. (2016). A comparison of three online recruitment strategies for engaging parents. *Family Relations*, 65(4), 550–561. doi:10.1111/fare.12206

Ebrahim, S. A., Poshtan, J., Jamali, S. M., & Ebrahim, N. A. (2020). Quantitative and qualitative analysis of time-series classification using deep learning. *IEEE Access*, 8, 90202–90215. doi:10.1109/ACCESS.2020.2993538

Edwards, R., & Mauthner, M. (2012). Ethics and feminist research: Theory and practice. In T. Miller, M. Birch, M. Mauthner, & J. Jessop (Eds.), *Ethics in Qualitative Research* (2nd ed.). London: Sage.

EC (European Commission). (2013). Ethics for researchers. Retrieved from http://ec.europa.eu/research/participants/data/ref/fp7/89888/ethics-for-researchers_en.pdf

Eisenberg, J., Glikson, E., & Lisak, A. (2021). *Multicultural Virtual Team Performance: The Impact of Media Choice and Language Diversity*. Small Group Research, 1046496420985614. doi:10.1177/1046496420985614

Eriksson, P., & Kovalainen, A. (2008). *Qualitative Methods in Business Research*. Thousand Oaks: Sage. https://doi.org/doi: 10.4135/9780857028044

ESRC (Economic and Social Research Council) (2021). *ESRC Framework for Research Ethics*. Retrieved from https://www.ukri.org/councils/esrc/guidance-for-applicants/research-ethics-guidance/consent/

European Union (2018). What is GPDR, the EU's new data protection law? Retrieved from https://gdpr.eu/what-is-gdpr/

Eysenbach, G. (2008). Medicine 2.0: Social networking, collaboration, participation, apomediation, and openness. *Journal of Medical Internet Research*, 10(3). doi:10.2196/jmir.1030

Farley-Ripple, E. (2020). Wordplay or paradigm shift: The meaning of 'research impact'. *International Journal of Education Policy and Leadership*, 16(11).

Fetterman, D. M. (2020). *Ethnography: Step-by-Step* (4th ed.). Thousand Oaks: Sage.

Flewitt, R., Price, S., & Korkiakangas, T. (2019). *Multimodality: Methodological Explorations*. London: Sage.

Fox, N. (2008). Postpositivism. In L. M. Given (Ed.), *The SAGE Encyclopedia of Qualitative Research Methods*. Thousand Oaks: Sage.

Finefter-Rosenbluh, I. (2017). Incorporating Perspective Taking in Reflexivity: A Method to Enhance Insider Qualitative Research Processes. *International Journal of Qualitative Methods*. https://doi.org/10.1177/1609406917703539

Finnegan, R. (2006). Using documents. In V. Jupp & R. Sapsford (Eds.), *Data Collection and Analysis* (2nd ed., pp. 138–153). London: Sage.

Fontana, A., & Frey, J. H. (2003). The interview: From structured questions to negotiated text. In N. K. Denzin & Y. S. Lincoln (Eds.), *Collecting and Interpreting Qualitative Materials* (2nd ed.). Thousand Oaks: Sage.

franzke, a. s., Bechmann, A., Zimmer, M., Ess, C. M., & The Association of Internet Researchers (2020). *Internet Research: Ethical Guidelines 3.0*. Retrieved from https://aoir.org/reports/ethics3.pdf

Freeman, R. (2007). Epistemological bricolage: How practitioners make sense of learning. *Administration & Society*, 39(4), 476–496.

Fritz, R. L., & Vandermause, R. (2018). Data collection via in-depth email interviewing: Lessons from the field. *Qualitative Health Research*, 28(10), 1640–1649.

Gallagher, J. R. (2019). A framework for Internet case study methodology in writing studies. *Computers & Composition*, 54. doi:10.1016/j.compcom.2019.102509

Gardner, B. (2020). [Online research: Interview.]

Gaudet, S., & Robert, D. (2018). *A Journey Through Qualitative Research: From Design to Reporting*. London: Sage.

Geddes, A., Parker, C., & Scott, S. (2018). When the snowball fails to roll and the use of 'horizontal' networking in qualitative social research. *International Journal of Social Research Methodology*, 21(3), 347–358.

George, G., Haas, M. R., & Pentland, A. (2014). From the editors: Big Data and management. *Academy of Management Journal, 57*(2), 322–326.

Giaxoglou, K. (2017). Reflections on internet research ethics from language-focused research on web-based mourning: Revisiting the private/public distinction as a language ideology of differentiation. *Applied Linguistics Review, 8*(2/3), 229–250. doi:10.1515/applirev-2016-1037

Giorgi, A. (2009). *The Descriptive Phenomenological Method in Psychology: A Modified Husserlian Approach*. Pittsburgh: Duquesne University Press.

Godinho, A., Schell, C., & Cunningham, J. A. (2020). Out damn bot, out: Recruiting real people into substance use studies on the internet. *Substance Abuse, 41*(1), 3–5. doi:10.10 80/08897077.2019.1691131

Goldstein, B. M. (2007). All photos lie: Images as data. In G. C. Stanczak (Ed.), *Visual Research Methods: Image, Society, and Representation*. Thousand Oaks: Sage.

Goldstein, R. S., Vasques, R. A., & Santos, M. C. L. d. (2020). Doing design research with youth at/from the margins in pandemic times: Challenges, inequalities, and possibilities. In H. Kara & S.-m. Khoo (Eds.), *Researching in the Age of COVID-19 Volume III: Creativity and Ethics (Vol. III)*. Policy Press.

Gordon, R. L. (1980). Interviewing: Strategy, techniques and tactics. Dorsey.

Grahe, J. E., & Bernieri, F. J. (1999). The importance of nonverbal cues in judging rapport. *Journal of Nonverbal Behavior, 23*(4), 253–269.

Gratton, N. (2020). [Interview: Online research.]

Gratton, N., Fox, R., & Elder, T. (2020). Keep talking: Messy research in times of lockdown. In H. Kara & S.-m. Khoo (Eds.), *Researching in the Age of COVID-19. Volume 2: Care and Resilience*. London: Policy Press.

Gubrium, J., & Holstein, J. (2003). From the individual interview to the interview society. In J. F. Gubrium & J. A. Holstein (Eds.), *Postmodern Interviewing*. Thousand Oaks: Sage.

Gray, D. (2004). *Doing research in the real world* (2nd ed.). SAGE Publications.

Gray, D. (2018). *Doing Research in the Real World* (4th ed.). London: Sage.

Gray, B., Hilder, J., Macdonald, L., Tester, R., Dowell, A., & Stubbe, M. (2016). Are research ethics guidelines culturally competent? *Research Ethics, 13*(1), 23–41. doi:10.1177/1747016116650235

Greeff, M., & Rennie, S. (2016). Phronesis: Beyond the research ethics committee – a crucial decision-making skill for health researchers during community research. *Journal of Empirical Research on Human Research Ethics, 11*(2), 170–179. doi:10.1177/1556264616650070

Gruber, T., Szmigin, I., Reppel, A. E., & Voss, R. (2008). Designing and conducting online interviews to investigate interesting consumer phenomena. *Qualitative Market Research, 11*(3), 256–274. doi: 10.1108/13522750810879002

Guerrero, L. K., DeVito, J. A., & Hecht, M. L. (Eds.). (1999). *The nonverbal communication reader: Classic and contemporary readings*. Prospect Hills: Waveland Press.

Guillemin, M., & Gillam, L. (2004). Ethics, reflexivity, and "ethically important moments" in research. *Qualitative Inquiry, 10*(2), 261-280. doi:10.1177/1077800403262360

Guthrie, G. (2010). *Basic Research Methods : An Entry to Social Science Research*. New Delhi, India: Sage.

Code of Federal Regulations: Protection of human subjects, Part 46 C.F.R. (2005).

Hammersley, M., & Traianou, A. (2014). Foucault and research ethics: On the autonomy of the researcher. *Qualitative Inquiry, 20*(3), 227–238. doi:10.1177/1077800413489528

Hargrove, R. (2001). *E-Leader: reinventing leadership in a connected economy*. Cambridge: Perseus Publishing.

Hastings, S. L. (2010). Triangulation. In N. J. Salkind (Ed.). Thousand Oaks: Sage.

Hawkins, J. E. (2018). The practical utility and suitability of email interviews in qualitative research. *The Qualitative Report*, 23(2), 493–501.

Hay, C. (2008). *Theory of Knowledge : A Coursebook*. Cambridge: Lutterworth Press.

Henderson, T., Hutton, L., & McNeilly, S. (2012). Ethics and online social network research: Developing best practices. Paper presented at the People & Computers XXVI: Conference on Human Computer Interaction, Birmingham.

Hennell, K., Limmer, M., & Piacentini, M. (2020). Ethical Dilemmas Using Social Media in Qualitative Social Research: A Case Study of Online Participant Observation. *Sociological Research Online*, 25(3), 473–489. https://doi.org/10.1177/1360780419888933

Hesse-Biber, S. N., & Leavy, P. (2006). *The Practice of Qualitative Research*. Thousand Oaks: Sage.

HHS. (2005) *Code of Federal Regulations: Protection of human subjects*, Part 46 C.F.R.

HHS (2017). *Federal Policy for the Protection of Human Subjects*. Washington, DC: Government Publishing Office. Retrieved from www.hhs.gov/ohrp/regulations-and-policy/regulations/common-rule/

Hibbert, P., Coupland, C., & MacIntosh, R. (2010). Reflexivity: Recursion and relationality in organizational research processes. *Qualitative Research in Organizations and Management*, 5(1), 47–62. doi:10.1108/17465641011042026

Hine, C. (2011). Internet research and unobtrusive methods. *Social Research Update*, 61 (Spring). Retrieved from https://sru.soc.surrey.ac.uk/SRU61.pdf

Hine, C. (2013). *The Internet: Understanding Qualitative Research*. Oxford: Oxford University Press.

Hine, C. (2020a). Ethnographies in online environments. *SAGE Research Methods Foundations* (Eds. P. Atkinson, S. Delamont, A. Cernat, J. W. Sakshaug, & R. A. Williams). doi:http://dx.doi.org/10.4135/9781526421036784565

Hine, C. (2020b). *Ethnography for the Internet: Embedded, Embodied and Everyday*. Abingdon: Routledge.

Holstein, J. A., & Gubrium, J. F. (2003). Active interviewing. In J. F. Gubrium & J. A. Holstein (Eds.), *Postmodern Interviewing*. Thousand Oaks: Sage.

Hsu, C., & Sandford, B. (2010). Delphi technique. In N. Salkind (Ed.), *Encyclopedia of Research Design*. Thousand Oaks: Sage.

Hursthouse, R. (2012). Virtue ethics. In E. N. Zalta (Ed.), *The Stanford Encyclopedia of Philosophy*. Stanford: Stanford University Press.

infoDev. (2008). Glossary. ICT Regulation Toolkit (Vol. 2008).

Iordache, C., Mariën, I., & Baelden, D. (2017). Developing digital skills and competences: A quick-scan analysis of 13 digital literacy models. *Italian Journal of Sociology of Education*, 9(1).

Ishii, K., Lyons, M. M., & Carr, S. A. (2019). Revisiting media richness theory for today and future. *Human Behavior and Emerging Technologies*, 1(2), 124–131.

Jackson, K., & Bazeley, P. (2019). *Qualitative Data Analysis with nVivo* (3rd ed.). London: Sage.

Jacobson, D., & Mustafa, N. (2019). Social identity map: A reflexivity tool for practicing explicit positionality in critical qualitative research. *International Journal of Qualitative Methods*, 18. doi:10.1177/1609406919870075

James, N. (2016). Using email interviews in qualitative educational research: Creating space to think and time to talk. *International Journal of Qualitative Studies in Education*, 29(2), 150–163.

James, N., & Busher, H. (2009). *Online Interviewing*. London: Sage.

Johnson, R. B., & Onwuegbuzie, A. J. (2004). Mixed methods research: A research paradigm whose time has come. *Educational Researcher*, 33(7), 14–26.

Johnsson, L., Eriksson, S., Helgesson, G., & Hansson, M. G. (2014). Making researchers moral: Why trustworthiness requires more than ethics guidelines and review. *Research Ethics*, 10(1), 29–46. doi:10.1177/1747016113504778

Jupp, V. (2006). Exploratory research. In V. Jupp (Ed.), *The SAGE Dictionary of Social Research Methods*. London: Sage.

Kalman, Y. M., Ravid, G., Raban, D. R., & Rafaeli, S. (2006). Pauses and response latencies: A chronemic analysis of asynchronous CMC. *Journal of Computer-Mediated Communication*, 12(1), 1-23.

Kant, I. (1785). *Grounding for the Metaphysics of Morals*.

Kant, I. (2008). *Grounding for the Metaphysics of Morals* (J. W. Ellington, Trans., 2nd ed.). Indianapolis: Hackett Classics.

Karamshuk, D., Shaw, F., Brownlie, J., & Sastry, N. (2017). Bridging big data and qualitative methods in the social sciences: A case study of Twitter responses to high profile deaths by suicide. *Online Social Networks and Media*, 1, 33-43. doi:https://doi.org/10.1016/j.osnem.2017.01.002

Kaufmann, M., & Tzanetakis, M. (2020). Doing Internet research with hard-to-reach communities: Methodological reflections on gaining meaningful access. *Qualitative Research*, 20(6), 927–944. doi:10.1177/1468794120904898

Kennedy, B. L. (2018). Deduction, induction, and abduction. In U. Flick (Ed.), *The SAGE Handbook of Qualitative Data Collection*. London: Sage.

Keusch, F. (2020). Gamification in web surveys. SAGE Research Methods Foundations (Eds. P. Atkinson, S. Delamont, A. Cernat, J. W. Sakshaug, & R. A. Williams). doi:http://dx.doi.org/10.4135/9781526421036888649

Knoblauch, H., Tuma, R., & Schnettler, B. (2014). Video analysis and videography. In U. Flick (Ed.), *The SAGE Handbook of Qualitative Data Analysis* (Ch. 30). London: Sage.

Koerber, A., & McMichael, L. (2008). Qualitative sampling methods: A primer for technical communicators. *Journal of Business and Technical Communication*, 22(4), 454–473.

Kotlyar, I., & Ariely, D. (2013). The effect of nonverbal cues on relationship formation. *Computers in Human Behavior*, 29(3), 544–551. doi:http://dx.doi.org/10.1016/j.chb.2012.11.020

Kozinets, R. V. (2019). *Netnography: The Essential Guide to Qualitative Social Media Research* (3rd ed.). Thousand Oaks: Sage.

Kress, G. (2003). *Literacy in the New Media Age*. London: Routledge.

Kress, G. (2005). Gains and losses: New forms of texts, knowledge, and learning. *Computers and Composition*, 22(1), 5–22.

Kress, G. (2010). *Multimodality: A Social Semiotic Approach to Contemporary Communication.* London: Taylor & Francis.

Kress, G., & Selander, S. (2012). Multimodal design, learning and cultures of recognition. *The Internet and Higher Education*, 15(4), 265–268.

Krishnan, A., & Hunt, D. S. (2021). TTYL :-) … Nonverbal cues and perceptions of personality and homophily in synchronous mediated communication. *Information, Communication & Society*, 24(1), 85–101. doi:10.1080/1369118X.2019.1635183

Kuckartz, U. (2014). *Qualitative Text Analysis: A Guide to Methods, Practice & Using Software.* Thousand Oaks: Sage.

Kumar, P., Follen, M., Huang, C.-C., & Cathey, A. (2020). Using laddering interviews and hierarchical value mapping to gain insights into improving patient experience in the hospital: A systematic literature review. *Journal of Patient Experience.* doi:10.1177/2374373520942425

Kvale, S. (2003). InterViews: An introduction to qualitative research interviewing. In J. Ritchie & J. Lewis (Eds.), *Qualitative Research Practice: A Guide for Social Science Students and Researchers.* London: Sage.

Kvale, S. (2007). *Doing Interviews.* Thousand Oaks: Sage.

Kvale, S., & Brinkman, S. (2014). *InterViews: Learning the Craft of Qualitative Research Interviewing* (3rd ed.). Thousand Oaks: Sage.

LaBanca, F. (2011). Online dynamic asynchronous audit strategy for reflexivity in the qualitative paradigm. *The Qualitative Report*, 16(4), 1160–1171. doi:10.1080/13645570802156196

Larsen, R. (2020). Mapping Right to be Forgotten frames: Reflexivity and empirical payoffs at the intersection of network discourse and mixed network methods. *New Media & Society*, 22(7), 1245–1265. doi:10.1177/1461444820912534

LeCompte, M. (2008). Secondary participants. In L. M. Given (Ed.), *The SAGE Encyclopedia of Qualitative Research Methods.* Thousand Oaks: Sage.

Ledin, P., & Machin, D. (2018). *Doing Visual Analysis: From Theory to Practice.* London: Sage.

Lee, N., & Lings, I. (2008). *Doing Business Research: A Guide to Theory and Practice.* London: Sage.

Lincoln, Y. S., & Guba, E. G. (1985). *Naturalistic Inquiry.* Thousand Oaks: Sage.

Lieberman, A., & Schroeder, J. (2020). Two social lives: How differences between online and offline interaction influence social outcomes. *Current Opinion in Psychology*, 31, 16–21.

Litman, L., & Robinson, J. (2020). *Conducting Online Research on Amazon Mechanical Turk and Beyond.* Thousand Oaks: Sage.

Livingstone, S., & Locatelli, E. (2012). Ethical dilemmas in qualitative research with youth on/offline. *International Journal of Learning and Media*, 4(2), 67–75. doi:10.1162/IJLM_a_00096

Locke, K. (2010). Abduction. In A. J. Mills, G. Durepos, & E. Wiebe (Eds.), *The SAGE Encyclopedia of Case Study Research.* Thousand Oaks: Sage.

Lockyer, S., Coffey, A., Atkinson, P., Fielding, J., Strauss, A., & Corbin, J. (2004). Coding qualitative data. In M. S. Lewis-Beck, A. Bryman, & T. F. Liao (Eds.), *The SAGE Encyclopedia of Social Science Research Methods.* Thousand Oaks: Sage.

Lomborg, S. (2013). Personal internet archives and ethics. *Research Ethics*, 9(1), 20–31.

Loseke, D. R. (2013). *Methodological Thinking: Basic Principles of Social Research Design.* Thousand Oaks: Sage.

Loue, S. (2000). *Textbook of Research Ethics: Theory and Practice*. Hingham: Kluwer Academic Publishers.

Mallery, M. (2015). Whiteboard. Retrieved from http://www.techdictionary.com/search_action.lasso

Margolis, E., & Pauwels, L. (2011). An integrated conceptual framework for visual social research. In L. Pauwels (Ed.), *The SAGE Handbook of Visual Research Methods*. London: Sage.

Markham, A., & Buchanan, E. (2012). *Ethical Decision-making and Internet Research: 2012. Recommendations from the AoIR Ethics Working Committee*. Retrieved from http://aoir.org/reports/ethics2.pdf

Mason, J. (2017). *Qualitative Researching* (3rd ed.). Thousand Oaks: Sage.

McCaslin, M. L. (2008). Pragmatism. In L. M. Given (Ed.), *The SAGE Encyclopedia of Qualitative Research Methods* (pp. 517–522). Thousand Oaks: Sage.

McKee, H. A., & Porter, J. E. (2009). *Ethics of Internet Research: A Rhetorical, Case-Based Process*. New York: Peter Lang.

Meho, L. I. (2006). E-mail interviewing in qualitative research: A methodological discussion. *Journal of the American Society for Information Science & Technology*, 57(10), 1284–1295. doi:10.1002/asi.20416

Merriam, S. B. (2009). *Qualitative Research: A Guide to Design and Implementation*. San Francisco: Jossey Bass.

Metros, S. E. (2008). The educator's role in preparing visually literate learners. *Theory Into Practice*, 47, 107–109.

Miller, K. (2013). Respectful listening and reflective communication from the heart and with the spirit. *Qualitative Social Work*, 13(6), 828–841. doi:10.1177/1473325013508596

Miles, M., Huberman, A. M., & Saldana, J. (2014). *Qualitative Data Analysis: A Methods Sourcebook* (3rd ed.). Thousand Oaks: Sage.

Mill, J. S. (1871). *Utilitarianism*. London: Longmans, Green, Reader, and Dyer.

Miller, T., & Bell, L. (2012). Consenting to what? Issues of access, gatekeeping and 'informed consent'. In T. Miller, M. Birch, M. Mauthner, & J. Jessop (Eds.), *Ethics in Qualitative Research* (2nd ed.). London: Sage.

Moeller, S. (2013). Numbers are never enough (especially when dealing with Big Data). blogs.worldbank.org (Vol. 2014). The World Bank.

Montiel, M. (2020). [Online research: Interview.]

Mor Barak, M. E. (2018). The practice and science of social good: Emerging paths to positive social impact. *Research on Social Work Practice*, 30(2), 139–150. doi:10.1177/1049731517745600

Morgan, D. L. (2007). Combining qualitative and quantitative methods paradigms lost and pragmatism regained: Methodological implications. *Journal of Mixed Methods Research*, 1(1), 48–76.

Morgan, D. L. (2008). Sampling frame. In L. Given (Ed.), *The Sage Encyclopedia of Qualitative Research Methods* (pp. 801–802). Thousand Oaks: Sage.

Morgan, D. L. (2014). Pragmatism as a paradigm for social research. *Qualitative Inquiry*, 20(8), 1045–1053. doi:10.1177/1077800413513733

Morris, M. C., & Morris, J. Z. (2016). The importance of virtue ethics in the IRB. *Research Ethics*, 12(4), 201–216. doi:10.1177/1747016116656023

Moss, J. (2011). 'Virtue makes the goal right': Virtue and phronesis in Aristotle's ethics. *Phronesis*, 56(3), 204–261. doi:10.1163/156852811X575907

Moser, A., & Korstjens, I. (2018) Series: Practical guidance to qualitative research. Part 3: Sampling, data collection and analysis. *European Journal of General Practice*, 24(1), 9–18. doi: 10.1080/13814788.2017.1375091

Moustakas, C. (1994). *Phenomenological Research Methods*. Thousand Oaks: Sage.

Mulhall, A. (2003). In the field: Notes on observation in qualitative research. *Journal of Advanced Nursing*, 41(3), 306–313. doi:10.1046/j.1365-2648.2003.02514.x

Munzert, S., & Nyhuis, D. (2020). Web scraping. SAGE Research Methods Foundations (Eds. P. Atkinson, S. Delamont, A. Cernat, J. W. Sakshaug, & R. A. Williams). doi:http://dx.doi.org/10.4135/9781526421036905588

Näykki, P., & Järvelä, S. (2008). How pictorial knowledge representations mediate collaborative knowledge construction in groups. *Journal of Research on Technology in Education*, 40(3), 359–387.

Nørskov, S. V., & Rask, M. (2011). Observation of online communities: a discussion of online and offline observer roles in studying development, cooperation and coordination in an open source software environment. *Forum: Qualitative Social Research*, 3(5). doi:https://doi.org/10.17169/fqs-12.3.1567

O'Connor, D. (2009). Apomediation and the significance of online social networking. *American Journal of Bioethics*, 9(6/7), 25–27. doi:10.1080/15265160902893981

O'Connor, D. (2013). The apomediated world: Regulating research when social media has changed research. *Journal of Law, Medicine & Ethics*, 41(2), 470-483. doi:10.1111/jlme.12056

O'Connor, H. (2006). Sampling issues in online interviewing. Exploring online research methods: Online Interviews. Retrieved from http://www.geog.le.ac.uk/ORM/interviews/intsampling.htm

O'Connor, S. (2019). Virtual reality and avatars in health care. *Clinical Nursing Research*, 8(5), 523–528. doi:10.1177/1054773819845824

Okumus, F., Olya, H., Van Niekerk, M., Taheri, B., & Gannon, M. J. (2020). Innovative mixed and multi method approaches to hospitality and tourism research. *Journal of Contemporary Hospitality Management*, 32(4), 1385–1391.

O'Leary, Z. (2007). *Deductive/inductive Reasoning: The Social Science Jargon Buster*. London: Sage.

Oleszkiewicz, A., Karwowski, M., Pisanski, K., Sorokowski, P., Sobrado, B., & Sorokowska, A. (2017). Who uses emoticons? Data from 86702 Facebook users. *Personality and Individual Differences*, 119, 289–295. doi: 10.1016/j.paid.2017.07.034

Ollerenshaw, J. A., & Creswell, J. W. (2002). Narrative research: A comparison of two restorying data analysis approaches. *Qualitative Inquiry*, 8(3), 329–347. doi:10.1177/10778004008003008

Ong, W. (1990). Writing and reading texts are speech events. The Walter J. *Ong Collection: Language as Hermeneutic*. Retrieved from http://libraries.slu.edu/sc/ong/digital/lah.html

Onwuegbuzie, A. J., & Leech, N. L. (2007). Sampling designs in qualitative research: Making the sampling process more public. *The Qualitative Report*, 12(2).

Oostveen, A.-M., Hjorth, I., Pickering, B., Boniface, M., Meyer, E., Cobo, C., & Schroeder, R. (2012). Cross-disciplinary lessons for the future internet. In F. Álvarez, F. Cleary, P. Daras, J. Domingue, A. Galis, A. Garcia, A. Gavras, S. Karnourskos, S. Krco, M.-S. Li, V. Lotz, H. Müller, E. Salvadori, A.-M. Sassen, H. Schaffers, B. Stiller, G. Tselentis, P. Turkama, & T. Zahariadis (Eds.), *The Future Internet* (Vol. 7281, pp. 42–54). Berlin: Springer..

O'Reilly, M., & Parker, N. (2012). 'Unsatisfactory Saturation': a critical exploration of the notion of saturated sample sizes in qualitative research. *Qualitative Research*. doi:10.1177/1468794112446106

Ouariachi, T., Gutiérrez-Pérez, J., & Olvera-Lobo, M. D. (2018). *The Use of the Delphi Method to Define Criteria for Evaluating Online Climate Change Games*. Retrieved from https://methods.sagepub.com/case/delphi-method-define-criteria-for-evaluating-online-climate-change-games. doi:10.4135/9781526438317

Ouariachi, T., Olvera-Lobo, M. D., Gutiérrez-Pérez, J., & Maibach, E. (2019). A framework for climate change engagement through video games. *Environmental Education Research*, 25(5), 701–716. doi:10.1080/13504622.2018.1545156

Owens, R. L. (2010). Informed consent. In N. Salkind (Ed.), *Encyclopedia of Research Design* (pp. 603–608). Thousand Oaks: Sage.

Paechter, C. (2013). Researching sensitive issues online: Implications of a hybrid insider/outsider position in a retrospective ethnographic study. Qualitative Research, 13(1), 71–86. doi:10.1177/1468794112446107

Pangrazio, L., & Selwyn, N. (2018). 'It's not like it's life or death or whatever': Young people's understandings of social media data. *Social Media + Society*, 4(3). doi:10.1177/2056305118787808

Pascale, C.-M. (2011). *Cartographies of knowledge: Exploring qualitative epistemologies*. Thousand Oaks: Sage.

Patton, M. Q. (2014). *Qualitative Research & Evaluation Methods* (4th ed.). Thousand Oaks: Sage.

Paulus, T. M., & Lester, J. N. (2021). *Doing Qualitative Research in a Digital World*. Thousand Oaks: Sage.

Paulus, T. M., & Wise, A. F. (2019). *Looking for Insight, Transformation, and Learning in Online Talk*. New York: Routledge.

Pauwels, L. (2011). An integrated conceptual framework for visual social research. In Pauwels, L. & Mannay, D. (Eds.), *The SAGE Handbook of Visual Research Methods* (pp. 3–23). SAGE Publications. https://www.doi.org/10.4135/9781446268278

Pauwels, L. (2020). An integrated conceptual framework for visual social research. In L. Pauwels & D. Mannay (Eds.), *The SAGE Handbook of Visual Research Methods*. London: Sage.

Pink, S. (2021). *Doing Visual Ethnography* (4th ed.). London: Sage.

Poth, C. (2021). *Research Ethics*. London: Sage.

Prandner, D., & Seymer, A. (2020). Social media analysis. SAGE Research Methods Foundations (Eds. P. Atkinson, S. Delamont, A. Cernat, J. W. Sakshaug, & R. A. Williams). DOI: http://dx.doi.org/10.4135/9781526421036921823

Preissle, J. (2008). Ethics codes. In L. M. Given (Ed.), *The SAGE Encyclopedia of Qualitative Research Methods*. Thousand Oaks: Sage.

Quigley, E., Michel, A.-S., & Doyle, G. (2020). *Vignette-based Interviewing in the Health Care Space: A Robust Method of Vignette Development*. Retrieved from https://methods.sagepub.com/case/vignette-based-interviewing-health-care-vignette-development. doi:10.4135/9781529735970

Rallis, S. F., & Rossman, G. B. (2012). *The Research Journey: Introduction to Inquiry*. New York: Guilford Press.

Ravitch, S. (2020). *Qualitative Research*. Thousand Oaks: Sage.

Reed-Danahay, D. (2019). Autoethnography. SAGE Research Methods Foundations (Eds. P. Atkinson, S. Delamont, A. Cernat, J. W. Sakshaug, & R. A. Williams). doi:10.4135/9781526421036815143

Reichertz, J. (2014). Induction, deduction, abduction. *In The SAGE handbook of qualitative data analysis*, pp. 123–135. SAGE Publications Ltd, https://www.doi.org/10.4135/9781446282243

Rheingold, H. (2000). *The Virtual Community: Homesteading on the Electronic Frontier* (2nd ed.). Cambridge: MIT Press.

Rheingold, H. (2012). Stewards of digital literacies. *Knowledge Quest*, 41(1), 53–55.

Ritchie, J., & Lewis, J. (Eds.). (2003). *Qualitative Research Practice: A Guide for Social Science Students and Researchers*. London: Sage.

Rocco, T. (2010). Criteria for evaluating qualitative studies. *Human Resource Development International*, 13, 375–378. doi:10.1080/13678868.2010.501959

Romare, J., & Collste, G. (2015). *Principles and Approaches in Ethics Assessment Human Subjects Research*. Retrieved from https://satoriproject.eu/media/1.d-Human-subjects-research.pdf

Roper, J. M., & Shapira, J. (2000). *Ethnography in Nursing Research*. Thousand Oaks: Sage.

Rose, G. (2016). *Visual Methodologies: An Introduction to Researching with Visual Materials* (4th ed.). London: Sage.

Rowbotham, M. C., Astin, J., Greene, K., & Cummings, S. R. (2013). Interactive informed consent: Randomized comparison with paper consents. *PLoS ONE*, 8(3), 1–6. doi:10.1371/journal.pone.0058603

Rubel, D., & Villalba, J. A. (2009). How to publish qualitative research in JSGW: A couple more voices in the conversation. *Journal for Specialists in Group Work*, 34(4), 295–306. doi:10.1080/01933920903251964

Rubin, H. J., & Rubin, I. S. (2012). *Qualitative Interviewing: The Art of Hearing Data* (3rd ed.). Thousand Oaks: Sage.

SAGE Research Methods (2021). Methods Map: Induction. Retrieved from https://methods.sagepub.com/methods-map/induction.

SAGE Research Methods (2021). Project Planner. https://methods.sagepub.com/project-planner

Saldaña, J. (2014). *Thinking Qualitatively: Methods of Mind* (3rd ed.). Thousand Oaks: Sage.

Salmons, J. (1992). Cultural democracy. MA dissertation, Empire State College, State University of New York.

Salmons, J. (2007). Expect originality! Using taxonomies to structure assignments that support original work. In T. Roberts (Ed.), *Student Plagiarism in an Online World: Problems and Solutions*. Hershey: IGI Reference.

Salmons, J. (2010). *Online Interviews in Real Time*. Thousand Oaks: Sage.

Salmons, J. (Ed.) (2012). *Cases in Online Interview Research*. Thousand Oaks: Sage.

Salmons, J. (2013). *New Social Media, New Social Science: Research Ethics in the Digital Age.* Retrieved from New Social Media, New Social Science Project Report.

Salmons, J. (2014). *The ethics of social media research: Moving our practice forward*, New Social Media, New Social Science: Social Media and Research Ethics London.

Salmons, J. (2015). *Qualitative Online Interviews.* Thousand Oaks: Sage.

Salmons, J. (2016). *Doing Qualitative Research Online.* London: Sage.

Salmons, J. (2019a). *Learning to Collaborate, Collaborating to Learn: Engaging Students in the Classroom and Online.* Sterling: Stylus.

Salmons, J. (2019b). [Qualitative Data Analysis with NVivo: Author Interview.]

Schensul, J. J. (2008). Methodology. In L. M. Given (Ed.), *The Sage Encyclopedia of Qualitative Research Methods* (pp. 517–522). Thousand Oaks: Sage.

Schreier, M. (2012). *Qualitative Content Analysis in Practice.* London: Sage.

Schutt, R. K. (2006). *Investigating the Social World: The Process and Practice of Research* (5th ed.). Thousand Oaks: Pine Forge Press.

Schwandt, T. A. (Ed.) (2007) *The SAGE Dictionary of Qualitative Inquiry* (3rd ed.). Thousand Oaks: Sage.

Schwinn, T., Hopkins, J., Schinke, S. P., & Liu, X. (2017). Using Facebook ads with traditional paper mailings to recruit adolescent girls for a clinical trial. *Addictive Behaviors*, 65, 207–213.

Seidman, I. (2019). *Interviewing as Qualitative Research: A Guide for Researchers in Education and the Social Sciences* (5th ed.). New York: Teachers College Press.

Shank, G. (2008). Deduction. In L. M. Given (Ed.), *The SAGE Encyclopedia of Qualitative Research Methods.* Thousand Oaks: Sage.

Sharpe, S., Kool, B., Whittaker, R., & Ameratunga, S. (2019). Hawthorne effect in the YourCall trial suggested by participants' qualitative responses. *Journal of Clinical Epidemiology*, 115, 177–179.

Silverman, D., & Marvasti, A. (2008). *Doing Qualitative Research: A Comprehensive Guide.* Thousand Oaks: Sage.

Sinnott-Armstrong, W. (2011). Consequentialism. In E. N. Zalta (Ed.), *The Stanford Encyclopedia of Philosophy.* Stanford: Stanford University Press.

Southerton, C., & Taylor, E. (2020). Habitual disclosure: Routine, affordance, and the ethics of young people's social media data surveillance. *Social Media + Society*, 6(2). doi:10.1177/2056305120915612

Spencer, L., Ritchie, J., & O'Connor, W. (2003). Analysis: Practices, principles and processes. In J. Ritchie & J. Lewis (Eds.), *Qualitative Research Practice: A Guide for Social Science Students and Researchers.* London: Sage.

Spencer, L., Ritchie, J., Ormston, R., O'Connor, W., & Barnard, M. (2014). Analysis: Principles and processes. In J. Ritchie, J. Lewis, C. M. Nicholls, & R. Ormston (Eds.), *Qualitative Research Practice: A Guide for Social Science Students and Researchers* (2nd ed.). London: Sage.

SRA (Social Research Association) (2021). Ethical guidelines. Retrieved from https://the-sra.org.uk/common/Uploaded%20files/Resources/SRA%20Research%20Ethics%20guidance%202021.pdf

Stake, R. E. (1995). *The Art of Case Study Research.* Thousand Oaks: Sage.

Stanczak, G. C. (2007). *Visual Research Methods: Image, Society, and Representation*. Thousand Oaks: Sage.

Stebbins, R. A. (2001). What is exploration? In R. A. Stebbins (Ed.), *Exploratory Research in the Social Sciences*. Thousand Oaks: Sage.

Stern, S. R. (2009). How notions of privacy influence research choices: A response to Malin Sveningsson. In A. N. Markham & N. K. Baym (Eds.), *Internet Inquiry: Conversations About Method*. Thousand Oaks: Sage.

Stiver, A., Barroca, L., Minocha, S., Richards, M., & Roberts, D. (2015). Civic crowdfunding research: Challenges, opportunities, and future agenda. *New Media & Society*, 17(2), 249–271. doi:10.1177/1461444814558914

Straus, A. L. (1987). Qualitative research for the social scientist. In D. Gray (Ed.), *Doing Research in the Real World*. London: Sage.

Streeton, R., Cooke, M., & Campbell, J. (2004). Researching the researchers: Using a snowballing technique. *Nurse Researcher*, 12(1), 35–45.

Stommel, W., & Rijk, L. D. (2021). Ethical approval: None sought. How discourse analysts report ethical issues around publicly available online data. *Research Ethics*, 17(3). doi:10.1177/1747016120988767

Sumner, M. (1995). Interpretivism. In V. Jupp (Ed.), *The SAGE Dictionary of Social Research Methods* (pp. 249–251). London: Sage.

Taylor, V. J., Valladares, J. J., Siepser, C., & Yantis, C. (2020). Interracial contact in virtual reality: Best practices. *Policy Insights from the Behavioral and Brain Sciences*, 7(2), 132–140. doi:10.1177/2372732220943638

The Nuremberg Code (1949). Trials of War Criminals before the Nuremberg Military Tribunals under Control Council Law. U.S. Government Printing Office.

Thomas, G. (2016). *How to Do Your Case Study* (2nd ed.). London: Sage.

Thornberg, R., & Charmaz, K. (2014). Grounded theory and theoretical coding. In U. Flick (Ed.), *The SAGE Handbook of Qualitative Data Analysis*. London: Sage.

Tracy, S. J. (2010). Qualitative quality: Eight 'big-tent' criteria for excellent qualitative research. *Qualitative Inquiry*, 16(10), 837–851. doi:10.1177/1077800410383121

Trevisan, F., & Reilly, P. (2014). Ethical dilemmas in researching sensitive issues online: Lessons from the study of British disability dissent networks. *Information, Communication & Society*, 17(9), 1131–1146. doi:10.1080/1369118X.2014.889188

Turner, D. (2020). Can a computer do qualitative analysis? *Big Qual Analysis Resource Hub*. Retrieved from http://bigqlr.ncrm.ac.uk/2018/08/14/guest-post-17-dr-daniel-turner-can-a-computer-do-qualitative-analysis/

UW Human Subjects Division (2012). *Does Your Research Involve Human Subjects?* Retrieved from www.washington.edu/research/hsd/do-i-need-irb-review/does-your-research-involve-human-subjects/.

Van de Ven, A. H. (2007). *Engaged Scholarship: A Guide for Organizational and Social Research*. Oxford: Oxford University Press.

van Gelder, M. M., van de Belt, T. H., Engelen, L. J., Hooijer, R., Bredie, S. J., & Roeleveld, N. (2019). Google AdWords and Facebook ads for recruitment of pregnant women into a prospective cohort study with long-term follow-up. *Maternal and Child Health Journal*, 23(10), 1285–1291.

Velasquez, M. G. (2012). *Business Ethics: Concepts and Cases* (7th ed.). Boston: Pearson.

Velasquez, M., Andre, C., Shanks, T., & Meyer, M. J. (2014). Ethical Decision Making: Ethics and virtue. Markkula Center for Applied Ethics. Retrieved from doi:http://www.scu.edu/ethics/practicing/decision/ethicsandvirtue.html

Vogt, W. P., Vogt, E. R., Gardner, D. C., & Haeffele, L. M. (2014). *Selecting the Right Analysis for your Data: Quantitative, Qualitative and Mixed Methods*. New York: Guilford Press.

Waight, E. (2020). Using photovoice to explore students' study practices. In H. Kara & S.-m. Khoo (Eds.), *Researching in the Age of COVID-19 Volume 3: Creativity and Ethics*. London: Policy Press.

Waldron, J. (2013). YouTube, fanvids, forums, vlogs and blogs: Informal music learning in a convergent on- and offline music community. *International Journal of Music Education*, 31(1), 91-105. doi:10.1177/0255761411434861

Walsh, M. (2003). Teaching qualitative analysis using QSR NVivo. *The Qualitative Report*, 8(2), 251–256.

Weiss, R. S. (1994). *Learning From Strangers: The Art and Method of Qualitative Interview Studies*. New York: The Free Press.

White, C., Woodfield, K., Ritchie, J., & Ormston, R. (2014). Writing up qualitative research. In J. Ritchie, J. Lewis, C. M. Nicholls, & R. Ormston (Eds.), *Qualitative Research Practice: A Guide for Social Science Students and Researchers* (2nd ed.). London: Sage.

Whiteman, N. (2012). *Undoing Ethics: Rethinking Practice in Online Research*. New York: Springer.

Wiles, R. (2013). *What Are Qualitative Research Ethics?* London: Bloomsbury Academic.

Williams, M. (2007). Avatar watching: participant observation in graphical online environments. *Qualitative Research*, 7(1), 5–24. doi:10.1177/1468794107071408

Wilmot, A. (2005). Designing sampling strategies for qualitative social research. Survey Methodology Bulletin-Office for National Statistics, 56, Newport, UK. {Archived] Available at https://tinyurl.com/pe2m4bze

Winskell, K., Singleton, R., & Sabben, G. (2018). Enabling analysis of big, thick, long, and wide data: Data management for the analysis of a large longitudinal and cross-national narrative data set. *Qualitative Health Research*, 28(10), 1629–1639. doi:10.1177/1049732318759658

WMA (World Medical Association). (2013). Declaration of Helsinki: Ethical Principles for Medical Research Involving Human Subjects. Retrieved from https://www.wma.net/policies-post/wma-declaration-of-helsinki-ethical-principles-for-medical-research-involving-human-subjects/

Wozney, L., Turner, K., Rose-Davis, B., & McGrath, P. J. (2019). Facebook ads to the rescue? Recruiting a hard to reach population into an Internet-based behavioral health intervention trial. *Internet Interventions*, 17. doi: 10.1016/j.invent.2019.100246

Yin, R. K. (2011). *Qualitative Research from Start to Finish*. New York: Guilford Press.

Yin, R. K. (2018). *Case Study Research and Applications* (6th ed.). Thousand Oaks: Sage.

Yoshikawa, H., Weisner, T. S., Kalil, A., & Way, N. (2008). Mixing qualitative and quantitative research in developmental science: Uses and methodological choices. *Developmental Psychology*, 44(2), 344–354.

INDEX